Google *Second Edition*

THE MISSING MANUAL

*The book that
should have been
in the box*

Google Second Edition

THE MISSING MANUAL

Sarah Milstein, J.D. Biersdorfer, and Matthew MacDonald

POGUE PRESS™

O'REILLY®

Beijing • Cambridge • Farnham • Köln • Paris • Sebastopol • Taipei • Tokyo

Google: The Missing Manual, Second Edition

by Sarah Milstein, J.D. Biersdorfer, and Matthew MacDonald

Copyright © 2006, 2004 O'Reilly Media, Inc. All rights reserved.
Printed in the United States of America.

Published by O'Reilly Media, Inc., 1005 Gravenstein Highway North, Sebastopol, CA 95472.

O'Reilly books may be purchased for educational, business, or sales promotional use. Online editions are also available for most titles (*safari.oreilly.com*). For more information, contact our corporate/institutional sales department: (800) 998-9938 or *corporate@oreilly.com*.

Printing History:

May 2004:	First Edition.
March 2006:	Second Edition.

 This book uses RepKover™, a durable and flexible lay-flat binding.

ISBN: 0-596-10019-1

[M]

Table of Contents

Part Two: Google Tools

Chapter 3: Googling Further: Images, News, Maps, and More 81

Chapter 4: Googling with Others: Groups and Answers 119

Chapter 5: Shopping with Google 159

Part Three: Google for Webmasters

Part Four: Gmail

GOOGLE: THE MISSING MANUAL

Part Five: Appendix

The Missing Credits

About the Authors

Sarah Milstein (author and editor) is O'Reilly Media's Managing Editor for Consumer Books. Previously, she was the Missing Manual series editor and a freelance business and technology reporter. She has been a regular contributor to the *New York Times* and a slew of other publications, most of them now defunct. When not planted at the keyboard, she likes to take epic walks, play poker, watch baseball, and rearrange the furniture. Email: *milstein@oreilly.com*.

J.D. Biersdorfer (author, Chapter 11 and revisions throughout the book) is the author of *iPod & iTunes: The Missing Manual* and *The iPod Shuffle Fan Book* and sometimes even writes about things other than iPods. She does the weekly computer Q&A column for the *New York Times* and is equally obsessed with the *BBC World News* and the banjo in her spare time. Email: *jd.biersdorfer@gmail.com*.

Matthew MacDonald (author, Chapter 10 and revisions in Chapter 9) is an author, educator, and programmer extraordinaire. He's the author of *Excel: The Missing Manual*, *Creating Web Sites: The Missing Manual*, and over a dozen books about .NET programming. Web: *www.prosetech.com*.

Rael Dornfest (author, Chapters 8 and 9, previous edition) is O'Reilly Media's Chief Technology Officer. He has co-authored various O'Reilly books, including *Mac OS X Hacks*, *Google Hacks*, *Essential Blogging*, and *Peer to Peer: Harnessing the Power of Disruptive Technologies*, and he is program chair for the O'Reilly Emerging Technology Conference. Email: *googlemm@raelity.org*.

About the Creative Team

Adam Goldstein (editor, technical reviewer) is the teenage founder of Goldfish-Soft, a Macintosh software company. He is the author *AppleScript: The Missing Manual*; co-author of *Switching to the Mac: The Missing Manual*, Tiger Edition; and contributor to *Mac OS X: The Missing Manual* and *Mac OS X Power Hound*. Email: *mail@goldfishsoft.com*. Web: *www.goldfishsoft.com*.

Aaron Swartz (technical reviewer, previous edition) is a teenage writer, coder, and hacker. He's also the guy behind the Google Weblog (*http://google.blogspace.com/*). Email: *me@aaronsw.com*. Web: *www.aaronsw.com*.

Rose Cassano (cover illustration) has worked as an independent designer and illustrator for 20 years. Assignments have ranged from the nonprofit sector to corporate clientele. She lives in beautiful Southern Oregon, grateful for the miracles of modern technology that make working there a reality. Email: *cassano@highstream. net*. Web: *www.rosecassano.com.*

Acknowledgements

Thanks to Jude, Adam, and Matthew for making this edition thorough, accurate, and entertaining. Special thanks to Brian Jepson for help with Google Wireless, to Glenda Dougherty for checking all the URLs, and to Michele Filshie for help with the details. And of course, thanks to my coworkers at O'Reilly for your patience and good humor in making this book possible.

—Sarah

The Missing Manual Series

The Missing Manuals are conceived as superbly written guides to computer products that don't come with printed manuals (which is just about all of them). Each book features a handcrafted index, cross-references to specific page numbers (not just "see Chapter 9"), and an ironclad promise never to use an apostrophe in the possessive word *its*. Current and upcoming titles include:

Access 2003 for Starters: The Missing Manual by Kate Chase and Scott Palmer

AppleScript: The Missing Manual by Adam Goldstein

AppleWorks 6: The Missing Manual by Jim Elferdink and David Reynolds

Creating Web Sites: The Missing Manual by Matthew MacDonald

Dreamweaver 8: The Missing Manual by David Sawyer McFarland

eBay: The Missing Manual by Nancy Conner

Excel: The Missing Manual by Matthew MacDonald

Excel for Starters: The Missing Manual by Matthew MacDonald

FileMaker Pro 8: The Missing Manual by Geoff Coffey and Susan Prosser

FrontPage 2003: The Missing Manual by Jessica Mantaro

GarageBand 2: The Missing Manual by David Pogue

Home Networking: The Missing Manual by Scott Lowe

iLife '05: The Missing Manual by David Pogue

iMovie HD & iDVD 6: The Missing Manual by David Pogue

iPhoto 6: The Missing Manual by David Pogue

iPod & iTunes: The Missing Manual, Fourth Edition by J.D. Biersdorfer

iWork '05: The Missing Manual by Jim Elferdink

Mac OS X Power Hound, Panther Edition by Rob Griffiths

Mac OS X: The Missing Manual, Tiger Edition by David Pogue

Office 2004 for Macintosh: The Missing Manual by Mark H. Walker and Franklin Tessler

PCs: The Missing Manual by Andy Rathbone

Photoshop Elements 4: The Missing Manual by Barbara Brundage

QuickBooks 2006: The Missing Manual by Bonnie Biafore

Quicken 2006 for Starters: The Missing Manual by Bonnie Biafore

Switching to the Mac: The Missing Manual, Tiger Edition by David Pogue and Adam Goldstein

Windows 2000 Pro: The Missing Manual by Sharon Crawford

Windows XP Power Hound by Preston Gralla

Windows XP for Starters: The Missing Manual by David Pogue

Windows XP Home Edition: The Missing Manual, Second Edition by David Pogue

Windows XP Pro: The Missing Manual, Second Edition by David Pogue, Craig Zacker, and Linda Zacker

Introduction

By now there's no way to have missed the Internet. Over the past twelve years, it's become a major factor in communications and business—arguably revolutionizing both. You can harness the Internet's awesome power to find recipes for ginger maple fudge ice cream and send the best one to your grandmother on another continent. You can use it to pay bills, look up your high school sweetheart's current phone number, and find out the common side effects for your allergy shots. You can do your grocery shopping, check your baseball team's box scores, or auction off the Rollerblades you used only once.

In fact, you can do practically everything online these days, thanks to a Web that's truly worldwide and growing by millions of pages *per day*. But all those goodies are useful only if you can find them—which would be no problem if the Internet had a complete index or a tidy table of contents…but it doesn't. Not even close.

A Little History

The Internet is really just an ever-growing series of interconnected computer networks that has been around since the late 1960s. Initially, the people who roamed the Internet were military officials, scientists, computer programmers, and other geek types who could deal with what was then a user-hostile system. All you saw were endless lines of words, and everything you did required an arcane text command. There were no photos, and there was no clicking. Instead, there were a lot of dull amber monitors and a ton of typing.

By the early 1990s, people had begun developing not only useful systems that ran on the Internet, like email and newsgroups, but also programs that made them easier to use (think Outlook and Eudora). Among the nifty new Internet systems was the *World Wide Web*, a network of documents and databases that, when viewed through a software program called a *Web browser*, let people share information visually and use a mouse to navigate around it. Clicking turned out to be a pretty intuitive way for people to sift through information, and Web surfing was born.

But before the Internet could become commonplace in civilian life, people needed an easy way to find other people and things on the Internet. In 1994, researchers at Carnegie Mellon University introduced Lycos, the first Web-based *search engine*—a program to help you find stuff on the Web. And the people rejoiced.

Actually, the geeks rejoiced. Seeing tremendous opportunity in providing search services on the Web, a mess of technology companies sprung up and launched search sites. Some sites, like Yahoo, were *directories* that slotted Web pages into predetermined categories that people could then browse through. Others, like HotBot, AltaVista, Excite, and Infoseek, ran *full-text search engines,* programs that tracked the words on Web pages and then, when you searched for a word or phrase, sent you to the pages it knew contained them.

Unlike directories, which let *people* create categories and assign Web pages to them, full-text search engines use *computers* to record the words on Web pages. In fact, such search engines rely on two automated programs to track Web pages. First, *spiders,* also known as *robots* or *crawlers,* go out and methodically trawl the Web, downloading copies of pages as they go. Second, programs called *indexers* record the text on the downloaded pages, along with important information that's encoded in them—things like the page title, links to other pages, and so forth. Indexers store all this stuff in a database, helpfully called an *index* or sometimes a *catalog.* To keep up to date, spiders return once a month or so to the pages they've visited, making note of dead links and handing off new or changed pages to the indexers for recording.

When you use a full-text search engine to look for something, it actually searches its index—not the entire live Web, which would be impossible.

Note: Google's index currently has more than eight billion Web pages, according to the company.

By the late 1990s, both kinds of searches—directory and full-text—were widespread and user-friendly, and non-geeks began taking to the Internet like cats take to tuna fish.

How the Web Was Won: Google's Technology

In the Web's early days, full-text searches ranked their results according to information contained on Web sites themselves—like the prominence of a certain word. If, for example, you wanted to learn about buying a small dog and you searched for *dachshund,* your list of sites was likely to be organized by which ones had the most instances of the word "dachshund." That might well have been a site set up by a woman in Boise who painted cartoon dogs onto sweatshirts, the schedule for a group of people in Sacramento who have dachshunds with ingrown toenails, and the Daytona Dachshunds Little League roster. You could search through thousands of pages before you hit any useful information.

Even if you narrowed your search to something like *"dachshund breeders,"* you might still have gotten sites run by pet food conglomerates or veterinarians or any company that set up its Web pages to draw people with an interest in dogs. In short, it was maddeningly hard to get *relevant* search results.

Enter Google. In 1995, Sergey Brin and Larry Page met in the graduate computer science program at Stanford University. Their idea was to create a search engine that would rank search results not on data that could be manipulated by Web masters, but by using the strength of the Internet itself—community input. Their technology evaluated a site primarily on how many other sites linked to it, and ranked search results accordingly. Thus, their searches tended to return results that lots of other people found useful, resulting in a surprisingly valuable system.

By 1998, Brin and Page had dropped out of Stanford to start Google. In its first year, the company—run by four employees out of a garage in Menlo Park, California—answered about 10,000 search requests per day. Today, the Web is home to about a dozen very popular search sites and likely thousands of less well-known ones, but Google's computers handle more search requests than anyone else's—over 250 million per day.

Google is the reigning search champ not because the company has clever marketing (it doesn't) or a killer online dating service (again, no dice), but because the site is easy to use and effective.

Tip: Wonder what all those people are searching *for*? Google provides snapshots of its search activity, by month and by year, at Google Zeitgeist, *www.google.com/press/zeitgeist.html.* This is the perfect place to find out if anyone still cares about Martha Stewart or whether *The Apprentice* is declining in popularity.

How the Ranking Works

Google uses a number of elements to decide whether a Web page is a good match for a particular search. First, it looks at links. Links from one Web page to another don't appear spontaneously; people have to make them—in effect saying, "Look *here* and *here* and *here*." Because each link thus represents a decision, Google infers that a link from one page to another is tantamount to a *vote* for the second page. Pages with lots of votes are considered more important than other pages. For example, if a million baseball-fan Web sites all have links to MLB.com (home of Major League Baseball), Google's logic is, "Hey, that's an important site for people searching for the word *baseball.*"

In addition, Google ranks the pages that *cast* the votes, based on their own popularity, and gives more weight to the votes from heavily linked-to pages. Finally, Google uses this information to assign Web pages an appropriate *PageRank*—Google's term for status—which it calculates on a scale from one to ten. (Page 277 explains PageRank further and tells you how to find it for any given site.)

Note: The term PageRank is actually based on the name of one of Google's founders, Larry Page, not on the idea of Web pages.

But all that jazz would lead to nothing more than an interesting hierarchy of Web popularity if it didn't take into account the words you're searching for. So when you query Google, it combines PageRank with an additional system for matching text—which looks not only at the content on a first layer of pages, but at the content on pages linking to them—to produce a list of pages that is, more often than not, relevant.

In all, the Google equation, or *algorithm*, incorporates 500 *million* variables looking at everything from links to the position of your search terms on a page. And most searches run in much less than a second.

Because the site's methods are so complex, it's tough—though not impossible—to jigger a page in order to improve its rank in a Google search. (See Chapter 8 for more on getting Google to find your site.)

Comparing Google with Other Searches

Most of the time, you'll probably decide which search site to use based on the relevance of its results. But these days, many search sites return similar results, which means you might want to make your choice based on factors like speed and site design. It's akin to buying a car today: most automobiles will get you where you want to go, but they differ in reliability, smoothness, and style. Figure I-1 compares two site designs.

For many researchers, Google is the no-brainer choice for searching the Web because it's fast, neat, smart, and fun (Figure I-2).

About This Book

If you're the sort of person who hasn't quite figured out how to get to the Google home page—and you're too embarrassed to ask any 8-year-old of your acquaintance—this book will help you not only get there but start using Google like a pro, too. If, on the other hand, Google already feels like an extension of your brain, and you've considered tattooing the site's colorful logo across your forehead, this book can elevate you to search guru, helping you exploit the little-known but powerful features of Google. For example:

- Most people who use Google every day have no idea why the results include links named "Cached" or "Similar pages" (see pages 26 and 28).

- Practically nobody knows what happens when you throw the term *inurl* into your search string—but it's a very handy trick (see page 67).

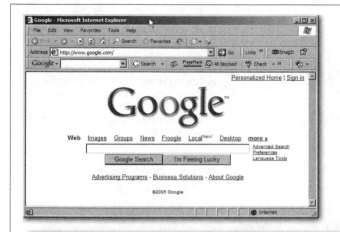

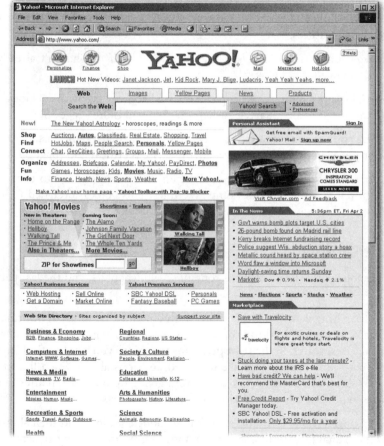

Figure I-1:
Top: The Google home page.

Bottom: The Yahoo home page. For many queries, different search sites will give you similar results because most search engines have adopted some variation of Google's method of analyzing links. But Google's unusually clean design makes it faster to load and easier to read than many other search sites.

Figure I-2:
The Google home page changes from time to time. To commemorate holidays and oddball celebrations (like Michelangelo's birthday), Google puts up special, themed logos, drawn by Dennis Hwang, a Web designer at the company. This is the logo Google used to celebrate the leap year on February 29, 2004. (The site still works the same, no matter the logo design.) The special logos are more popular than the Beatles, and you can see the whole back catalog of them at www. google.com/holidaylogos.html.

- Froogle (page 159) is a link right on Google's home page, but a lot of people never click through to find out the nifty things it can do.

- Google Answers (page 141) is a wicked cool service and may be one of the site's most underused features.

- The Google Toolbar (page 171) is a total lifesaver, and if you haven't already installed it, you need it right away.

- And a woefully small number of people know that you can easily make Google work as a calculator, a dictionary, a package tracker, and more (page 38).

Really knowing your way around Google lets you search smarter and faster. And knowing when *not* to use Google and try something else is critical, too (page 34).

Of course, the Google site has help pages. But frankly, explaining how to use the site, and use it well, is not where the company shines. This book is designed to be the manual you wish came along with such a great search site.

About the Outline

This book has four parts. The first three contain several chapters, and the last part has just one:

- **Part One, Searching with Google,** is all about finding the diamonds of information on the Web, even in its dusty corners. These chapters help you craft powerful search queries, search in the right places for the things you want to find, and interpret your search results to make informed decisions about which links to follow. This section of the book takes you from giving up on a search after one or two tries to holding a bagful of tricks for successful quests.

- **Part Two, Google Tools,** introduces you to the Google toolbar and then shows you how it can change your life, saving you tons of time and putting an array of search options at your fingertips. This section also covers buttons, little-known search systems, and other features that can help you search more efficiently. And it teaches you how to use a wireless gizmo to take Google everywhere you go.

- **Part Three, Google for Webmasters,** shows you the best ways to help Google—and other people—find your site. It demystifies AdSense and AdWords, Google's programs to help you make money and influence people. And it teaches you how to make great use of Google Analytics, the company's new program for researching your own site.

- **Part Four, Gmail,** covers Google's excellent, free email system.

At the end of the book, the Appendix provides information on Web sites *about* Google.

The Very Basics

To use this book, and indeed to use Google, you need to know a few basics. This book assumes that you're familiar with a few terms and concepts:

- **Clicking.** This book gives you three kinds of instructions that require you to use the mouse that's attached to your computer. To *click* means to point the arrow cursor at something on the screen and then—without moving the cursor at all—press and release the clicker button on the mouse (or your laptop trackpad). To *double-click,* of course, means to click twice in rapid succession, again without moving the cursor at all. And to *drag* means to move the cursor while pressing the button.

- **Menus.** The *menus* are the words at the top of your browser: File, Edit, and so on. Click one to make a list of commands appear, as though they're written on a window shade you've just pulled down.

  Some people click and release the mouse button to open a menu and then, after reading the menu command choices, click again on the one they want. Other people like to hold the mouse button down after the initial click on the menu title, drag down the list to the desired command, and only then release the mouse button. Either method works fine.

- **Keyboard shortcuts.** Every time you take your hand off the keyboard to move to the mouse, you lose time and potentially disrupt your workflow. That's why many experienced computer fans prefer to trigger menu commands and other features by pressing certain combinations on the keyboard. For example, in most word processors, you can press Ctrl+P on a PC (⌘-P on a Mac) to print. When you read an instruction like "press Ctrl+P," start by pressing the Ctrl key, then, while it's down, type the letter P, and finally release both keys.

About → These → Arrows

Throughout this book, and throughout the Missing Manual series, you'll find sentences like this one: "Choose View → Explorer Bar → Search." That's shorthand for a much longer instruction that directs you to choose three nested commands in sequence, like this: "In your browser, you'll find a menu item called View. Choose that. Inside the View menu is a choice called Explorer Bar; click it to open it. Inside *that* menu is yet another one called Search. Click to open it, too." Figure I-3 shows you the menus this sequence opens.

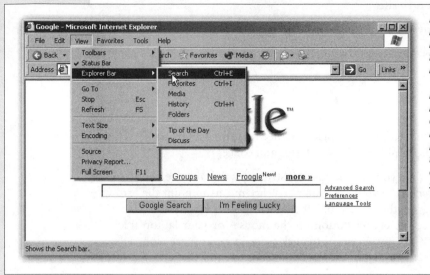

Figure I-3:
In this book, arrow notations help to simplify folder and menu instructions. For example, "Choose View → Explorer Bar → Search" is a more compact way of saying, "From the View menu, choose Explorer Bar; from the submenu that then appears, choose Search," as shown here.

Similarly, this kind of arrow shorthand helps to simplify the business of opening nested folders, such as Favorites → Links → Search Engines.

Late-Breaking News

As this book was going to press, Google was announcing new features nearly every day. The company is growing fast, and it's quickly expanding from a search service into a much broader Web-based information and communications company.

Now, in addition to helping you find news on Britney Spears and holiday gifts for your postal carrier, it also lets you talk with your friends (Talk), post content of various kinds (Google Base), analyze your Web site traffic (Google Analytics), and much, much more. Cool new services appear in Google daily, and the interface for Gmail and other core Google services change constantly. Google is becoming a major part of daily life and big business. (The fact that many Google features now require you to have a free account with the company is one sign of its shift from search tool to info-comm provider.) It's exciting stuff.

But frankly, it's maddening for book publishers trying to cover Google. Just as a book on the service comes off the press, Google updates the look of its homepage, making a bunch of figures slightly out of date. Or the company offers a new feature after the book is already on bookstore shelves.

The book in your hands is no exception. It covers *nearly* all of Google's services, and it absolutely helps you get the most out of Google. But as you read through it, you may discover that Gmail has some new labeling feature that this book doesn't cover—because the feature didn't exist at the time of the writing. Or you may find that Google has a brand-new service not discussed in these pages (Google Base is one such service; it came out too late to be included in real detail in this version of the book). Those small omissions are a drag. But they won't prevent you from gaining great Google skills with this Missing Manual. And if you can't find something Google-related in this book that you want to learn about, let us know. We'll add it to the next edition and consider putting it online in the meantime.

About MissingManuals.com

At *www.missingmanuals.com*, you'll find news, articles, and updates to the books in this series.

But the Web site also offers corrections and updates to this book (to see them, click the book's title, then click Errata). In fact, you're invited and encouraged to submit such corrections and updates yourself. In an effort to keep the book as up to date and accurate as possible, each time we print more copies of this book, we'll make any confirmed corrections you've suggested. We'll also note such changes on the Web site, so that you can mark important corrections into your own copy of the book, if you like.

In the meantime, we'd love to hear your own suggestions for new books in the Missing Manual line. There's a place for that on the Web site, too, as well as a place to sign up for free email notification of new titles in the series.

Safari® Enabled

 When you see a Safari® Enabled icon on the cover of your favorite technology book, that means the book is available online through the O'Reilly Network Safari Bookshelf.

Safari offers a solution that's better than e-books. It's a virtual library that lets you easily search thousands of top tech books, cut and paste code samples, download chapters, and find quick answers when you need the most accurate, current information. Try it for free at *http://safari.oreilly.com*.

Part One:
Searching with Google

1

Google 101

If you've never used Google before, you're in luck: it's incredibly easy to run a simple search. But if you've been using Google since the day it debuted, and you've never tried an image search or clicked the "Similar pages" link, consider yourself part of the vast Underusers Club.

Google is appealing because it's so straightforward. But you can get a lot more out of the site by knowing your way around the unobvious details and using the less prominent features. This chapter guides you through basic search techniques, and helps you analyze search results in ways that would surprise many power users.

The Heart of Google: Basic Text Searches

The Google home page (*www.google.com*) is as plain and friendly as Web pages get—loading quickly both for dial-uppers and broadband jockeys. As Figure 1-1 shows, it features tons of white space, a blank search box awaiting your command, two buttons, and a handful of links. What less could you want?

Google is about as hard to use as your refrigerator. To run a search, just follow this simple procedure:

1. **Point your browser to *www.google.com*.**

   In most browsers, you can even skip the "www" part and just type *google.com* in the address bar, and then press Enter.

   As shown in Figure 1-2, the address bar is the space at the top of the browser where you can type in a new URL. *URL* (pronounced "You Are El"), which stands for Uniform Resource Locator, is the unique electronic address assigned

Figure 1-1:
The launch pad for a million dreams. In Windows browsers, if you click Make Google Your Homepage, Google automatically sets www.google.com as the site your browser opens to and the place it heads when you click your browser's Home button. (If Google is already your home page, or if you're using a Mac, the Make Google Your Homepage link disappears.)

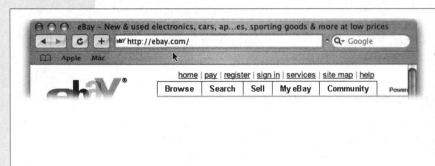

Figure 1-2:
To move to a new Web page, highlight the current address (in most browsers, clicking once in the address bar does the trick), type your new URL right over the old one, and then press Enter. Your browser jumps to the new page.

to every Web page, and it tells computers where to find that page on the Internet. A URL looks like this: *http://www.missingmanuals.com,* or sometimes just *www.missingmanauls.com,* or even *missingmanuals.com.* Google's URL is *www.google.com.* URLs are also known as Web addresses, and you'll see a lot of them as you surf around.

Once you've entered Google's address, its home page—shown in Figure 1-1—snaps to attention, with a blinking cursor in the blank search box, ready to receive your search words.

2. **Type in the word or words you want to search for (up to ten of them), and then press Enter or click Google Search.**

Google looks for Web pages that contain the words you type (you may hear these words called *keywords, search terms,* and *queries,* but they all mean the same thing). If you put in *Britney Spears,* you get not only Britney's official Web site (*www.britneyspears.com*), but a couple million fan sites and media outlets that have mentioned her, too.

Common searches include proper nouns like celebrities' names, company names, places in the news, the name of your high school, and your own name. You can also look for things like *New York subway map,* or *prostate cancer support group,* or *hemp wholesalers.*

3. **Scroll through your results, and click any link to jump to that page.**

Links appear underlined and blue, and when you mouse over them, the cursor turns to a hand. Figure 1-3 shows you a typical results page.

Tip: In most browsers, you can right-click or Ctrl+click (⌘-click) a link to open it in a new window, thereby preserving your list of results for further exploration.

---

4. **To return to your Google results, click the Back button on your browser (or, if you preserved your results window, simply switch back to it).**

In other words, if you don't find what you want on one page, you don't have to type Google's URL again and retype your search, too. You can just click back to the original results.

Tip: A lot of browsers, including Internet Explorer, have a little down arrow *beside* the Back button. If you click it, it displays a list of the pages you've most recently visited. It's super-handy when you've clicked your way down into a site and want to jump back to your Google results—or anywhere else you've been—without backing through every page along the way.

Congratulations. You've just used one percent of Google's power. And that's as far as 99 percent of the population ever goes.

The rest of this chapter gives you tips on extracting more power from Google using less effort, including a tour of a typical results page highlighting the little-visited corners of Google that hold many treasures (page 24).

How to Get More out of Google

What makes Google so amazing is that, more often than not, you get what you're looking for right away. Google figures out that the pages you're mostly likely to want are the pages other people link to most often.

Why's It Called Google?

"Google" is a cute name, but does it mean anything?

The thing that stands out most on the Google home page is the company's colorful signature. Which raises the question: Why does this search service sound like it's named after a Muppet?

In fact, "Google" is an adaptation of the word *googol*, which is the number 1 followed by one hundred zeroes, or 10^{100}, and brings to mind the stupendously large number of Web pages that it searches.

Incidentally, the word *googol* was coined around 1938 by the 9-year-old Milton Sirotta, the nephew of mathematician Edward Kasner.

Tip: In fact, the system's so reliable that Google offers an I'm Feeling Lucky button, described below, that takes you directly to the page that would appear at the top of your results.

Still, depending on what you're looking for, you may have a hard time finding what you want. And as the Web grows, you can easily get *too many* results. A search for *dog biscuit recipes,* for example, turns up more than 90,000 pages. How do you choose?

Filtering is the name of the game. To prevent an attack of Futile Search Frustration, a few simple techniques help ensure that no matter what you're looking for, you'll get to the stuff you really want—not just somewhere near it. Here's a handful of tricks to keep in mind.

Getting Specific

Google is a smart Web site, but it can't read your mind. If you search for *apple,* Google doesn't know whether you're more interested in the fruit, the computer company, the Beatles label, New York City, the singer Fiona, or something else altogether. (In this case, Google guesses you want to find the computer company, because—thanks to the techie types who hang out online—many more sites link to Apple Computer than to other sites with the word "apple." For more on how Google judges relevance, see page 3.)

Search engines live by the maxim "Garbage in, garbage out." So give Google hints to get what you want—the more specific, the better. Try *apple nutrition, Apple software, Apple Records, the Big Apple,* or *Fiona Apple.* You can take your query a step farther and go for *"how many calories does an apple have?"* Or *Fiona Apple lyrics.*

Tip: Actually, instead of asking Google *"how many calories does an apple have?"* put your search in the form of an answer: *"an apple has * calories"* (the asterisk stands in for the word you don't know, as explained on page 22). After all, you want Google to find *answers*, not *questions*, so you're more likely to hit pay dirt if you search for answers. Here's another example: Instead of the query *"Where does Oscar the Grouch live?"* try *"Oscar the Grouch lives in."* Or, rather than *"Why is Snuffleupagus invisible?"* try *"Snuffleupagus is invisible because."* (When you're searching for specific phrases, use quote marks, as explained on page 19.)

Keep in mind that Google cares about the details of your search terms. A few cases stand out:

- **Singular is different from plural.** As Scrabble mavens know, the "s" is a key letter. Searches for *apple* and *apples* turn up different pages. Try both the singular and plural forms of a word if you're not sure which is more appropriate for your search.

- **The order of words matters.** Google considers the first word most important, the second word next, and so on. Thus, *brown bear* brings up a lot of pages related to big, furry animals first, while *bear brown* starts off with a children's book.

- **Google ignores most little words.** To stay speedy and focused on the most important terms in a search, Google ignores a bunch of common words, known to search aficionados as *stop words*. These include "I," "where," "how," "the," "of," "an," "for," "from," "how," "it," "in," and "is," among others, and certain single digits and letters. Most of the time, this is a good thing. When it's not (say you want to find *The* King, not just king), use quotation marks, described in the next section.

Note: Google doesn't give out its official list of stop words. But after you run a search, it tells you if it has excluded a common word by displaying a message on the results page, right below the search box, something like this: "'the' is a very common word and was not included in your search."

- **Google ignores most punctuation, except apostrophes, hyphens, and quote marks (discussed next).** Google treats *Paul's, Pauls'* and *Pauls* as three different searches (though it acts as if *Senator P. Simon* and *Senator P Simon* are the same guy). And when you hyphenate a word, like *bow-tie*, it also searches for "bowtie" and "bow tie." Google does the reverse, too: If you search for *bowtie*, it also finds "bow-tie" and "bow tie," but it shows you the results in a different order. So for commonly hyphenated or compound words, it's sometimes worth running the search a few different ways to bring up a variety of results.

The other kind of punctuation that Google recognizes is two periods in a row, as explained in the box below.

GEM IN THE ROUGH

Home on the Number Range

Most people use Google to search for *words*. But it also lets you search for a host of identification numbers, like package tracking IDs, as described on page 42. Even more exciting, Google lets you search for a *range* of numbers or dates. Just type two periods between the numbers at either end of the range, and Google shows you results that include those numbers and everything in between.

For example, if you want to find references to New York City in the first half of the 19th century, try *1800..1850 "New York City"*. Google shows you results mentioning the Big Apple during that entire span of years. This trick is also good for prices (*$50..75 Tiffany*) and for other types of numbers (*45..55 MPG Honda* or *400..600 thread count cotton* or *200..300 watt bulbs*).

To Quote a Phrase

If you type in more than one keyword, Google automatically searches for all the words anywhere they appear on a Web page, whether they're side by side or scattered throughout. For example, if you search for this:

```
to be or not to be
```

then Google gives you results that contain those words anywhere on the page, including a page called "Hot or Not?" and the National Do Not Call Registry. Probably not what you had in mind.

If you want only Web pages that contain your words in order, as a complete phrase, let Google know by enclosing your words in quotes. Google calls this a *phrase search*. But despite the fancy name, it's really the most elemental search trick on the planet.

So if you search for *"to be or not to be"*, Google gives you matches only for pages that include that whole, exact phrase. You get links for lots of articles and movies with the famous phrase in their titles, and a bunch of Shakespeare-related sites, too.

Searching Within Your Results

You wanted to see if you could find the text of *Hamlet* online. So you searched for *"to be or not to be,"* enclosing the phrase in quotes, and you got 770,000 results—most of which didn't even mention Denmark.

Google has a great feature for helping you narrow down your results to find the really relevant pages, although almost nobody uses it. Double your Google effectiveness simply by using the "Search within results" link at the bottom of any results page. Figure 1-4 shows you how.

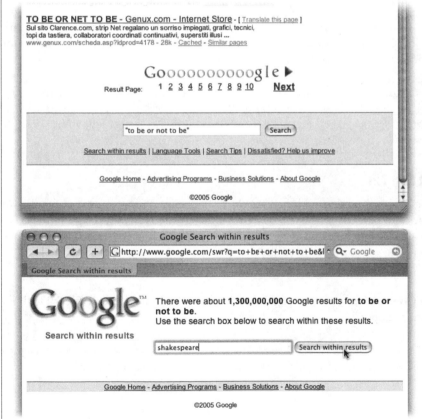

Figure 1-4:
Top: At the bottom of every results page is a link called "Search within results." If you click it, Google offers you a new, blank search box that lets you search for new terms within your results pages only.

Bottom: Enter your new search term here, and then press Enter or click "Search within results" to have Google narrow down your search.

And vs. Or

When you run a search, Google assumes that you want to find *all* of the search words you type. For example, if you search for this:

```
chimps "Los Angeles" trainer
```

then Google finds a list of Web pages containing the words *chimps,* the phrase *Los Angeles,* and the word *trainer.* (Put another way, Google automatically inserts the word AND between each term.) Google does *not* include Web pages that are just about Los Angeles, or just about Los Angeles chimps. A Web page must include all three phrases, or it doesn't make the cut.

If, on the other hand, you want to find pages that have *either* one term or another, type OR between them, like this:

```
"Ben Affleck" OR "Matt Damon" OR chimps
```

In this case, Google gives you pages that include any *one* of the three terms.

Finally, if you want one term plus any of several other terms, group the options in parentheses, like this:

```
chimps ("Ben Affleck" OR "Mark Wahlberg")
```

Now Google shows you pages that include the name "Ben Affleck" or "Mark Wahlberg," plus the word "chimps." Handy when you can't remember which actor was in the 2001 remake of *Planet of the Apes.*

Tip: You can use the | (pipe) character instead of OR, as in: *chimps ("Ben Affleck" | "Mark Wahlberg").* The pipe is above the backslash on your keyboard; to get it, press Shift + \. (This tip's brought to you by the National Society of Unix Gurus and Other Geeks Who Use the Pipe Symbol in Their Programming All the Time.)

Just Say No

Google doesn't understand the word NOT, a programming command familiar to techies and parents of 2-year-olds. But it does let you use a minus sign (or dash) to indicate that you don't want a certain term to appear in your results. For example, if you type:

```
"Ben Affleck" -"Jennifer Lopez"
```

then Google gives you only pages that contain mentions of "Ben Affleck" without "Jennifer Lopez."

Tip: The minus sign must appear *directly* before the word or phrase you want to exclude. If you put a space after the symbol, Google ignores it. Do, however, put a space *before* the minus sign.

This negation trick is most useful when you're searching for a term, like *compact*, that has more than one meaning. (Cocktail-party trivia: These words are called *homographs*.) If you want results about political agreements like the Mayflower Compact, which have nothing to do with small cars or makeup cases or CDs, try something like:

```
compact -car -makeup -disc
```

In addition to weeding out homographs, the minus sign is also handy when you're searching for people or places that share the same name but you want results for only one. For example, when you need to make sure that a search for William Perry, the former defense secretary, doesn't include results for William Perry, the former defensive tackle for the Chicago Bears, try this:

```
"William Perry" -"the Refrigerator"
```

Similarly, if you want to exclude reams of pages focusing on one particular aspect of your subject, like posters of The Refrigerator, go for:

```
"William Perry" "The Refrigerator" -poster
```

Just Say Yes

Because Google ignores certain common words (described above), it sometimes misinterprets a phrase. For example, *omen* and *The Omen* aren't the same thing. If a common word or number is critical to your search, you can tell Google to include it. Simply place a plus sign (+) directly in front of the term you want to include, like this:

```
+the omen
```

which gives you results for hundreds of thousands of pages that mention the classic devil-baby movie.

Tip: Another way to force Google not to ignore little words is to use quotes, as described above. For example, if you put quotes around *"of thee I sing,"* Google gives you pages with the whole phrase, not just the words *thee* and *sing*.

FREQUENTLY ASKED QUESTION

Case Sensitivity

Does Google care if I capitalize my search words?

No. Some search engines, including those on many intranets (private Web sites), are case-sensitive, meaning they search for your terms based on how you capitalize the words. In a case-sensitive world, the query *"ALFRED HITCHCOCK"* wouldn't find Web pages containing the term "Alfred Hitchcock," "alfred hitchcock," or "aLfREd hiTCh-CoCk."

Google, on the other hand, doesn't care about capitalization. If you search for *Pugs, pugs, PUGS,* or even *pUGs,* you get the same results. So give your pinkies a rest and type your queries in all lowercase letters.

Getting Lucky

After the Google Search button, the most prominent feature of Google's home page is the I'm Feeling Lucky button. It's enticing—does it mean you can win the lottery?—but it doesn't tell you what it really does. In fact, the Lucky button takes you directly to the first Web page that you'd see in the listings if you clicked the regular Search button (Figure 1-5). In other words, the Lucky button operates on the premise that it can guess where you want to go.

Figure 1-5:
If you search for Coke *and then hit I'm Feeling Lucky, you land right on Coca-Cola's corporate home page—the same place you'd go if you did a regular search for* Coke *and then clicked the first result. Typing* Excel *and clicking Lucky takes you to Microsoft's main page for its spreadsheet program. Even* president *and Lucky zooms you to* www.whitehouse.gov.

The Lucky button is a fabulous click saver when you're looking for something fairly obvious, like the examples in Figure 1-5. On the other hand, the Lucky button is more like roulette if you're searching for something obscure, like *"purple umbrellas,"* or something generic, like *"pot roast recipes,"* because so many pages can seem equally relevant.

Two Important Google Quirks

Much of the time, Google does what you expect. Quotes, "and" and "or," special symbols—they're all familiar from other search features you've probably used. But Google has two quirks worth noting: weird wildcards and a ten-word query limit.

Wildcards

A lot of search engines let you use *wildcards*. Wildcards are special symbols—usually an asterisk (*) but sometimes a question mark (?)—that you add to a word or phrase to indicate that you want the search to include variants of your query. The wildcard stands in for the possibilities. For example, it you're not sure whether the Culture Club singer was Boy George or Boy Gorge, you might search for *Boy G** to see how other people have completed the word.

But Google doesn't let you include a wildcard as *part* of a word like that. Which, frankly, is a drag. (In programming circles, you may hear the partial-word wild-card referred to as *stemming.*)

Google does, however, offer *full-word* wildcards. While you can't insert an asterisk for part of a word, you can throw one into a phrase and have it substitute for a word. Thus, searching for *"chicken with its * cut off"* could find: "chicken with its head cut off," "chicken with its hair cut off," "chicken with its electricity cut off," and so on.

Tip: A single asterisk stands in for just one word. To set wildcards for more words, simply include more asterisks: *"three * * mice"* leads to "three blind fat mice," "three very tough mice," and so on.

The full-word wildcard isn't as useful as the partial-word wildcard. But it can come in handy for filling in the blanks and when your memory fails. For example, you've always wondered exactly what Debbie Harry was singing in the first line of "Heart of Glass." You think it might have been "Once I had a lung and it was a gas," but you're not sure. Maybe it was "Once I had a lunch and it was a gas." Type in *"Once I had a * and it was a gas"*; Google gives you 1,090 links suggesting the lyric is actually "Once I had a love…" In short, the asterisk combined with quote marks is good for finding quotations, song lyrics, poetry, and other phrases.

The full-word wildcard is also cool when you want the answer to a question. For example, if you're wondering how often Haley's comet appears, you can use the asterisk to stand in for your X factor by running this query:

```
Haley's comet appears every * years
```

If you type your query as a question (*"How often does Haley's comet appear?"*), then Google searches for instances of the question, which is a nice way to find other people with a thin knowledge of astronomy, but might not actually turn up the answer.

Tip: For a search engine that does allow partial-word wildcards, try Altavista (*www.altavista.com*).

The Ten-Word Limit

Quite possibly, you've been using Google since Bill Clinton was president and you've never noticed that the site has a strict limit of ten words per search. Indeed, for most people, this limitation isn't a problem. But if you're the type who likes to search for long phrases, it can be maddening.

For example, if you're looking for *"There's a lady who's sure all that glitters is gold and she's buying a stairway to heaven,"* Google cuts you off after "gold." If that's a problem because, say, you want only instances of the whole sentence, or if you want to add additional query words (e.g. *"live recording"*), you can employ a couple of tricks to circumvent the limit.

Obscurity rules

You can get relevant results without wasting precious keywords by limiting your query to the more unusual keywords or phrase fragments you want to find. In this case, a query that included:

```
"glitters is gold" "buying a stairway"
```

would probably keep you on track while conserving eleven words. If that doesn't fly, try adding words in, one or two at a time (*"buying a stairway to heaven"* instead of *"buying a stairway"*).

Playing the wildcard

Google doesn't count wildcards as part of your ten-word limit. So the full-word wildcard, described above, can really help you out here. Just toss in wildcards for common words, and you're in business. For example:

```
"* * lady * sure * * glitters * gold * she's buying * stairway * heaven"
```

looks strange if you're a person, but Google is a mess of computers, and it eats that query right up while saving you nine big keywords. This is a particularly good trick if you're looking for something with a lot of common words, like *"year *, year *,"* or *"easy *, easy *."*

Interpreting Your Results

Google search results are deceptively simple. Google lists the links from what it believes are most relevant to least relevant, and each link includes snippets of text from the page that included your search terms. Google uses a variety of factors to determine relevance; see page 4 for an explanation.

Each link also includes detailed, useful information—provided you know how to read it. For example, the *cache* you see as part of most results lets you view slightly outdated versions of those pages, which sounds unappealing but can be a *huge* benefit when the grail you're looking for is on a page that somebody has altered or removed from the Web. (Page 26 tells all about using the cache feature.)

Results pages also sometimes contain sponsored links (that is, ads), spelling suggestions, links to news stories, and other stuff that can help you focus your search. Figure 1-6 points out the components.

Google underusers overlook the many parts of a result, but the details are worth knowing about. (Of course, not every result includes all the possible components.)

Interpreting your results is like conducting a basic search: you could spend your whole life never bothering to learn the details, but you'd be missing out on the true power of Google. And by knowing a few tricks, you can, over your life, shave years off your search time.

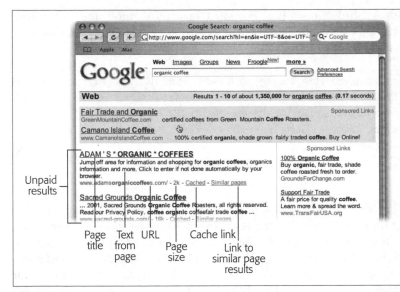

Figure 1-6:
You can easily tell which links are your true, unpaid results: They appear along the left side of your window, and there are often a ton of them. The paid results (or, in common parlance, "ads") are always separate—along the top and/or right side—and they're labeled Sponsored Links.

Your Actual Results

The pages that Google found for you—as opposed to those that somebody paid to have you see—are usually the most important results. Here's how a listing breaks down (Figure 1-6 shows all the parts).

Tip: If you find the text in your Google results listing too small to read, squint no further: Your browser lets you adjust the text size. On a Mac, try ⌘-plus sign or ⌘-minus sign. On a Windows machine, try Ctrl+plus sign or Ctrl+minus sign, or use View → Text Size.

Page title

The first line of each result is a Web page title, usually descriptive and hyperlinked to the actual page. Sometimes, if a page has no title or if Google hasn't yet indexed it, a URL appears instead. Either way, click the link to head over.

Text from the site

The next line or two gives you a few excerpts from the site, with your search terms in bold letters. Usually, this is the most important part of your results because it gives you a sense of the context in which your query appears and whether you want to click through or not. Often, the text itself can serve as the end of your search, especially if you're looking for a quick piece of information.

URL

Next, Google serves up the Web address for that page. Sometimes, the URL is more revealing than the page title. For example, if you're looking for *Café Canopy,* the page title is "Shade Grown Bird Friendly Organic and Fair Trade Coffee from Tree…"—but the URL is simply *www.cafecanopy.com*. If your search words appear in the URL itself, Google bolds them.

Tip: Sometimes, the reverse is true: The page title is useful, but the URL is long and complicated—and not working. You can type a shorter version of the URL directly into your browser, which sometimes gets you to a live part of the same site. Working from the end of the URL, lop off sections after each slash (/). For example, if *http://www.coca-cola.com/usa/ourBrands/sprite.html* doesn't work, try typing *http://www.coca-cola.com/usa/ourBrands/*.

Size

This number is the size, in kilobytes, of the *text* part of the page. (If Google is aware of a site but hasn't yet indexed its text—as explained on page 274—it doesn't offer size data.) Of course, text is usually the least voluminous part of a Web page, so this isn't a reliable indicator of how long a site takes to load. Instead, think of it as a clue to the contents. If the page is just one or two kilobytes, and you're looking for detailed information, it may not be much help. On the other hand, if you're seeking out pages that have lists of links to other pages, look for pages of 20 KB and up.

Date

Occasionally, a result listing displays a date between the size and the cached links. This date is the last time Google *crawled* the page—that is, the last time its automated software went around, confirmed that the page still existed, noted any changes since the last time it visited, and made a copy of it (explained next). Google keeps track of over eight billion Web pages, crawling each of them more than once a month. The date tells you how fresh that copy is, which can give you a clue as to whether it'll be helpful or not.

Cached

As Google tracks Web pages, it keeps copies of them in a repository called a *cache*. While the page-title link takes you to the current site, the Cached link delivers you to the copy Google made when it recorded the page. Google rerecords most pages every few weeks. This time difference is significant because if a page has changed recently, you can still see a slightly older version, which might include the nugget you're looking for or some info you remember from a previous visit.

Note: Webmasters can set up a site so that Google won't cache it. As a result, you may not be able to reach a previous version of every page you find in a list of Google results. In such cases, you simply won't see a Cached link. For a discussion of setting up your site to ward off caching, see page 283.

Google's cache is also handy when a page you need has been deleted or its link is broken. Just click the Cached link, and Google takes you into its time machine. Figure 1-7 shows you what a cached page looks like.

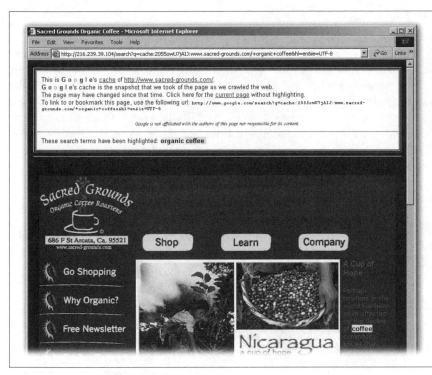

Figure 1-7:
*In addition to showing
you the page when
Google last indexed it,
Google also highlights
your search terms on the
cached page (here you
can see the word "coffee"
highlighted in the lower-
right corner). You can
use the Google toolbar to
create the highlighting
effect on live pages (see
page 188). It's a quick-
and-dirty way to find
your terms fast,
especially on large
pages.*

Google's cache feature is notorious for bringing deleted Web pages back from the grave. For example, in early 2003, Microsoft accidentally published codes on its site that let people crack into its software. Googlers are still hailing the cache feature for helping them find those codes for a couple of weeks after Microsoft pulled down the offending pages.

The cache can save you not only when you're searching for something you recall seeing earlier or something you've heard somebody else wants to hide, but also when you've deleted a page from your own site by mistake. Just hit the cached link, right-click the page to get the source code, copy it, upload it, and you're back in business.

But the cache isn't a cure-all for Web staleness. First of all, a cached page lasts only until Google rerecords the live page, usually every few weeks. And second, cached pages often include dead links. So if you're reading a hot article on a cached page, and it flows to a second page, clicking the Next Page link may get you nowhere. Consider yourself forewarned.

Tip: The Wayback Machine (*www.waybackmachine.org*) is a searchable archive of the Web. Unlike Google, however, it keeps track of Web sites in perpetuity—making it kind of a permanent cache. It's a great resource when you need to find a site that's been defunct for more than a few weeks and has therefore fallen off Google's radar.

Similar pages

The "Similar pages" link searches the Web for pages that fall into the same general category as that result. For example, the pages related to ConsumerReports.org include ConsumerWorld.org, the site for the Better Business Bureau, and other consumer advocacy groups and agencies. Similarly, if you want to find a particular marathon training program, and you've clicked through to the New York Road Runners' site (*www.nyrrc.org*) to no avail, try "Similar pages" to get links to Runner's World, the Boston Athletic Association, and more. In short, "Similar pages" is a really good way to find pages in a category—including those that don't necessarily contain your original keywords.

Indented results

When you run a search and Google finds more than one page with your terms *within the same Web site,* it lists what it thinks is the most important page first, and then it indents less relevant pages, as shown in Figure 1-8.

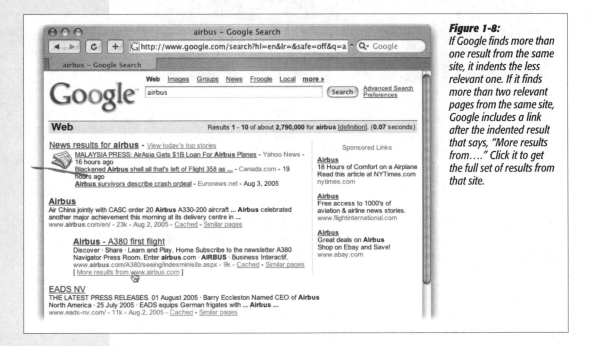

Figure 1-8:
If Google finds more than one result from the same site, it indents the less relevant one. If it finds more than two relevant pages from the same site, Google includes a link after the indented result that says, "More results from…." Click it to get the full set of results from that site.

File format

Web sites often store documents that you can download by clicking a link. Google searches those documents—provided they're in any of 12 common formats—and tells you if something you're looking for is in such a file.

When your query matches words that Google finds in a formatted document, it lets you know by placing a little format marker before the page title, as Figure 1-9 shows.

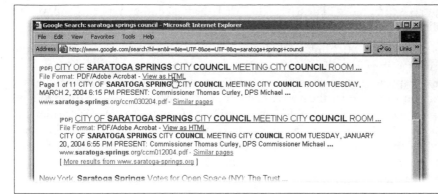

Figure 1-9:
When a Google result is a formatted document instead of a regular Web page, Google abbreviates the file format in brackets before the page title. Directly under that, Google includes a line that starts with File Format and the full name of the file type.

Here's a list of the file types Google recognizes, along with their abbreviations (page 52 gives you tips on searching for specific file types):

• Adobe Portable Document Format (pdf)

• Adobe PostScript (ps)

• Lotus 1-2-3 (wk1, wk2, wk3, wk4, wk5, wki, wks, wku)

• Lotus WordPro (lwp)

• MacWrite (mw)

• Microsoft Excel (xls)

• Microsoft PowerPoint (ppt)

• Microsoft Word (doc)

• Microsoft Works (wks, wps, wdb)

• Microsoft Write (wri)

• Rich Text Format (rtf)

• Text (ans, txt)

Note: PDF, Adobe's Portable Document Format, allows anyone–using any operating system–to create documents that anyone else–no matter *his or her* operating system–can read. To read a PDF, you need Adobe's free Acrobat Reader program, which you can download from *www.adobe.com*. (If you're on a Mac, you can also use Mac OS X's built-in Preview program.)

But what if the page with your critical gem is a PowerPoint document, and you don't happen to own PowerPoint? You're in luck. Google not only keeps track of documents on the Web, it also converts them to HTML—a code your browser can read (see the box on page 30)—and keeps a copy of the HTML for your viewing pleasure. Below the page title is the unassuming link, "View as HTML," which might as well be called "Life Saver." Just click the link, and in a split second, you're reading the file on your browser as a normal Web page.

The "View as HTML" link is also ideal when you don't want to spend half the morning waiting for a file to download and open. For example, if you want to view an Excel spreadsheet, your computer first has to download the spreadsheet file and open it in Excel. Under the best circumstances, this process can take 10 or 20 long seconds. And if the file contains a lot of graphics, it can take a couple of semesters. Click the HTML link to bypass this morass, and you're reading the file immediately. (If the HTML version of a document displays in a font too small to read, look around your browser for a feature that lets you zoom in on a page—something like View → Text Size.)

Note: Sometimes the HTML version of a file appears super-scrambled. If that's the case, no harm, no foul: You can always go back and download the primary version. But if you don't have the right program to read it, you can probably glean most of the info you need from the scrambled-HTML version.

UP TO SPEED

What is HTML?

HTML stands for Hypertext Markup Language, which sounds more complicated than it is.

In fact, HTML is a pretty simple system for encoding text or pictures so that Web browsers can read the information. For example, to make text on a Web page appear in bold, you'd put HTML *tags* around it, like this: <b>Beet juice makes a lousy cleaning solution.</b> And it would appear like this: **Beet juice makes a lousy cleaning solution.** The <b> tag turned on bold formatting, and </b> turned it off.

People create HTML code using word processors, browser-based composing features, and special software like Dreamweaver and FrontPage that automatically tags elements as you build a Web page. In the end, though, HTML ends up as plain text documents stored on computers connected to the Web. Your browser knows how to read these files and display them with fancy formatting rather than ugly tags.

The Things You Didn't Ask For

Along the top and right side of your results page, Google gives you a handful of things you didn't explicitly ask for. But just because they're extra doesn't mean they're not useful. Figure 1-10 maps out the goodies.

Tip: At the top of a results page, above the search box, Google gives you links for the Web, Images, Groups, News, Froogle, Local, and More. Google's standard search looks for your terms on the Web, but Google can also search other electronic collections for the same terms. Each link represents a different place Google can search; if you click one, Google runs the same search there. For example, if you searched for *organic coffee,* and you're wondering what the plant looks like, try the Images link. (Chapter 3 tells you all about Google's different collections.)

Figure 1-10:
Across the very top is the search box with your query, plus the familiar links from the Google home page. You can change your query by clicking in the box and adding more terms or by deleting what's there and running a new search. Under that is the summary bar—and sometimes ads.

The summary bar

The summary bar has two important elements:

- **Each word in your search, underlined.** Click one, and Google takes you to a site with a definition for that word, often with handy audio pronunciation, too. You can use this feature, of course, just to get a definition—even if you don't care about the search results.

- **An estimated number of results and the time it took Google to perform your search.** People like to use the number of results as a measurement of something's popularity or importance, but given the vagaries of the Web and the idiosyncrasies of Google searches, Ouija boards might be more accurate. Still, that number is worth a glance when you're trying to decide whether to look through all 350,000 results or not.

Sponsored Links

Sometimes, below the summary bar and along the right side of the page are short listings with small labels identifying them as *Sponsored Links*. "Sponsored link" is Google-ese for *ads*, and they're a big part of how Google makes its money. Part of Google's allure is that it clearly distinguishes these links from your regular results.

Here's how ads work: When you search for a keyword that people have paid to be associated with, Google displays their ads on the Sponsored Links list. On Google, ads always appear separate from your regular results, and they look different, too, as Figure 1-11 shows. These ads don't affect your results in any way. In fact, a lot of terms don't have any ads associated with them, so you won't always see ads.

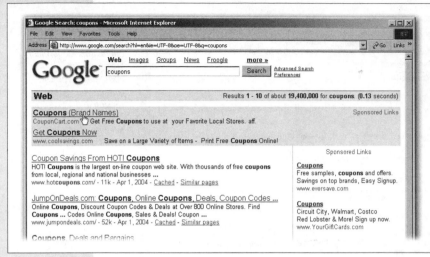

Figure 1-11:
A search for coupons gives you ads—labeled Sponsored Links—above and to the right side of your regular results. Up to two ads can appear above your results (they have colored backgrounds), and as many as eight along the side. If you click anywhere on an ad, Google takes you to the site for the URL displayed in the ad (though it may take you to a page within that site, rather than the home page).

If, for example, you search for *Harry Potter books*, your search results might include ads from BooksAMillion, Amazon, Buy.com, and a half-dozen other places that sell Harry Potter books. If you search for just *Harry*, you get no ads.

Note: Neither Google nor the people who buy the ads are tracking your Google searches; they're simply displaying Web-based ads for anyone who searches for certain words.

A lot of the time, you can ignore the ads. But because they're associated with a specific search you've run, sponsored links are good resources, particularly if you're looking to buy something. Bear in mind that if Google has more than ten advertisers for your keywords, the sponsored links can change on successive results pages. You also might see different ads if you run the same search more than once. So if you're looking for something that might have a useful sponsored link, keep a close eye on them because the one that might help you could be gone the next time you run the same search.

Note: Google's ad program is called AdWords, and advertisers pay only if somebody clicks through their ad. The cost per click varies from 50 cents to $50. If you're interested in placing your own ads on Google, head to Chapter 9.

Other things that can show up: news links and spelling suggestions

If you're looking for something timely—like the latest trial scoop on a deposed CEO—Google often gives you a link called something like, "News results for Martha Stewart," which takes you to Google's own news service. Clicking such a link does the same thing as clicking the News tab on the summary bar. Below that link, Google gives you a few direct links for related news stories on media Web sites. (Google News is explained in depth in Chapter 3).

Note: Google is increasingly incorporating its various collections and search services into the regular search results. So instead of News links, you might find other Google stuff near the top of your results page, things like Froogle results (Chapter 5) or Google Print results (Chapter 3). Sometimes, you'll even get more than one set of extra links.

The other thing you might find under the summary bar is a big question in red letters: "Did you mean: *XYZ?*"

XYZ is an alternate—sometimes corrected—spelling of your search terms (see Figure 1-12). For example, if you searched for *"blue suede shoos,"* Google asks if you meant "blue suede shoes." (On the other hand, if you searched for *"blue suede shoes,"* Google assumes you know what you're doing, and it doesn't offer another spelling.) If you click Google's suggestion, it runs your search again with the alternate spelling.

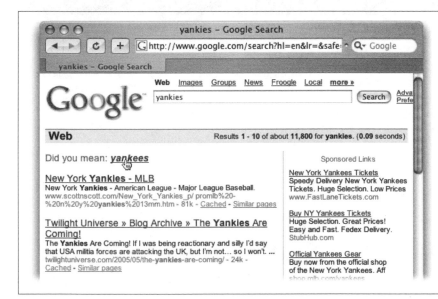

Figure 1-12:
If you spell the famed New York baseball team, "yankies," Google gives you more than 11,000 sites created by other people who think that's a perfectly fine spelling. But Google also suggests an alternate spelling just above your results. Click the suggested spelling to have Google run that search.

The Stuff at the Bottom of the Results Page

The important links at the bottom of a Google results page, shown in Figure 1-13, are those that let you click through to the next page of results. The big blue arrow, the Next link, the number 2 (on the line labeled Result Page), the first yellow "o" in the word Goooooogle, and the "le" at the end of the word all take you to the next page of results. Click each of the subsequent "o"s or any of the numbers under the loooooooogo to jump ahead to that page of results.

At the bottom of the page, you get another chance to retype your query if your first attempt didn't work, and you can narrow down your search by clicking the "Search within results" link, described on page 19.

When Misspelling Is Your Friend

Running a *misspelled* search can sometimes be to your advantage. Because anyone's free to misspell anything on the Web, a lot of pages can wind up left out of a search if you check only the *correct* spelling. Proper names are particularly worth checking a few ways. For example, thousands of Web sites mention *Arnold Schwarznegger,* though the governator spells his name "Schwarzenegger."

And names that orginate in another alphabet (Hebrew, Arabic, Cyrillic) almost always have many valid transliterations. "Mohammed," for example, can be spelled dozens of ways in English.

Unfortunately, Google doesn't offer alternate *mis*spellings or alternate valid spellings. If you search for *Mohamed Atta,* you get 947,000 results and no alternate spellings. Similarly, if you search for *Mohammed Atta,* you get 959,000 results, but Google doesn't suggest "Mohamed Atta" or any other variation on the name.

The bottom line? If Google doesn't give you an additional choice, you have to get creative with spelling.

Figure 1-13:
The links at the very bottom of the page are pretty self-explanatory: They take you to various help and information pages on the Google site.

Note: The Google logo at the bottom of the page grows extra "o"s when a search has more results. The maximum, however, is ten "o"s, even if a search has more than ten pages worth of results. (Links to pages 11 and higher appear magically as you click through the first few pages).

Below the search box is a link with a question: "Dissatisfied? Help us improve." The link takes you to a form where you can tell Google what you were looking for, why you were disappointed, and whether you wanted to find a particular URL. You're not likely to hear back from the company, but they say they read their mail.

When Not to Use Google

Google this, Google that. Is it *always* the best search engine?

No. Here are some reasons to use other search sites:

- **Google simply doesn't perform every search trick you might need.** For example, Google doesn't cluster results. Clustering is a hugely useful feature in which a search engine groups results by topic, as shown in Figure 1-14. (Vivisimo.com is the clustering king.) Nor does Google allow partial-word wildcards (page 22); try nearly any other search engine for that feature.

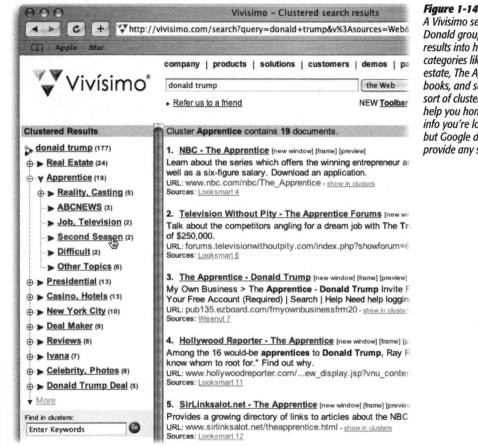

Figure 1-14:
A Vivisimo search for Donald groups the results into helpful categories like real estate, The Apprentice, books, and so on. This sort of clustering can help you home in on the info you're looking for, but Google doesn't provide any such feature.

- **Many sites perform deeper, more specialized searches than Google.** For example, to find a person's email address, you could try typing his or her name into Google. But if you get back random results with no clear email connection, you might try MetaSearchEmailAgent, or MESA, at *http://mesa.rrzn.uni-hannover. de/.* MESA simultaneously queries the major Web-based email search engines, like WhoWhere and Switchboard.

  Similarly, Google is a quick way to find out what an acronym stands for. Or it can return a morass of confusing and unrelated results. For example, when you search Google for *"PDQ"*, you get links for cancer-related sites, printing, yachts, phones, and something called "Touch Free vehicle washes." Even if you narrow it down by trying *"PDQ stands for,"* you still get links about printing, dental work, catamarans, and the Physician Data Query. Pretty Damn Quick shows up, but it's hard to tell how meaningful that is. Acronym Finder (*www. acronymfinder.com*), on the other hand, generates a tidy list of possibilities, with the most common at the top (Figure 1-15).

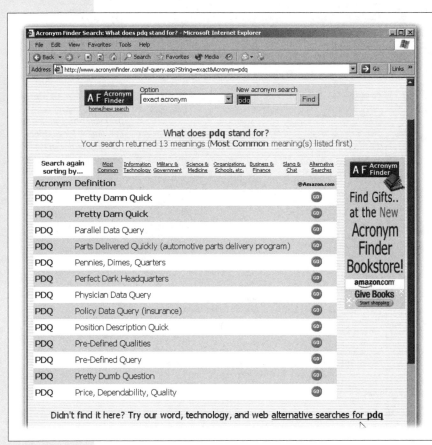

Figure 1-15:
Sometimes Google isn't the best place to do a search. When you want to find what an abbreviation stands for, Acronym Finder cuts through the BS.

- **Some topic-specific directories are simply more fine-tuned than Google's regular full-text search.** For example, you can click through the Google Directory (page 107) to News → Newspapers → Regional → United States → California and come up with dozens of direct links to publications, plus subcategories for College, High School, Kern County, Los Angeles County, San Diego County, and a related category for Regional → North America → United States → California → News and Media.

But if you want more helpful subcategories and more papers, try NewsLink (*http://newslink.org*), a directory for newspapers around the world. Under Newspapers → By State → California, the site lists hundreds of papers grouped by Major metro, Daily, Business, Non-daily, Alternative, Specialty, Limited, Promotional, Campus, Association, and Inactive. The Glendale Gazette may be gone, but its memory lives on.

Still, Google has a ton of links for California papers, probably plenty for the average search. Which is a good example of why Google is nearly always a sound place to start—especially if you don't know where else to turn.

• **When working on an in-depth research project (like a college thesis), Google doesn't help you catalog multiple search results, or let you take notes on interesting sites.** By contrast, Amazon's A9 search service (*a9.com*) is quite a nimble research assistant. You can save and organize your searches, make bookmarks, and take notes on sites you find during your surfing travels (Figure 1-16).

Even if you use A9, though, you're not straying too far from the Good Ship Google. A9 incorporates Google findings right in the search results—along with film facts from the Internet Movie Database, reference results from GuruNet, and Amazon's own "Search Inside the Book" feature for peeking inside the pages of books you haven't bought. All in all, a lot of helpful information.

Figure 1-16:
An A9 search rounds up images as well as Web sites, right in the same window. If you use the A9 Toolbar and sign in (you can use your Amazon.com account name and password), you can even save your search data on Amazon's servers, where you can get to it from any computer in the world. If you're a college student who does research from a different library computer each day, you've just found a new friend.

Nine Very Cool Google Tricks

Google has a handful of tricks up its sleeve. Here are nine special and useful things you can do with Google—several of which even search hounds tend to overlook.

Definitions

When you can't remember what "sedulous" means, or you want to find out what a "wireless LAN" is, you don't have to bother opening the dictionary or calling your friendly neighborhood IT guy. Instead, Google can come to your rescue. Type *define* into the blank search box, followed by your term, like this:

```
define sedulous
```

and then press Enter to have Google include a definition at the top of your search results. (The definitions come from Web sites Google tracks.)

If you want a list of definitions and no other results, type in *define* followed by a colon and your terms, with no spaces on either side of the colon, like this:

```
define:wireless LAN
```

You can also get a list of definitions by typing your term into the Google Deskbar (described on page 221) and pressing Ctrl+D (not available for the Mac). Alternatively, if you use Safari as your Web browser, you can type *define:* followed by your term in the Google search box (not available in Windows) to get the definitions for a word.

Google Definitions aren't just English-only, either. If you ask the site to define a multilingual word like "rouge," for example, and then click "all languages," you get definitions for what the word means in English, French, and German—all on the same results page.

Tip: If Google doesn't come up with a definition that helps you—or in rare cases, if it doesn't come up with one at all—try searching for your terms at *www.OneLook.com,* which aggregates definitions from nearly 1,000 dictionaries. That ought to do it.

Calculator

This trick is extra cool: You can use the blank Google search box as a calculator. Just enter an equation, like *2+2,* and then press Enter to have Google tell you *2 + 2 = 4.* For multiplication, use the asterisk (*), like this: *2*3.* For division, use the slash (/), like this: *10/3.* You can also use the search box to perform unit conversions, like this: *5 kilometers in miles* or *how many teaspoons in a cup?* For a chart listing of units of measure Google can convert, check out Nancy Blachman's site, GoogleGuide, at *www.googleguide.com/calculator.html.*

The calculator works for simple equations and for some seriously complex operations, too, like logarithms and trigonometric functions. You can find a rundown of all its capabilities at *www.google.com/help/calculator.html.* And if you know what a physical constant is—or the phrase "base of the natural system of logarithms" makes your heart pitter patter with joy—GoogleGuide does a terrific job of steering you through these features.

Tip: For a great alternative interface to Google's calculator, check out Soople at *http://soople.com/ soople_intcalchome.php*. Page 59 tells you all about it.

Phonebook

Google provides a phonebook service, letting you look up a phone number and address (with corresponding map) for business or residential listings. You can make it work in two ways: either as part of your regular search results (with a cute phone icon indicating that something is a phonebook listing), or as a separate set of listings. Figure 1-17 shows the difference.

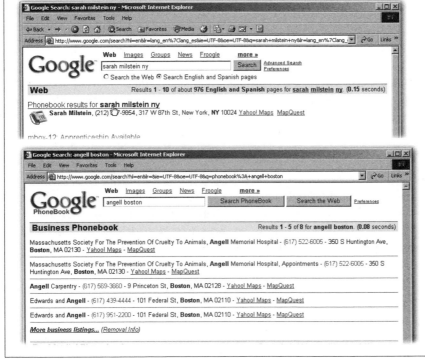

Figure 1-17:
Top: You get just one or two results when you know lots of details beforehand—like the full name of the person or business, and their state or Zip code—so you're likely to hit the right result.

Bottom: A full listing is the way to go when you have only a partial name and a state. (Either way, the listings are sometimes out of date, as shown at top.)

To have a single residential listing appear at the top of a regular results page, try typing any of the following into the Google search box:

- First name (or first initial), last name, city (state is optional)
- First name (or first initial), last name, state
- First name (or first initial), last name, area code

- First name (or first initial), last name, Zip code

- Last name, city, state

- Last name, Zip code

For a single *business* listing, typing in the company name along with city and state or Zip code ought to do the trick.

Tip: You can also type an area code and phone number—business or residential—to get the name and address associated with it in Google's phonebook. You don't need to include any punctuation.

To get a page of nothing but phonebook listings, type the word *phonebook* followed by a colon, then a space, and then the name and state you want to look up. (Weirdly, you can't capitalize *phonebook*.) The phonebook listings give you about 600 results, so if you're looking for a common name, add the city (if you know it) to narrow your search. Your query should look something like this:

```
phonebook: ansonia veterinary center NY
```

or:

```
phonebook: ansonia veterinary center new york NY
```

You can also narrow your search by telling Google whether you want to search for business listings or residential listings only. To limit your search to residential listings, type *rphonebook* before the name and state. For business listings, use *bphonebook*. (If you don't specify one or the other, and your results have both types, Google gives you five of each and lets you pick which you'd like the full set for.)

Note: Google has a parallel service, Google Local, that provides contact information for businesses anywhere in the U.S. Unlike the phonebook feature, which requires that you know a name, Google Local works more like a Yellow Pages, letting you search by business type (eyeglasses, or bagels, or dog walkers) in a specific Zip code or town. The results look similar to phonebook listings. (Sometimes, when you run a search even *with* a business name, you get results from Google Local, which has a compass logo rather than a phone icon. See page 62 for the details.)

The phonebook trick has a couple of quirks:

- **You can't use the minus sign to exclude terms.** For example, if you want to find every New Yorker with the last name Doe except those with the first name John, you can't run the search *rphonebook: doe -john new york NY*.

- **You can't use OR to find listings in more than one state.** For example, the query *bphonebook: espn (NY OR NJ)* gives you listings only in New Jersey, since Google reads the rightmost part of your query. On the other hand, you *can* use OR with the name of a person or business. So if you want to find an array of chain restaurants in the heart of Manhattan, try *bphonebook: (espn OR hooters) new york NY*.

Tip: If you want to remove your listing from Google's phonebook, head over to *www.google.com/help/ pbremoval.html,* which provides a delisting form for residences and a snail-mail address to send delisting requests for businesses.

Street Maps

If you enter a U.S. street address—including city and state, or Zip code—Google usually tops your results with links to several maps.

Stock Quotes

If you enter a ticker symbol for a company or mutual fund listed on the New York Stock Exchange, NASDAQ, or the American Stock Exchange, Google begins your results with a link for that corporation or fund; when you click the link, Google takes you to a page with tabs of stock information from Yahoo Finance, Quicken, and other companies. You can enter one symbol, like this: *msft* (for Microsoft). Or several symbols, like this:

```
msft gm dis
```

If you don't know the ticker symbol for a company, try the full name. If Google recognizes it as a public company, it provides a link for stock quotes at the end of the result for that company (Figure 1-18).

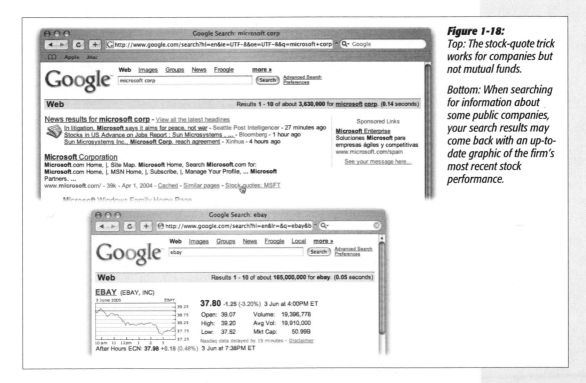

Figure 1-18:
Top: The stock-quote trick works for companies but not mutual funds.

Bottom: When searching for information about some public companies, your search results may come back with an up-to-date graphic of the firm's most recent stock performance.

Even when you're not specifically looking for the financial lowdown, stock quotes and charts may show up in your regular search results. Type in *ebay,* and you often get the stock's most recent daily performance results from NASDAQ, atop links to all other things eBay on your search results page (see Figure 1-18).

Tip: Sometimes, adding the word *company* or *corporation* after the proper name in your query (like *Microsoft Corporation*) can prompt Google to recognize that you want stock info.

Patents, Tracking IDs, and Other Numeric Goodies

Hardly anyone knows this, but Google lets you search for *numbers* on the Web. And not just any numbers, but specific tracking IDs: U.S. patent numbers, FAA airplane registration numbers, FCC equipment ID tags, Universal Product Codes, maps by area code or Zip code, and vehicle identification numbers. When Google comes up with a match for your number, it shows you a special listing at the top of your results page, as shown in Figure 1-19.

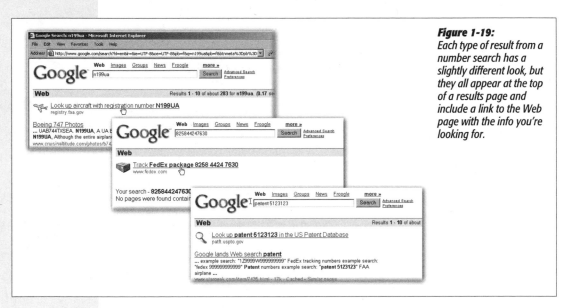

Figure 1-19:
Each type of result from a number search has a slightly different look, but they all appear at the top of a results page and include a link to the Web page with the info you're looking for.

Here's how to run the specific searches:

- **UPS, FedEx, and U.S. Postal Service tracking numbers.** Looking up package tracking numbers and finding out whether your Lands' End long underwear is stuck in a warehouse in Kentucky has long been a major benefit of the Web. The process just got easier. Simply type your tracking number in a blank search box, and Google provides a link to a Web page with your item's transit history.

- **Patent numbers.** If you look up patent numbers regularly—or ever—you know the U.S. Patent and Trademark Office makes you jump through a lot of hoops to find a patent by number. Stave off a few gray hairs by using Google to look them up instead. Just preface the number with the word "patent," like this: *patent 5123123.*

- **Universal Product Codes (UPCs).** For some basic information on consumer products, like their manufacturer, try looking up the UPC, like this: *036000250015* (no need to include UPC first). Most of the time, you can find UPCs under an item's barcode.

- **Federal Communications Commission equipment ID numbers.** If you're an engineer at a wireless phone company, and you want inside info on a competitor's product, check out the FCC's database. To get there, type *fcc* into Google, followed by the ID number, like this: *fcc G9H2-7930.*

- **Flight numbers.** Want to find out if your cousin's flight from Ottawa is on time? Check flight status by typing in the airline and flight number, like this: *continental 501.*

- **Federal Aviation Administration airplane registration numbers.** If you're the head of a startup airline, and you're considering buying a used plane from one of the big industry players, this feature's for you! Just type in the registration number directly, like *n233aa,* and Google gives you a link to the FAA site with some details about the manufacturer and history of that plane.

Tip: You can typically find airplane registration numbers on the tail of a plane.

- **Vehicle identification numbers (VINs).** If you're buying a used car, you can use the VIN to learn more about that individual auto's history (the VIN is usually on a small metal tag at the bottom edge of the windshield). Type in a number, like *JH4NA1157MT001832,* and Google provides a link to the Carfax info for that car.

- **Maps by area code or Zip code.** Type in an area code, like *212,* or a Zip code like *95472,* and the top of your Google results includes a link for a MapQuest map of that region. The maps generally cover a larger area than the area code, but they can give you a sense of whether 609 is in New Jersey or Idaho.

Note: If you'd like Google to add another type of number to its search service, let them know: *suggestions@google.com.*

Weather

You don't need a weatherman to know which way the wind blows, thanks to Google's weather forecast feature. Just search for *weather,* followed by the name of the U.S. city you're meteorologically mulling, as in *weather fargo.* Google pops up current conditions and the four-day forecast for your specified burg, as shown in Figure 1-20. (The info comes courtesy of the Weather Underground site.)

Figure 1-20:
Your four-day forecast is just a few keystrokes away in Google's search box; just type in weather, *followed by the name of an American city. And if four days isn't far enough ahead for you, click the first link to jump to an even more foresightful forecast.*

Most of the time, just a city name is enough information, but you can also add in the state and Zip code if you don't get the results you had in mind. (There are more than a few Portlands, after all.) And although you can easily get the weather for London (in Kentucky) and Paris (in Tennessee) if you include the state abbreviations, Google's weather feature usually refers you to CNN or BBC links for international weather.

Q&A

If you find yourself in need of fast facts, Google's Q&A feature may help fill the bill. The trick's to phrase your question as a *fact*.

If you want to know how many people live in South Korea or who the president of Mexico is these days, for example, just search for *population of south korea* or *president of mexico*. Google brings back the answer at the top of your results page.

Movies

Don't waste time rustling up a newspaper or waiting through Mr. Moviefone's yammering over the phone: You can find out what's playing down at the nearest multimegaplex by asking Google. If you live in Phoenix, just type *movies phoenix* or *showtimes phoenix* in the search box, and you'll get a list of films playing in theaters around Phoenix. If you click the film title you're considering, Google gives you a list of theaters and screening schedules.

You can search directly for a movie currently playing in your town, too. If you typed in *star wars phoenix* during the summer of 2005, you would've gotten a list of the theaters showing *Star Wars Episode III: Revenge of the Sith* around Arizona's capital.

If you've already told Google where you live using Google Local (page 62), you can leave off the city name and just type *movies, showtimes,* or *star wars* to get theaters, schedules, and showtimes (respectively) for your area.

Google's movie mania isn't limited to listing showtimes. If you remember vague details about a film but can't remember its title, try using the *movie:* operator in front of any factoids you remember, like directors, actors, or plot points in the production. The search *movie: holy grail* delivers a long list of films focusing on the Arthurian legend, including *Excalibur, Indiana Jones and the Last Crusade,* and, of course, *Monty Python and the Holy Grail.* Figure 1-21 shows how obscure you can get.

Figure 1-21:
The movie search operator does more than just round up theaters and showtimes for current flicks playing around town. Feed it a few facts from movies you can't fully remember, and Google brings back the title and other information like reviews and pop-culture cross-references. You can also use the movie: operator in front of actors' names to pull up a partial filmography of the stars' noted roles.

A Final Tip: Googling Google

If you find yourself staring at a Google feature you've never heard of before, or if you're wondering when Google introduced the calculator, or if you want to know about getting a job at the company, head to the bottom of the home page or any search results page and click About Google. The links there take you to all four corners of the Google universe—if you can figure out where to look. For example: Is the calculator under Web Search Features or Services & Tools?

Half the time, it's easier to simply Google Google. There's a blank search box on almost every page within About Google, usually labeled "Search our site" or "Find on this site." When you run a search (like *a google job*) you get a regular page of Google results, complete with handy snippets. It's a terrific timesaver—letting you learn within seconds that the place to send your résumé is *www.google.com/jobs*, for example. Too bad they don't make Google for your life.

Tip: Cheaters may never win, but cribbing with the Google Cheat Sheet (*www.google.com/help/ cheatsheet.html*) provides a quick hit of instant gratification when you can't remember a particular Google command. The Cheat Sheet keeps essential Google information stashed on one simple Web page, including a quick recap of common Google search operators, calculator functions, and the URLs for other Google services.

Superior Searching

Searching the Web is like panning for gold. There's a lot of dirt out there, and you need the right tools to get at the shiny nuggets. The previous chapter provided the sieve. But to become a real search jockey, you need tweezers. And forceps. And maybe a staple gun.

It may help to think of every search as a problem, and to bear in mind that different problems require different solutions. "How do I find out which Web sites link to mine?" needs a different approach than "I want to find sites about Miss Piggy—but only those in Urdu."

This chapter sets you up with an array of techniques that you can use to run different kinds of searches or get more specific results from any search. Because Google's preference settings can affect all of your results big time, this chapter covers them, too.

Have It Your Way: Setting Preferences

Software programs almost always let you change some settings, like the way Microsoft Word lets you choose the standard font or turn spell checking on and off. Google lets you set some preferences, too. Unlike Word and other programs that hang out on your hard drive, Google remembers your settings with a *cookie,* a tiny file that a Web site can place on your computer and communicate with.

You can reach Google's settings page by clicking Preferences on the home page or at the top of any results page. Figure 2-1 shows the Preferences page, from which Google lets you control five settings: interface language, search language, filtering, number of results, and which window the results appear in. You have to click Save Preferences to activate the new settings.

Tip: If you change your settings and return to Google only to find they didn't take, your browser could be set to reject cookies. Check your browser's security or privacy settings. In Internet Explorer, for example, choose Tools → Options and then click the Privacy tab. You can move the slider to change the intensity with which the program blocks cookies (anything below the highest setting works for Google). Or you can click Edit to specify a Web site from which you want to allow cookies—in this case, *www.google.com*.

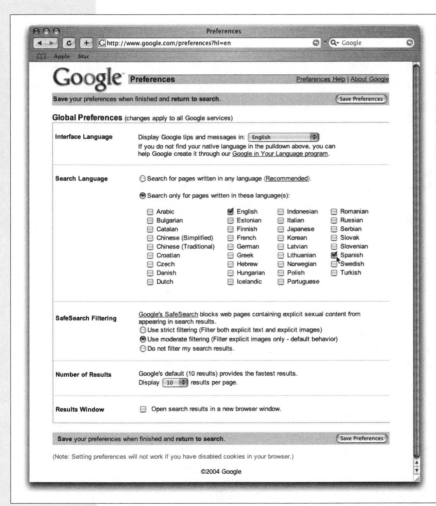

Figure 2-1:
The changes you make on Google's Preferences page affect every search you do. You can tweak the settings for individual searches on the Advanced Search form (page 50) and other places described throughout this chapter.

Interface Language

The interface language controls the language Google uses to display tips and messages. Google sets itself to use English, but you can change it to anything from Afrikaans to Zulu. If you want to add some zing to your Google experience, try

Bork, bork, bork! (the Swedish Chef), Elmer Fudd, or Hacker. For the less adventurous, Google provides Tamil and Scots Gaelic.

Search Language

The *search* language is different from the *interface* language. Instead of affecting the way Google talks to you, the Search Language limits your results to pages that are written in the language you specify. Google assumes you want sites in any language, but if you'd prefer sites only in Finnish and Catalan, this is the place to say so. Just click the blank box next to a language.

Note: You can choose as many languages at once as you like.

The tricky part is that this setting really, *really* limits your results. Unless you know for certain that you always want to search in one language, you're probably better off using Google's Language Tools (page 58) to fine-tune individual searches.

SafeSearch Filtering

It's no secret that the Web is home to a lot of explicit text and pictures. If you want your search results to avoid some or possibly all of that material, you can filter it out with SafeSearch, which has three modes:

- **Moderate filtering** removes results with explicit images, but not explicit language. Google comes set to Moderate.

- **Strict filtering** nixes both explicit images *and* language.

- **No filtering** blocks nothing.

Moderate filtering usually works fine for most casual Web surfers. Because Google tries to give you the most relevant pages first, a search for *breast cancer* or *impotence* is unlikely to yield inappropriately salacious results in the first few thousand listings when you've got moderate filtering on. But occasionally, moderate filtering can cause you to miss something important. If you don't mind surprises every now and then, turn the filtering off. Those of you who *want* particularly spicy content, or none at all, know who you are.

Number of Results

Google is set to display 10 results per page. Studies have shown that most people never click past the first page of results on any search site. You can increase your changes of finding your Holy Grail if Google shows you more results at once: just change the setting to 20 results per page.

Note: You can change this setting to get up to 100 results per page, but it can get hard to read really long results pages. And if your computer is very slow, it may take it an annoyingly long time to display a big list. Ten to 30 results per page is probably a good range.

Results Window

Unless you tell it otherwise, Google displays your results pages in the same browser window where you ran your search. So when you click a link on the results page, Google replaces your results list with the page you've decided to explore. But when you turn on "Open search results in a new browser window," Google leaves your results page intact and starts up a new window in your browser when you click a result. (After it's opened the second window, Google doesn't *keep* opening new windows when you click results links; it just switches what you see in the second one.)

Note: If you're using a browser with tabs (page 196), this setting may make your search results open in a new *tab,* rather than a new window altogether.

Google comes with this setting turned off, but it's a great one to turn on, as it lets you use one window to view the Web pages you've found and the other to keep track of your results. If you often explore more than one result, or if you find yourself clicking deep into sites or following links to new pages, this setting can save you a lot of hassle getting back to your results. (If your computer is getting geriatric and struggles to keep open a lot of windows, then leave this setting off.)

Tip: In most browsers, you can open additional windows on a case-by-case basis by right-clicking any link and choosing something like "Open in new window," or "Open link in new window." (On Mac browsers, you can often ⌘-click a link to achieve the same result.)

Advanced Search

On every Web page it tracks, Google records a handful of things, including the URL, body text, links to other pages, files in particular formats, and other goodies (Chapter 1). A simple Google search tells you when those things exist on the pages in your results. But if you want to *restrict* your search using those nit-picking criteria—to find only PowerPoint presentations for the terms you're using, for example—you may feel lost.

Google's Advanced Search page can help you sort things out. You can get to it by clicking the Advanced Search link on Google's home page or at the top of any results page. Figure 2-2 shows the straightforward form.

Refining Your Search

Advanced Search can be a quick way to build a complex query. It's particularly handy when you want to run a *multipart search*—like one that looks for either *Ren* or *Stimpy,* but returns only results that are also in PDF format.

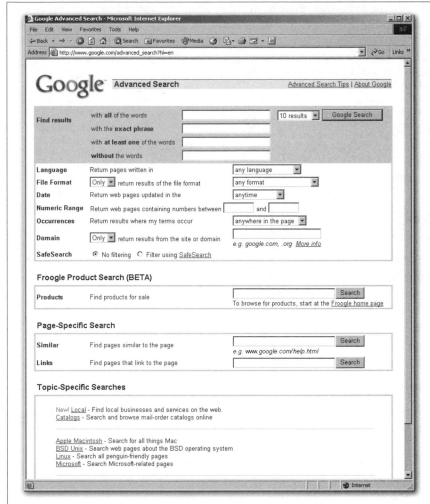

Figure 2-2:
Google's Advanced Search lets you take a piece of fine-grit sandpaper to your search results, brushing away superfluous results to leave you with just the ones you want. (If you're familiar with database queries, this form probably looks familiar.)

Tip: Occasionally, multipart queries from Google's Advanced Search page simply don't work. If that happens to you, consider using special Google *syntax* (described in detail on page 65), which is sometimes more flexible. For example, the keyword *define*, followed by a colon and another word (as in, *define:vintner*) tells Google to search for a definition of the second word (in this case, *vintner*). Other syntax features let you restrict your search by file type, language, and so on.

Query words

At the top of the page, in the shaded gray section labeled "Find results," Google gives you four choices for how you would like it to treat your search terms. In order from top to bottom, these mimic the results you can get by using the operators AND, quote marks, OR, and the minus sign. The helpful thing here is that you can use these puppies in combination—which is nice when you want to do something like search for two phrases simultaneously, or search for one and exclude the other. Figure 2-3 shows one possibility.

Figure 2-3:
This search gives you results that include the phrase "Miss Piggy" and either the words "Kermit" or "frog" but not the phrase "Jim Henson."

Language

The language menu lets you specify whether you want your results to include pages written in any language, or just one particular language.

Tip: The language tools explained on page 58 give you a lot more control over this feature.

File Format

The cool thing about the File Format option is that not only can you search for specific file types, like Word or PowerPoint documents, but you can *exclude* them, too. If you're looking for an example of a table of contents in any format other than PDF, this is the place to let Google know.

On the other hand, this Advanced Search feature lets you specify only PDF, Postscript, Word, Excel, PowerPoint, and Rich Text Format. It doesn't let you choose from the many other file types Google indexes. For those, you have to use the *filetype* syntax, described on page 71.

Date

The Date option lets you limit your search results to pages that Google has recorded in the last three months, six months, or year. This search has nothing to do with the date a page was created, but rather *when Google indexed it.* (For an explanation of Google's indexing process, see page 274.) If you created a page on March 15 but Google didn't record it until August 29, for example, it shows up in a date search for August 29.

Note: Google rerecords pages regularly—usually every few weeks. But if a page's content doesn't change from one recording to the next, Google doesn't update the index date.

So what's the use of this feature? Google indexes the Web regularly enough that specifying a range can help filter out irrelevant results. If you're wondering what Lance Armstrong has been up to since the Tour de France, try searching for pages indexed in the last month (or however long it's been since the Tour).

To zoom in on any date range beyond the last three months, six months, or year, see the box on page 71.

Specifying where on a page to search

Google keeps track of text in the body of a page, in the URL, in the links to other pages, and in the page's title (which is different from the URL). The Occurrences pop-up menu lets you tell Google when you're looking for results from only one of those places. Here's when you may want to use them:

- **In the title.** A Web page's URL isn't the same thing as its title. A URL is an address that your computer can read, and sometimes you can read, too (for example, *www.npr.org*). But often, URLs are super-long and contain a slew of characters and symbols that make no sense unless you're a droid. In those cases, it's useful when a page has a separate, readable title that a Webmaster has written to help you understand what's on that page. The first line of a Google result is usually a page's title, for example, as Figure 2-4 illustrates.

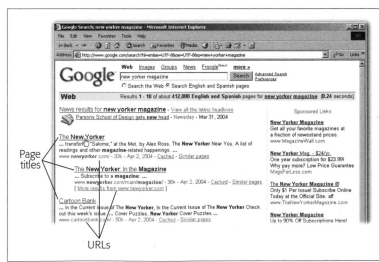

Figure 2-4:
Titles and URLs usually say different things, though sometimes a URL is the title for a page. When you click a title, it takes you to the page for the URL listed.

A word that's mentioned in the title of a page is more likely to indicate what's on that page than a word that shows up randomly in the text. For example, a page called "File sharing for fun and profit" is more likely to explain how to go about file sharing than a page that simply mentions the topic as part of a side discussion. Use this feature, therefore, to get a smaller, more focused list of results.

- **In the text.** Asking Google to ignore titles, URLs, and links is useful when you want to search for keywords or phrases that are likely to show up all over the place. For example, if you want only sites that discuss those bumpkins known as yahoos, and you don't want pages from Yahoo.com or links to that site, use this feature to help filter out references to the Web site.

- **In the URL.** Want to find out how many sites have already used the word "sneaker" in their URLs? Here's the place to check. Happily, this feature doesn't limit you to simple Web addresses, like *www.sneaker-nation.com*; it also gives you back more complex results, like *www.cynosure.com.au/isp/sneaker.*

Note: Searching for a term within a URL yields only results with whole words. In the example above, Google would give you back *www.sneaker-fetish.com* or *www.sneaker.fetish.com,* but not *www. sneakerfetish.com.*

- **In the links.** This feature simply searches for the text in hyperlinks that connect pages. It's useful in two situations. First, if you want to find out what pages have links to a certain person, phrase, or site, the "in links to the page" option can give you a rough idea.

Note: The *text* of a link may have nothing to do with the page it links to. Most commonly, you see sentences like, "To read about Barry Bonds, click here." If "here" is the text for the link, your search for *Barry Bonds* isn't going to bring up this page; only a search for *here* would do it—but since tons of Web sites use the word "here" in their links, you're very unlikely to find what you want that way.

Second, the links search can help you find a person's email address because on most Web pages, an email address *is* a link. If the person's name is part of the email address, or if the page says something like, "For more information, email Brad Pitt," you're in business.

Domain

The Domain feature lets you restrict your search to a single site or to a domain (like .edu or .com). The site restriction is useful when you want to look up specific keywords on a site that has no search function (or that has a lousy one). It's also good for a site whose search function is seriously annoying—maybe it displays results confusingly, or it doesn't let you use the OR operator. And sometimes a Google site search turns up goodies you simply can't seem to reach through a regular on-site search. To see the difference, try running a query with NYTimes.com as the site, and then try the same search terms using the *New York Times*' own search feature.

Note: The site search doesn't search related Web sites. For example, if you want to search all of Google's sites, restricting your query to Google.com means you'll miss anything in *www.answers.google.com, http://labs.google.com,* and so on. To make sure you hit those sites, too, try searching for *Google* in the URL, described above.

Limiting your search results to a particular domain can help, for example, sift out sites that want to sell you things. Figure 2-5 shows you what a difference it can make to limit your results to the .org domain—thus filtering out the common .coms and other flotsam.

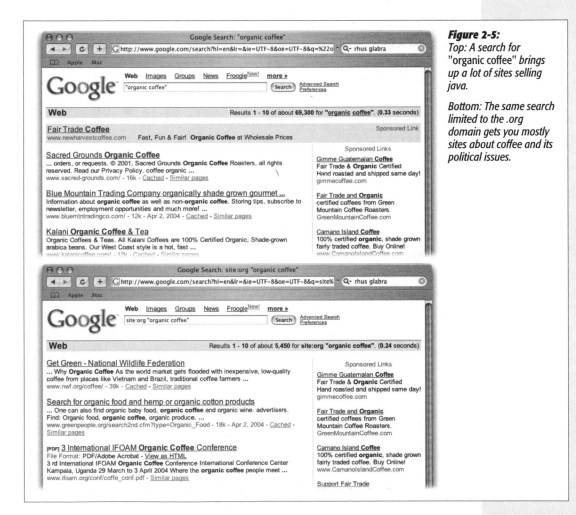

Figure 2-5:
Top: A search for "organic coffee" *brings up a lot of sites selling java.*

Bottom: The same search limited to the .org domain gets you mostly sites about coffee and its political issues.

The domain option also lets you *rule out* a particular site or domain—handy if your results are overwhelmed by one site that you know doesn't contain the info you want.

SafeSearch

As described in the discussion of preferences on page 49, SafeSearch lets you filter out offensive content. If you normally keep it turned on, but you want it off for a single search that may suffer from filtering (like *bra sizes*), you can make the change here.

Page-Specific Search

Google lets you run two special searches for any particular page.

Similar

When you type a URL in the "Similar" box, Google searches for pages in that general *category*. For example, the pages related to *www.nascar.com* are parts of sites like NFL.com, MLB.com, NBA.com, ESPN.com, PGA.com, and so on.

Note: The Similar feature runs the same search as the "Similar pages" link that shows up in a Google result (see page 28).

Links

If you have a Web site, you could spend fully half your waking hours wondering who has linked to your pages. Just type in a URL here, and Google spits out a list of pages linked to it. (Obviously, this works even if the URL isn't for your own site.)

Topic-Specific Searches

Your first two choices here, Google Print and Google Scholar, take you to the search pages for those specialized Google searches, described on pages 115 and 117, respectively.

Below that are links for a few broad categories in which Google has already done a little filtering for you. These topic-specific searches are all just common subsets of the Google database and help keep your searches focused. From Apple Macintosh to the U.S. Government, the topics are self-explanatory. The link for Universities takes you to a page with a handy alphabetical listing of school sites Google has recorded.

Advanced Search on Steroids

Google provides a useful advanced search form, but you can also run more specific searches from Fagan Finder, a site that has no official relationship with Google (Figure 2-6). It works best from Internet Explorer (*www.faganfinder.com/google.html*),

but an alternate version that works with other browsers is well worth a try, too (*www.
faganfinder.com/google2.html*).

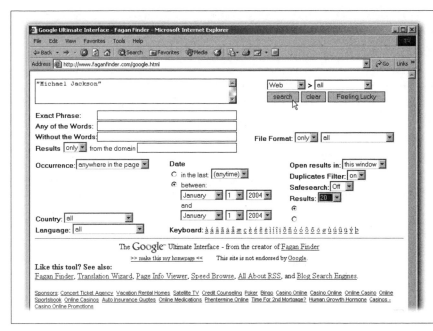

Fagan Finder has all the choices you can specify on Google's advanced search
page—things like the type of file you want to find and the domain you'd like to
restrict your search to. But unlike Google, Fagan Finder has put several other variables on the same page, letting you run a highly specialized search without using
syntax or multiple searches. The extra choices include:

• A menu that lets you specify the *type* of Google search you want to run (it's
above the Search button). For example, you can search Google's Directory,
Groups, Images, News, Catalogs, Froogle, or a few other oddball Google types
(the Alternate option lets you run your query on other search sites, like Yahoo).
What makes Fagan Finder's system notable is that *one* page lets you run an
advanced search in any of these special collections; on Google's site, each special collection has its own advanced search page, forcing you to recreate your
search if you want to check in on several areas. And Google's advanced search
pages don't include as many detailed choices as Fagan Finder's.

• A menu that lets you specify *subsets* of the Google search you want to run (it's
above the Feeling Lucky button). For example, if you're searching the Web, you
can choose to run your query through Google's keyboard shortcut page (choose
"all-shortcuts") so you can navigate your results without a mouse. Or you can
choose to search just Google's own site (handy if you're looking for help on a
particular feature), or a bunch of other narrow slices of the Web. For each type
of Google search, the subsets change (the Directory search, for instance, lists the

categories you'd find on Google's main directory page), but note that not all searches have subsets (News, for instance, has none).

Tip: Choose your type of search and subset before setting up the rest of your search. Some of the types and subsets don't have the choices the regular search does, so you could waste time setting options that disappear when you pick a search type.

- **The country** from which you'd like your results to hail.
- **A specific date or date range** for your results. Google lets you give a general range, like "past three months." Like Google's date feature (on the Advanced Search form), this option searches for pages that Google indexed or re-indexed within the period you specify.
- **Special characters,** handy for quests in languages other than English. When you click a letter on the Fagan Finder page, it appears in the general search box.

Tip: If you're trying to type a long query into the Exact Phrase box or any of the other search boxes, formulate your query in the regular box—which gives you a lot more breathing room and lets you make changes easily—and then cut and paste into whichever search box you'd like to use.

- **The ability to turn off the duplicates filter.** You may have noticed that from time to time when you run a search in Google, your list of results is rather small, but Google inserts a message at the bottom that says something like, "In order to show you the most relevant results, we have omitted some entries very similar to the 5 already displayed. If you like, you can repeat the search with the omitted results included." Google gives you this option because it automatically represses sites it thinks may be duplicates. Fagan Finder lets you run a search with this filter turned off from the start, which is useful if you frequently click to see the omitted results message in Google.
- **A choice to open results in the same window you're already in or in a new window.** Google lets you set this option on its preferences page (as explained on page 47).

Note: The Fagan Finder Google page has an I'm Feeling Lucky button. Mostly, you don't need this for advanced searches, but if you make Fagan Finder your home page, it's nice to have the Lucky choice available.

Fagan Finder has a mess of non-Google features worth exploring, too. Head over to the home page, *www.faganfinder.com*, for a full menu of search tools.

Searching by Language and Country

Google's Language Tools are a collection of features that let you fiddle with the language and location of your search. For example, you can limit an individual

GEM IN THE ROUGH

Soople Your Google for a Great Calculator

While Fagan Finder lets you do some fancy searching, it isn't the only site that has an alternate interface for Google's advanced search features. Another site, *www.soople.com,* provides a very straightforward set of search boxes for each of Google's special features. And like Fagan Finder, it gives you the same high-quality results you'd get from Google itself.

For example, on Soople under "Filter search for filetype," you can type in your search words and pick the type of document you'd like to search for: Word, Excel, PowerPoint, or Acrobat, for example. An added bonus is that in the title of each type of search, Soople includes a link called "explain," which opens a box that gives a clear description of that feature and how to use it.

Soople is easier to use than Google's advanced search or Fagan Finder, but it doesn't provide *quite* as many options in most cases. For example, Google can search for two more document types not mentioned on Soople (Adobe PostScript files and Rich Text Format files). And Fagan Finder lets you cross-examine Google in unique ways.

But Soople stands out for its calculator page, which you can get to from the main Soople page by clicking the Calculator link at the top, or by pointing your browser to *www.soople. com/index.php?p=&sub=calculator.* Google's built-in calculator function lets you do some really, really complex stuff, but you have to remember a bunch of weird symbols and phrases to use most of those features (explained at *www.google.com/help/calculator.html*).

Soople, on the other hand, lays out each function in its own easy-to-use search box. Want to know the square root or percentage of something? This is your stop. It's also handy for logarithms, trigonometric functions, and other geeky stuff.

search to pages written in a particular language or pages from a country you specify. You can also translate text you type or entire Web pages. And you can try out a new interface language or run a search from a Google site in another country.

To find these features, click Language Tools on Google's home page or any results page, or point your browser to *www.google.com/language_tools.* Here are the tools and what you can do with them:

- **Search Specific Languages or Countries.** This feature, shown in Figure 2-7, lets you narrow a search to pages written only in a certain language, with or without limiting it to pages from one country. If you're looking to learn what

Korean students at Bulgarian universities have to say about American pop stars, this is the tool to use.

Note: This feature is like any advanced search on Google: it works for just one search. If you *always* want to search for pages written in a language other than English, change your Google preference settings, as described on page 47.

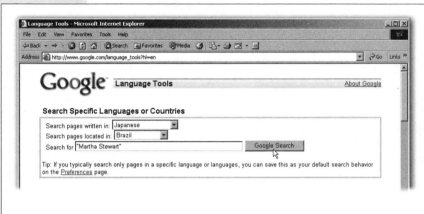

Figure 2-7:
Use the menus to change either or both choices, type in your search terms, and then press Enter. When Google says, "pages located in," it means a page whose URL specifies a country, like www.amazon.fr, Amazon's site in France. You can find a list of URLs by country at the bottom of the Language Tools page (see the chart called "Visit Google's Site in Your Local Domain").

• **Translate.** You can type in a single word or lots of text into the "Translate text" box. Use the menu to choose the languages you're translating from and to, and then press Translate to have Google display your results in a box like the one in Figure 2-8. Alternatively, you can type a URL into the blank box below "Translate a web page," choose the languages you're translating from and to, and then press Translate to have Google show the original Web page with its text in the new language.

Tip: If you run a regular Google search and your results include pages in languages Google can translate, it provides a "Translate this page" link next to the title of any page it can convert for you.

Google's translation feature, like nearly all computerized translation tools, is pretty crude. After all, a machine doesn't know that when you want to translate an Italian newspaper page about New York Mets catcher Mike Piazza, you're not actually looking for a story about Mike Public Square. And grammar can take a hit, too. A recent page from a German site on Michael Jackson comes out like this: "In order to become fair the music-historical value of the sieved child of the family Joseph Jackson, one can either good chronologically precious metal honors list or the absolute high point of its work with a superlative on the point bring: Thriller." As it turns out, ABC may not be easy as 1, 2, 3.

Figure 2-8:
After you've translated something, you can search for the translated text simply by clicking Google Search on the translation-results page.

Still, the translation tool can be helpful. It can give you the gist of a page in another language, and it can usually give you reasonable interpretations of single words or phrases.

Tip: If Google's translation tool doesn't include the language you need, try *http://babblefish.com/babblefish/language.htm*.

• **Use the Google Interface in Your Language.** Like Google's preferences page, this tool lets you pick the language in which Google displays buttons, messages, and links (it has nothing to do with the language of pages on the Web). If you pick an interface language here, however, it lasts only for the current browser session—a good way to check out the different options. For a permanent change, select your interface language from your preferences page.

Note: If you don't see your favorite lingo on the list of interface languages, you can volunteer to translate for Google. Check out *https://services.google.com/tc/Welcome.html* for details.

• **Visit Google's Site in Your Local Domain.** Google runs sites that are primarily for searching pages whose URLs specify a country, like *www.yahoo.co.jp*, Yahoo's site for Japan, and for searching sites in a country's local language. This

---

feature is helpful if you're going to, say, Bilbao, and you want to find only Spanish pages about the Guggenheim Museum there.

Like the interface tool, this domain choice lasts only as long as the current browser session. If you close the browser and then reopen it, you're back to your earlier settings. To make a permanent domain change, you must install the Google toolbar if you haven't already done so (page 171). Then click Options to open the Toolbar Options dialog box, and at the top of the Options tab, choose your domain from the menu labeled "Use Google site."

Searching by Town

Being able to limit a search to sites from a particular country can help you filter out a lot of noise. But Google actually lets you limit searches to pages about a particular U.S. *town*—which is a total godsend. Whether you're looking for a neighborhood magician to perform at your cat's birthday party or for a bed-and-breakfast that takes pets in a town six states away, Google Local can be your online Yellow Pages.

In fact, Google Local is a *hybrid* of the Google index and standard phonebook data. When you include in your search an address with city and state or Zip code, Google cross-checks its index against various online Yellow Pages, giving you a batch of results from your specified area only. But because it incorporates its own relevance rankings, Google sometimes lists a place 10 miles away from you before a place only 2 miles away.

Still, it's a super-handy search tool, and you can use it to search for general things (Italian restaurants in Boise, ID) or a specific business (Fiesta Market in Sebastopol, CA).

You can run a Google Local search two ways:

- **From the regular search box.** Just type in your search terms plus city and state or Zip code. At the top of your search results, Google includes a few local links, signaled by a compass icon (Figure 2-9, top). If you click through those results, you'll wind up on a page that looks like the one shown at bottom in Figure 2-9.

Note: If your business is listed incorrectly or is missing altogether, shoot off a note to *local-listings@google.com* and give them the proper info.

- **From the Google Local page at** *http://local.google.com/*. This page (Figure 2-10) is a handy way to use Google Local. When you run a search here, you get a full page of results listings, like the ones shown at bottom in Figure 2-9.

Tip: If Google can't find you a business within 15 miles, it shows you a page with the choice to expand your search out 30 or 45 miles.

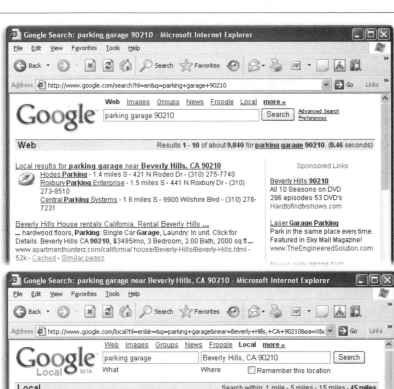

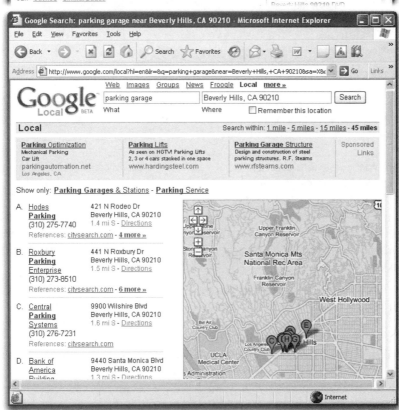

Figure 2-9:
Top: A search for parking garage 90210 finds where you can safely leave your vintage Pinto in Beverly Hills. If you click the first link (the line that starts "Local results for…"), Google takes you to a full page of local listings (shown below).

Bottom: On the local listings page, Google shows you a map with the locations of all the nearby businesses that match your search criteria. Along the left is a list of businesses; click the name of one to see it isolated on its own map, along with links for directions and references to it from other Web sites. (The results listed horizontally across the top of the map, subtly labeled Sponsored Links, are ads. Page 31 tells you more about them.)

Figure 2-10:
If you frequently search for businesses in one town—your own, your sister's, your vacation destination—you can make that search the default setting on this page. Just type in the address, city and state, or zip, and then turn on "Remember this location." You can save only one location at a time; to save a new one, just type it in and click "Remember this location" again.

Thanks to Google's mapping prowess (described in detail on page 100), your Google Local search results now arrive with an interactive map pinpointing the geographical locations of the listed businesses.

Tip: If you want to get all aerial about it, there's also a link in the upper-right corner of the window to see a satellite photo of the location.

You can scroll through the map to see the surrounding area, either by clicking the arrows or dragging the map. You can also change the map's scale (use the + and – buttons), or click View Larger Map to open a much larger, more detailed map in its own window.

Google labels each company with a letter, which corresponds to a marker on the map. If you click a marker, a balloon pops up giving you the exact street address and a link to get directions to and from the location. In the upper-right corner of the window, there are even links for searching other distances (one mile, five miles, and so on); click one, and Google gives you new listings that fall within that area.

Tip: The business listings also include a link for directions, but if you click it, you get directions from the center of the town where the business is—not very helpful. Instead, click the marker on the *map*, and in the balloon that opens, use the direction links to specify where you're coming from. (To learn more about getting directions from Google, see page 103.)

When you click through a company name, you get a new version of the location map with the address marker, along with more information, like which credit cards the business accepts, reference URLs for other Web pages mentioning the company, and links to the sites where Google gleaned all that info. Some business listings, especially those for restaurants, even include reviews that Google has collected from other sites. These reviews are color-coded: a green square is positive, yellow is a neutral opinion, and red means *somebody* is expressing a less than glowing critique of the establishment.

If you want to fine-tune your search, at the top of the Local results pages, Google gives you search boxes to change the business (What) or location (Where). Just under that, if you turn on the checkbox next to "Remember this location", Google keeps that location in the Where box every time you open Google Local. To make that behavior stop, just remove the checkmark.

Tip: Looking for a lift? Google RideFinder (*http://labs.google.com/ridefinder*) helps you hail a taxi, shuttle, or limousine in more than a dozen U.S. cities by displaying vehicle locations (and telephone numbers) in real time on an interactive map. The service works with Internet Explorer for Windows, plus the Firefox, Netscape, and Mozilla browsers for Linux, Mac, and Windows systems but doesn't yet track that sometimes-elusive automotive creature: the Manhattan yellow cab.

Getting Fancy with Syntax

When you type in a query, you can add words known by the geek term *syntax,* also called *operators*, that tell Google something specific about the search you want to conduct. For example, the operator *inurl* tells Google to look just in URLs for your search terms. Operators are great for honing results, easy as pie, and are the primary uncharted territory of the Google Underusers Club. In some cases, syntax replicates the results you can get via Google's Advanced Search page, but it's often more specific, and it almost always saves you some clicking around.

To use any syntax, simply type the operator and a colon before each of your terms, and don't put spaces before or after the colon. For example, a search using the operator *inurl* (described on page 67) should look like this:

        inurl:whammy

or:

        inurl:"double whammy"

or:

        inurl:double inurl:whammy

Note: URLs never contain any spaces, like the one between "double" and "whammy," so if your query is *inurl:"double whammy"*, Google automatically searches for variations like *double-whammy*; *double.whammy*; and *double,whammy*—all of which are perfectly kosher in URLese.

If you type in a space before or after the colon, though, Google can't read your query.

Searching Titles

As explained in the Advanced Search section earlier in this chapter, titles are different from URLs, and they're handy to search when you want pages that really focus on your topic. To search titles, use the operator *intitle*, like this:

```
intitle:file intitle:sharing
```

or:

```
intitle:"file sharing"
```

The first example finds titles that contain both of your words. The second example finds titles that contain the exact phrase "file sharing."

A variation of this syntax, *allintitle*, finds pages that have all your keywords or phrases in the title, in any order. For example:

```
allintitle:file sharing
```

finds titles that contain both file and sharing, without your having to put an operator before each word (as in *intitle:file intitle:sharing*).

Tip: If you try to mix *allintitle* with some other syntax and the search conks out, put *intitle* before each keyword or phrase (*intitle* plays better with other syntax than *allintitle*).

Searching Text

The *intext* operator searches only the body text of Web pages, ignoring links, URLs, and titles. Use this syntax when you want to find a word that may crop up in zillions of URLs or links, like this:

```
intext:amazon
```

or:

```
intext:amazon.com
```

Its cousin, *allintext*, works similarly to *allintitle*, but it, too, has unpleasant issues when mixed with other syntax.

Searching Anchors

Link anchor is HTMLese for the words and pictures on a Web page that serve as links to another page. Mostly, a link anchor is just what you think of as a link (a

---

blue, underlined word or phrase that describes a related, linked page), but a lot of times an anchor turns up as a button or icon or image.

Note: The term "anchor" is confusing because anchors don't usually refer to both a starting-off point and a destination. But that's HTML terminology for you.

The *inanchor* operator searches for text in link anchors. It's a nifty way to get an idea of which or how many pages link to a person, place, or thing. And sometimes, it can help you find a person's email address, because most Web pages consider email addresses as links. Use it like this:

```
inanchor:"Charles Mingus fans"
inanchor:"Richard Stallman"
```

Unsurprisingly, Google also has an *allinachor* option. (The keywords you specify for *allinanchor* must all appear in a link anchor in order to show up in your results.)

Searching Within Sites and Domains

Like the Domain feature on the Advanced Search page, the *site* operator lets you specify a site or domain you want to search. It makes a quick and handy search function for sites that don't have a search feature.

Unlike the previous operators, the *site* syntax has two parts. First, you have to attach a site name or domain name to *site:* And second, you have to include the keywords or phrases you want to search for. Here are a couple of examples:

```
site:nba.com "larry bird" magic
site:gov "agricultural subsidies"
```

Tip: You don't have to include http:// or www in the site name. Also, you don't have to put it in quotes.

You can also use *site* to exclude a particular Web site from your search. For example, if you want to look for sites about books, but you don't want to wade through zillions of results from Amazon, this query:

```
books -site:amazon.com
```

does the trick. Mostly. It doesn't block Amazon's international partners, like Amazon.co.uk, because that's not the site you specified. To nix all instances of Amazon in a URL, use the *inurl* operator, described below.

Searching URLs

The *inurl* operator searches solely URLs for your query words. No body text. No titles. Just URLs. Unlike the site operator, *inurl* doesn't require additional query words: *inurl:"great pumpkin"* is perfectly acceptable. (Remember, a URL can't contain any spaces, like the one between "great" and "pumpkin," but if your query

---

includes an exact phrase that has spaces, Google automatically searches for variations that work in URLs, like *great.pumpkin* and *great-pumpkin*.)

Inurl is also handy when you want to *exclude* a site from your search. For example, this search:

```
books -inurl:amazon
```

lets you find pages that sell or discuss books, but it blocks any site with Amazon in its URL, which includes the giant retailer *and* its international partners.

Allinurl is a variation that finds all your keywords, but it doesn't mix well with some other special syntax.

Who Links to Whom?

Want to find out which sites link to your Web site, or to Friendster.com, or to a particular page on Friendster? The *link* operator is for you (it does the same thing as the Links feature on the Advanced Search page [page 50]). If you type in *link:friendster.com*, Google spits out a list of pages linked to Friendster.com.

Tip: One nice thing about *link* is that it works with subdirectories, too. Thus, if you wanted, you could see who's linked to *poundy.com/journal/04-01/4-11.html*.

Caching Up

Google keeps a copy of each page as it records it (called a *cache*), discussed in detail on page 26. The *cache* operator lets you view Google's last cached copy of a page, even if the page has moved from its original URL or changed radically. Thus, this query:

```
cache:espn.com
```

gets you the ESPN home page on the last day Google checked it. Figure 2-11 compares a Google cache to a current site.

Tip: If your own site changes regularly, you can use the *cache* operator to find out the last time Google recorded it.

The *cache* operator does pretty much the same thing as clicking one of the Cached links on a Google results page, except that using the *cache* syntax doesn't highlight your search terms on the cached page. Also, the *cache* syntax works only with top-level domain names (like *giants.com*), not with subdirectories (like *giants.com/tickets*).

Daterange

The *daterange* operator lets you search for pages that Google indexed during a specific time frame. Like the Date option on the Advanced Search page (page 50), this

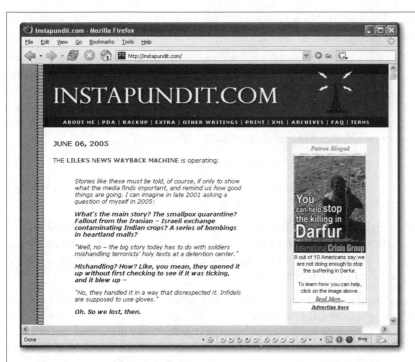

Figure 2-11:
Top: Current InstaPundit.com page.

Bottom: The result of the query cache:instapundit.com.

operator has nothing to do with the date a page was created, but rather when Google *recorded* it.

So seeing as Google's Advanced Search page lets you narrow down results, why bother with *daterange*? Because the Advanced Search lets you limit your results only to the last three months, six months, or year. The *daterange* operator is a lot more powerful, letting you specify a single day for which you'd like results, or a date before or after which you'd like results (for example, you can search for "terrorism" before and after September 11, 2001).

In fact, *daterange* can be useful in a few other situations:

- **Stale results.** If you tend to run searches that pull up a lot of old, useless pages, you can use *daterange* to ensure freshness.

- **Too much current news.** For your doctoral dissertation on weight lifting and masculinity, you want to find some older writings on Arnold Schwarzenegger, but your results are all gummed up with news about the governator. Use *daterange* to filter out the recent news.

- **Finding trends.** You can use *daterange* to see how results for a particular query have changed over time. Comparing the number of results for *"mad cow"* in 1995 to the number in 2005, for example, could make for illuminating study. Plus, the content of certain queries can change over time. What would Google give you if you searched for *"Tom Cruise"* in 1999 vs. today?

In theory, *daterange* is easy to use. You just type *daterange:startdate-enddate keywords*. You have to specify a start date and end date; if you want only one day, use the same date for start and end. In practice, *daterange* is a power user's operator because the dates must be in the *Julian date* form, a continuous count of days since noon on January 1, 4713 BC. In the Julian scheme, July 8, 2002 is 2452463.5.

Though it may seem ridiculous to base an electronic search on a dating system that started thousands of years ago, computers like Julian dates because each is just one number, regardless of leap years, days in a month, and other things that confuse machines. People, on the other hand, tend to take to the Julian calendar like ducks to molasses.

Fortunately, you can easily convert dates from Gregorian (the calendar you're familiar with) to Julian, and vice versa, at several Web sites. Just run a Google search for *"julian date"* to get a current list of converters. Even better, you can use the Fagan Finder Google interface at *www.faganfinder.com/google.html* to specify dates using pop-up menus with Gregorian dates. (For more info about Fagan Finder, see page 56.)

Note: Google doesn't officially sanction *daterange* searches. So if you get funky results, you can't complain.

You can use *daterange* in combo with most of Google's special operators, except the *link* syntax. Also, the stocks and phonebook operators described in Chapter 1 on pages 41 and 39, respectively, don't fly with *daterange*.

Searching by Content Creation Date

Searching for pages based on when they were *created* or *updated* seems like it should be a no-brainer. Don't computers routinely stamp a date on every file they open or change?

Well, yes and no. While Word documents and email messages get dated automatically, not all Web pages do. Some pages have information about when somebody created and updated them, but others have neither. And *some* files are tied to software that date-stamp them every day, regardless of whether their content changes.

Even when a site has a date, it's not in any standard format. People understand "September 2003," "2003 September,"

"9/03," "03/9," "September 21, 2003," and "21 September 2003" as the same thing, but computers don't.

Because not all pages have dates, therefore, you risk missing important results any time you run a search with a date in it. But if you want to give it a whirl, try adding your date in a *few* common formats, like this:

```
("September * 2003" OR "September 2003" OR
09/03 OR 09/*/03)
```

If this approach impinges too far on your ten-word limit (page 23), try each format individually.

Searching by File Type

The *filetype* operator searches for file name extensions, like .doc or .pdf. Unlike the similar feature on Google's Advanced Search page, *filetype* lets you specify HTML pages (and those encoded as *htm*, which may give you different results). Geeks can also use *filetype* to search for *page generators*—like *asp*, *php*, and *cgi*—little programs that render Web pages suitable for your browser.

You use *filetype* with keywords or phrases, like this:

```
"chocolate soymilk ingredients" filetype:ppt
```

or this:

```
tofu filetype:xls
```

to get PowerPoint slides on chocolate soy milk ingredients or Excel spreadsheets on tofu, respectively.

Searching for Related Content

The *related* operator performs the same search as the "Similar pages" link that appears in a Google result (page 28). It's a good way to find pages in a category, rather than with your particular keywords. For example, *related:"sesame street"* brings up a list of pages on children's TV shows, while a straight search for *"sesame street"* yields a lot of sites selling Cookie Monster merchandise.

Synonyms

If your keywords describe a concept, you may want your results to include synonyms for your query. For example, if you're looking for technical help, it's useful to automatically include synonyms for "help"—like "support" and "customer service"—without having to type them all in.

The ~ symbol tells Google to look for synonyms. You can find this squiggle near the top of your keyboard, on the key to the left of the number 1 (type it by pressing Shift+`). Use it like this:

```
~help "Microsoft Word"
```

to get a list of pages with tips on using the popular word processing program.

Most of the Kit and Caboodle

The *info* operator provides you with a tidy summary of the details Google can give you about a URL—including links to that page's cache, similar pages, linked pages, and pages containing the words in your search. Figure 2-12 shows you what to expect.

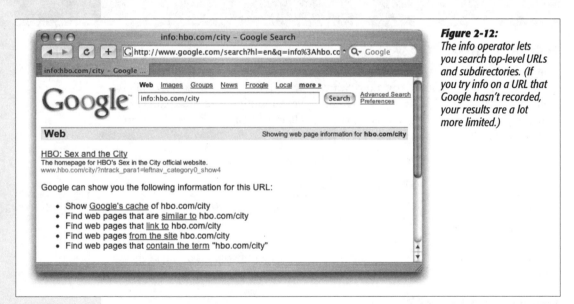

Figure 2-12:
The info operator lets you search top-level URLs and subdirectories. (If you try info on a URL that Google hasn't recorded, your results are a lot more limited.)

Mixing Syntax

As noted above, some syntax operators work only on their own, while some play well with others. For the many you can combine, cleverly splicing them together can narrow your search results in the most satisfying manner. Although you'll probably have to experiment a lot to find out what works for your searches, the tips below can help, too.

Tip: If you find Google's syntax confusing to combine at first, stick with the Advanced Search page for now. Then, after performing an advanced search, take a look at the search box on your results pages, where Google has converted your query into syntax. This trick can help you learn which operators do what.

How Not to Mix Syntax

The most important rules to keep in mind are those dictating which syntax *not* to mix. For starters, a few operators don't get along with any of the others: *allinurl, allintitle, allintext, allinanchor,* and *link.* In addition, there are a few general principles of mixology described below.

Canceling yourself out

Basic safety tip: Don't mix operators that cancel each other out. For example:

```
site:bluefly.com -inurl:bluefly
```

tells Google that you want all your results to come from bluefly.com, but that the results shouldn't include the word "bluefly" in the URLs. As you'd expect, this search yields exactly zero results.

Doubling up

You can also run into trouble by doubling up a single operator. This query:

```
"trading spaces" site:com site:edu
```

might look like you're asking Google to give you results from either .com or .edu sites, but in fact, you're telling it that your results should come from sites that are simultaneously part of *both* domains. Unfortunately, there's no such thing as a URL like *www.google.com.edu.*

To get what you want, try this:

```
"trading spaces" (site:edu OR site:com)
```

Getting carried away

If you want to run a very narrow search, something like:

```
intitle:curtains site:ebay.com inurl:funkyfresh
```

you're likely to get nothing in return. Instead, start with a broader search, like this:

```
intitle:curtains site:ebay.com
```

and then narrow it down by searching within your results (page 19).

How to Mix Syntax Correctly

Some syntax combinations work very well. Here's an example to get you started: *intitle* and *site*. If you want to get a sense of the forms available from the United States Department of Agriculture, for example, you could run this search:

```
intitle:form site:usda.gov
```

If you want to narrow that down, you can add a keyword, too, like this:

```
cattle intitle:form site:usda.gov
```

Tip: You can put keywords at the beginning or the end of your query, but it's easier to keep track of them if you put them first.

Remember that the site operator lets you specify subdomains (like *maps.google.com*), so if you want to know what kind of forms the National Agricultural Library has on tap, you could run a search like this:

```
intitle:form site:nal.usda.gov
```

Another classic combo is *intext* along with *inurl*, described on page 67.

Anatomy of a Google URL

As you've probably noticed, URLs are often long, complicated, and weird. You certainly don't have to become an expert in what goes into those addresses. Indeed, millions of people live happy lives never wondering why some URLs are eighteen characters and some are longer than Beowulf.

But after you've run a Google search, the URL in your browser bar contains some characters that you can change on the fly to refine a quest without taking a long trip to the Advanced Search page. Plus, once you can read URLese, you can fiddle with URLs to produce results you can't get any other way.

The URL for a Google results page can vary depending on the preferences you've set, but mostly, they look similar (see page 47 for more on preferences). Say you run a search for the phrase *"over the river"*; your results URL should look something like Figure 2-13.

Changing the Number of Results

In the middle of a Google results URL, you can sometimes find *num=,* which tells you the number of search results Google gives you per page of results. You can temporarily change the number of results to anything from 1 to 100 simply by altering the number in the URL and then pressing Enter. Most of the time, search results are easiest to read when you've got 10, 20, or 30 per page (page 49). But this trick is a quick way to amp up the number of results on a page for the rare times when you want to review a lot of them at once or compare results 1 and 100 on one page.

What Basic URLs Are Made of

URLs have a few parts, each of which helps your Web browser find the right Web page. Take *http://www.nytimes.com/pages/national/index.html*, for example.

The first part, *http,* tells your computer to communicate with other computers using the *hypertext transfer protocol,* which is simply a way computers communicate when transmitting Web pages to each other. (Sometimes, this section appears as *https*; the "s" tells the computers that the transmission is secure.)

The second part, *www.nytimes.com,* is the address of the computer, known as a *Web server,* that hosts that site. The ".com" in a URL is what's known as an *extension* or *domain,*

and different extensions change the address completely. Common extensions include .edu (for schools), .org (for nonprofits), and .net (anything). Thus, *www.stanford.edu* is the Web site for the university, *www.stanford.com* could be a consulting company, *www.stanford.org* could be a homeless shelter, and *www.stanford.net* could be the home page for a porn star.

The next sections, */pages* and */national/*, are the names of folders (also called *directories*) that live on the Web server, much the way folders reside on your hard drive.

Finally, *index.html* is the actual page your Web browser shows you.

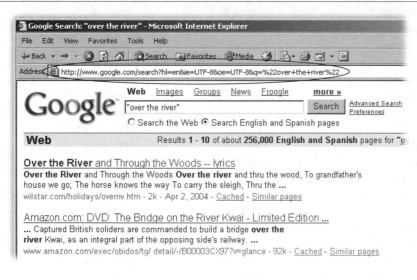

Figure 2-13:
The "q" toward the end signals the query itself, in this case, "over the river". And the %22 on either side of the terms is the URL version of double quotes. Two more chunks appear in every URL: codes for the language you're surfing, and for the number of results you see per page. The rest of the stuff varies wildly, and can include information on the browser you're using, the page where you initiated your search (perhaps you ran a Google search from Amazon.com), and some other stuff Google doesn't reveal.

Tip: If you don't see *num=* in your URL, you can click the end of the URL in your browser's address bar, add an ampersand (&) and then type in *num=whatever.* For example, to set the number of results to 50 per page, add *&num=50.* (Actually, this works even if you can *already* see the *num=* setting in your URL, because Google reads URLs from right to left.)

As long as you have the same browser window open, Google keeps your number of results at the new setting. However, Google doesn't remember the change *after* you've closed the browser; to make the change permanent, see page 49.

Changing the Interface Language

In addition to a setting for the number of results, the URL contains a setting for the interface language—that is, the language Google uses on things like buttons and instructions. The setting's prefix is *hl=*, followed by a language code. For example, English is denoted thus:

```
hl=en
```

Like the number of results, you can alter the URL for a temporary change of interface language. This is most useful when you find yourself in front of a computer that's set to a language you don't know—a common problem for exchange students and diplomats. If the language is something other than English but you want English, just change the code to *en*.

Here's a list of the codes for the other languages Google knows:

Afrikaans. af	Filipino. tl	Kyrgyz. ky
Albanian. sq	Finnish. fi	Laothian. lo
Amharic. am	French. fr	Latin. la
Arabic. ar	Frisian. fy	Latvian. lv
Armenian. hy	Galician. gl	Lithuanian. lt
Azerbaijani. az	Georgian. ka	Macedonian. mk
Basque. eu	German. de	Malay. ms
Belarusian. be	Greek. el	Malayalam. ml
Bengali. bn	Guarani. gn	Maltese. mt
Bihari. bh	Gujarati. gu	Marathi. mr
Bork, bork, bork! (Swedish Chef). xx-bork	Hacker. xx-hacker	Mongolian. mn
Bosnian. bs	Hebrew. iw	Nepali. ne
Breton. br	Hindi. hi	Norwegian. no
Bulgarian. bg	Hungarian. hu	Norwegian (Nynorsk). nn
Catalan. ca	Icelandic. is	Occitan. oc
Chinese (Simplified). zh-CN	Indonesian. id	Oriya. or
Chinese (Traditional). zh-TW	Interlingua. ia	Persian. fa
Croatian. hr	Irish. ga	Pig Latin. xx-piglatin
Czech. cs	Italian. it	Polish. pl
Danish. de	Japanese. ja	Portuguese (Brazil). pt-BR
Dutch. nl	Javanese. jw	Portuguese (Portugal). pt-PT
Elmer Fudd. xx-elmer	Kannada. kn	Punjabi. pa
Esperanto. eo	Klingon. xx-klingon	Romanian. ro
Estonian. et	Korean. ko	Romansh. rm
Faroese. Fo	Kurdish. ku	Russian. ru

Scots Gaelic. gd	Sundanese. su	Twi. tw
Serbian. sr	Swahili. sw	Uighur. ug
Serbo-Croatian. sh	Swedish. sv	Ukrainian. uk
Sestho. st	Tagalog. tl	Urdu. ur
Sindi. sd	Tamil. ta	Uzbek. uz
Sinhalese. si	Telugu. te	Vietnamese. vi
Slovak. sk	Thai. th	Welsh. cy
Slovenian. sl	Tigrinya. ti	Xhosa. Xh
Somali. so	Turkish. tr	Yiddish. yi
Spanish. es	Turkmen. tk	Zulu. zu

Two More URL Tricks

By now you've probably noticed that you can temporarily change Google's behavior by placing an ampersand at the end of the results URL and then adding a *modifier,* which is simply a term or code that alters your results slighly. Here are two more handy modifiers.

- **Fresh results.** By adding *&as_qdr=m#,* you can alter the maximum age of the results, in months. Just change the # symbol to anything between 1 and 12.

  Google's Advanced Search page lets you say you'd like results that have been updated anytime, within the past three or six months, or year. Yet this trick is an excellent way of narrowing down results to only the *freshest* pages, and it's very handy when you're looking for a page that you're sure has been changed recently.

- **Unsafe searching.** The SafeSearch filter tells Google to remove potentially offensive links from your results (for more on the filter, see page 49). The problem is, sometimes the filter gets carried away and removes things you need (for example, you're searching for information on sex education, and Google hides some important sites). Or maybe what you want *is* XXX sites. To make sure the filter is off, add this to the end of your URL: *&safe=off.* To make sure it's on, add *&safe=on.*

Part Two: Google Tools

2

Googling Further: Images, News, Maps, and More

Normally, when you run a Google search, you're asking Google to look for your search terms on any Web page it's tracked. But the Web can be sliced in many ways, and Google has created a bunch of alternative systems for helping you find things.

For example, when you want to find a picture of somebody, you could type in his or her name followed by a few file types used for images, like *"Mick Jagger" jpeg gif*, and hope for the best. Problem is, Google gives you any site that mentions Mr. Jagger *and* that has JPEG or GIF files—but not necessarily pictures *of* the thick-lipped star. You could be drowning in photos of Keith Richards for days before you get any search satisfaction. Better to use Google Images, a special search that finds only pictures.

But the fun doesn't end with images. Google News lets you search for and organize news stories. Google Maps helps you find addresses, directions, and businesses all over the country. The Google Directory gives you a way to find information by category rather than keyword. And Google Print lets you search inside *books*.

This chapter explains all these features, and the following two chapters cover a few other Google goodies: Groups, Answers, Froogle, and Catalogs. Figure 3-1 shows you where to find all of these services.

Knowing how to use Google's alternative searches can help you tap amazing resources most people overlook.

Figure 3-1:
You can reach Google's alternative search services several ways. From the home page, click one of the links above the search box. Or, on the home page, click More to get the page of service options shown here. You can also run a regular search and then, from your results page, have Google run the same search in a different service by clicking the appropriate link above the search box. Finally, the Google toolbar (Chapter 6) has buttons for each of the search services.

Google Images

Google's primary search looks for *text* on the Web matching your keywords. But Google also lets you search through a bank of billions of *images* on the Web. Because most pictures have keywords associated with them, you can type in text to find them. (To figure out what a picture contains, Google reads the text on the page around it, the caption if there is one, and other variables, producing surprisingly accurate results.)

The Image Search is terrifically useful when you want to find drawings or photos for use on your Web site, or for inspiration or imitation in your own artwork. It's even a good way to find things like desktop icons, maps, and posters. It can help you figure out if that familiar looking guy on the Stairmaster next to you at the gym was actually Benicio del Toro, and it can show you instantly what a Smart Car looks like. It can also be handy if you're a collector: The objects you're interested in may well be featured in pictures on Web pages. Figure 3-2 shows how image searching works.

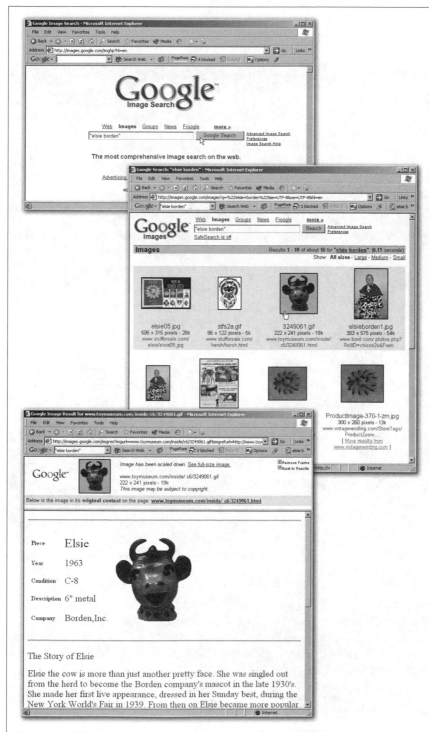

Figure 3-2:
Top: The Google Images search page (http://images.google.com) looks almost identical to the home page.

Middle: A search for "Elsie Borden" shows thumbnail pictures of the cow as well as memorabilia in her image. To view an image, click the thumbnail, and Google takes you to a page like the one below.

Bottom: The close-up page has two parts. At top, a version of the image floating alone; at bottom, the image on the page where Google found it, so you can see it in context.

Note: If you have a Web site with pictures that you don't want Google to find, *http://images.google. com/remove.html/#images* tells you how to remove the images from Google's orbit.

NOTE FROM THE LAWYERS

Using Pictures Legally

Google can legally help you find images on the Web, but its service doesn't give you the right to *reuse* the pictures. Many—perhaps most—pictures on the Web are protected by copyright, though the way you want to use them can determine whether you need permission.

First, the issue of copyright. If somebody creates a picture, they own the rights to it. In the same way you can't legally copy text—say, somebody's blog entry on the benefits of synthetic-fiber dog coats—and post it under your own name on your Web site or sell it to The New York Times op-ed page, you can't simply copy his picture of a dog coat and post or sell that, either. While many people believe that they can copy text or images as long as they *credit* the source or if they *modify* the picture, in many cases that's not true. You need explicit permission to use most material, even if you say who originally created it and even if you alter it.

A major exception to the "look don't touch" rule is artwork that's in the *public domain.* Public domain means that the work is not protected by intellectual-property laws such as copyright and trademark, so anyone can use it without getting permission. An image usually falls into the public domain because its copyright has expired (though the length of a copyright can vary), or because the creator specifically placed the copyright in the public domain. For a clear explanation of when material becomes part of the public domain, see *http://fairuse.stanford.edu/.*

But even if a picture is copyrighted, the way you *use* it and the nature of the original material can affect whether you need permission or not. Under the *fair use* doctrine, you can use part of somebody else's work without permission if your use meets certain criteria. For example, if you download a copyrighted picture of an Appaloosa horse from an encyclopedia and then you display it in a nonprofit educational setting like a third-grade classroom, your use without

permission would probably be OK. If you use the same picture for commercial purposes, like pasting it into your travel-agency brochure, you may well be in violation of the copyright.

The tricky thing about fair use is that the criteria are only guidelines. A fair-use analysis helps you determine a relative level of risk of infringement, not an absolute answer on whether a particular situation qualifies as fair use. To get your head around the standards of fair use, check out the copyrights section of *www.nolo.com.*

If you want to use a picture for something other than fair use, and it's not in the public domain, you need permission from the rights holder. And it's important to remember that even if a work *appears* to be in the public domain, it can still have restrictions associated with it. For example, a 200-year-old portrait of Thomas Jefferson might be in the public domain, but a recent photograph of that painting could be copyrighted—and you might not be able to tell the difference without asking. In addition, just because you can see an image on a site doesn't mean you can necessarily tell who owns it, because the Webmaster may not have the legal right to permit others to use the picture, even if she's authorized to use it on her own site.

Google recommends that when you want to copy a picture for some reason other than fair use, you contact the site owner and ask for permission. That's a good place to start. But if the owner doesn't have the authority to grant you permission, you're not off the hook. In the end, it's your responsibility to secure any necessary licenses or permissions. The Stanford and Nolo sites both have excellent discussions of copyright and fair use, and you can also check the government site *www.copyright.gov.* If you can't figure out whether your intended use is legal, consider contacting a lawyer who specializes in copyright law.

Searching for Images

Searching for pictures is as easy as typing a keyword or two into the blank search box at *http://images.google.com* and then pressing Enter. Image searches are not, however, as reliable as text searches. And, unfortunately, multiword queries tend not to work well in Google's Image Search. But single-word queries can give you thousands of results, which is often too many to be useful.

Here are a few tips for finding what you want:

- **Keep it short (but not too short).** When you can be both brief and specific, you're most likely to get what you want. For example, if you need a drawing of a male Muppet, a search for *Bert* turns up an overwhelming 314,000 results. A search for *Bert Ernie* gets you more than 6,500 pictures. And *Bert Sesame Street* weighs in with just over 1,700 images.

- **Experiment and be patient.** The keywords Google associates with images are not always consistent. Thus, while it's generally a good idea to use very specific search terms, trying out variations can pay off, too—especially when your attempt to be brief and specific, as suggested above, doesn't fly. For example, if *vintage Cadillac convertible* and *1953 El Dorado* don't pan out, try *1953 Cadillac convertible* or *Cadillac El Dorado*.

- **Try the Advanced Image Search feature.** Google's Image Search has its own advanced search page, explained next, that's separate from the advanced page for regular Web searches. It can help you narrow down a search by file type, size, or coloration (black and white, grayscale, or full color). And, as explained in the box on page 89, Advanced Image Search also lets you change the level of filtering Google uses for your results. Finally, the page guides you through keyword choices and lets you specify a site or domain Google should restrict your image search to.

Tip: Want to see how other people use their digital cameras? Cruise over to Flickr (*www.flickr.com/ photos*) to browse the photographic journeys of people who've signed up for the free photo-sharing service. You can see everything from moody art shots to casual cellphone snaps—and lots and lots of pictures of member's dogs.

- **Use syntax.** Google lets you use four syntax elements to focus your image searches. All four are the same ones used in Google's regular Web search (page 65). Keep in mind that because image searches are something of a crapshoot, you'll probably have to fiddle with these syntax elements till you find exactly what you're looking for.

  Intitle can be a good way to hone searches because it looks for your keywords in Web page titles, which removes some of the guesswork for Google about what a page contains. Use it like this: *intitle:"taj mahal"*.

  Inurl works strangely in Google's Image Search, because when Google records the text on a Web page, it considers certain elements—like JPG extensions—as

---

part of the URL. Thus, if you search the image bank for *inurl:poker,* Google might show you a picture from the URL *www.dogsplayingcards.com/velvet.html* because that page contains a picture called *poker.jpg.* That weirdness aside, *inurl* is like *intitle* in that it can whittle your results from tens of thousands of images down to a manageable number, like a few hundred.

Filetype is available as a choice in the Advanced Image Search, too, although you can use it to search only for the formats Google keeps track of—JPG, GIF, and PNG. The one trick with this operator is that you can specify *filtetype:jpeg* and *filetype:jpg,* which give you different results (the advanced page includes only an option for JPG). Use it like this: *"poker chips" filetype:jpg.*

Site is also part of the Advanced Image Search, and you can use it to limit your searches to particular sites or domains, which include segments of the Web, like .com and .net, and also countries, like .au (Australia) and .fr (France). The *site* syntax is especially handy when you want to restrict your results to images from Web sites from a certain country, like this: *sitcom site:UK,* which gives you pictures from British sites. And if you know that something you want to see is somewhere on one large site, use it like this: *friends site:nbc.com.*

Tip: To find country codes for the Web, look on Google's Language Tools page (*www.google.com/ language_tools*). About halfway down the page, the section labeled Visit Google's Site in Your Local Domain shows you the URLs for dozens of countries. The last two-letter segment of each is the country code.

Advanced Image Search

You can get to the Advanced Image Search via the Images main page, which has a link to it on the right side of the screen. Alternatively, every Images results page has a link to it above the search box at the top of the screen. Figure 3-3 shows the advanced search page.

The Advanced Image Search has six elements you can tweak. SafeSearch is explained in the box on page 89; the others are:

- **Find Results.** This section is where you type in your keywords. You can use all or any of the four search types, which work as follows:

  — **"Related to all of the words"** means Google looks for every word or phrase you ask for, but not necessarily in order. This option works nicely when you don't care whether a picture is of a 1953 Cadillac or simply a picture of a Cadillac taken in 1953.

  — **"Related to the exact phrase"** is like putting quote marks around your terms, and means Google looks for all your words in the order you type them in. If you typed *1953 Cadillac* here, you'd most likely get only pictures of 1953 Cadillacs.

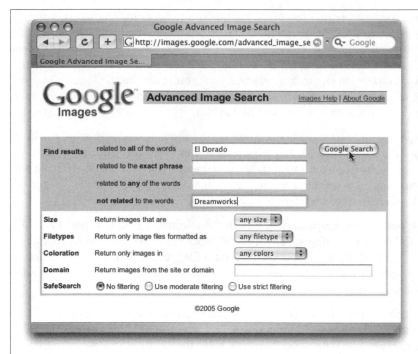

Figure 3-3:
The Find Results section lets you fill in query words that are related to the picture you want to find. Because the Web has no standard technical system for labeling images, and because two different Web sites could legitimately call the same picture "car" and "Cadillac," Google has to perform search jujitsu and look at the text near images to figure out which pictures might match your terms.

— **"Related to any of the words"** means Google shows you pictures that are near at least one of your words, but not necessarily all of them. This search gives you 1953 Cadillacs, but also Cadillacs from other years, and pictures of other things from 1953 or taken in 1953.

— **"Not related to the words"** leaves out pictures that are near the words you type in here. For this search to work, however, you have to have some keywords in one of the other boxes in Find Results. For example, if you want pictures of a vintage El Dorado, but you're not interested in the Dreamworks movie *El Dorado,* try typing *Cadillac El Dorado* in either of the first two boxes, and type *Dreamworks* in this last one. Google gives you lots of pictures of cars and excludes cartoon stills from the movie.

Tip: This feature is also great if you're phobic of snakes and you're searching for feather boas. Type *snakes* into the "Not related to the words" search box to prevent Google from showing you serpent pictures by accident.

• **Size.** People measure electronic images in two ways: by *dimension* (which can be in inches, centimeters, pixels, and so on) and by the amount of space a picture takes up on your hard drive, usually expressed in *kilobytes.* Google lets you narrow down your results to include only images with rough dimensions, measured in pixels. (Google also tells you how big a file is in kilobytes, but it doesn't let you search for this factor.)

Dimension matters in a few cases. First, if you're accessing the Internet over a dial-up connection, image searching can be slooooow. While dimensions are no guarantee of weight in kilobytes, smaller pictures are often made up of less data—and therefore load faster. Second, some things, like maps and posters, tend to show up in larger dimensions. And if you're specifically looking for pictures to use on your desktop icons or to fill a space of a certain size on your Web site, this feature can help you hit pay dirt.

Google has three sizes to choose from: small (about 100×100 pixels), medium (around 200×200 pixels), and large (everything else). You can simply pick the one you want from the menu. Like all elements that narrow down an image search, picking a certain size can lead to maddeningly few or sometimes no results, so it's best to stay flexible when you can.

- **File types.** Google keeps track of files in three formats: JPG, GIF, and PNG. It's best to leave this setting at "any filetype" since choosing one eliminates lots of results. But, obviously, if you need a certain file type and you don't have access to a graphics program that can convert images, this feature is crucial for successful searching.

- **Coloration.** Your choices here—black and white, grayscale, or full color—can produce wildly different results. Black and white images tend to include diagrams, charts, line drawings, symbols (like the outline of a woman from a restroom door), cartoons, sheet music, and maps. Sometimes photos show up in a black-and-white search, and sometimes they don't. Grayscale searches, however, often produce photos as well as drawings of various kinds. And full-color searches usually give you primarily photos, followed by cartoons and other drawings.

  In addition to helping you find different kinds of pictures, the coloration feature can be a boon to dial-up searchers. Both grayscale and black and white pictures are often much, much leaner than color pictures and thus load significantly faster.

- **Domain.** If you know the picture you want is on a particular Web site, you can use the domain feature to limit Google to that site. For example, if you want to see official pictures of Microsoft's Windows logo, try *windows* as your keyword, and then in the domain box, type *www.microsoft.com.*

  Of course, you can also use the domain feature to tell Google you'd like to search only in one country, like .de (Germany) or .sp (Spain), or in a particular segment of the Web, like .edu, .org, or .com. This option is handy when, for example, you're looking for things to buy (try limiting your search to the .com domain). Want to find computer science department logos? Try looking only in .edu.

Note: Even when you're just doing a regular Google text search and not purposely searching for images, you might see a few thumbnail images atop your results page, especially if you've searched for something wonderfully photographic like *1966 Ford Mustang* or *leprechauns.*

Too Hot to Handle

The results of an image search have one potentially tricky aspect: what Google delicately calls "mature content." If the Web has revealed nothing else about human nature, it's shown that people can make nearly *anything* into porn, and then post electronic pictures of it online. Thus, an innocent search for pictures of toasters could turn up a toaster fetish photo. If you're concerned about seeing something objectionable, you can block some such pictures, as explained below, though Google doesn't guarantee that it will nix them all.

The Image Search has a filter that comes set with moderate filtering on, which means Google tries to exclude most potentially offensive pictures. If you want to ratchet up the filtering to strict mode, in which Google tries to prevent anything questionable from sneaking through, or if you want to turn off the filtering altogether, you can do so on a search-by-search basis, session-by-session basis, or permanently. Bear in mind that either moderate or strict filtering can restrict your results in undesirable ways, particularly if you're looking for something that could be either legit or seamy, like *sex education.* If you can deal with the seamy (and steamy) stuff, it's better to turn the filtering off permanently.

To adjust the filter for an individual search or for a full session of searching (that is, while you still have the browser open), hit the Advanced Image Search page (the Images home page has a link to it on the right side of the screen, and every Images results page has a link to it above the search box at the top of the screen). At the bottom of the Advanced Image Search page, you can choose "No filtering," "Use moderate filtering," or "Use strict filtering." The setting—which doesn't affect regular Web searches—holds until you change it, or until you turn off your browser and turn it back on, at which point Google reverts to moderate filtering for images.

If you want to set the filtering to hold from one browser session to the next, you can adjust the mode in your Google preference settings under SafeSearch Filtering (*www.google.com/preferences*). Choose the level you'd like, and then click Save Preferences. In this case, the filtering applies not only to pictures but to regular Web searches, too.

The results page for every image search includes a link above the thumbnails telling you what level of filtering you have set. If you click the link, Google takes you to your general preferences page, where you can change the setting. Remember that by changing the global preference, you not only keep the change in place after you've turned off your browser, but you also change the setting for all different types of Google searches.

Reading Your Images Results

It's pretty easy to navigate through a page of image results. You get a bunch of thumbnail-sized pictures, you click one you want to see, and Google shows you a larger picture of the image and the page it came from. But the image results have a few nooks and crannies you might miss. Figure 3-4 shows you what to look out for.

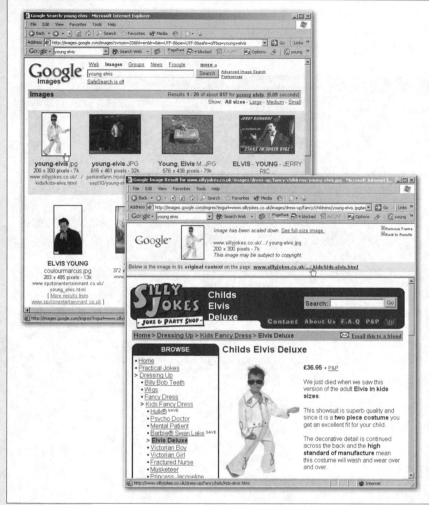

Figure 3-4:
Top: Below each picture is its name and file type (JPG, GIF, or PNG), followed by its dimensions in pixels and its size in kilobytes. Under that is the URL for the page where Google found the picture. And if Google knows that a site contains more pictures that might match your keywords, it includes a link for "More results from www.whatever.com," as you can see under the first image in the second row; click the link to get another page of results.

Bottom: When you click a picture, Google shows you a page like this, which has your image isolated at the top, and below that, the page where Google found it. If you click the URL between the two parts of the page, or Remove Frame in the upper-right corner, Google displays the Web page alone. If you click the image or "See full-size image," Google shows you the picture alone.

Tip: If you have a broadband Internet connection and a fairly large screen, image results are usually easiest to flip through if you've got about 20 or 30 on a page, rather than the 10 Google comes set to. From the preference page (*www.google.com/preferences*), you can change the number of results Google shows you for every search. Once you've made the change, Google saves that setting unless you change it again.

Google News

Most of Google's services help you find things on the Web only when you ask for them. Google News (*http://news.google.com/*) does the opposite: It goes out and finds news stories throughout the day, continuously updating its news page (Figure 3-5), or even sending you email as stories develop. Google culls articles from thousands of online news sources, and then presents them by topic ("Fans, Industry Mourn Johnny Cash") and by category (Entertainment).

Figure 3-5:
Google organizes news stories into eight categories: Top Stories, World, U.S., Business, Sci/Tech, Sports, Entertainment, and Health. The first section of the page has a smattering of top stories, but if you scroll down, you can find three recent stories in each category, plus three more top stories at the very bottom of the page. If you don't like this arrangement, you can shake things up and move sections around—or even add your own topics, as explained on page 97.

Zooming In and Out

Most of the time, browsers don't let you zoom in and out on images. But you might want to see the details of a picture up close, or pull back to view the whole thing, especially in pictures with large dimensions. Or you might just want to see what a picture looks like at a different size. The secret is the *Print Preview* feature, which opens a new window with your current Web page, and lets you zoom in and out. This trick works equally well in nearly all browsers, though it's hit-or-miss in Internet Explorer for the Mac (try using Safari instead).

The first step is to isolate the image you want to see on a page of its own, so you can zoom in and out on the picture only and not the rest of the gunk on the page. If you're looking at a picture on its native Web page, or looking at it as a thumbnail on a Google image search results page, right-click it (Control-click on the Mac) to pull up a contextual menu, and then select something like View Image or Open Image in New Window (or Open Link in New Window, or View Link in New Tab). If you found your picture via a Google image search and clicked the thumbnail on the results page to get the two-part page shown in Figure 3-4, simply click "See full-size image" to open the picture on its own page.

Once you've got the picture separated out, you can open it in Print Preview. In most browsers, you can find Print Preview in the File menu; in Safari, you first have to select File → Print, and then in the dialog box that opens, click Preview. In Print Preview, look for buttons to zoom in and out, or for a menu that lets you change the scale of an image. Mess with the size to your heart's content.

Unlike most other news services, Google News uses sophisticated computer algorithms, rather than sophisticated humans, to group and categorize stories. The advantage to this system is that Google can gather a lot more stories a lot faster than most news aggregation services. In addition, because people aren't involved, the service isn't influenced by politics or ideology, so you get a range of viewpoints on most stories. The disadvantage is that sometimes, those computerized editors misunderstand things and post a story about, say, the Gaza Strip in Entertainment.

Note: Google considers the news service to be a *beta* offering, which means the company does not claim that it's ready for prime time. In practice, this means very little. Google News works so consistently, you may never notice any glitches.

Google News is great for learning about breaking news, for comparing the way different news organizations cover the same story, or for seeing how a story has developed over the past month (the service archives stories for 30 days). You can also run a keyword search in Google News, as described in the next section.

ALTERNATIVE REALITIES

News Sites of Note

If you're a news junkie, Google News might not give you a big enough fix. Fortunately, the Web is crammed with news sites.

A good place to start is Yahoo Daily News (*http://dailynews. yahoo.com*), a thorough, well-organized directory with links to tons of stories and other news sites. You can also search for stories or news photos. And don't miss the "Oddly Enough" link to irresistibly weird stories, like "Thieves Return Cranky Alligator" and "She Closed Airport to Avoid Vacation with Boyfriend."

For localized searches, Topix (*www.topix.net*) can't be beat. It's also an excellent all-around news aggregator, with terrific category breakdowns covering zillions of topics (including Google).

To search for news coverage on blogs or regular Web pages, Daypop (*www.daypop.com*) is a good bet. It also keeps running tabs on the words that appear most frequently in the news.

Searching Google News

You can run a search in Google News just the way you would run any regular Google search of the Web. If you type your terms into the blank search box at the top of any Google News page and then press Enter, Google gives you a list that looks like the results in Figure 3-6, including results up to a month old.

If you find yourself with tons of irrelevant results, you can take two courses of action to narrow things down. Either use the advanced search feature described in the next section, or use one of these two syntax elements:

- *Intitle* searches for your words in the article title. Use it like this: *intitle:"presidential hopeful"*.

Figure 3-6:
Google News is set to show you 30 listings on a page, sorted by relevance (as assessed by Google). You can also sort the results by date, which lets you track a story's development. Simply click "Sort by date" toward the upper-right corner of the page, which reorders the stories from most recent to oldest. If you want to change the number of results on the page, move your cursor to the end of the URL in your address bar and type in: &num=50 (make that number however many listings you'd like to see). To read a full story, click its title.

- *Source* restricts your results to stories from one news outlet, like the *Washington Post* or CNN. If your source has more than one word in its title, you have to use underscores to link them together, not quote marks, like this: *SpongeBob source:newark_star_ledger*.

Maddeningly, Google does not publish a list of the sources it gathers stories from, so you have cull sources from existing stories or do some guessing (if *source:times* doesn't work, try *source:new_york_times*).

Advanced News Search

When you want to limit your keywords or home in on results from a particular time frame or location, the Advanced News Search page, shown in Figure 3-7, is the place to head. You can either point your browser to *http://news.google.com/advanced_news_search,* or you can jump to it from the main Google News page—there's a link near the top.

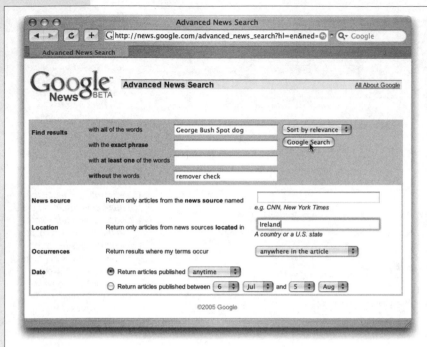

Figure 3-7:
The advanced search page for Google News is a real boon when you're sifting through a haystack (stories about George W. Bush) to find a needle (a description of Spot, one of his dogs). It's also great when you want perspectives from a particular state or country, or when you're looking for breaking news and you want to see only results from the last day or hour. (When you jump to the Advanced News Search from a page of results, Google transfers your original search settings to the form, so beware of residue that you don't want.)

Here are the elements you can fine-tune with the Advanced News Search:

- **Find results.** As in the regular advanced search (described on page 50), this section gives you four ways to specify the keywords you'd like Google to search for. If you want to exclude something by filling in the last box ("without the words"), you also have to fill in one or more of the first three boxes. Exclusion is one of the strongest tools you have at your disposal, letting you search, for instance, for *Art Garfunkel* without *Paul Simon*. This section also includes a menu that lets you select whether Google shows you results listed by relevance or by date.

- **News source.** Like the *source* operator, this option lets you tell Google which news outlet you'd like results from. To use this feature, you also have to fill in at least one of the keyword boxes; you can't simply say you'd like to see stories from Al Jazeera for the past week without giving Google some search terms, too.

- **Location.** When you're searching for articles on potatoes, here's the place to tell Google that you want stories only from news sources in Idaho. This is also a handy feature if you're trying to track events in other countries, like soccer matches in Spain, that aren't likely to be covered by U.S. sources.

- **Occurrences.** This menu gives you the choice to search for your keywords anywhere in an article, in the headline only, in the body text only, or in the URL only. This feature is useful when you're searching for something that simply gives you too many results and you want to weed out a few thousand. Use the headline or URL options when you have a sense that your topic may be the main idea in a story (*Ozzy Osbourne injured*); limit your search to the body text if you want something offbeat (*fifth place in British pop charts*).

- **Date.** In this section, a menu lets you choose to see articles from the last hour, day, week, or month. Alternatively, you can specify stories from a single date or range of days during the last month. Unfortunately the Google News archive goes back only 30 days.

Tip: To see stories from only one day in the past, choose the same start and end date.

This feature is seriously helpful, because a normal Google Web search lets you narrow your results down only by the day on which Google last recorded the page, or possibly on the day a page was last changed—neither of which is too useful for most searches. Here you can see what Tiger Woods has won since the beginning of the month, what Justin Timberlake was doing on New Year's Day, or get the very latest on the return of *AbFab*.

Browsing Google News

To browse through recent stories, you can simply scroll down the main page to see the top stories in each category. Or you can click the colored links on the left to jump to a full page of stories for each category.

Tip: If you have a dial-up connection, you can speed up the delivery of Google News considerably by viewing the service without photos. In the upper-right corner of the page, click Text Version. To return to the version with photos, click Graphical Version near the top of the page.

Google helpfully clusters stories together by topic. An individual story consists of a headline you can click to go to the original site (if that site requires registration, Google makes note); the first paragraph of the story; links for related headlines from several other news sources; links to other sources that have covered the story; and a link for a listing of related stories, which takes you to a page of results like that shown in Figure 3-6.

Tip: How fresh is the news Google is feeding you? There are two ways to tell: 1) Toward the top of the page, under the search buttons, is a note, "Auto-generated 4 minutes ago," or however recently Google updated the page (usually very recently); and 2) each story tells you when its native Web site posted it.

If you want your news from sources based primarily in another country, or in another language, Google News comes in other flavors: Australian, Canadian, French, German, Indian, Italian, and so on. The links for the international versions are at the bottom of the main page.

Customizing Google News

Some people don't care about sports, and others could really do without entertainment news dominated by constant coverage of celebrity couples going out to dinner. Fortunately for the headline hound with a discriminating nose for news, Google News can be *customized*—meaning you can rearrange your topics and sections on the page in the order you want to see them, delete subjects you don't care about, and make your own sections to gather news on any topic of particular importance to you.

To customize your Google News, click the "Customize this page" link on the top-right side of the main page. This opens a pane like the one shown in Figure 3-8 that displays the current layout of the page and where each section is positioned.

Figure 3-8:
News page design is as easy as dragging the section boxes around the page. To fine-tune each section further, click the name for another palette of options.

The Top Stories area is anchored to the top of the page, but you can change up the categories below. Drag the topic blocks into the order you want to read them, and if you want to ditch a topic entirely, just click it and then on the screen that appears, turn on the checkbox next to "Delete section".

You can pick the international edition of Google News to use for a section's stories as well: Click the section name and then choose the country of origin for the news you wish to see. This can be very helpful if you want to keep up with the latest entertainment news from Germany, or keep tabs on what French scientists are working on.

If you click the Save Changes button, the Google News page rejiggers itself to your specifications.

Tip: You can spread your version of the Google News page around to your pals or even to your other computers. Scroll to the very bottom of your customized page and click on "Share your customized news with a friend." The URL for your version of Google News pops up onscreen, and once you cut and paste it into an email message and send it off, you can use that link to lead yourself (or your friends) back to your personalized page.

Adding your own news sections

Customizing Google News means more than just shoving sections around on the page. You can create completely new sections based on a few keywords pertaining to a topic you want to keep an eye on, like the hurricane forecast (if you live in Florida) or the antics of the British royal family (if you happen to be an Anglophile). You can have up to 20 standard and customized sections on your Google News page.

It takes just a few steps to add your own section from scratch:

1. **Click the "Customize this page" link on the main Google News page**

   The link may be labeled "Edit the customized page" link if you've already been in there tinkering. At any rate, the page-editing panel appears.

2. **Click the link for "Add a custom section."**

   In the box like the one shown in Figure 3-9, you can add the keywords that you want to appear in the collected news, like *florida hurricanes* or *tennis tournaments*.

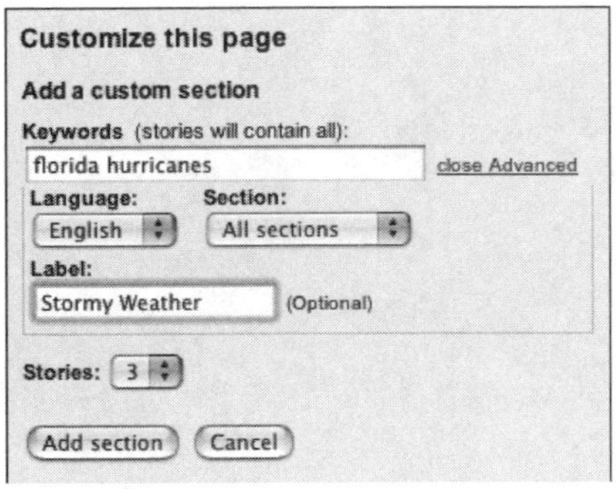

Figure 3-9:
In addition to keywords, you can modify your news-gathering further by clicking the Advanced link in the "Customize this page" box and then specifying things like label, language, and number of stories on the page.

3. **Select the number of stories you want to appear on the page.**

   Use the drop-down menu to choose between one and nine stories to be displayed on the page.

4. **Click the Advanced link to further finesse your section.**

   In the Advanced area, you can add a custom label for your new section, like *Scary Weather* or *Grand Slam*, to describe this collection of news stories you're gathering. The menus in the box let you choose the language you want to use for your news stories and the section you want to draw them from. For

---

example, you if you want to watch for stories about Apple Computer's fiscal health, use Apple Computer as your keyword and select Business from the drop-down menu under section.

5. **Click the Add Section button.**

This pops you back out to the panel where you can rearrange your news blocks. Position your new section where you want to see it and click the Save Layout button. To fold up the page-editing panel, click the Close link at the top.

Once your new section lands on the Google News page, you can tweak its settings by clicking the Edit link next to its label, as shown in Figure 3-10.

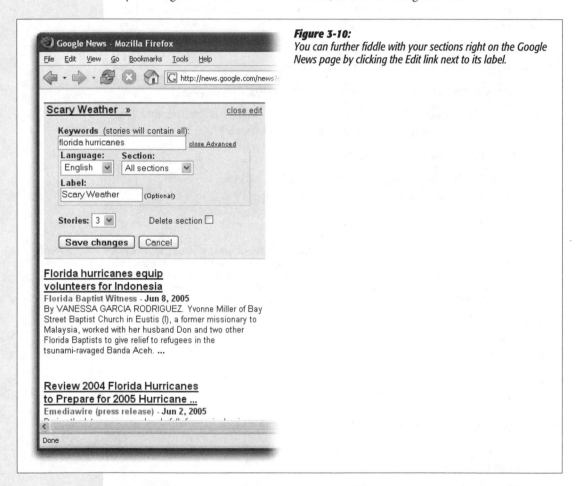

Figure 3-10:
You can further fiddle with your sections right on the Google News page by clicking the Edit link next to its label.

If you decide that you've bungled up the works or want to revert back to the generic Google News page, click the "Edit this customized page link" and tap the "Reset page to default" line at the bottom of the panel.

Tip: For a really fast read, customize your Google News page to show only the headlines by clicking the option at the bottom of the page-customization box.

Getting the News Delivered

Browsing and searching for stories is all well and good if you're serving ten years to life. But if you're too busy to click around Google News looking for breaking stories all the time, you can have Google email you updates, either as they appear or once a day, as a digest. Google calls these notices *alerts,* and as it points out on the sign-up page, alerts are great for keeping track of a business competitor's activity, watching action in your industry, tracking a news story as it develops, and keeping up to speed on your favorite sports teams and celebrities.

Tip: You can also use news alerts to keep track of *yourself* in the news. To see who's saying what about you, sign up for alerts that let you know when Google's found news mentioning or featuring you (or someone famous who shares your name).

Signing up is a cinch. On the left side of the main news page, click the link for News Alerts to get the page shown in Figure 3-11.

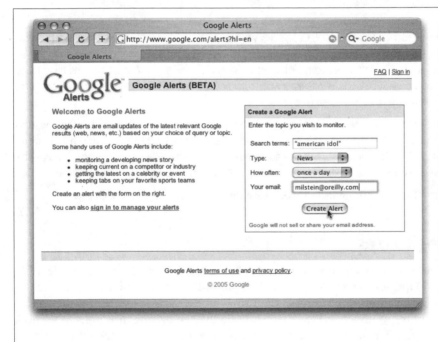

Figure 3-11:
In "Search terms," fill out your keywords. In "How often," select "once a day," "as it happens," or "once a week." And in "Your email," type in the address where you'd like to receive the alerts. Then click Create News Alert. Google sends you an email with a link to click, verifying that you want to sign up for the alert. Click it, and you're done. (Google says that it does not sell email addresses or use them for any purpose other than the one you designate—in this case, receiving news alerts. For more information, see http://www.google.com/help/faq_newsalerts.html#q11.)

The keywords you choose for your alerts can have a big effect on the stories Google sends you. For example, if you live in Salt Lake City and you're a big basketball fan, signing up for alerts with the keyword *Jazz* is also going to get you stories about Louis Armstrong's house in Queens and the new Lincoln Center auditorium. For better results, try *Utah Jazz.*

Tip: You can create a pretty complex query using the Advanced News Search page, described above, and then transfer that query to a news alert. Simply set up an advanced search, and run it. Then, at the top of the results page, copy all the words that appear in the search box and then paste them into the blank box in a fresh news-alert setup page. Complete the alert as usual, and you're done.

If you sign up to get alerts as they happen, you can wind up with a ton of email in a short period of time if your topic heats up. If the onslaught is overwhelming, consider creating a separate folder in your email program for messages from Google News and using message rules (which nearly all email programs have) to automatically file incoming alerts into that folder. Your other alternative is to shut off the flow entirely: Each alert you receive has a handy cancellation link at the bottom, which you can click to instantly kill that stream of messages.

If you want to change your keywords or the frequency of news delivery, sign into the Google Alerts box (click the "Sign in" link in the upper-right corner), and then click the Edit link next to the alert you want to alter. You can delete outdated alerts here as well.

Note: In addition to news alerts, Google lets you sign up for *Web* alerts, which tell you when Google finds a page that mentions your terms. Web alerts are great for tracking comments other people make about you, your company, your competitors, your sister-in-law, and so on. You can also use them to discover new pages on a topic, or to find out when somebody has linked to your site (use the link syntax like this: *link:www.[your website's name here].com*).

Head over to *www.google.com/alerts* (you may already be there) and fill in the form, specifying whether you want to receive the alerts daily or weekly. Now the important part: From the Type pop-up menu, choose Web (instead of News). Your alert now sends you email when there are new *search results,* rather than news events. (To get both in the same alert, pick News & Web from the Type pop-up menu.)

You can fill in the search box with advanced queries, too, using the syntax described on page 65.

Google Maps

Online map sites are among the most useful services on the World Wide Web. With MapQuest, Yahoo Maps, and their ilk, you can quickly plot your driving trip from start to finish by typing in the two addresses—no matter where they are in the country. With a graphical map and step-by-step driving directions, it's a heck of a lot faster than schlepping down to AAA and picking up a marked-up TripTik before you hit the road.

Google Maps wasn't the first online map site, but in typical Google fashion, it's one of the fastest, easiest, and most versatile sites in the cartographic category. Unlike other map sites, Google Maps is *dynamic* and *interactive*. In other words, if you want to see the next few streets over from your house, you can just *drag* the map to pull the adjacent neighborhood into view, rather than having to wait for the whole page to refresh. No other free map service comes close.

You have your choice of views with Google Maps, too. You get the standard road and street grids, of course, but if you're feeling omniscient, you can switch to a *satellite* (that is, photographic) view of the same area with just one click. You can even get a "Hybrid" map that combines the two views, superimposing street maps on a satellite photo of your destination.

Even if you're not actually going anywhere, it's easy to lose yourself in Google Maps for hours, just wandering around and looking at close-ups of your neighbors' houses. You can even annotate your maps with the location of the nearest tapas bar in town—a stunt that, 20 years ago, would have required an *actual* map and thumbtack.

Using Google Maps

If you want to see a map of a certain location with Google Maps, browse on over to *http://maps.google.com*. You can zoom right in on the map of the United States and use your mouse to drag through until you find your town, but it's quicker to just type your address in the box at the top and then click the Search button (Figure 3-12). Google Maps presents you with a street diagram, complete with a little pushpin icon pointing to the address you provided. A comic-book-style balloon displays your address and lets you get directions to or from the location.

Figure 3-12:
If you type in an address for just about any location in the country, Google Maps takes you there in a flash—and thoughtfully pinpoints your location. To close the balloon (so you can see what streets are behind it, for example), click the X in its upper-right corner.

If you just want to see a general city map, you can type in the name of the town, like *Salt Lake City* or *Fargo*. (Add a state abbreviation if you're looking for a place with a common name, like Columbus or Springfield.) You can also just type in the Zip code of a town to get its map.

When your Google Map appears, use the slider along the left side of the image to zoom in (to see details like minor street names) or out (to get a better lay of the land). If you want to wander around town, you can either use the four directional arrows in the top-left corner, or just drag your way through the streets with your mouse cursor.

Tip: To return to the original map, click the small button between the four directional arrows.

Satellite view

For many of its maps, Google also offers a satellite photograph, as shown in Figure 3-13. Click the Satellite link in the top-right corner of the page to switch views. (Your address remains pinpointed even in this bird's-eye view.) Unfortunately, this Satellite view isn't updated in real time, so you can't spy on your neighbors to see what's causing such a ruckus in their backyard.

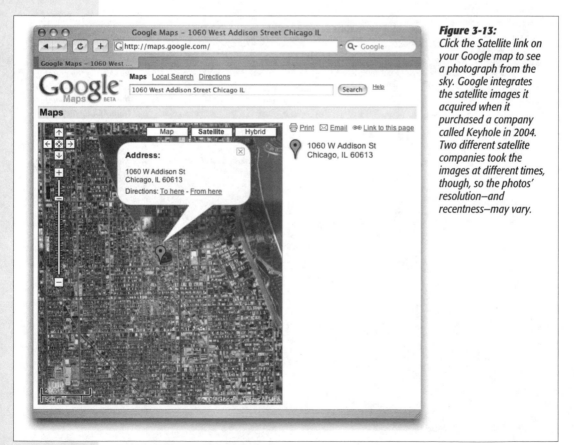

Figure 3-13:
Click the Satellite link on your Google map to see a photograph from the sky. Google integrates the satellite images it acquired when it purchased a company called Keyhole in 2004. Two different satellite companies took the images at different times, though, so the photos' resolution—and recentness—may vary.

You can usually zoom in pretty close on maps of popular areas, as shown in Figure 3-14. Google Maps doesn't have satellite close-ups for some less-traveled parts of the country, though, so you'll see a grayed-out area instead.

Tip: You can take your hands off the mouse and zoom through your onscreen streets with several convenient keyboard shortcuts. Once you've clicked on the map, press the + (plus) key to zoom in closer and the − (minus) key to zoom out farther away. You can use the Page Up and Page Down keys to take big leaps up and down the map, and the Home and End keys to take big jumps left or right. (For smaller movements, just use your keyboard's arrow keys.)

Figure 3-14:
Look, it's Wrigley Field! Zooming in gives you a bird's-eye view of your location on the satellite map. It's not a live image, but most photos were taken within the last year.

Getting Directions

Finding a location is one thing, but getting there is a whole different ball of wax. Google can help. If you know you're going to need directions right off the bat, click the directions link at the top of the Google Maps page (Figure 3-15) and type in your origin and destination addresses. After you click the Search button, Google Maps returns a detailed map highlighting both locations, along with the driving directions needed to navigate from start to finish, and an estimate of the time it'll take to make the trip.

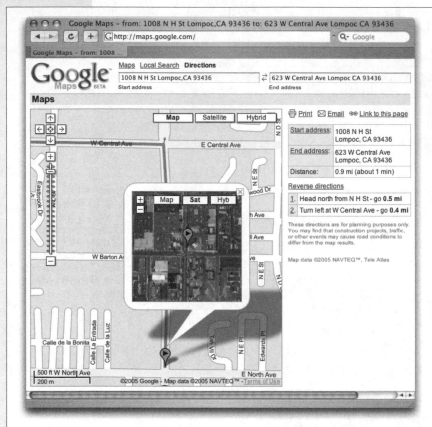

Figure 3-15:
When you ask Google Maps for directions, you get an interactive diagram explaining each turn along the way and an estimated driving time. Click either the start thumbtack (the green one with an arrow on it) or the end thumbtack (the red one with a box on it) for a close-up of the corresponding location.

As shown in Figure 3-16, Google marks up your map just like the folks down at AAA and annotates turn-by-turn driving instructions along the right side of the screen. To see a close-up of a turn—as a map (Map), satellite photo (Sat), or hybrid (Hyb)—click the number next to the turn you're curious about. Don't overlook this feature; it's a great way to anticipate any funky traffic interchanges or potential bottlenecks along the way.

You can print out your customized map or email its link to a friend using the choices on the right side of the window. There's even a "Link to this page" option to generate a URL for the map, so you can link to it from your *own* Web page. That's something to keep in mind if you're ever making an online guide— for example, to tell your family how to get from your wedding to the reception after.

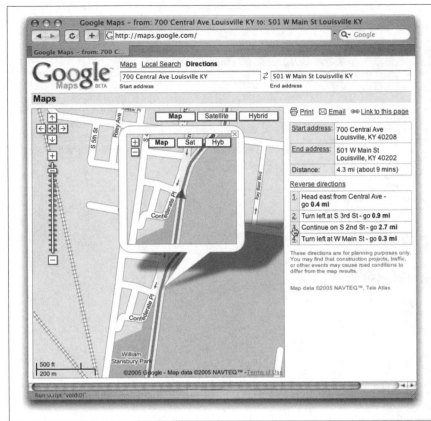

Figure 3-16:
Click one of the directions along the route to see a detailed view of the corresponding turn or interchange. You can switch between views using the three buttons at the top of the balloon, and even zoom in and out with the + and – buttons, respectively.

If you type only a *single* location into Google Maps—and then later decide you want directions for it—all is not lost. Just click the link for your desired directions in the address balloon, and a mini Get Directions section appears (Figure 3-17).

***

Tip: If anybody asks you if you know the way to San Jose, sit 'em down in front of Google Maps and type in *37.37 N, 121.92 W* in the Search box. That's right: Google Maps can recognize and translate latitude and longitude coordinates, and convert the numbers into a location on a map.

***

Using Local Search and Maps Together

Google Maps are integrated with Google Local (page 62), so you can find nearby coffeehouses, eyeglass-repair shops, and wireless-network hotspots—and then get directions. That can be extremely helpful if you're staying in an unfamiliar town, for example, and need to find a wireless network or locate a java joint where you can get a double-shot of espresso.

To search for shops, stores, hotels, or other destinations, click Local Search at the top of the Google Maps page. Type in the kind of place you are looking for and what town you want to find it in—like *barbecue* in *Tuscaloosa, AL*—and then click the Search button (Figure 3-18).

Tip: You can also use just the Zip code of the town.

Google gives you a list of places in the area. Click the one you want—and then, in the balloon that floats up, click the link to get directions to or from the establishment. If it's a restaurant or hotel you're looking at, Google may even provide links to reviews of the place.

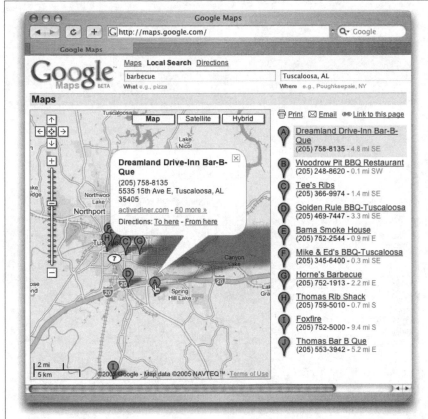

Figure 3-18:
Google can search globally and map locally, so if you find yourself in a strange city and want to find out what's around, click the Local Search link on the Google Maps page and tell it what you want to know. (For more on what kinds of places Google Local can find, see page 62.)

Google Directory

When you run a good old-fashioned Google Web search, Google checks its massive index of Web pages and shows you every single one that has your search terms on it. That Web index, described on page 274, is created by software that regularly combs the Web and records everything it finds; no humans judge or categorize the pages. The index system is great when you're searching the Web for something specific—like the name of the 1983 Wimbledon women's champ and how many errors she made that year.

But when you want to learn about something more general (like tennis) or you want to find out what kind of Web sites exist for a particular topic (like skincare tips), an index-based Web search can't give you an *overview*. You could, of course, type *tennis* or *skincare* into the Google search box in order to get a few thousand pages that mention those terms. But if you want a survey of a topic, the Google Directory (*www.directory.google.com*) is much more useful.

GEM IN THE ROUGH

Google Earth: Get the World on a Screen

If the bird's-eye view of the U.S. in Google Maps Satellite view gets you all a-tingle, check out Google Earth (*earth.google.com*) for an even more exhilarating experience. Using 3-D technology, animation, and satellite imagery from all over the world, Google Earth lets you swoop in like Superman from outer space and zoom into maps so detailed that you can pick out specific buildings from just a few hundred feet above.

As with Google Maps, you can find nearby restaurants, hotels, and other places of interest, along with driving directions, for many cities in North America. With Google Earth, though, you can tilt and rotate the maps to see buildings and terrain in 3-D, and you can add your own annotations to points of interest for other Google Earth users to see. You can then print, email, or save the images from your virtual travels.

As its name suggests, Google Earth covers the *earth*, so you can travel the world in just a few clicks and keystrokes. Every place on the globe isn't here quite yet, but most major world cities are. For instance, type in Dublin, Ireland, and you soon find yourself hovering over the River Liffey, where you can float close enough to see the roof of the Custom House. Landmarks like the 44-meter-high column in Place Vendôme, Paris, or the docks of Hong Kong, are also visible. And as you type in a new address or city, Google Earth dramatically pulls back and whisks you over the expanse of continents, oceans, mountains, and whatever lies between your current and future location.

As cool as Google Earth is, though, it's not for everybody's computer. Google Earth for Windows demands at least Windows 2000, a Pentium III 500 megahertz processor, a 3-D-capable graphics card, and a broadband Internet connection. Mac users will need OS X 10.4, a 500 megahertz processor, and a 3-D-capable graphics card. (The faster your computer, the better the program will run; see *http://earth.google.com/downloads.html* for Google's recommendations.)

There are three different versions of the program: the free Google Earth, the $20 Google Earth Plus (which gets you better-quality images and the ability to download information from a location-tracking device you own), and the $400 Google Earth Pro. Aimed at commercial users, Google Earth Pro gives you even *higher*-resolution photos, the ability to overlay architectural blueprints on the existing world, and plenty of technical-support hugs and kisses from Google.

Although it's still in beta, Google Earth has the potential to be one of the company's most fun and educational applications.

The Google Directory organizes more than 1.5 million Web pages into categories by topic, like an encyclopedia. Beginning with 16 main categories—ranging from Arts to World—the Directory includes subcategories and sub-subcategories and sub-sub-subcategories, with a list of related Web pages at every level. Figure 3-19 has more.

Figure 3-19:
Top: Looking for diet help? Start at the Google Directory and click Health.

Middle: The Health category. The top section has subcategories (the most popular are in bold). General sites about health are on the bottom.

Bottom: The Weight Loss subcategory. You can either dig deeper into the sub-subcategories, or just use the links at the bottom of the page to jump to a Web site about weight loss.

Note: The World category of the Directory contains sites in languages other than English—and the listings *themselves* are in other languages, too.

Unlike Google's main index of Web pages, the Google Directory is created by people who decide what the categories are and which sites go into them. (For more on how the Google Directory is maintained, see the box on page 111.) As a result, pages usually wind up in categories directly related to their main topic, rather than showing up in tangential searches.

Note: A directory is sometimes called a *searchable subject index* because it lets you browse for pages by subject rather than by keywords.

When to Use the Directory

Because directories sometimes miss the details of Web sites' content, and because they rely on human judgment, they're not always the best tools for finding information. Still, there are a number of good reasons to use a directory:

- **Getting the big picture.** Directories excel at showing you the lay of the land for a given topic. For example, if you want to find information on ecotourism, you'd follow the links in the Google Directory for Recreation → Travel → Specialty Travel → Ecotourism. This page lists a few dozen top ecotourism sites—plus subcategories for associations, birding, and fall foliage. Because each subcategory tells you how many sites it contains, you can also get a sense of the *scope* of a topic.

- **Narrowing down a search.** Directories are great guides when you want to search within a broad category but don't know what direction to head in. For instance, if you want to take a vacation, but you're not sure what kind of trip would be fun, the Travel page of the Google Directory suggests about a dozen ways to think about your vacation—and each of those categories has subcategories, and so on.

- **Seeing how other people approach a topic.** Because a directory is organized by people with experience in their fields, it can give you a good sense of how others see a topic—a useful way to broaden your thinking. For instance, if you want to write for television but you're not sure what kinds of shows you'd like to pitch, take a look at the Google Directory page for Arts → Television → Programs, which lists several dozen thought-provoking genres.

- **Finding related topics and search terms.** Because directories list many topics connected to a category, they can tip you off to related ideas and search words you might not have thought of. For example, if you have friends coming in from Melbourne and you want to make them feel at home without renting a herd of kangaroos, head over to the Google Directory and follow the links in succession for Sports → Football → Australian Rules. You'll find subcategories for things you may never have heard of, like "tipping," and related categories for info on Australian sports and international football. If you'd done a regular Web search, you might never have discovered tipping, or that Australia and Ireland have a longstanding competition in a game that combines the rules of Australian and Gaelic football.

- **Searching within a category.** The Google Directory has a blank search box that lets you search for keywords within any category or subcategory. For example, if you want to look up studies that discuss the way people use the mouse to interact with their computers, but you don't want any results about rodents, you could search for *mouse* within the Computers → Hardware subcategory. For studies of the way live mice react to eating a lipstick a day for three years, search for *mouse* within the Science category.

- **Getting appropriate and ranked results.** Google's normal Web search shows you pages that a sophisticated algorithm deems most relevant. And most of the time, it comes through. But if you'd like the human touch, too, the Google Directory gives you the best of both worlds. People choose the sites that it includes (see the box below), and then Google applies its PageRank technology to the directory listings. So you see sites that an editor has deemed worthy, but Google presents them in order of importance, based on its ranking algorithm.

Tip: Because directories are designed by people, each one has different categories and unique ways of organizing information. When you want to use a directory, try more than one to get a few perspectives. Yahoo, for example, is another good place to start.

Where Google's Directory Listings Come From

Because directories rely on people to review and categorize Web sites, they are seriously labor-intensive to create. Rather than employ hundreds of staffers to develop its directory, Google uses listings from the Open Directory Project (*http://dmoz.org*), which is edited and maintained by a cadre of thousands of volunteers—much the way open source software is developed.

The Open Directory contains about 1.5 million URLs, and sites in it are purely the choice of editors—you can't pay to have your site included. (If you want them to consider your site, head over to *http://dmoz.org/add.html*.) So it's important to remember that when you're using Google's Directory, you're browsing through a much smaller collection of Web pages than you get using Google's regular Web search tool. Still, because the directory is edited by *people,* you're a lot less likely to get junk results.

Note that the Open Directory Project offers listings only. Search services like Google, Lycos, HotBot, and others provide the actual search *mechanism* you can use to find things within the directory.

Browsing the Directory

Like Google Groups and News, the Directory is set up so that you can browse through the categories from its main page. Just click a link, and you're off to that category—which gives you more categories you can investigate (Figure 3-20), and so on, until you hit the bottom level, which has no subcategories, just page listings.

When you drill down as described in Figure 3-21, the top of every Directory results page offers a handy path showing where you currently are within the Directory (for example, Sports → Football → Australian Rules). If you click any of the links in

---

the path, Google takes you directly to that Directory page, making it easy to navigate around.

Note: Most of the time, Web sites listed in the Directory come with a useful description of what you'll find on that site. The quality of this information, however, varies from category to category.

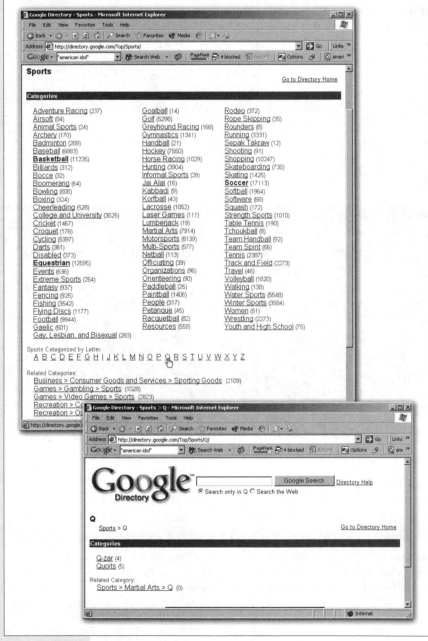

Figure 3-20:
Top: In the list of categories, the number after each link tells you how many sites or subcategories the Directory lists under that subject. Below that, a list of Related Categories indicates that other Directory categories also include sites that cover the current topic. Click a link to jump to a different category.

Bottom: If a category has too many subcategories to display at once, Google instead gives you a list of the alphabet; each letter links to subcategories starting with that letter. Here, the Sports category didn't explicitly list any "Q" sports, but clicking the letter "Q" on that page brings you to this handy listing.

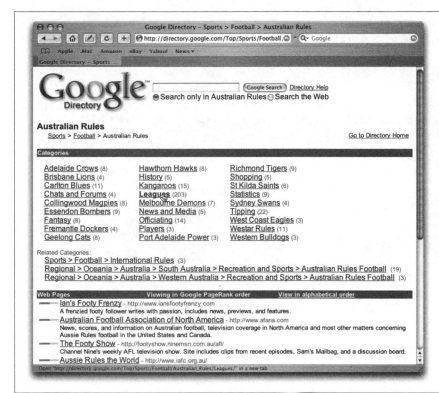

The bottom half of a Directory results page lists Web sites that fall under the current category. Google applies its PageRank system to the Directory search results, listing the Web sites in order from highest rank to lowest. The green bar to the left of each Web site gives you a sense of how high Google's algorithm ranks that site overall (see page 3 for more on how PageRank works). If you want to see the sites listed alphabetically instead, simply click "View in alphabetical order."

Tip: If you want to return to the main Directory page, click the Google logo in the upper-left corner of every Directory page.

Searching the Directory

When you want to home in on something and there's no obvious starting point on the main Directory page, or when you want to find out which categories include your search terms, it's time to run a *keyword search*. You can do so from the Directory home page or from any level of the Directory. When you run a query in the Directory, your results look similar to regular Google listings (Figure 3-22), but they include only sites in the Directory, and each listing shows the category where you can find that Web page. Click a category path to jump to that Directory page and see more related sites.

Note: A Directory search for *"chocolate recipes"* gets you around 15,000 results. A regular Google search gets you more than 3,500,000. While it might seem like the Directory limits you, more likely it's helping you find some of the 15,000 *best* sites. And be realistic: You're not likely to sift through all 15,000 sites–let alone the millions Google normally shows you.

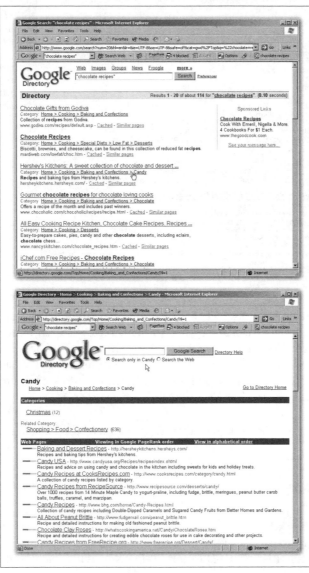

Figure 3-22:
Top: You can type your keywords into the blank search box to get a results page that includes a category path in each listing. Here, a search for "chocolate recipes" shows that results can appear in several categories.

Bottom: Click a category path to find yourself on a tidily arranged page offering recipes of many kinds. Now the search box at the top of the page lets you search within that category only.

The Google Directory has no advanced search page, but you can use two syntax elements to refine your searches: *intitle* and *inurl*, both of which help you narrow down results to pages that really focus on your keywords. See page 66 for more on these keywords.

Google Print

As if you didn't have *enough* to read on the Web, Google Print can let you peek and search between the covers of thousands of actual books that have been scanned in and cataloged on its ever-expanding virtual shelves.

The works available on Google Print aren't just home-published ventures or rejects from the remainder shelf at the discount book barn; they're contributions from major publishers working with Google to get a broader audience for their wares. Some of the texts in the collection come from the libraries of Harvard, Stanford, the University of Michigan, and Oxford University. The types of books available include fiction, nonfiction, children's books, textbooks, medical and reference volumes, and other educational tomes. You can even find some old classics and out-of-print books.

Searching for Books

To use Google Print, just point your browser to *http://print.google.com* and type in your search terms. Google Print quickly gives you a list of books that contain your terms in the title or text, as shown in Figure 3-23.

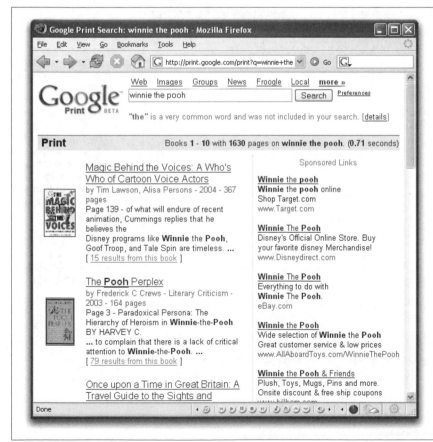

Figure 3-23:
Don't get confused—Google Print isn't channeling Amazon.com here; it's merely taking a spin through its database of digitized book excerpts in an attempt to match your keywords. As with most Google pages, there's also a column of paid-advertising links off to the right side.

If you click a book title, you can browse some or all of its pages (the exact amount varies depending on how many pages the books publisher has opted to allow). In some cases, you may just get a snippet or two of text and a dash of bibliographic info to help you track down a copy of the book itself.

Aside from the academic and research folks who spend most of their days rolling around in massive amounts of data, Google Print might appeal to any kind of book lover who likes to browse. Say, for example, you're looking for books suitable for your 8-year-old's reading level and can't remember if A.A. Milne's *Winnie-the-Pooh* series is too advanced for younger readers. Stroll over to Google Print, type in *winnie the pooh*, and start your search.

As shown in Figure 3-23, Google Print shows you more that 1,600 book pages that have some mention of Winnie-the-Pooh. Scan the list, and you can find an excerpt from the first Pooh book in *The Kingfisher Treasure of Classic Stories* (see Figure 3-24). In addition to children's titles, you also get Pooh excerpts for grown-ups like "The Paradoxical Persona: The Hierarchy of Heroism in 'Winnie-the-Pooh'" mixed in with your results, which might be too boring for your 8-year-old.

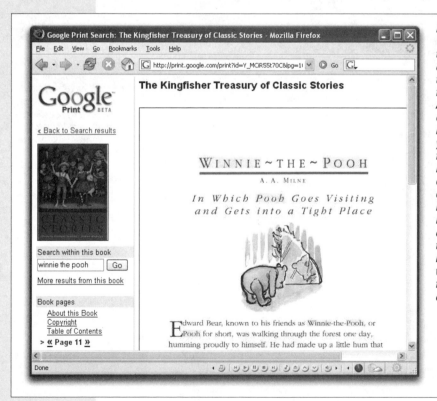

Figure 3-24:
When you click a book-title link, Google Print displays a few pages of the text that it scanned in from the original source. Although you usually can't read the whole book from cover to cover, you can get a sense of it from the sample pages. Here, for example, you can read enough to find out that "Winnie-the-Pooh" is an alias for one Edward Bear. If you scroll down to the bottom of the Web page, you'll see links to online stores where you can buy the full version of the book displayed on the page.

Studying With Google Scholar

Academics and the World Wide Web have intertwined for years. The original Web was partially *invented* to allowed scientists and researchers to easily share information stored on different computers. Today, however, finding specific scholarly journals, articles, and papers in the sprawling mass of online documents can be like finding a sentence on needles in a haystack-sized pile of history books.

Google Scholar (*http://scholar.google.com*) slips inside the ivory tower and performs targeted searches on much of the vast trove of academic literature on the Web, including peer-reviewed papers, abstracts, books, and theses—many of which are tucked away behind subscription services and members-only archives.

Yes, you still have to pay to see full versions of this sort of protected material, but thanks to agreements with many academic publishers, Google Scholar alerts you to the basic fact that these materials even *exist*, as they're usually shielded from standard search engine spiders crawling the Web for fresh data to index.

Opening the archives to Google Scholar has its advantages for academic publishers, as it increases the number of potential buyers for the material. Google is also working with university libraries and other research-oriented institutions to make even more scholarly works available for the service.

Google requests that publishers supply at least an *abstract* (a short summary) so searchers have a good idea what the article is about. (In some cases, search results may yield unclickable items tagged as *citations*, which means Google Scholar has seen references to the article in other sources but has yet to index the full document.)

Using Google Scholar is similar to using the rest of Google. If you have an idea of what you're looking for, you can use the *author* operator in the search box and add keywords for the topic you're seeking. For example—

```
author:castronova "virtual words"
```

—brings back many of Edward Castronova's writings on virtual worlds, including a 44-page paper titled "On Virtual Economies" written for the Center for Economic Studies and Ifo Institute for Economic Research. Within Google Scholar's Advanced Search area, you can refine your search on authors and publications (including fine journals like *Annual Review of Plant Physiology and Plant Molecular Biology* and *Social Semiotics*) and narrow down publication dates.

Although professional researchers, librarians, and others with access to expensive databases probably won't find much use for Google Scholar, the service is free, which is just the right price for most amateur academics.

Google Print is still in the testing stage, and your search results can be very unpredictable. You'd think if you searched for *Kurt Vonnegut*, you'd get a stack of books written by the famed novelist and essay writer; instead the top results are books *about* Kurt Vonnegut and his influence on American literature.

There are some very good reasons for this. First, Google Print is still in its early years, and it doesn't have every book out there scanned in. Another equally important reason is that Google follows the laws for the reproduction and distribution of copyrighted material. That's why you see only a page or two on most modern titles, but may find the complete text for older works that have outlived their copyright.

But even if you can't read the whole book, Google Print can be extremely useful if you want to get the sense of a title you're thinking of buying or borrowing from a library. It's like being able to stroll down to your local Borders bookstore and flip through thousands of pages on a topic, all without having to leave the comfort of your own computer.

If you like what you find, just click the links for Amazon.com and other online booksellers. (Google doesn't earn a nickel from those courtesy links, but they do profit from the sponsored links on the other side of the page.) Some books also include a "Find It in a Library" link; click the link, provide your Zip code, and see if there's a copy of the book in your local library branch.

Note: Google Print keeps a few pages of some books under tighter security to help enforce copyright protection. If you stumble across these restricted pages, log in to the site with any Google account you may have created—like a Gmail (page 377) or Google Groups (page 119) account—to see the material.

Until you log in, Google doesn't care what you look at, but the company starts to keep tabs on how many pages you've pored over once you sign in—and it may cut you off if you get greedy with the copyrighted pages. If you don't have an account, don't want to log in, or don't want to create one in the first place, click on the "View an unrestricted page" link to see another sample from the book.

Googling with Others: Groups and Answers

Most Google searches help you find text and pictures on pages anywhere on the Web. But two Google services, Groups and Answers, are actually sites hosted by Google, and they primarily help you connect with other *people* by providing forums for online conversations.

Google Groups lets you participate in or search through the archives of Web-based discussion groups—and if you find the conversations boring, you can even start your own discussion group and invite people all over the world to join you. Google Answers can help you bypass the discussions and find expert research on nearly every subject known to humankind.

Both services have a cyber-community feel, and this chapter reveals how to participate or how to read along without posting a peep yourself.

Google Groups

Back before the Web, when dinosaurs like the Commodore 64 roamed the Earth, the Internet had a cousin called Usenet. Like the Internet, Usenet was a decentralized global network of computers. But unlike the Internet, Usenet was designed solely to carry the traffic of a massive collection of text-based discussions, or *newsgroups*. The groups were organized by topic, and anyone could jump in at any time (the messages stayed online, like a bulletin board, as opposed to a live chat). Hundreds of thousands of people participated in newsgroups, making Usenet one of the first popular systems for online communication.

More than 20,000 groups are still active today, and about 100,000 have archives, covering everything from Abraham Lincoln to Intel microprocessors to organic chemistry to civic issues in Winnipeg. And most of the messages in Usenet—also called *posts, postings,* or *articles*—are saved in perpetuity, making it a rich source of information, and history, too.

Note: Usenet has had a role in the evolution of English: A number of terms that are widely used today, like *spam* and *FAQ,* first appeared in newsgroups.

Since 2001, Google has hosted Usenet newsgroups under the name Google Groups (see the box on page 122). By the end of 2004, Google had overhauled Groups with a redesigned interface and added tools to let users easily create fresh new discussions. The company also gave the whole enterprise a speed boost; new postings to the boards now pop in about 10 seconds and are indexed within 10 minutes. Google Groups includes thousands of live groups, plus Usenet archives since 1981, totaling a *billion* messages—and counting.

The biggest advantage is that, as part of Google, the groups and their archives now appear as Web pages with the power of a Google search built right in. So you can look up information by keyword, by date, or by author, and you're bound to find something juicy every time you dive in. And, of course, you can jump into the fray and post messages for discussion, too.

Figure 4-1 shows you the front page of Google Groups (*http://groups.google.com/*), which is similar to the Google Directory (page 107) in that it lets you either browse by topic or run a keyword search.

When to Use Google Groups

Groups are handy for finding arcane bits of knowledge (how to use an old Atari console as a Web server), for connecting with people who share an interest of yours (Renaissance cat paintings), or for talking to an expert who might be able to answer a question (where can you get the best tuna on rye in Dubuque?).

Even better, while a regular Web search doesn't let you target the date a page was created, a search in Google Groups might yield gold because you can specify results from any day or range of days from May 12, 1981, to the present. Groups are thus a good place to find out what people are thinking about today's news (Jennifer Aniston: hot or not?) and yesterday's news (Valerie Bertinelli: hot or not?)

If you need tech support, consider heading over to Groups, where you can search existing messages for help, and post questions and answers. In fact, the archives and regular participants in many groups have become a primary technical support system for lots of software programs. But even if the software you use has more formal help systems, groups can be quicker (nothing beats a successful keyword search), cheaper (free), and more thorough (other people can be surprisingly willing to help you through a difficult problem, and you can get assistance from several people at once). Microsoft alone has nearly 300 Usenet groups in the hierarchy *microsoft.public.*

Figure 4-1:
Top: As part of its new design, the Google Groups home page has replaced the dotty old Usenet system of organization with friendlier categories. The old Usenet system is still around and accessible in the "Browse all of Usenet" link, where you can stroll down Internet memory lane and still find the old chestnuts like alt.tv.dinosaurs.barney. die.die.die.

Bottom: A discussion on alt.tv.six-feet-under. Usenet groups like this one are still loud and proud, but there are plenty of newer discussion groups that have sprung up since Google gave Groups a face-lift. Like many Google services, a strip of Sponsored Links (page 31) adorns the right side of the page.

When Usenet Met Google

When Usenet was born in 1979, it was a network of its own, linking together servers that exchanged newsgroup messages. Internet service providers (ISPs) provided access to this network, and individuals who participated in newsgroups read and sent messages via software programs similar to email readers. In fact, many email programs have a newsgroup feature built in, so you can send and receive newsgroup messages just like email.

For technical reasons, however, Usenet was a hard network for providers to maintain. As a result, most ISPs wouldn't let you connect to all newsgroups, and some ISPs wouldn't let you connect to *any*. On top of that limitation, the email-like interface was a convenient way for individuals to get messages, but it didn't provide a good way to search newsgroups. And if you participated in a lot of active groups, you could clog up your phone lines forever sending and receiving messages.

But while Usenet was experiencing growing pains, the Internet was turning into a better environment for online communication—both for computers and for humans. In particular, people liked using the Web (which is a part of the Internet), and in 1995, Deja News created a Web site for Usenet groups. DejaNews.com let people search for keywords in articles and group titles, and read and join groups without getting their email involved. It was a glorious development.

But Deja, as it was known, folded during the Internet bust. Happily, Google bought Deja in 2001, and it now hosts the service under the name Google Groups. Thanks to the change in stewardship, the Deja/Usenet picture has become clearer, as you can now find all newsgroups—and their archives since 1981—in Google Groups.

For more on the significant history of Usenet, see *http://en. wikipedia.org/wiki/Usenet* and *http://groups.google.com/ googlegroups/basics.html.*

Tip: You can often find groups that discuss software from defunct companies or outdated programs—a real boon when you can't figure out how to print in dBaseII.

Newsgroups are also known for providing a sense of community on the Internet. If you like connecting with other people around a common interest, be it vermiculture or vintage porn, you can find a clique in Google Groups—or start your own club (the box on page 139 gives some examples of why you might want to). Many Usenet groups have active participants who've known each other electronically for years (page 120 tells you how to figure out which those are, but in general, the Alt section of Usenet has the most gregarious groups), and you can start new groups, too (*http://groups.google.com/googlegroups/help.html#added* tells you how to request a new group).

Back in Ye Olde Days of Newsgroupes, the way the messages and responses were displayed looked kind of like a trippy email/Web hybrid, which could be confusing. With New Improved Google Groups, however, user-interface experts obviously had their say in redesigning the service with a cleaner, less cluttered look. You have your choice of an easy-on-the-eyes *proportional* font (each letter takes up a different amount of space, which helps your brain recognize them) or an old-fashioned *fixed* font (each letter is the same width) to display the onscreen text. The old-style Usenet look is still available if you opt for "tree" view, but newcomers may prefer the standard, more straightforward design. The next few sections will get you surfing any style of group like a pro.

How Google Groups Are Organized

When Google revamped Groups, it added the power to create your own online discussion groups and invite as many or as few people as you want. Sure, the hearty old Usenet groups are still around (and explained starting on page 124), but Google has moved its own version of Groups front and center.

Note: Google is still tinkering with the service and trying new things. So for now, Google Groups is still considered a beta project (that is, there might be some rough edges).

As you saw back in Figure 4-1, the Google Groups main page has a list of ten general categories, with dozens of subtopics contained within:

- **Arts and Entertainment.** Movies, music, television, and entertainers are all in this category, as are arts-related discussions about technology, computers, education, and business.

- **Business and Finance.** Here, you'll find people talking about investing and financial markets, business and consulting issues, and financial news.

- **Computers.** The geeks shall inherit this category, as everything from artificial intelligence to programming to systems and security are covered in the more than 8,000 different groups here.

- **Health.** Addictions, alternative medicine, diseases, and medicine are here, along with topics like beauty and fitness.

- **Home.** Martha Stewart would like this category, which contains discussions on cooking, gardening, shopping, home improvement, and so on.

- **News.** You'll find current events, breaking news, and gab on the latest developments in the world right here.

- **Recreation.** Sporty subjects like camping, autos, and outdoor sports are here, along with groups devoted to animals, antiques, astrology, games, travel, and other leisurely pursuits.

- **Regions and Places.** Want to find people talking about Newfoundland? This is the category for you. You'll also find information on what to do in Marrakech and how to set up a business in Guatemala.

- **Science and Technology.** All those subjects you either loved or hated in school—math, astronomy, biology, chemistry, physics, philosophy—are under discussion here, along with space, weather, agriculture, and other serious topics.

- **Society and Humanities.** Items of cultural interest dominate this group, with areas devoted to education, activism, government, law, languages, religion, and more.

Once you click a category, the next screen presents you with all the topics within the category; keep clicking until you drill down to the group that interests you. You can also search specifically for groups that focus on topics you're interested in, like ferret care or mandolin playing.

Note: Some Google Groups have restricted membership lists, while others allow anyone to join. The description on each group's page gives the details.

Most categories include discussions centered on different geographical regions (Dungeons & Dragons in Ireland, for example) and in multiple foreign languages (boating in France—in French), along with the thousands of English-language groups.

How the Usenet Groups Are Organized

The old-school Usenet groups are organized by categories, each of which has sub-categories and sub-subcategories (and sometimes sub-sub-subcategories and beyond). Each topic has many discussions (also known as *threads*) associated with it, and each discussion is made up of one or more *posts*.

That's easy enough, but newsgroups have a peculiar naming system. Top-level categories, like those listed on the Google Groups Usenet page (Figure 4-2), are called *hierarchies*. All newsgroups fit into a hierarchy, as indicated by first part of a group's name. Subsequent parts of a name consist of subcategories and specific topics, and each part is separated by a period (*dot*). For example, the Sci (science) hierarchy has a subcategory called Agriculture, which has four separate topics: *sci.agriculture.beekeeping, sci.agriculture.fruit, sci.agriculture.poultry,* and *sci.agriculture.ratites.* In the beekeeping topic, a recent thread was called "Swarm prevention by foundation in the brood nest," and it had ten posts.

Note: Usenet group names always have at least two parts—a hierarchy and a subcategory—and sometimes five or more (for example, *alt.collecting.beanie-babies.discussion.moderated*).

The Usenet area of Google Groups has more than 950 hierarchies listed, but here are ten of the most common:

- **Alt.** This category's name stands for "alternative," but might as well mean "anything goes." The topics are sometimes very specific (*alt.animals.goats.pygmy*), and the conversations are often freewheeling.

- **Biz.** This category is supposed to have discussions about business products, services, and reviews. But there aren't many groups in Biz, and the ones that *are* there typically aren't very active. Not to worry: A lot of business topics are covered in other hierarchies.

- **Comp.** Computers: hardware, software, operating systems, theory, and more, all in one place. Geek city.

Figure 4-2:
Usenet used to take center stage in Google Groups, and even though Google has changed things up a bit on the Groups home page, you can still find all your quirky Usenet faves in their own section.

- **Humanities.** In theory, this hierarchy covers fine art, literature, philosophy, culture, and other liberal-artsy topics. In practice, nearly all that stuff is discussed much more actively in Alt and Rec. Humanities has a few active groups, however, including *humanities.classics, humanities.lit.authors.Shakespeare,* and *humanities.philosophy.objectivism.*

- **Misc.** This category is supposed to cover the miscellaneous—which is odd, because most Usenet hierarchies carry pretty random groups. Notably, Misc contains some employment and for-sale groups, plus *misc.kids, misc.health,* and *misc.immigration.*

- **News.** This hierarchy is all information about Usenet. (For current events, see the Talk hierarchy.)

- **Rec.** This hierarchy covers recreation and entertainment, including arts, aviation, food, games, hobbies, humor, knives, music, outdoors, sports, travel, and so on.

- **Sci.** Here you'll find science of all kinds: aeronautic, cognitive, cryonic, environmental, linguistic, and physical, just to name a few. You'll also find larger discussions of science, like *sci.skeptics.*

- **Soc.** Social issues. A few groups here get lots of activity, including *soc.geneology, soc.culture* (which covers countries, like *soc.culture.afghanistan* and *soc.culture. yugoslavia*), *soc.history,* and *soc.religion.*

- **Talk.** Current issues, especially those that lend themselves to controversy and debate, go here. Politics and religions are hot. *Talk.meow,* however, appears defunct.

Tip: Alt is *by far* the largest hierarchy, with thousands of groups. The rest have only a few hundred—or fewer—groups.

In addition to the ten main hierarchies, Usenet has a slew of more specific hierarchies, covering regions (everywhere from Alabama to York), companies (Microsoft alone has set up hundreds of groups that discuss its products and provide forums for technical support), computer languages and products (Perl, Debian), and organizations (Navy, Yale, you name it). To see them all, pull on your Internet hip waders and click the link on the Google Groups home page for "Browse all of Usenet".

Note: When you see an asterisk in a group name, you've found a group that has multiple subcategories or subgroups. For example, *Microsoft.** means that the Microsoft hierarchy has multiple subcategories, *Microsoft.public.** means that *Microsoft.public* has several subgroups, and so on.

The asterisk is a wildcard (page 22), and this is the one place on Google where a wildcard can be attached to other words.

Navigating Google Groups

You can find things in Google Groups by searching for words that you type in the Google Groups search box (just like a regular Google search) or by browsing through the categories until you hit a discussion you want to read. If you want to find something specific, or if you want to find out which groups discuss a particular topic, your best bet is to run a keyword search.

Browsing

To browse Google Groups, start on the main page and click either a category link or the "Browse complete list of groups" link. Either way, Google takes you to a list of groups, like the one shown at top in Figure 4-3. From there, you can click a subcategory and a sub-subcategory (and so on) until you get to a thread you want to read.

Figure 4-3:
Top: When you opt to browse all of Usenet from the Google Groups home page, you can wander through the hierarchies until you find one that suits your fancy. If you've clicked on "rec." on your Usenet travels, you wind up here—a complete, alphabetical listing of groups in the Rec hierarchy. You can see the rest of the list by clicking Next in the bottom-right corner. To dig deeper, click a group name.

Middle: Clicking a group name brings you to the subgroup page. In this case, it's all the subgroups under rec.aviation that explore a topic within aviation.

Bottom: Clicking a sub-subgroup name takes you to a page that has nothing but threads (rec.aviation. student).

On any page listing groups, the gray/green bar under some group names tells you how popular that group is. The greener the bar, the more members belong to the group. Usenet groups, all open to the public, typically have huge memberships; unfortunately, some boards have become vast wastelands of spam. If a group name has an asterisk and a number next to it—for example, *rec.aviation.** (23)—Google is telling you how many subgroups the group has.

> **Tip:** You can jump around the levels of a hierarchy by using the path at the top of the page next to the search box. The path tells you where you are now (for instance, Group: *rec.aviation.student*), and each part of the name is a link that takes you to the corresponding subgroup (click "rec." to jump back to the full listing of Rec groups). If you click the Google Groups logo in the way-upper-left corner of any page, you wind up back on the Google Groups home page.

When you're finally facing a list of threads (as shown at bottom in Figure 4-3), note that they're posted in reverse chronological order, with the most recent at the top. In newsgroups, *most recent* means the thread that has the most recent message in it—not the thread that was started most recently. For example, if a thread started in 1993 but had a new post yesterday, it appears at the top of list—just below a thread that started today.

Like an email message that gets batted back and a forth, a thread retains the same subject title until somebody changes it (at which point it becomes a new thread). Thus, when you see a subject title ("Tejon pass questions") followed by a number ("13 messages"), you know all those posts are on the same topic.

If you click a subject title, Google displays the most recent message in the thread, as shown in Figure 4-4. What's confusing here is that Google shows the list of *threads* with the most recent activity at the top, but it shows the list of *messages* within a thread in the opposite manner: The most recent message is at the bottom of the list.

Although Google takes you directly to the last message—which is handy if you're actively keeping up with a thread—it's often more intuitive (and useful) to start reading at the *top* of a thread, especially if you're new to a topic. To jump to the top, click the first name in the list on the left or click the "go to top" link on the right side of the page.

> **Tip:** If you're looking at a short thread, you can often just scroll up the main window to reach the first post.

Each individual message has a few moving parts, as shown in Figure 4-5.

Because a newsgroup thread can contain a few subthreads, and because you can find and read messages individually (and therefore out of context), people posting to threads commonly include a snippet of the message they're responding to. Quoted text appears in a different color and sometimes under a "Show quoted text" link that serves to tuck up the text so you can read down the threads faster.

Figure 4-4:
The main window displays the actual messages in this thread. The pane on the left shows who posted a message and when; click a name, and you jump to that post. (If you don't see the left pane, scroll up and click "No Frames"). The orange arrow indicates which message you're currently looking at in the main window, and the orange lines above or below it tell you which posts appear if you scroll up or down the main window.

Figure 4-5:
Top: If you click the "show options" link next to the colored block showing the author's nickname, you'll get choices to act on the message. In the gray header at the top of each message, you can find the name and email address of whoever posted the message (to see a list of all the messages that person has posted to Google Groups, click the name). You also get the subject title, a link back to the list of threads for that newsgroup, and the date and time the person posted the message.

Bottom: Click the "Show original" link, and Google takes you to a page showing just this post—handy primarily if you want the post's Message ID (page 136), as this is the only place to find it.

> **Tip:** If you find the left pane distracting, click "No frame." You can always get it back by clicking "View as tree." (just below the thread name).
>
> If you have the left pane open, you can *supposedly* use the Back link like the Back button on your browser. But Google can lose track of your progress, so it's usually better to stick with the familiar Back button.

That's it for the ins and outs of browsing Google Groups—but because the system has a lot of odd corners, it can take a while to get comfortable clicking around. After a session or two, though, you'll be zipping through messages like a pro.

Searching

Of course, a lot of the time, browsing can't help you pinpoint a piece of information. For those times when you need to zero in on a query, you can run a search that looks for your keywords in all Google Groups, or you can search within a single hierarchy or any subcategory.

To search the whole newsgroups enchilada, simply type your query into the search box on the main groups page. As Figure 4-6 shows, a Google Groups results page looks a lot like a regular Google listing, with your results along the left and a few ads (Sponsored Links) along the right.

Figure 4-6:
At the top of your listing are links for "Related groups," which are newsgroups that Google thinks have something to do with your keywords. Click a link to jump to that group. Below that, Google shows you snippets from posts that contain your keywords. Each result is headed up by the title of that discussion (which is like the subject header in an email message), followed by the snippet, and then a line with a link to the group that contains the message, the date that message was posted, the user name of the person who posted it, and the option to view the whole thread that contains that post. If you click the title, Google takes you directly to that individual message.

Tip: Google Groups ignores stop words (page 18) even when you put them in quotes. Thus, it reads *"The Shining"* the same as *The Shining*—which, since Google ignores "the," is the same as *Shining*. If you want Google Groups to include a common word, you have to put a plus sign (+) before it, like this: *+The Shining* (remember, no space between the plus sign and the search term).

Unlike regular Google results, you can sort Google Groups results by *date*. That's because when somebody posts a message to a newsgroup, the system automatically date-stamps it (the Web has no equivalent method for dating regular pages). Google normally shows groups results listed by relevance—just like regular results. But in many cases, sorting by date—which puts the most recent post at the top, followed by the most recent post before that, and so on—gives you *much* more useful listings.

For example, if you're searching for a person or event that's been in the news lately, sorting by date—which you can do by clicking the link in the upper-right corner—gives you the freshest messages first. Figure 4-7 shows you how big the difference can be.

Figure 4-7:
These messages are more recent than those in Figure 4-6, which Google sorted by its own estimate of relevance. Sorting by date also gives you new related groups at the top of the listings. To return to the relevance sorting, just click "Sort by relevance."

When you've found a snippet that intrigues you and you want to read the whole message, click the subject title to jump to a page that holds just the message with your search terms highlighted (Figure 4-8, top). If you click "show options" and then View Thread, Google takes you to a page that looks like the one at bottom in Figure 4-8.

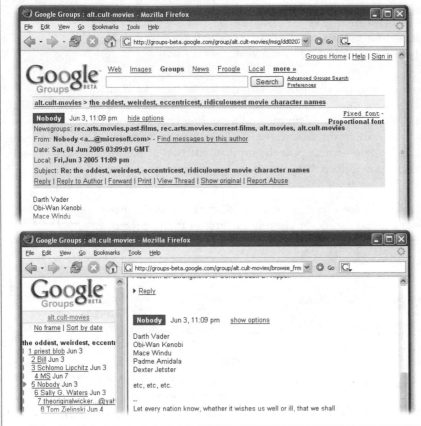

Figure 4-8:
Top: This view shows you the message alone. If you click View Thread just above the message body (click "show options" next to the poster's name if you don't see it), Google opens the left pane, showing who posted messages and when; the orange arrow shows you where your message fits on the thread.

Bottom: If you want to see the rest of the messages in the thread, click "See this message in context" at the bottom of the screen (not shown here).

If you're looking at an article in a thread that has no other posts, Google doesn't give you the option to view the complete thread, because you're already looking at it.

Note: When you look at a message on its own, the link in the upper-right corner ("show options" → "Show original") shows you the message with no formatting, which is handy if you want to cut and paste it into an email or other document. The original format also lets you see the header with the routing information, which is handy if you're a geek.

Refining your search

A weird quirk of newsgroup results is that Google shows you up to only four links in the Related Groups listings at the top of the page. A lot of the time, you can tell that you're not getting the whole picture—which is a drag if you're trying to find the groups that cover your topic. For example, if you search for information on Condoleezza Rice, it's pretty unlikely that the group with the most to say about Condi—in one such search—is *alt.fan.art-bell* (Art Bell is a talk show host). Where are the Republican or Democrat groups? Why don't you see *talk.politics*?

FREQUENTLY ASKED QUESTION

What's My Line?

In the left pane on a page of messages, why are some names indented?

When you're on a page that shows you the messages in "tree view," the left-side pane uses indentation to *try* to show you who's responded to whom. This system is maddeningly hard to read, but it can give you a sense of how a conversation is progressing. The two pictures here show how it works.

In the figure on the left, person 1 posted the original message. Person 2 responded to that message, and Person 3 then responded to that. Person 4 responded to the original message. Person 5 replied to Person 4, and those two went back and forth with each other for several messages. Person 13 got the discussion back on track by replying to Person 1's original post, as did Persons 15, 18, and 22, while various people replied to *their* posts, as shown by the indents, until the person that started the whole conversation chimed in at the very end. (Hopefully, they all went out for a drink afterwards.)

In the figure on the right, Person 1 asked a question ("How can I make KDE my default environment?"), and most of the people answered him directly.

To make the pane on the left wider or narrower, mouse over the bar in the middle until you see the double-headed arrow, and then drag the frame to your desired size. You can also make the list on the left appear as a neat, chronological column by clicking "Sort by date" at the top of the frame.

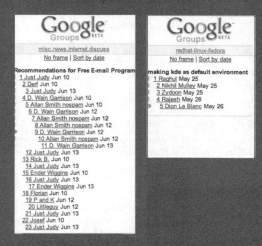

A good trick here is to search within the hierarchies and *second-level* categories in your results. For example, searching for Condoleezza Rice in Alt or Soc—or, better yet, in *alt.fan*, *alt.politics*, *soc.culture*, and so forth—gives you good results (including additional related groups).

You can limit your search to a particular hierarchy, group, or subgroup in a few ways:

- **Using syntax.** Remember Google's special operators from Chapter 2? A few of them work here. You also have a new one at your disposal—*group*—which you can use to specify any area of Google Groups. Use it like this (with no space on either side of the colon):

      condoleezza rice group:alt.*

  or:

      condoleezza rice group:soc.culture.*

  or:

      condoleezza rice group:talk.politics.misc

In the first two examples, the asterisk tells Google to look in any subgroup, sub-subgroup, and so on, within that hierarchy or subcategory. In the last example, the query tells Google to look *only* in the group *talk.politics.misc,* since there's no asterisk.

Note: To learn about other operators you can use in a Google Groups search, see "Advanced Groups Search" below.

- **Using a category-specific search box.** As explained in the earlier section on browsing Google Groups, you can navigate to a page for each category and sub-category. For example, if you're on the Google Groups home page and you click "alt.", you wind up on a page listing all the Alt groups. Similarly, if you click through to *alt.politics,* you get a listing of all those subgroups. If you click a link, as shown in Figure 4-9, the search box changes to look only within this group.

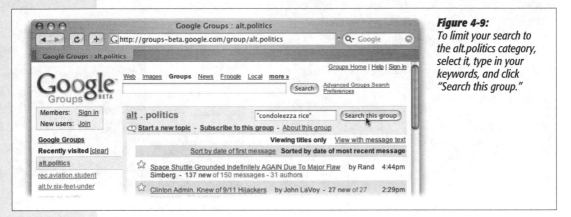

Figure 4-9:
To limit your search to the alt.politics category, select it, type in your keywords, and click "Search this group."

- **Using the Advanced Groups Search form.** Just like the Advanced Search for a regular Google query, Google Groups has its own Advanced Search page. See the next section for a full rundown.

Warning: Occasionally, group names are misspelled. There is, for example, a group called *alt.poltics.** You might land in a misspelled group without realizing it and miss valuable discussions in the properly spelled group (*alt.politics.socialism.democratic* is more active than *alt.poltics.socialism.democratic*).

Advanced Groups search

Almost every Google Groups page has a link that takes you to the Advanced Groups Search form (shown in Figure 4-10), which lets you narrow down your search in a number of useful ways, including by date (or date range), by language of the post, and by author. This form is particularly handy for mixing and matching elements—like looking for messages by one author in a single hierarchy before May 1, 2003.

Figure 4-10:
When you jump to the Advanced Groups Search from a page of results, Google transfers your original search settings to the form. Thus, if you searched for how to eat pizza with a spoon in group alt.*, and you click from your results directly to the Advanced Search page, the form comes up with "how to eat pizza with a spoon" in the "with all of the words" slot, and "alt.*" in the Newsgroup slot. Here's your opportunity to clear any settings you don't want, and to add new ones.

By now, you're probably familiar with the first four options, all of which let you choose the way Google treats your search terms (for a refresher, see page 50). To the right of the top search box, a pop-up menu lets you decide how many results appear on a page. Below that, you can choose to sort by relevance or sort by date (either way, you can re-sort your listings from the results page).

In the next section, you can choose:

• **Newsgroup.** This slot is just like the *group* operator described above. Use it to limit your search to a particular hierarchy, subcategory, or group.

• **Subject.** The subject refers to the title of a thread. Use this when you want to restrict your search to one discussion or when you want to find a discussion on a particular topic.

Tip: You can also use the *insubject* operator for the same purpose. For example, if you type *Condoleezza Rice insubject:"hot or not"* into any Groups search box, Google looks for her name only in threads that contain the phrase "hot or not."

• **Author.** Every post has a "From" line (like email) that lists a name and email address. If you want to find all the messages posted by somebody you know, or somebody whose articles you admire, this is the field to use. Type a name, an email address, or part of either:

```
Curiousgeorge
```

or:

```
George
```

or:

```
george@whitehouse.gov
```

Tip: If you're one of those syntax types, the *author* operator lets you do the same thing.

Bear in mind that posters often use nicknames and fake email addresses, both to protect their privacy and to prevent spammers from adding them to mailing lists. You can, of course, still search by author, but you can't always find out a poster's real identity or how to reach the person directly.

- **Language.** The place to tell Google what language you want the messages in your results to be in. This option doesn't translate messages; it just specifies which, if any, languages to restrict your search to.

- **Message Dates.** Here's where newsgroups really shine. The first menu lets you search for messages posted anytime, within the past 24 hours, the past week, month, three months, six months, or year. This is a quick way to find the freshest posts. But if you want to search for messages posted on a particular day, or a within a range of days (anytime from May 12, 1981, until today), you can use the second set of menus to get *really* specific. This awesome feature is lacking on most of the Web, making newsgroups the ideal place to find ideas and comments from a specific time period.

- **SafeSearch.** Although it's usually smart to keep SafeSearch turned off (page 49), it can be handy for filtering out the waves of sexually explicit spam that plague a lot of newsgroups. Use it with caution, and keep in mind that it doesn't block other potentially objectionable posts.

- **Message ID.** When somebody posts a message, the system automatically assigns it a unique Message ID. Most of the time, you can ignore this field. But if somebody tells you the ID for a particular post—which happens occasionally with historic articles—you can zoom in on that single message.

For example, Linus Torvalds, the inventor of the Linux operating system, first announced his creation on Usenet in 1991. The message is legendary, and you can find it by searching for the Message ID *1991Aug25.205708.9541@klaava. Helsinki.FI.* (Figure 4-5 tells you how to find any other post's Message ID.)

Serious Newsgroup Analysis

The headers on newsgroup posts contain a lot of information about topics people are discussing and who participates in the discussions. To look for trends, Marc Smith, a research sociologist at Microsoft Research, has started Netscan (*http://netscan.research.microsoft.com*). The site uses the data from message headers to create charts that can help you decide which of the existing millions of messages you might want to read or respond to, or to help you find a popular expert on a topic.

Dr. Smith explains that in real life, a person walking into a party can use social cues to decide which conversations to join or start. Similar cues exist in newsgroups, he says, and you can discover them by mapping out discussion threads to reveal trends like whether a group tends to have lots of regulars who return often—a likely sign of a lively discussion.

Similarly, if you can see that a particular person tends to post often in a group or two, and you find that other people tend to reply to that person, you have a clue that she's a valued member of the community. People who start lots of threads and get little response may not be as helpful.

Netscan is rich with such social details, but it has two significant drawbacks. First, if your computer is slow, or if you use a dial-up modem, don't count on getting any satisfaction from the site; the data is simply too intense for lesser systems to handle. Second, the site is complex and can be hard to figure out. You might get lucky and find your way just by clicking onto something useful from the home page. If not, hit the About and Help pages for guidance. You can also check *microsoft.public.research.netscan.discussion* or search Google Groups for Netscan threads.

Posting Messages in Google Groups

Posting messages on Google Groups is a snap. The first time you do it, Google asks you to register with a user name and email address; after that, you're free to shout out to the world. In fact, Google Groups reach people all over the planet, and a lot of those people believe in following Usenet etiquette—a set of posting guidelines that help keep electronic conversation flowing smoothly. People who violate the rules are not looked upon with kindness—even newsgroup neophytes (known as *newbies*). That doesn't mean fresh faces aren't encouraged; they are, and you should feel free to post up a storm. But before you dive in, familiarize yourself with the newsgroups' style of exchange by reading a bunch of threads and checking Google's dos and don'ts of posting messages (*http://groups.google.com/googlegroups/posting_style.html*). Google also has a Posting FAQ that's worth three minutes of your time: *http://groups.google.com/googlegroups/posting_faq.html*.

If you want to reply to an existing message, find the bottom of that message and click Reply (the link disappears if the message is more than a month old). A box unfolds on the page so you can type your response to the message. Click Preview to see what your polished prose will look like on screen, and then click Post to share your views with the world—or at least, the folks in this newsgroup.

Tip: You can follow up on a message that's more than a month old—and thus has lost its Reply link. Simply post a new message in that group and use the same subject line as the thread you want to add to. Google appends it to the existing discussion under that name.

Many groups required you to "join" up by clicking a button on the page to add your name to the roster before you can post, so don't be shy. When you join a Google-created group (as opposed to a Usenet group), you have the option of participating via email if you don't want to check in on the Web. As you join different groups, a list of your subscriptions appears when you go to the Google Groups home page and log in.

If you want to start a new thread, navigate to the main page of the group you want to post in, and click "Start a new topic." In either case, Google opens a page, shown in Figure 4-11, that lets you specify or change the header, write out your message, and preview or post it directly. If you reply to an existing message, Google copies that message into the "Your message" box; you can delete any of that text as you see fit.

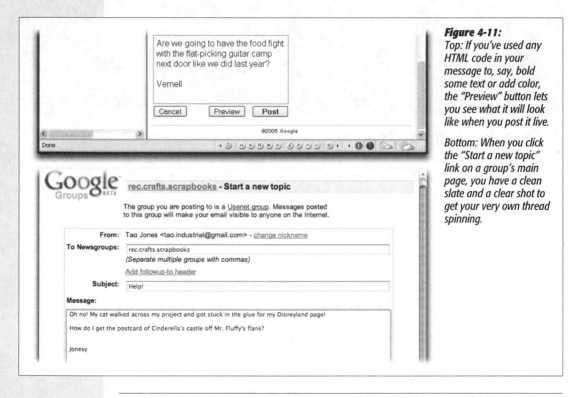

Figure 4-11:
Top: If you've used any HTML code in your message to, say, bold some text or add color, the "Preview" button lets you see what it will look like when you post it live.

Bottom: When you click the "Start a new topic" link on a group's main page, you have a clean slate and a clear shot to get your very own thread spinning.

Tip: When browsing the Google Groups you belong to, you can tag certain threads that interest you with little yellow stars so they stand out from the other kinds of text filling the screen. There's also a "Show my Starred topics" link on the left side of the page that lets you cut right to the conversational chase.

Gmail (Chapter 11) is another Google service that lets you see stars. There, you can use the five-point beacons to highlight your favorite mail message topics as well.

In a nod to privacy (and lack thereof on the Internet these days), Google Groups slaps a mask over your email address so the spambots slithering around the Web can't harvest it for nefarious purposes. Your address doesn't get the mask, however, if you post to a Usenet group (which are hosted on servers around the world, including some used by spammers themselves), or if you participate in a group by email instead of using the Web interface. Snagging an email address just to use for posting (say, a Gmail address, which you can read about on page 377) can help separate your Group mail from your other correspondence.

Once you click "Post message" it takes about 10 seconds for it to appear in Google Groups, compared to the hours it could take for the poor thing to show up before Google revamped the service. If you have a sudden change of heart and you want to remove your message, the Posting FAQ tells you how to do it (*http://groups.google.com/googlegroups/posting_faq.html*).

How to Create a Google Group

Before Google gave Groups a makeover, you could post to existing newsgroups, many of which were unwieldy or full of spam and *trolls* (those aggravating message-board members who like to pick fights in public forums) or not exactly the topic you were looking for. Nowadays, though, you can create your very own group on any topic you can think of. You can make it wide open for anybody in the world to join, or restrict the membership to just you and your pals.

Creating your own group is as easy as clicking the "Create new groups" link on the main Google Groups page. It's a simple two-screen process:

1. **Give your group a name.**

   As shown in Figure 4-12, you need to give your group a name so people can find it. The page automatically fills in a similar email address on the next line that your members can use to post messages. Based on the name, Google also generates a URL for the group's Web page, and you have the chance to type in a short description of what your group's all about. If you plan to discuss topics off-limits to children, turn on the checkbox below the group description so your page will display an adult-content warning.

   In the last section, you can set the access level for your group: Public (open to everyone to join and post), Announcement-only (anyone can join and read, but only the creator can post messages), and Restricted (invite-only to join and read, plus your group's archived posts don't appear in Google search results). Click the "Create my group" button to continue.

2. **Add some people to your group.**

   Here, as shown in Figure 4-13, you can add the email addresses of friends and colleagues you'd like to join your online social circle. After you add their email addresses, you can decide how they can join (immediate membership from the get-go or a membership requiring a response to your initial invitation email) and in what form their messages initially appear (just on the Web site or by various email delivery methods). Add a welcome message, and you're done!

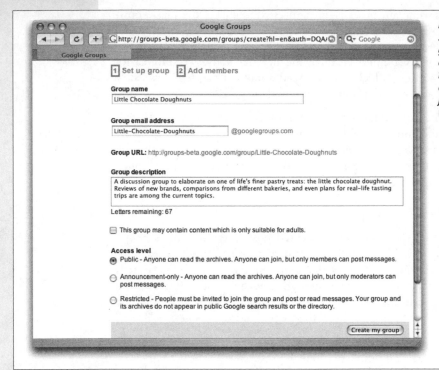

Figure 4-12:
Starting a group means giving it a name and an address so people can find it. You need to decide how people can join and participate as well.

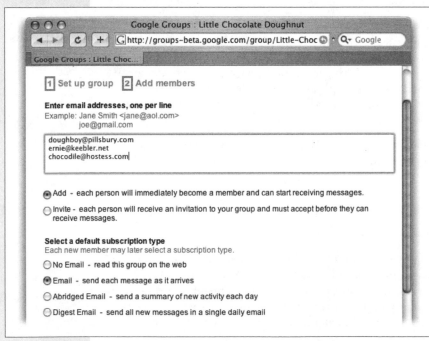

Figure 4-13:
Once you create your group, fill out the guest list of email addresses for those joining you and set a delivery option for the messages that get posted to your group.

Google sends a long email to your account with information about your group and links for articles on managing your new group. Google Groups has an elaborate Help section covering all the ins and outs of group ownership and management at *groups-beta.google.com/support*.

Groups Therapy

Starting a Google Group is like inviting your friends—no matter where they are—into a communal space, but a group can be more than just a virtual living room to hang out and shoot the breeze. A Google Group can be a place of refuge for people who can't meet in person to share stories—or even political ideas deemed dangerous by their governments.

You might want to start your own Google Group if you belong to a Usenet forum with like-minded members who want to create a "private room" to discuss a sensitive topic in further detail or to ditch harassing members of a Usenet newsgroup. (Many a girls-only group has been created in this manner.)

Groups have been started by friends who want to keep in touch, high school reunion committees, or people in recovery groups (and because you can restrict access to your group, you can make it private to members and keep Google from archiving its contents).

Despite the fact that you're getting to know people through text on a computer screen, deep relationships can be formed that last for decades. People who've been longtime members of Internet mailing lists, online bulletin-board systems (like the Well in San Francisco or New York's ECHO communities), and Usenet pioneers can tell you: Just because it's virtual doesn't mean it's not real.

Google Answers

Google Answers may be the most underused corner of the entire site. But that doesn't mean *you* have to miss out on this incredibly useful tool. If you've tried searching for something and all you've got to show for your work is eye fatigue, or if you simply don't have time to seek out a piece of information, Google Answers (*http://answers.google.com*) may be your knight in electronic armor. The service lets you ask questions that real, *actual* people answer—for a fee. The people are research experts, and you set the fee, based on how much you're willing to pay— anywhere from $2 to $200—plus a 50-cent listing charge. If you're not satisfied with your answer, you can apply for a refund.

Without a doubt, the service sounds a little weird. Why pay strangers to look up things you could probably find yourself, *gratis*? Of course, you *can* use the service as a super-fancy search feature. But it's better to think of it like hiring a research assistant, or having access to more than 500 friends with expertise in a range of topics. The people who work for Google Answers aren't simply good at using Google's Advanced Search form to find obscure Web sites and references. They're seasoned researchers who can answer complex questions methodically, thoroughly, and clearly. There's no better proof than their existing answers, which you can browse through or search from the Google Answers home page.

For example, a first-time writer working on a musical that he wanted to get produced recently asked: "What are the best theaters around the Seattle area to contact about developing the musical and putting it onstage? Any venues that are particularly friendly to newbies who are enthusiastic though inexperienced? At a minimum, what do you need to shop a musical around?" He offered $20 for the answer.

An hour and a half later, a Google Answers researcher posted a well-written 1,400-word reply (that's about three single-spaced pages in Word) answering each part of the question with specific details, examples, and advice. The researcher also listed, as many do, the sources of the information—in this case, "personal knowledge and experience," plus The Dramatists Sourcebook and some phone directories. (To see the question and answer, search Google Answers for *Question ID: 327256.*) A week later, another researcher chimed in—for free—with two additional suggestions.

That's not necessarily the kind of information you could find in one and a half hours on your own—or by asking around among your friends. Nor are you limited to asking questions about musicals. Recent queries have included:

- "How is the value of a bond determined? What is the value of 1-year, $1,000 par value bond with a ten percent annual coupon if its required rate of return is 10%?" (Question ID: 330297.)

- "Is it true that the real Goth followers sleep in coffins?" (Question ID: 324406.)

- "Is membership in private clubs [such as golf or yacht clubs] generally declining or increasing?" (Question ID: 323385.)

- "My 24-year-old gorgeous [daughter] could use a date to go with her to the Masters golf tournament in two weeks. She wants to meet a film or sports personality. There are several hundred people that would probably be golf nuts who would love to go. How do I contact such a person? Time is factor here. PS. A list of sports agents would be best." (Question ID: 323706.)

- "I have been diagnosed and am being treated with 'Procrit' for Sideroblastic Anemia. I have been told that this disease is a 'Precursor' possibly for Leukemia. Is there any validity to this statement?" (Question ID: 329758.)

- "Can I curse police? According to the First Amendment we have the right to free speech but where is the line drawn when police are involved?" (Question ID: 330406.)

Tip: To read a bunch of questions that researchers particularly enjoyed answering, see Question ID: 204301.

Figure 4-14 shows what a question and answer look like.

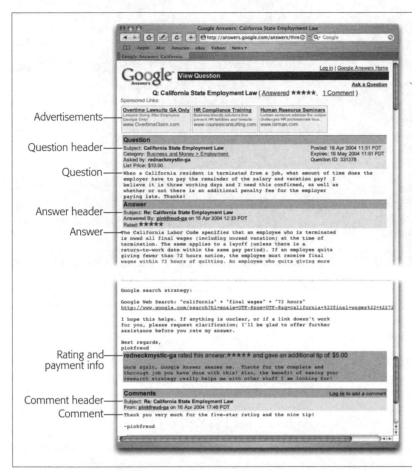

Figure 4-14:
An answered question starts with a header supplying summary information about the post, including when it appeared (in Pacific Time) and its ID number (right side). Below that is the answer header, telling you who answered the question and when (in this case, about 45 minutes after somebody posted the question). The actual answer includes explanations, links to related resources, and, toward the bottom, the researcher's search strategy. The lavender bar below that shows you how the asker rated the answer (five stars is best), whether he paid a tip (tips are optional, but outstanding answers often provoke generosity), and usually a note of thanks. At the bottom of the page are comments, which anyone can post and which sometimes include additional information.

And that's just the tip of the inquiry iceberg. Since Google Answers began in April 2002, people have posed more than 300,000 questions on the site. Researchers pick the questions they want to answer, so not all questions draw a response. But of the questions that researchers do answer—more than half—most reply within a day, and many respond within a couple of hours.

Note: The questions that aren't answered tend to be underpriced (say, $2.00 for a complete discussion, with citations, of the nature vs. nurture debate), inappropriate for the service (see the box on page 145), or unclear ("What's the best way to teach math?").

When to Use Google Answers

Google Answers is a versatile service, letting you pose questions in categories like Arts and Entertainment, Business and Money, Family and Home, Health, and

The People Who Do the Research

Who answers the questions?

Google Answers has more than 500 researchers, and they're independent contractors paid by the answer, not company employees. But they're not a random crowd. Google screens and tests prospective researchers for their ability to answer questions quickly and thoroughly. And they have filled the ranks with experts in many different subjects—though there are no special credentials required for the gig. (Google is not currently in the market for more researchers.)

Google also keeps an eye on researchers. Editors randomly check answers for quality. And a researcher who consistently gets poor ratings (Google encourages questioners to give feedback), or whose answers get several requests for refunds, can lose his position.

On the other hand, some researchers have gained cult status by regularly supplying great answers. Occasionally, you may see a question whose subject says something like, "Private question to Bobbie7-ga," or just, "Bobbie7" (all user names on Google Answers receive the tag "ga"). Click a researcher's name to find her average rating, the number of questions she's answered, and the number of refunds granted for her answers.

Researchers pick the questions they want to answer (Google doesn't assign questions), and if an answer is satisfactory, the researcher gets 75 percent of the fee.

Science. While you can find similar categories in Google Groups, the information you can get on Google Answers is likely to be more relevant and of higher quality. (It's also going to cost you, of course.) The service tends to be particularly useful for a few kinds of help:

• **Timely answers.** You *may* be able to find an answer yourself. But if your afternoon includes attending your son's soccer game, taking the dog to get her nails trimmed, negotiating the lease on your company's office, and designing a new space shuttle, you might want to get somebody else to look into the best shape for wings. Many questions are answered within a few hours.

• **Research assistance.** You remember seeing a Web site with tasty sauerkraut recipes, but you can't find it anywhere. Google Answers can help you track it down.

Tip: Most researchers tell you how they found your answer (for example, the search terms they used), which can help you hone your own search skills by showing you how the experts seek information. In addition, if you were looking for something that required more than a Google query or two, most answers include links to the sites where they found your info, helping you learn where you can look for obscure stuff.

• **Embarrassing questions.** Although you have to register for the service and create a screen name, your true identity is hidden—making Google Answers the perfect place to ask your question about octopus sex.

• **Market research.** The service is a good place to get in-depth information on industries, products, and business processes.

- **Computer support.** If you're looking for help with a defunct product, or you were stymied by Microsoft's Web site and don't want to sit on hold for two hours waiting to speak with a tech support agent, you may be able to get a faster—and possibly cheaper—answer here.

- **Numbers and facts.** You can get good value asking for statistics that are hard to find. Questions of fact about science, history, and notable people are also good candidates.

- **Background information on legal, financial, or medical issues.** Google Answers does not give definitive advice in these areas, but researchers can steer you toward relevant resources and information.

WORD TO THE WISE

Things You Can't Ask

While you can ask almost anything you want, the service has a few restrictions. Google may remove your question if:

- **It requests private information about individuals.** Don't bother asking the net worth of your Friday-night blind date.

- **You're asking for assistance conducting illegal activities.** The service is not the best way to learn where you can profitably sell heroin, for example.

- **You mean to sell or advertise products.** Put another way: Don't spam Google Answers. (If you do, Google may prevent you from posting more questions.)

- **It refers or relates to adult content.** Porn is a no-no.

- **You ask homework or exam questions.** You can ask for resources to help you find answers, but you can't ask researchers to do your schoolwork for you. In fact, if you're looking for homework help, say so; that'll give the researchers a sense of what you need.

- **You're looking for specific information about Google or Google Answers.** If you have questions about the service, shoot a note to *answerssupport@google.com.*

Before You Ask a Question

Wondering if hippos walk backwards? You're not the first (Question ID: 324775). People have asked questions of every kind, so it's worth looking around Google Answers to see if your problem already has a posted solution. It's also a good idea to search the existing questions to get a sense of the going rate for your kind of question and to learn how to write an effective question (see page 148 for more about question technique).

You can either run a keyword search or browse by category. (You don't need a Google Answers account to search the site.)

Searching Google Answers

You can run a keyword search from the box on the main Google Answers page (Figure 4-15), or you can browse by subject (explained in the next section) and then search within a category only.

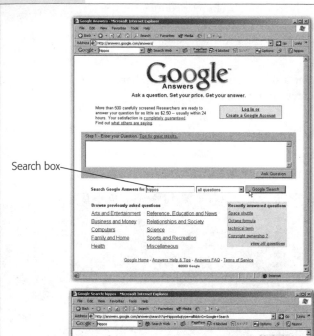

Search box

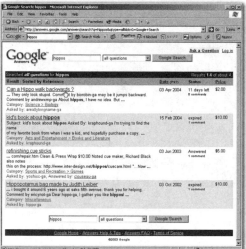

Figure 4-15:

Top: To run a keyword search, type your terms into the blank search box (not the question box, which is the big rectangle with the lavender outline). Use the menu to the right of the box to choose whether you want to search unanswered questions, answered questions, or both. Then press Enter or click Google Search to get a list of entries with your search terms.

Bottom: Each result is a separate question. The first line of an entry is the subject (click it to jump to that whole question and answer), followed by a snippet from the question. Below that is the question's category, then the screen name of the person who posed the question and the person who answered it, if there is one. On the right, you can see when the question was posed, whether anyone answered or commented on it, and how much the questioner was willing to pay for an answer.

Tip: When you want to find out whether anyone has ever asked for something specific, the tricky part is figuring out what they would have asked *for*. For example, if you're looking for an elementary school classmate, you might benefit from what researchers told somebody looking for a tenth grade sweetheart. Try search terms that will get you a broad range of responses. Rather than searching for "how to find third grade friend," try "people search." If you get too many replies, you can always narrow down your results.

The keyword search is handy when you want to zero in on all the questions relating to, say, hippos. Because you can search by unanswered questions, it's also a good way to learn the kinds of queries and prices that don't draw any researchers. Conversely, searching *answered* questions gives you not only juicy hippo info, but a sense of how to phrase a question in order to get a useful answer and how much to pay for answers.

Google automatically sorts your results by *relevance*, or how closely each result matches your search terms. You can, however, sort by date or by price, either of which can be handy if you wind up with a long list of results and you want info from a particular time period or to compare prices. In the upper-right corner of your results listing, click the link for Date or Price. After you do, Google displays a little arrow next to the link, telling you whether your list is sorted in ascending or descending order. Click it again to sort in the other direction.

Tip: To return to the listing by relevance, click the Results link that appears on the left side of the page.

Browsing Google Answers

The other way you can find things on Google Answers is by browsing the categories, just the way you would sift through the Google Directory (page 107). Start on the Google Answers main page and click a category to get a list of subcategories and results (Figure 4-16).

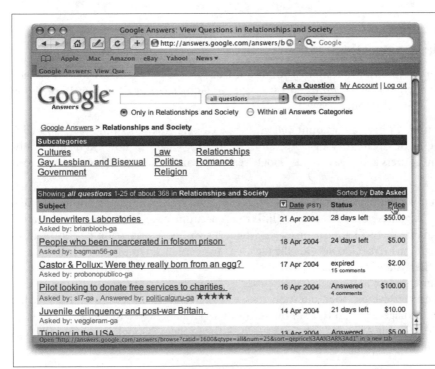

Figure 4-16:
When you click the "Relationships and Society" link, Google shows you this page. At the top is a search box that lets you limit a keyword search to this category. Below that is a path showing you the page you've navigated to, followed by links for subcategories, and then a list of questions in the current category, sorted by date (most recent first). You can sort by oldest first—or by price—by clicking the links in the upper-right corner of the list. The bottom of the page has a link to take you to the next 25 results.

If you want to see the kinds of questions that are hot right now, you can browse all the questions asked in the last month. On the main Google Answers page, the box in the lower-right corner, "Recently answered questions," has the four most

---

recently *answered* questions and then a link to "view all questions." If you click that link, Google takes you to page of results called "Questions currently being asked," as shown in Figure 4-17.

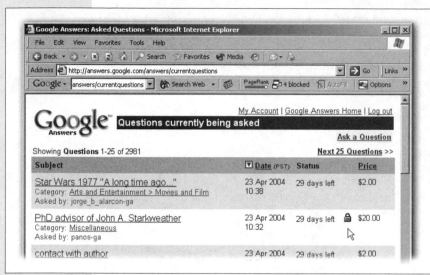

Figure 4-17:
The list of recent questions looks like most Google Answers results, but here you often see little locks on the right side of the page. A lock icon tells you that a researcher is currently working on a question—which is how Google prevents more than one person from answering it.

Asking a Question

In order to post a question, you need a free Google Account, which you already have if you've signed up to post messages in Google Groups (page 119), or if you have a Gmail account (page 377).

If you *don't* have an account yet, go to the Google Answers home page and click "Log in or Create a Google Account," then click "Sign up now" and fill in your email address and a password. Google sends you an email with a link to verify your account.

When you click that link, Google takes you to a Web page saying you're verified. That page lets you click *another* link to an account page, where you can create a nickname that will appear onscreen whenever you post a question or comment in Google Answers (Google adds the tag "-ga" to every nickname). This page also asks whether you want to receive email from Google when somebody has answered or commented on a question you've posed. (If you choose not to get email, you have to keep an eye on your question to see if there's been any action.) Finally, the account page asks you to read the terms of service and agree to them. Click "Create My Google Answers Account" to finish the process. (Google automatically logs you in.)

If you already have an account, you can log in either before you create a question or during the process. Here's how to get questioning:

1. **Come up with a good question.**

   This step may seem obvious, but a lot of questions go unanswered because the writer posed a confusing question or one inappropriate for the service (see the box on page 145). Google gives tips on asking good questions, along with examples, at *http://answers.google.com/answers/help.html.*

   In general, the more specific your question, the more likely you are to receive a satisfying answer—or any answer at all. For example, if you ask, "How do I get to Carnegie Hall?" the researchers have no way of knowing whether you're looking for travel directions, career advice, or ticket information. Similarly, "Who's the ninth U.S. Supreme Court judge?" doesn't reveal whether you want to know the ninth justice *ever*, or whether you want to find out who the most recently confirmed justice was.

   Tip: One of the best ways to be specific in your question is to explain what you're *not* looking for. For example, "I'm staying at a hotel in New York, on the corner of Canal and West Broadway, and I want to walk to Carnegie Hall tonight. How do I get there? No subway, bus, or cab directions, please."

   You can also help researchers understand your question by explaining *why* you want a piece of information. If you're looking for the going rate on rental castles in Spain, let them know if it's for your honeymoon in July or because you're thinking of renting out your own castle in Transylvania. The more detail you give, the more focused and relevant your answer will be.

   Note: It goes without saying that Google Answers thrives on good, friendly communication. You'll get faster, more thorough answers—and you'll make the researchers' lives a touch sunnier—if you're patient and clear in your messages.

   ---

2. **In the big box on the Google Answers home page, type your question, and then click Ask Question to jump to the page in Figure 4-18. Or, from any Google Answers page, click the link near the top, "Ask a Question" to get to the same page, and fill in your question there.**

   It doesn't matter where you start, though; Google still takes you to the page shown in Figure 4-18.

3. **Fill in the subject.**

   The subject is like the subject line on an email: It should give your reader a sense of what to expect.

4. **Set a price.**

   Your price should be based on the amount of time and effort it will take somebody to answer your question, and the amount of detail you need. Google gives very good guidelines at *http://answers.google.com/answers/pricing.html.* You

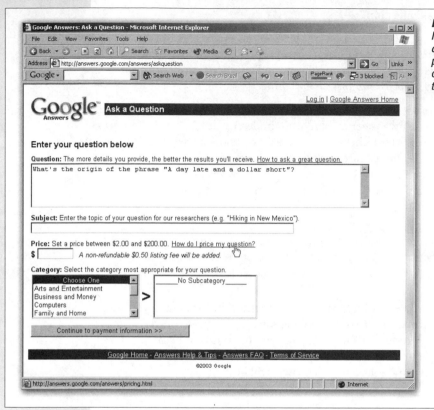

Figure 4-18:
If you typed your question in on the home page, Google carries it over here. Otherwise, type it in now.

can—and should—surf around Google Answers to find out what people have paid for answers similar to the one you seek.

5. **Choose a category.**

If the appropriate category is not immediately clear, you can research existing questions to find the right one—or go for Miscellaneous. Most categories have subcategories, but you can leave that blank (choose No Subcategory).

6. **Click "Continue to payment information."**

If you haven't already created an account or logged in, Google asks you to do so now. Once you're in, Google takes you to a page where you fill in your credit card and billing info.

The bottom of the screen shows you what your question will look like once it's posted, so take a gander, and if you don't like what you see, click "Go back and edit question."

When you're ready, click "Pay listing fee and post question."

Note: At this point, Google charges you only the listing fee (50 cents). When and if somebody answers your question, Google charges the answer fee, too. (Google tallies your charges and sends them to your credit card every 30 days, or every time your total fees reach $25, whichever comes first.)

That's it. You can lounge around and wait for somebody to answer your question, or you can post a new one. If nobody is trying to answer your question at the moment, you can tinker with it or cancel it, as discussed in the next section.

Note: Your question will stay open on Google Answers for 30 days or until it's answered—whichever comes first. After that, the question expires, but it remains in the listings, and people can comment on it.

While You Wait

After you've posted your question, Google gives the chance to jump to your account page (Figure 4-19), which you can also reach by clicking the My Account link at the top of any Google Answers page. My Account has three tabs: My Questions, My Profile, and My Invoices.

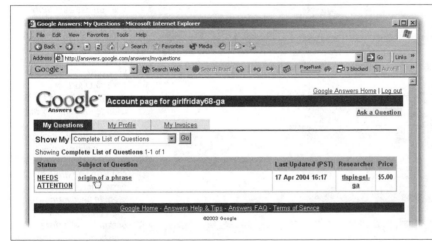

Figure 4-19:
The menu above the list of questions lets you filter for answered questions, unanswered questions, and cancelled or expired questions—a nice way to home in on a question if you have dozens listed.

My Questions is the important one right now, giving you a list of all the questions you've posted. There are three possible statuses for a question: open (not yet answered or expired), needs your attention (explained on page 153), and closed (answered satisfactorily, canceled, or expired). From the list, click any subject to jump to the View Question page, which shows the details of that post.

Hopefully, the question you just posted is clear and your price is intriguing enough to provoke a researcher to *lock* it. If somebody has locked a question, she's currently trying to answer it, and other researchers can't touch it. You can tell when your question is locked because padlock icons appear all over the View Question page and Google posts a big note at the top: "You cannot modify or comment on this question right now. It is currently being answered."

Note: Just because somebody has locked your question doesn't mean you'll necessarily get an answer; they may try and then give up. But researchers can't lock a question for more than four hours, so your query won't get sucked into a black hole.

If somebody has locked your question, you can't do much but wait to see whether they post an answer. But if a question is open and *unlocked*, you can make a few changes to it from the View Question page. Figure 4-20 explains.

Note: Quite possibly, a researcher will lock your question and try to answer it before you even have a *chance* to take any of these actions. That's just one more reason to phrase your question carefully from the start.

Figure 4-20:
Google doesn't let you edit the text of your original message, but you can use the Clarify Question button to jump to a form where you can add specific details or follow-up questions to your post. Similarly, use the Edit Question Parameters button to change the category in which you've listed a question or the price you're willing to pay. (Either of these factors can help you draw an answer if researchers seem to be ignoring you.) The Cancel Question button lets you close a question without paying the answer fee (Google still charges you the listing fee, however).

Getting an Answer

Your question can be resolved in any of a few ways.

Perfection

In Googletopia, a researcher locks your question and answers it immediately and thoroughly. You're happy with the answer, and all that's left is to rate and perhaps tip the researcher—which Google prompts you to do.

Note: As soon as a researcher posts an answer, Google charges your account.

When a researcher posts an answer to your question, Google changes the status (on your My Questions page) from "open" to "needs attention." Click the subject to reach the View Question page, where Google gives you two buttons: Request Answer Clarification, and Rate Answer. If you need no additional information from the researcher, click Rate Answer to jump to the form shown in Figure 4-21.

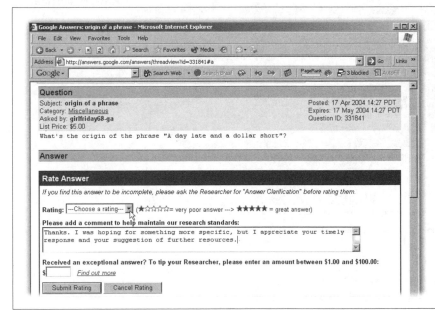

Figure 4-21:
Use the menu on this page to choose a rating (up to five stars), and then type in a brief note about the quality of the answer. If you thought the answer was outstanding, you can tip the researcher, too. When you're done, click Submit Rating.

After you've submitted the rating, Google changes the question's status from "needs attention" to "closed."

Note: Even after your question has been officially answered and closed, people can add comments at any time.

You need to clarify things

If a researcher doesn't understand all or part of your question, he can post a Request for Question Clarification, which asks you to jump in with more info, or he can communicate with you by adding a comment (page 156). Either way, it's up to you to respond to keep things moving—although other people can post comments at any time.

If you've got a Request for Question Clarification, the status of your question (on your My Questions page) changes from "open" to "needs attention." Click the subject to jump to the View Question page, where Google shows you the full request for more information. You also get a button that takes you to a page to type in and submit your clarification. Google adds both the request and your response to the public posting of your question (Figure 4-22).

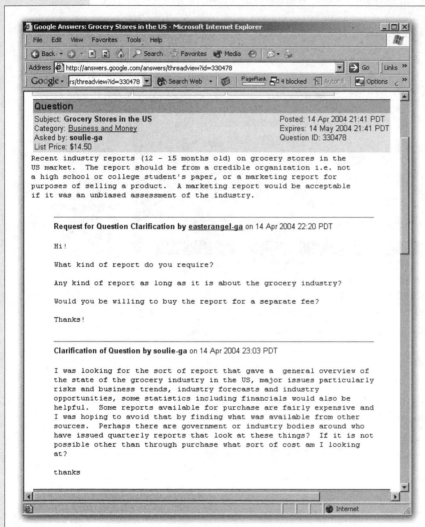

Figure 4-22:
You and the researcher may go back and forth a few times until you understand each other.

Once the researcher has posted an official answer, it's time to rate and possibly tip him, as described in the box on page 157.

Note: Because Google doesn't charge your account until an official answer appears, a researcher who's found something but isn't sure whether it meets your needs may show what she's got so far by posting it in a Request for Question Clarification or in a comment, asking if you approve. If you do, she can then post the information as an answer, which triggers the fee.

The researcher needs to clarify things

If a researcher posts an answer but it doesn't satisfy you, you should ask for more information before you rate the answer. Chances are, by explaining where he went wrong, you'll help the researcher figure out what you want.

To ask for further information, go to View Question page (choose My Account → My Questions, and then click the subject of the question). Then click Request Answer Clarification to jump to the form shown in Figure 4-23.

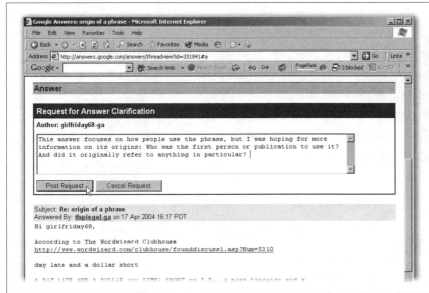

Figure 4-23:
If the researcher missed the mark, give more details about what you want and don't want. When you click Post Request, Google adds your message to the public posting of your message. If your note prompts a satisfactory response, go back to the View Questions page and rate the answer.

You're not satisfied

If you've had a few exchanges with the researcher, and you're getting nowhere, you have a few choices. You can accept the answer and give the researcher a moderate or low rating. You can repost your question, which allows another researcher to try to answer it. When you repost (which you can only do once per question), Google credits you for the original answer fee, and it doesn't charge a second listing fee. Finally, you can request a refund and cancel the question. If you choose this option—which you can do only within 30 days after the answer has been posted—Google requires you to give a reason, which it then posts publicly with your question.

Requests for reposts and refunds are serious business on Google Answers, and you should consider these options only after you've tried hard to resolve things with the researcher. The form for reposts and refunds is the same, and you can find it at *http://answers.google.com/answers/refundrequest.*

People answer your question by posting comments

Surprisingly often on Google Answers, the researchers or other civilians post comments that can answer your question. (Anyone with a Google Answers account, including you, can post a comment to any question.) If your question can have many answers, or if the answer is likely to be an opinion, you might draw a handful—or an avalanche—of comments. Researchers can also use comments to partially answer a question (Figure 4-24) or to point you to previous posts that answer your question.

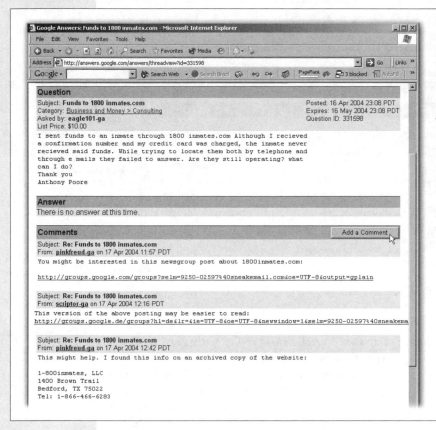

Figure 4-24:
If the comments answer your question before a researcher has posted an official answer, you can cancel your question from the View Question page. (Google still charges you the 50-cent listing fee, but it doesn't charge you for the comments.) Once you close a question, it remains in the listings, but nobody can answer it. (If you want your question removed for some reason, send a request, along with the Question ID, to answers-editors@google.com.)

Note: Sometimes, the researchers get a witty conversation going in the comments of a question, but they don't actually answer anything. You're not charged for comments, so enjoy the repartee.

Nothing happens

If everybody seems to be ignoring your question, or you've noticed that a few researchers have locked it but nobody's answering it, you might consider raising the fee, changing the category in which you've listed it so that different people might see it, or starting over with a simpler question.

Tips for Rating and Tipping

How do I choose a rating and a tip amount?

On Google Answers, ratings and tips are important, so don't blow off this step. Researchers work hard—often very hard—to provide high-quality answers. Ratings and tips are your tools for rewarding them.

Ratings contribute to a researcher's reputation—good or bad (you can see somebody's average rating by clicking his nickname from any page where it's highlighted; one star is the lowest, and five is the highest). A researcher who meets your expectations with a thorough answer or surprises you with a terrific write-up and lots of useful links deserves a rating of four or five stars. If you felt an answer was adequate, a three-star rating is probably appropriate. For unsatisfactory answers—or a researcher who refuses to provide follow-up information after you've requested it—consider one or two stars. (If, on the other hand, you didn't *bother* to ask for an answer clarification, don't punish the researcher by giving him a bad rating.)

Tips, of course, are a more concrete way to reward a great answer. While Google takes 25 percent of an answer fee, researchers get 100 percent of the tips. And Google believes you will tip for outstanding service (you can tip anywhere from $1 to $100). So while the expectation of a gratuity is not as high as it is at, say, a restaurant, a question that merits a five- or even a four-star rating often gets a tip, too. Check already answered questions to get a sense of the going rate for tips.

You can't revoke ratings or tips, so choose carefully before you submit them.

Changing Your Account Settings

Google lets you tweak your Answers account settings. To do so, click My Account from any Google Answers page, and then choose one of these tabs:

- **My Profile** lets you change your email, password, nickname, and billing info.

- **My Invoices** shows you what Google will charge your credit card, based on the status of your current questions. For example, if you have two open questions and one recently answered $15 question, Google shows the three listing fees at $.50 each, the answer at $15, and your total debits as $16.50.

Shopping with Google

Tracking news and finding answers to your burning science questions are nice benefits of the Web. But the real fun online is, as any human with a credit card can tell you, shopping. The Web has it all: belt sanders, pregnancy tests, *The Simpsons* Monopoly sets, Bulgari jewelry, cotton candy machines, ATV tires, wild fennel pâté. There's no limit to what you can buy.

But *finding* the goods is another matter. If dozens or hundreds of sites sell your desired item, you need a team of assistants and a complex spreadsheet just to figure out who has, say, the cheapest rubber chickens or the best deal on hole punchers.

Shave a few months off every product search, then, by clicking over to Froogle (*http://froogle.google.com*). Froogle—the word is a pleasing mix of Google and frugal—is a service to help you find things sold online and compare them by price. It's an indispensable shopping tool.

Note: Froogle isn't a *store*; it just brings you links, pictures, and product information from e-commerce sites across the U.S. If you want to buy something, you have to jump to the merchant's site. (Google doesn't get a cut of sales that come through Froogle searches, nor does it charge e-tailers to be part of Froogle listings.)

When to Use Froogle

Froogle is particularly good at finding specific products and at comparing prices. It's not, however, great at helping you decide *what* to buy. If you're in the market for a portable generator, for example, Froogle shows you about 20,000 of them, and it doesn't include reviews or other information to help you narrow the field. So while it can give you a sense of what's on the Web portable-generator-wise—and it can lead you to merchants you may never have heard of otherwise—it can't help you pick the best model. Do your product research at sites like Consumer-Reports.org, BizRate.org, Epinions.com, and Consumer.gov, and then head over to Froogle to search for a specific manufacturer or model.

Furthermore, while Froogle has information for thousands of products and e-tailers, it's not comprehensive. You may have heard that a hot woven golf bag is sold at eWicker.com, but you can't find the item or the store through Froogle. What gives? Froogle gets its information from two sources: Google's Web crawl (page 2) and data that merchants send in directly. Merchants have to sign up to send in data (*www. google.com/froogle/merchants/*), and Google doesn't quite keep track of every page on the Web. Moreover, even when Google does track a site, the site can store information like product details in a way that Google can't record (Chapter 8 tells you more about why Google ignores all or part of some sites).

Despite the gaps, Froogle is still a terrific way to start a shopping trip on the Web. It finds and organizes information in ways that can save you time, hassle, and money.

Finding Stuff with Froogle

Like all of Google's special searches, Froogle lets you run a keyword search or browse by category. Sort of.

At one time, the main page of Froogle had categories like Apparel & Accessories, Electronics, Health & Personal Care, and Sports & Outdoors. You could click a category to get subcategories until you hit the kind of product you wanted to shop for. But Froogle, like Google News, is what Google considers a *beta* service, which means it's still experimental, and the company may add or remove features without notice. In this case, Google pulled the categories from the front page of Froogle, instead showing you examples of recent Froogle searches (Figure 5-1).

The weird thing is that Google *still* assigns products to different categories. You can use a workaround to browse by category, and Froogle has a kind of browsing-and-searching hybrid mode, too, as explained on page 167.

Searching

When you know a specific item you want—say you've got a brand name, product name, or model number—a keyword search is the easiest way to perform your comparison-shopping search. Type your terms into the search box on Froogle's main page, press Enter or Search Froogle, and let 'er rip.

Figure 5-2 shows you what a results page looks like. If you click an individual result, Google takes you directly to the page selling that item.

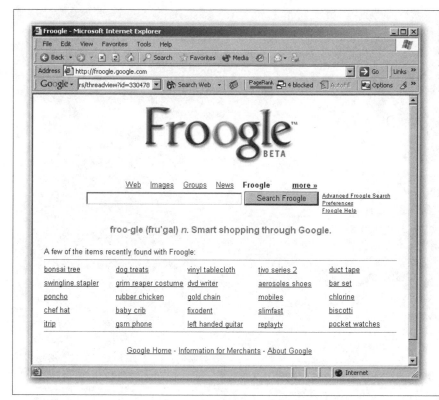

Figure 5-1:
If you click the Froogle logo, the recently found items change. It's fascinating to play with it for, say, several hours.

Tip: If you're searching for something with a well-known product name, including a brand name can sometimes narrow down your results too far. For example, a search for *Apple iPod* might net you *fewer* results than a search for *iPod*—and might exclude some good deals in the process. For best results, try your search both ways.

As Figure 5-2 shows, whether you choose "List view" or "Grid view," a Froogle results page has a few parts. At the top is a search box where you can refine your search terms or run the same search—on the whole Web, in Images, Groups, and so on. Below that is a green summary bar that tells you how many results Froogle found for your search terms. (It usually says something like, "Results 1 - 20 of about 293 confirmed / 9,810 total results for deep fryer." The *confirmed* results are from the data feeds that merchants send Google on a daily, weekly, or monthly basis. The rest of the results are from Google's Web search and may be less accurate.)

Under the summary bar, the bulk of the page is taken up by your listings. On the right are sponsored links (that is, ads) for the product you're searching for (those ads could be helpful, so don't overlook them), and on the left is a navigation bar.

GEM IN THE ROUGH

Google Catalogs

Froogle is a great way to find stuff for sale *online*, but what about when you want to browse through a good old-fashioned print catalog? Google Catalogs bridges the gap, bringing more than 6,600 conventional catalogs to your Web browser. To work this magic, Google electronically scans the pages of print catalogs and converts the text into a format that you can search like any other writing online. Google then posts each catalog at *http:// catalogs.google.com*.

The collection is a bit of an oddity, because most of Google's services help you find things that are already online, rather than bringing stuff from the outside world to the Internet.

Still, Google Catalogs can be really useful. You may have every mailer from Crutchfield to Victoria's Secret stacked in your bathroom, but Google Catalogs lets you browse by *category* or flip through each retailer's catalog individually. And, even better, you can run a search that looks for your item in all 6,600 catalogs. For example, you know that L.L. Bean sells sleeping bags, but who else does, too? Turns out Campor, Sierra Adventure Edge, Cabela's, Major Surplus & Survival, and at least a few hundred more all do—and you've probably never heard of a lot of them before. You can also run a search within an individual category or even in an individual *catalog*. And Google Catalogs includes retailers who don't have online ordering.

From the Catalogs home page, you can click through the links to browse by category until you hit an individual catalog you want to peruse. Each catalog has a navigation bar at the top that looks confusing at first but is really very straightforward, and it includes a search box that lets you look for stuff in that catalog alone. For a handy explanation of each feature on the navigation bar, see *http://catalogs. google.com/googlecatalogs/help.html*.

You can also run keyword searches. Search all catalogs from the main page, or click a category and run a search *within* that category, using the search box at the top of the page. Google Catalogs also has an advanced search form (look for the link next to any Catalogs search box), which lets you tailor your terms and include old catalog editions in your search.

If you run a keyword search, Google highlights your search terms in the results listings. (Because it uses an imperfect system for converting the words in a catalog into searchable text, you might sometimes get mismatches in your results.) But the listings don't look like regular results. Instead, you get pictures of pages from catalogs, and if you click a page, you jump to that individual catalog.

Once you find something you want to order, you have to contact the retailer directly. That's why, at the top of each page displaying an individual catalog, Google provides the retailer's phone number, URL, and even catalog code, which some stores like to have when you place an order.

Because it's so graphics-intensive, however, Google Catalogs isn't a great bet if you're reaching the Internet over a dial-up connection. And it also tends to have outdated catalogs, especially from retailers like J.Crew who send out new print editions more often than you exhale. Nonetheless, Google Catalogs can help you find stores and merchandise you might have otherwise missed, and it's fun to click around—although you can't do it from the bathtub.

The navigation bar is a little confusing at first, but it's easy to understand when you break it down into its five parts:

- **View.** Here's where you choose "List view" or "Grid view," as explained in Figure 5-2.

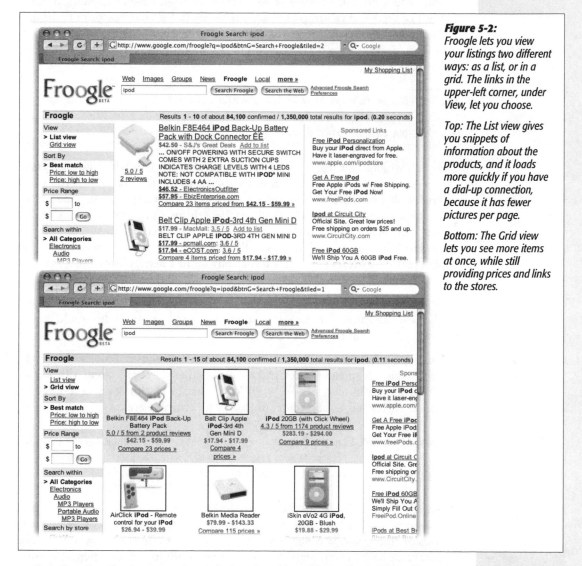

Figure 5-2:
Froogle lets you view your listings two different ways: as a list, or in a grid. The links in the upper-left corner, under View, let you choose.

Top: The List view gives you snippets of information about the products, and it loads more quickly if you have a dial-up connection, because it has fewer pictures per page.

Bottom: The Grid view lets you see more items at once, while still providing prices and links to the stores.

- **Sort By.** Google gives you three choices for the order in which it displays your results. "Best match" is Froogle's assessment of a product's relevance, calculated much the way Google decides the order to display regular Web page results. (Froogle shows you results sorted by best match, unless you re-sort things.) "Price: low to high" shows you lowest price first; "Price: high to low" is, obviously, the opposite. Toggle between the two price sorts to learn the range of prices for an item.

- **Price Range.** This option lets you type in the low and high prices you want to see. It's a great way to filter out stuff that matches your search terms but isn't what you want. For example, if you search for *iPod*, Froogle includes accessories like cases and cables, plus books on the iPod. Set your low price to around $199 (the bottom street price for iPods) and your high price to whatever you're willing to pay, and you cut your results by more than half without doing any tedious sifting.

Tip: Find just what you're looking for but have to wait until next month's paycheck to buy it? Sign up for a Froogle Shopping List (page 167) and click the "Add to list" link under the desired item to store a little reminder to buy it after that paycheck lands.

- **Search within.** This feature is part of the search/browse hybrid system on Froogle. And, frankly, it's not very intuitive to use. Here's the deal: When you run a Froogle keyword search, this section shows you the categories and subcategories that contain your results. So if you search for *iPod*, Froogle tells you that you can find iPods in the following categories: Electronics, Audio, Portable Audio, MP3 Players, and, um, MP3 Players. (How those last two categories are different is a total mystery.) If you click any of the category links, Froogle shows you the results in that category only.

  The feature isn't very useful for the iPod search, since an iPod really *does* fit in all those categories. Limiting your search to, say, Portable Audio would simply cut down on your legitimate results.

  But say you're trying to find a snazzy new pair of *glasses*. Froogle shows you beer steins, Champagne flutes, and a mess of other glassware, along with spectacles. To home in on the eyewear, click the link for Health & Personal Care (or Vision & Hearing, a subcategory of Health & Personal Care).

Warning: If you click a category link and *then* try to run a new search from the top of the resulting page, you can get some funky mixed-category results. Better to start fresh by jumping back to the Froogle home page. (Click the Froogle logo in the upper-left corner for the quickest ride back.)

- **Search by store.** Sometimes you're on the hunt for an item that comes in multiple varieties—like fruit baskets—and Froogle brings back scads of results from tons of stores. Say, you *sort of* like the pineapple-and-macadamia-nut sampler that came back in your search results, but you want to see other items the company may also sell in case there's another assortment you like better. To isolate the merchandise from that one store, click its name under the "Search by Store" list. Froogle keeps your same search terms but lists only items from that particular store.

Unfortunately, Froogle doesn't let you search for synonyms using the ~ character (page 72). So, for example, if you think your item might turn up as *shirt, blouse,* or *top,* you've got to run searches for all three—or use the OR operator to search for them simultaneously: *shirt OR blouse OR top.*

Tip: A general search term like *shirt* is a great opportunity to use the category links in the results, because they can help you focus on men's or women's, t-shirts or blouses, and so on.

In fact, any time you search for something broad—be it *necktie, digital camera,* or *steak*—Froogle can give you too many results to handle. In addition to OR, you can refine your query by using the minus sign (–), the plus sign (+), and quote marks. Quotes are, of course, useful for products with more than one word (*"denim jacket"* or *"my pretty pony"*). The minus sign is particularly handy, as it lets you tell Froogle to ignore certain things, like this: *steak -sauce.*

Note: Froogle, unlike other Google services, *does* include stop words like "the" in your searches (page 18).

Finally, you can use a few syntax elements (page 65) to separate the wheat from the chaff. Froogle lets you limit your search to a particular e-commerce site, which is a good way to search just for items from your favorite merchant. To use the *store* operator, leave off the .com (or whatever) after the domain name, like so: *shirt store:gap.*

Note: You *do* have to know the domain name for a store, because Froogle doesn't recognize store names. For example *store:the gap* gets you nowhere, because *the gap.com* isn't the right domain.

If you search for *store:gap* without specifying an item, Froogle shows you everything it finds from the Gap's Web site, in no particular order. But you can also sort by price or specify a price range—two tricks you might not be able to do on a store's actual site.

Tip: You can also filter products by category—at least in a limited way. Here's the trick: If you're in List view, each individual result includes a link to its category. Click that link to see all the results from that category. (You can switch to Grid view, if you like, once you've homed in on a category.)

The problem with this system is that you can't see a comprehensive *list* of categories, and if the overall results are extensive, you may not even be able to find the type of thing you're looking for without sifting through a lot of results.

Froogle also lets you use the *intitle* and *intext* operators. *Intitle* searches for your terms in the product name only, while *intext* searches in the description only. Use them like this:

```
intitle:robomower
```

or:

```
robomower intext:"replacement blades"
```

or mix them, like this:

```
intitle:robomower intext:blades
```

You can also use *allintitle* or *allintext* to have Froogle search for several words at once (*allintext:replacement blades*). But you can't mix these two elements. You can, however, toss the *store* operator into the mix, like this: *allintitle:robotic mower store:sears*, which prompts Froogle to show you all the robotic mowers Sears.com sells.

Tip: *Allintext* is a good way to list the features you want in a product, because it searches in *descriptions*. Think of it like telling a salesperson what you're looking for. For example, if you want to find a fancy phone, try this: *allintext:caller ID conferencing*.

Advanced Froogle Search

If syntax makes you woozy, try the Advanced Froogle Search (Figure 5-3).

Like the advanced search forms in other parts of Google, the Froogle form lets you create a complex query without using syntax. (See page 50 for a review of the ways an advanced search form can help you hone your search.)

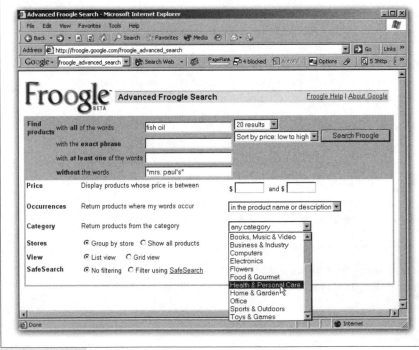

Figure 5-3:
To get here, click Advanced Froogle Search next to the search box on the Froogle main page or at the top of any results page.

In addition, the Advanced Froogle Search lets you *predetermine* the factors you'll be able to adjust on a results page, like the price range and how you want your listings sorted. (Whether you adjust the settings here or in your results, you get the same listings.) The one element that may be easier to set from Advanced Froogle Search is the category, which you can choose from a nice, familiar menu rather than from a confusing array of links.

Note: Advanced Froogle Search also lets you turn on or off SafeSearch filtering (page 49) for an individual search. After one search, however, all searches on Google revert to the SafeSearch setting on your general Google Preferences page (page 47).

Shopping Lists

If there's anything that's survived the test of time as an incredibly great idea, it's the *shopping list*; British scientists recently found ancient Roman shopping lists scratched on wooden tablets 2,000 years ago. (Clothes were just as expensive back then and they didn't even *have* Old Navy.)

Maintaining a shopping list in Froogle is infinitely easier and does not involve pointy sticks. All you need is the desire to buy things and some sort of Google account, like a Gmail address and password (page 377). And, unlike a shopping *cart*, where the online merchant expects you to check out and pay for the things you've picked up along your visit, a Froogle shopping list is just a *reminder* of the things you want to buy.

WORKAROUND WORKSHOP

Browsing Froogle

Most people find that *browsing* Froogle isn't the best way to use the service, because you often wind up with too much stuff to look through. But if you're in the mood to discover unknown corners of the Web and oddball products, here's a trick you can use to browse the Froogle categories.

On the Advanced Froogle Search page, choose a category you want to surf—for example, Home & Garden. Leave everything else blank and then click Search Froogle. Froogle takes you to the page shown here, which has links for subcategories that you can click—some of which have their *own* subcategories. Browse 'til you drop.

One note of caution: When you're in this backdoor browsing mode, the search box at the top of the page gives you the option to run a keyword search *within* that category (or subcategory), or to search all of Froogle. Froogle automatically sets itself to search within the category of the page you're on—which is great if that's what you want. But if you

want to run a general Froogle search, it's easy to forget the setting here and run a very limited search without even realizing it. For a full Froogle search, then, it's a good idea to get in the habit of jumping to the main page, where you'll avoid category snafus.

To start a Froogle Shopping List, click the My Shopping List link in the top corner of the Froogle home page. If you don't already have a Google account, the next page invites you to start one, and walks you through the steps. Your email address serves as your Froogle user name.

If you already have a Gmail or other Google account, just type in your account name and password, and click the Sign In button. After you agree to the obligatory Terms of Service/Privacy Policy screen that comes next, you've got yourself a Froogle Shopping List.

Now, when you're out on a capitalist tear through Froogle's search results, click the "Add to list" link under any item you've got your eye on. The links and descriptions for your collected items are neatly stored and displayed on your Froogle Shopping List for future reference, as shown in Figure 5-4.

Figure 5-4:
The Froogle Shopping List stores all of your future treasures in one convenient place. Turn on the In Wish List checkbox to make the selected item publicly visible to anyone who's searching Froogle, trying to find gift ideas for you.

If you want to write yourself a note on a particular item ("Get this for Sally's birthday but ask her husband if she likes taupe or teal better"), click the "edit" link under the product image to add some notes to your selected item. You can arrange the items on your list by their names, the date you added them, or their prices.

This information gets stored on Google's servers—not your own hard drive—so you can get to your Shopping List from any computer with a working Web browser. (Imagine: You can now shop at home and buy at work!) When you're ready to buy any or all the items on your list, sign in to your Froogle page and use the item links to finally seal the deal with the online merchant selling the product. If you change your mind about an item and don't want to buy it after all, just click the "delete" link next to the product to scratch it from your list.

Froogle Wish Lists

The Wish List feature over at Amazon.com has saved thousands of marriages from husbands who think an electric can opener makes a darn fine birthday gift. Froogle, therefore, includes the helpful Wish List feature for its shoppers as well.

With a Wish List, you collect—on your Froogle Shopping List—the items you would like to have and then turn on the In Wish List checkbox to make them appear on a version of your Froogle Shopping List that can be seen by the public— or at least the members of the public who thoughtfully look up your Wish List.

Tip: To get the direct link for your Froogle Wish List–so you can alert the gift givers in your life–click the My Wish List link under View on the left side of your Froogle Shopping List page. The link appears at the top of the Wish List page, ready for cutting and pasting into an email message.

To find somebody else's Froogle Wish List, just type in the person's email address on the Froogle home page and then click the Find button. The Wish List appears, with only the items marked for Wish Listing shown. Any items the person has *not* specifically marked stay hidden, so no one will know that your niece has, say, a secret desire to buy a lute.

The Google Toolbar

It's a fact: Google is fast. But if you have to pull up its home page every time you run a search, you're wasting valuable seconds. True pros use Google from a tool-bar you can install directly in your browser, and from the Google deskbar, which sits in the corner of your screen and lets you run a search without even opening your browser. This chapter covers the must-have toolbar; Chapter 7 covers the deskbar and a batch of other efficiency features and tricks.

The Google Toolbar: Search Faster

The Google toolbar, shown in Figure 6-1, can change your life. Easy to download and install, it sits at the top of your browser and lets you run a search without opening Google's home page. Simply type your search words into the blank search box, press Enter or click Search Web, and your browser takes you directly to the page of Google search results. No muss, no fuss.

But wait—there's more! The toolbar also lets you search a single site and run special Google searches (like News or Directory) without going to those pages first. And it adds some browser-type features that are more about surfing than searching: things like blocking pop-up windows, automatically filling in forms with your name and address, and a mess of other cool stuff.

If you take just one thing from this book, then, make it the Google toolbar.

The catch is that Google's toolbar requires Microsoft Windows 95, 98, ME, NT, 2000, or XP, *and* Internet Explorer 5.0 or later (to use the pop-up blocker, make that Internet Explorer 5.5 or later). Alternatively, a *beta* (still-imperfect) version of the Google toolbar is available for Firefox 1.0, regardless of whether you're using it on a Windows, Mac, or even Linux machine.

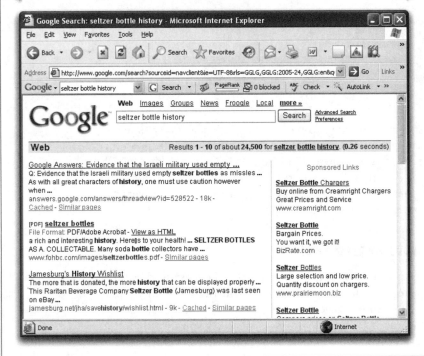

Figure 6-1:
Top: The Google toolbar lets you run a Google search no matter where you are on the Web (here, a page on BoingBoing.net).

Bottom: The toolbar results display exactly the way they would if you ran the same search from the Google home page.

Note: To find out what version of Internet Explorer you have, choose Help → About Internet Explorer. In the dialog box that opens, you'll see your version number. (If you're using Firefox, choose Help → About Mozilla Firefox.)

Fortunately, if you're on the Mac, you can use Apple's Safari browser, which has a simple Google search bar built right in. And several other browsers, such as Mozilla and Netscape, have their own GoogleBox that runs a lot like the official Google toolbar. (For more information, see "Other Browsers with Google Features" on page 192.)

Note: Firefox users actually have a choice: whether to use the official Google search bar or the Google-Box. Both toolbars are fast and free. The only advantage of Google's own toolbar is that it lets you view a page's *PageRank* (importance), as described on page 181.

Installing the Google Toolbar

If you've got the right operating system and browser, here's how to download and install the Google toolbar:

1. **Click over to** *http://toolbar.google.com/,* **shown in Figure 6-2.**

   You can also get to the installation page from Google's home page by clicking Services & Tools, or by clicking the same link at the bottom of any results page. Then scroll down the Services & Tools page and click the link for Google Toolbar.

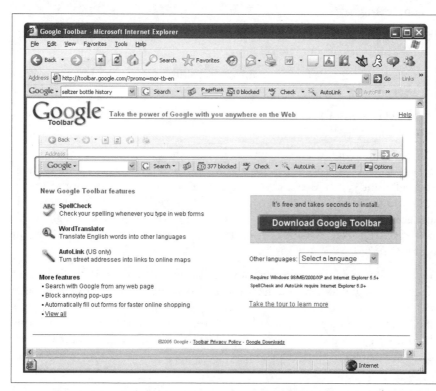

Figure 6-2:
The installation page shows you what the toolbar looks like and gives you a nice, fat button for downloading it.

2. **If you want Google to use an** *interface language* **other than English (so Google gives you instructions in French, for example), choose one from the menu on the right, and then click the giant Download Google Toolbar button.**

   In Internet Explorer, a dialog box appears asking if you want to save or open the file; click Open. When the file is done downloading, Google automatically opens a wizard for installing the toolbar. (If you're using a Mac, double-click the file once you've downloaded it.)

3. **The first page of the wizard asks you to agree to its terms of use.**

Scroll down to read them, and then click then click Agree to continue.

4. **The next page of the wizard asks you to choose your configuration.**

By *configuration,* Google means you can choose between what it calls "advanced features" and "no advanced features." Choosing "advanced features" lets Google collect and display a bunch of additional information about Web pages you visit, such as:

- **PageRank info** is Google's system for gauging results' relevance (page 181).

- **A Page Info button** can show you similar pages, backwards links, a cached version of your current page, and an English translation of the page if it's in another language.

- **Word Translator** displays the translation of an English word on a Web page into a language of your choice.

- **SpellCheck** catches and cleans up your spelling mistakes and typos in Web forms.

- **AutoLink** scans a Web page for street addresses and automatically links to maps of the location.

Of course, these options are nice to have, but when you sign on for them, you agree to let Google's computers see information about the pages you're visiting. After all, if the system doesn't know what page you're on, it can't, for example, show you the version of that page it cached two weeks ago. If you choose "no advanced features," your privacy will be fully protected, because Google won't look at the sites you're visiting. Instead, it just spits out search results when you ask for them.

However, if you *do* sign on for the advanced features, you're not divulging that much to Google. When you let Google's computers learn about the pages you're visiting, the company says it doesn't pay attention to your name or your email address, so they don't actually track *you.* Put another way, Google learns about the pages you've asked for, but it doesn't even know that you're the person who's looking at those pages.

Tip: If you install the advanced features now and become seized with a bout of paranoia later, you can turn off the features whenever you want (page 179). From that time on, Google stops receiving information about the sites you visit.

If you want to go the advanced-features route, the configuration page of the wizard lets you select "Enable advanced features." If, however, you wish to keep your site visits entirely private, simply select "Disable advanced features."

Tip: To learn more about Google's privacy policy for the toolbar, visit *http://toolbar.google.com/privacy.html*.

5. **The last page of the wizard asks you to choose three settings.**

   The first setting is the Google site you want to use for your searches (page 58). Leave it at Google.com, or scroll down and select the site you want.

   The next setting is whether you want to use Google to as your default search engine. If you choose this—and it's not a bad idea—you can run Google searches from the address bar and sidebar (pages 210 and 203, respectively).

   Finally, Google asks whether you want it to automatically close all Internet Explorer windows to finish up the toolbar installation. If you have some windows open that you don't want to lose, select "Don't close…"; otherwise, leave the first choice turned on. Click Next.

6. **Reopen Internet Explorer.**

   If you let Google close Internet Explorer, it does so now, and then reopens it automatically, too. If you didn't ask Google to take this step for you, go ahead and close all your Internet Explorer windows, then reopen one.

   That's it: The toolbar should be sitting near the top of your browser.

   If it's not, choose View → Toolbars (or right-click an existing toolbar), and then select Google from the list. If the Google checkbox is on and you still don't see the toolbar, it might be smushed over to the right, as shown in Figure 6-3.

Note: Older versions of Internet Explorer list extra toolbars as "Radio." If you see two Radio options, select the second one.

The missing toolbar

Figure 6-3:
To move the toolbar down to its own row—which gives you direct access to all of its glorious features—mouse over the bar to the left of the Google logo and when the cursor becomes a two-headed arrow, drag the bar to wherever you want the toolbar to reside. You can rearrange all the browser toolbars using this trick; it's up to you whether they share rows or not.

Working with the Search Box

Once you've got it installed, the Google toolbar is ready to go. Just type your search words into the blank box, press Enter or click the Search Web button, and savor the results Google delivers in your current browser window.

If you'd rather your results appear in a new window just this once, press Shift+Enter. If you want your results to appear in a fresh window *every* time, open the Toolbar Options dialog box, click the Options tab, and turn on "Open a new window to display results each time you search."

Tip: To get to the toolbar's search box in a mouseless hurry, press Alt+G.

Instead of typing words into the search box, you can also highlight and drag text from a Web page directly into the search box. (When you drag text, you might at first see the universal forbidden sign—the circle with a slash through it. The green light you're looking for—the plus-box sign—doesn't appear until your text is right over the search box.) This trick also works with text from a lot of word processing programs; highlight a word or two and try dragging the selection to the search box. If it works, great! If not, you've done no damage.

The Two Toolbar Buttons You Can't Get Rid Of

In addition to the search box, the toolbar comes loaded with a lot of features, all of which you can see at the bottom of Figure 6-4. But if you never use the optional stuff, or if you don't have room for the extra buttons, you can remove everything but the search box and two essential buttons, as shown at top in Figure 6-4.

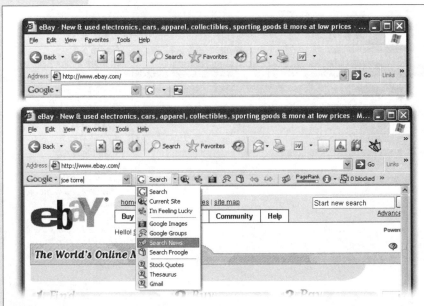

Figure 6-4:
Top: To get the toolbar down to this sleek profile, open the Toolbar Options dialog box (click the Options button), and on the Options and More tabs, turn off all the buttons listed.

Bottom: Toolbar with everything, hold the fries.

Tip: You can also change the size of the search box, making it just a few characters wide or nearly as wide as the whole screen. If you often search for phrases or lots of keywords at once, try a longer search box to see all your terms together. Simply mouse over the bar to the right of the search box until it turns into a two-headed arrow and then drag it right or left.

The two buttons you can't get rid of are Search Web and the Google menu.

Search

Once you've typed some words in the search box, you can press Enter or click the Search button (the one with the G for Google) to begin your search. But the down arrow on the right end of the Search button is the gateway to a handful of other searches Google can perform (Figure 6-4)—things like searching Google's image library and directory (both explained in Chapter 3). Just type in some terms, click the arrow, and select the special search you want to run.

Note: You can add Google's special subject searches (for Linux, BSD Unix, the U.S. Government, Apple Macintosh, and Microsoft, described on page 56) to the Search Web menu. Google provides no individual buttons for these searches, so it's good to add them to the menu if you use them a lot. Open the Toolbar Options dialog box, go to the More tab, and turn on "Include special searches on search menu."

Button Behavior

While the Search menu is handy if you're a toolbar minimalist, most people find it easier to keep individual buttons on the toolbar for the features they use regularly, including I'm Feeling Lucky, Google Images, Google Groups, Google Directory, and Froogle. ("The Optional Toolbar Buttons" on page 179 explains how to get 'em.)

But if you often run a particular alternate search (like Images or Froogle), and you don't have room on the toolbar for its button, you can set the Search button to remember the last kind of search you ran and use it for your *next* search. Open the Toolbar Options dialog box, go to the More tab, and turn on "Remember last search type."

Google menu

The Google button to the left of the search box contains a menu of links to Google's home page and its other search services (Advanced Search, Google Images, Google Groups, and so on)—most of which you can also get to via optional buttons on the toolbar, described in the next section. The menu also includes a choice for Options, which brings up the dialog box shown in Figure 6-5.

The Google menu has one feature—Clear Search History—that you can't get to any other way, and it's useful. Here's the story: The toolbar keeps a list of your searches, which you can find by clicking the down arrow on the right end of the search bar. That way, if you want to rerun a search, you don't have to retype your

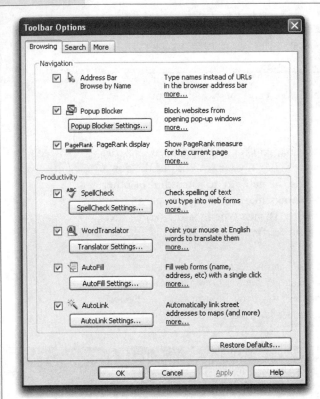

Figure 6-5:
The Toolbar Options dialog box lets you control which buttons appear on the Google toolbar and how some of the features behave. You can also choose whether the buttons have text on them or just icons. To do so, choose the More tab, and under Extras, click "All text," "Selective text only" (which puts words on a few key buttons), or "No text."

terms. Instead, you can just open the list to find and select your original search; you don't even have to press Enter to run it.

Note: If you want to use the history as a reference rather than a menu of choices, it may annoy you that Google runs a search automatically when you click in your search history. Happily, you can kill this feature. Open the Toolbar Options dialog box (to do so, click the Options button), choose the More tab, and turn off "Automatically search when you select from the search history."

But if you're trying to plan a surprise birthday party for your wife, and you don't want her to see you've been searching for *"novelty cakes"* and *"SpongeBob party favors"*, you can wipe clean the list of searches. Simply choose Google → Clear Search History. (You might also consider clearing the browser's history, which is a list of all the sites you've visited recently. In Internet Explorer, choose Tools → Internet Options, and on the General tab, click the Clear History button. To prevent it from ever storing the sites you've visited, set "Days to keep pages in history" to zero. [Other browsers work similarly; use their help files if you can't find where the Clear History button is.])

Tip: Ordinarily, the toolbar saves a list of your last searches—up to 20—when you close the browser. If you want it to clear this history every time you shut down the browser, open the Toolbar Options dialog box, click the More tab, and turn off "Save the search history across browser sessions."

Alternatively, you can stop the toolbar from keeping a list of your searches *at all* by opening the Toolbar Options dialog box, clicking the Options tab, and then turning off "Drop-down search history."

Finally, the Google menu gives you five links to Google help pages:

- **Help** takes you to Google's Toolbar help page, which includes links to Frequently Asked Questions, information about its features, and a page For Geeks Only—a history of revisions to the toolbar's features.

- **Privacy Information** opens up a dialog box that describes how Google's toolbar ensures your privacy. It also lets you turn off the advanced features, described above, which pass certain information about the sites you visit back to Google.

- **Contact Us** gives the email address for Google's toolbar team. You can use it if you have a problem with the toolbar that you can't resolve through the help pages. But keep in mind that Google doesn't respond to many people personally.

- **Uninstall** takes you to a page with a button that automatically removes the toolbar from your browser. If you find the toolbar takes up too much room or is otherwise not to your liking, uninstalling it is a snap. The uninstall page also includes a blank box where you can type comments to Google about why you're nixing the toolbar. If you've got a serious complaint—like the toolbar seemed to unexpectedly translate all Web pages into Korean—let 'em know.

- **About the Google Toolbar** opens a small window with the version number of the toolbar, and a treat for dead-language aficionados: the Latin *De parvis grandis acervus erit,* which translates loosely as "Out of small things a great heap will be formed."

The Optional Toolbar Buttons

This section explains the Google toolbar's additional buttons and features, from left to right across the toolbar. Some of these buttons and features don't appear on the toolbar at first, and some come turned on. You can, however, add or remove any of these features and buttons, and in some cases, you can change their behavior, too.

To customize the toolbar, click the Options button toward the right end of the toolbar, which opens the Toolbar Options dialog box, shown in Figure 6-5. This dialog box is command central for the toolbar. You can also click the Google logo button all the way on the left end of the toolbar and then choose Options to get the same dialog box.

Note: This dialog box has three tabs, each of which lets you control different features and buttons. If you don't see the item you're looking for on the first tab, try the other two.

If your monitor is small, or if you keep a ton of buttons on your Web browser's toolbar, some of the features can fall off the right end of the screen, leaving behind the little double arrow shown in Figure 6-6. Click the arrow to see the hidden stuff, and then select the button or feature you want to access.

Note: A few of the features, like AutoFill and the Previous and Next (arrow) buttons, stay grayed out when you're on a page where they aren't applicable.

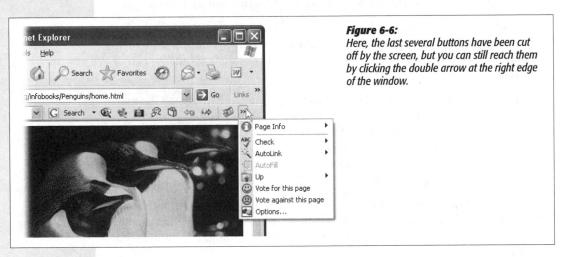

Figure 6-6:
Here, the last several buttons have been cut off by the screen, but you can still reach them by clicking the double arrow at the right edge of the window.

Search Site

Use this button when you want to find your search terms just on the pages of the current site open in your browser, rather than on the whole Web. For example, if you're on HBO.com and the site won't let you search for pages that mention Sarah Jessica Parker without Kim Cattrall, try the Google site search, which lets you construct any Google search for that site alone.

I'm Feeling Lucky

This button works just like the button on Google's home page (see page 22). It bypasses the results page altogether, which is a nice way to eliminate a few clicks when you suspect Google's first instinct will be the page you want to visit.

Tip: Even if you haven't added this button to the toolbar, you can run a Lucky search by typing in your terms and then pressing Alt+Enter.

Search Images, Search Groups, Search Directory, and Search Froogle

These buttons run your search in Google's alternate universes, described in detail in Chapters 3, 4, and 5. To use them, simply type your search terms into the blank box, and then click the button for the area you want to search. For example, to search for pictures of *wildfires*, type in the word and click the Images button. Instead of running your search on the whole Web—which could bring up definitions of wildfires, instructions for putting them out, and other flotsam—Google runs your search only in its listing of images.

Next and Previous results

These buttons are a *huge* timesaver. Suppose you've just run a Google search and, from the results page, you clicked through to a certain Web site. If, once you're there, you find you want to go to the next or previous page on your list of results, simply click the appropriate button—no need to return to the page of Google results. Even better, the buttons work after you've clicked deeply into a site.

Tip: To open a page in a new browser window, Shift-click the Next or Previous button.

So, for example, if you search for *movies,* your top results include Movies.com, The Internet Movie Database, Hollywood.com, and Yahoo Movies. If you click through to The Internet Movie Database and surf around the site for ten minutes, winding up on an obscure page that shows whether Cary Grant ever collaborated with Keanu Reeves, you can jump directly to Movies.com or Hollywood.com without backing up to your results page or running the *movies* search again. Just click Previous or Next, and Google takes you directly to that result.

News

The News button takes you directly to *http://news.google.com/,* Google's news culling service, described on page 90.

PageRank

PageRank is Google's system for determining the importance of every page it records (page 3). This toolbar icon displays a green bar that fills in to show you how Google ranks the site you're on right now. If you mouse over the icon, a small box appears, telling you what rank—on a scale from 1 to 10—Google gives the current page.

Checking PageRank is really a geek activity, of greatest interest to people who run Web sites and want to know how Google is rating them. For more on PageRank and Webmastering, see Chapter 8.

Tip: If you find PageRank isn't filling in the green bar for your results, and you know you're reaching the Internet from behind a *firewall* (software and/or hardware designed to deter hackers) and a *proxy server* (a computer that directs traffic between an intranet and the Internet), your network may be blocking the feature. To get PageRank back in order, you can try an experimental solution Google has devised. Open the Toolbar Options dialog box, click the More tab, and then turn on "Fix PageRank through proxies."

Page Info menu

The Page Info button opens a menu with four choices to see more information about the page you're currently on. It's a quick way to dig deep without returning to your results page (or creating one in the first place) or heading to the Advanced Search form (page 50). Here's what you can get:

- **Cached Snapshot of Page** lets you see the way the page looked when Google last recorded it. (For more on caching and when it's useful, see page 26.)

- **Similar Pages** gives you listings for pages with similar content. (For more on this feature, see page 28.)

- **Backward Links** gives you a list of pages that link to the page you're on. (For more on viewing links, see page 56.)

- **Translate into English** is handy, of course, if you're viewing a page that's not in English.

Pop-up blocker

Pop-up ads—the little advertisement windows that sprout like mushrooms in a damp basement—are a real impediment to productivity, forcing you to spend half the day closing them. Better to use a pop-up blocker, which prevents these annoyances from opening as you surf the Web. The Google toolbar has a built-in pop-up blocker that provides relief from this perpetual pest.

Note: Blocking pop-ups isn't strictly a search function; it's really a surf aid. But Google has endowed the toolbar with a handful of surfing features that make it easier to reach the things you want to find. If your browser doesn't have its own pop-up blocker (like older versions of Internet Explorer), the Google toolbar proves a nice stand-in.

When Google blocks a pop-up window, your cursor briefly displays a little Pow! symbol, the browser makes a noise, and the toolbar button tells you how many pop-ups Google has blocked. (You can turn off the counter if it annoys you. In the Toolbar Options dialog box, go to the More tab, and choose "Hide popup blocker count." You can also squelch the noise by turning off "Play a sound when blocking pop-ups.")

Tip: If you want to see how many pop-ups occur on a single site, you can reset the counter to zero by pressing Shift+Alt while clicking the pop-up button.

But not everybody wants to block pop-ups all the time. Some pop-ups aren't ads at all—in fact, they're an important part of certain Web pages. They can be coupons you want, forms you have to complete, or even email messages on a Web-based email system. To preserve these friendly pop-ups, you have two choices. You can tell Google to let *all* the pop-up windows through on a specific Web site. (Do so by clicking the pop-ups button while you're on that site.) Or you can allow pop-ups on *a case-by-case basis*: Leave the pop-up blocker on and Ctrl-click the link or button for a pop-up you want to see. (You'll know which link or button to Ctrl-click because, if you have pop-up blocking turned on, nothing will happen when you first try to click through.)

Persistent Pop-ups

Why do some pop-ups appear even when the pop-up blocker is on?

The pop-up blocker slams shut all windows that open when you click a link or button. But some Web sites install a small program on your hard drive that randomly opens pop-ups for its pages—a behavior that outsmarts the blocker and leaves you with a field of pop-up windows even when you've turned on the blocker.

If this behavior is threatening your sanity, consider installing and running AdAware, a free program that attempts to detect and delete software that's surreptitiously installed itself on your computer (*www.lavasoftusa.com/support/download*).

AdAware not only nixes pop-up launchers, but it also kills off *spyware,* software that companies can secretly place on your hard drive in order to track your behavior online. Spyware is generally not condoned by legitimate businesses, but file-sharing services have a history of deploying it.

SpellCheck

Even in this crazy world of point-and-click, you still have to do a fair bit of typing on the Web—think of your Web-based email program, your Amazon.com reader reviews, your Google Group discussions (page 119). If you've ever wished there were a way to check your online typing for typos and spelling errors, Google has heard your wishes and bestowed a spell checker in the latest version of the Toolbar.

As shown in Figure 6-7, after you click the "Check" button on the Toolbar, Google scans your text for errors and highlights any suspect words. To correct misspelled words automatically, click the green arrow next to the SpellCheck button in the Toolbar and choose AutoFix. If AutoFix is feeling neurotic about a word it doesn't recognize, it leaves it highlighted for you to deal with.

AutoLink

Wouldn't it be great if all companies had a map of their location on their Web sites so you wouldn't have to go mucking around on a map site? For those Web sites that are map-free, the Toolbar comes to the rescue with its AutoLink function. When you click the AutoLink button, the Toolbar scans the page for U.S. street

---

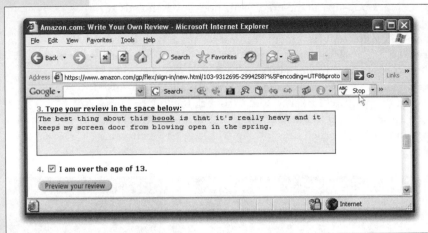

Figure 6-7:
The Toolbar's SpellCheck feature rats out those misspellings and typos on your Web forms and Web-based email. SpellCheck highlights suspicious words for you, and if you want to take a chance on the program's proofreading skills, click the AutoFix button to clean things up automatically.

addresses and then presents you with a link to click through for a map to the exact location.

AutoLink works for more than just finding that new Burmese restaurant in town—you can also use it to hunt down books, car information, and tracking and delivery info from FedEx and UPS. You just need to be on a Web page where a book's ISBN number, a car's VIN number, or a package-tracking number is displayed. Click the AutoLink button to see those numbers available as links, as shown in Figure 6-8. When you select one of those links, the Toolbar pops open a window of relevant information—the book's page on your favorite online bookstore, for example.

By default, AutoLink goes to Amazon.com for its book info, CarFax for its vehicle identification data, and Google Maps for its maps, but you can change these settings. To change the source where AutoLink gets its information, click the arrow next to the AutoLink button and then choose Change Default Provider. Use the drop-down menus to change the place that AutoLink uses for reference.

AutoFill

If you're the type who can't make it through the day without buying something online, AutoFill can save you scads of time filling out order forms and other pages on the Web. The feature lets you store your name, address, and other information in one place on your computer. Then, when you visit sites with blank forms, Google highlights in yellow the spaces it recognizes; when you press the AutoFill button, the yellow spaces fill in with your info (Figure 6-9). You could take an annual weeklong cruise with the time you save pecking through forms.

To set up AutoFill, open the Toolbar Options dialog box and click the Browsing tab (Figure 6-10). Click the AutoFill settings button and fill in as much of the form as you'd like. AutoFill stores your information on your computer—not on Google's, so the company never sees what you've written down. When you're ready to

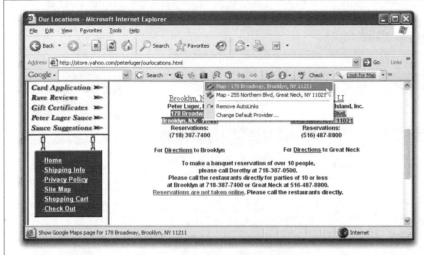

Figure 6-8:
AutoLink scans the page for a street addresses and then offers you a quick link to a map of your desired location.

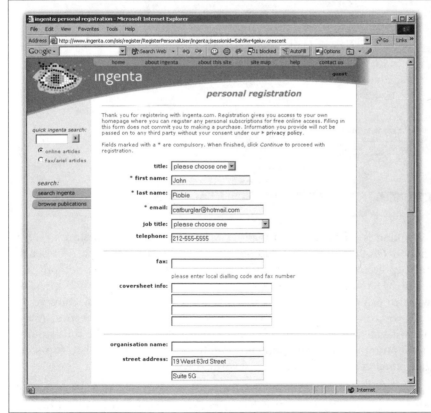

Figure 6-9:
When you click the AutoFill button, your computer fills in any highlighted boxes. Some Web pages have invisible boxes, however, and you can wind up sending, say, your phone number without even realizing it. To find out which info AutoFill is supplying, Shift-click the AutoFill button, which opens a small window telling you the data it's going to fill in.

use AutoFill, simply click the AutoFill button to work the magic. Bear in mind, though, that anyone else who uses your computer can see whatever you've typed on the AutoFill form.

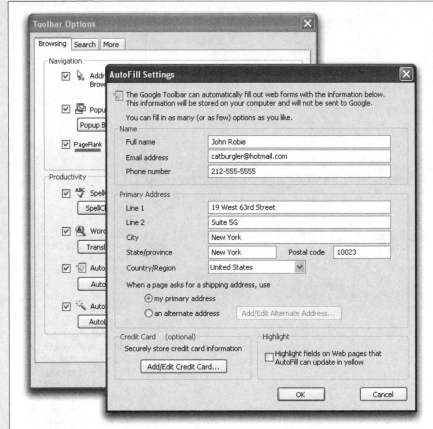

Figure 6-10:
The Google toolbar can fill in your name, address, phone number, and credit card information, among other things. For more information on what to put in each space, check out http://toolbar.google.com/autofill_help.html.

The exception is credit card information, which AutoFill lets you store in a way that nobody else can see or use without a password. This is fortunate, of course, because it prevents your 4-year-old from buying Barney CDs online without your permission. Here's how it works: After you fill out the credit card info, press Set Password to bring up a dialog box that lets you create a password. Once you've done so, you can't use or edit the credit card info without the password. And—cleverly—if you forget your password, AutoFill deletes the credit card number instead of prompting you (or a snooping family member) with a not-so-top-secret hint like "mother's maiden name" or "favorite pet."

The downside to storing credit card info on your computer is that it *may* be vulnerable to hackers. Although AutoFill encrypts your data when it saves it on your hard drive, and Google claims it's safe, some privacy experts believe it's smarter to keep your computer free of truly sensitive numbers. You'll have to let your tolerance for risk—and inconvenience—guide your decision.

Note: If you don't want AutoFill to highlight the spaces it can fill in (a reasonable desire if you share your computer with a lot of people and you don't want them to know how you've set AutoFill), open the Toolbox Options dialog box, click the More tab, and then turn off "Automatically highlight fields that AutoFill can fill."

Voting

The yellow and blue smiley and frowny faces are what Google calls voting buttons. If you particularly like or dislike a set of results from Google or a Web page you're visiting, you can tell Google by clicking one of these buttons. Weirdly, when you do so, nothing seems to happen—except for maybe a note's appearing at the bottom of your browser saying that Google has recorded your vote. So what does Google do with your votes? A company spokesperson says, "We use this information in aggregate to help us improve the overall quality of search results." The Pentagon gives more direct answers. Vote at your discretion.

BlogThis!

If you've never heard of a *blog* and suspect it's some kind of stain, see the box on page 188. But if you have a blog—whether hosted by the Google-owned Blogger service or any other blogging site—this button is a big old blogging bonus.

When you're visiting a Web page that you want to note on your blog, click BlogThis! to automatically create a new post that includes a link to the current page. Or highlight text on a Web page and click BlogThis! to create a new post that includes the whole selection. In either case, clicking the button opens a small window for your new post with its fresh link and/or text, ready to edit or publish directly.

Options

The Options button opens the Toolbar Options dialog box. It's handy to keep on the toolbar if you like to change your toolbar configuration often. Otherwise, you can open the dialog box from the menu under the Google button.

Up

The Up button lets you move through the *levels* of the site you're on, which means you can jump from a page deep within a site to a page closer to the home page without running a new search.

To understand the usefulness of this feature, it helps to think of the structure of a Web site like a family tree. At the top is the mother of all pages on that site (called the *home page*), and under it are a couple of branches that contain the other pages on the same site. Under *those* pages are branches filled with even more pages. In a

Blog-o-Rama

A *blog,* also known as a *Weblog,* is a journal published on the Web. Usually, a blog is created and maintained by one person, and blogs are often updated daily or several times a day, with the most recent posts appearing on the top of the page. Blogs commonly contain text, photos, and links to other sites, including other blogs. They can be personal or professional, public or private.

People who blog are known as *bloggers,* and the act of posting something to a blog is called *blogging.* Because bloggers often refer to each other's blogs, and because a number of noted pundits have gotten in on the game, the world of blogs is sometimes called the *blogosphere,* as in: "The recent Supreme Court decision outlawing green mousepads was widely derided in the blogosphere."

Blogs have been around since the late 1990s. Their numbers have grown quickly because unlike other types of Web sites, they're very easy to set up and maintain—you don't need to know any programming code at all—plus, a number of services let you create and run blogs for free.

In fact, in early 2003, Google bought Blogger (*www.blogger.com*), one of the first companies to offer blogging services. Blogger's basic service is free, easy to use, and chock-full of nifty features (for example, you can create draft posts and save them until you're ready to publish them). Other popular blogging services include TypePad.com, LiveJournal.com, and Xanga.com.

URL (for example, *www.raelity.org/gadget*), the levels of a site are separated by slashes (/). That's why some Web addresses look like this:

```
http://www.raelity.org/gadget/pda/palm/
```

(That site has tips on updating the memory on a certain PalmPilot.)

If your Google results take you to such a page, you could find yourself wondering what else the site has to say about gadgets or just what the *raelity.org* site is, exactly. Click the Up button to move through a site's levels one at a time. In this case, you'll move next to:

```
http://www.raelity.org/gadget/pda
```

and then to:

```
http://www.raelity.org/gadget
```

and then to:

```
http://www.raelity.org
```

Or click the arrow on the right side of the button to get a list of the current site's levels, as shown in Figure 6-11, and then select one to jump to that page.

Highlight

Sometimes, it's handy to highlight all the instances of a word or phrase on a page, making them easier to find or count. For example, if you're on a very long, text-heavy page, and you want to find any mention of *lobster* or *cryonics*, you could

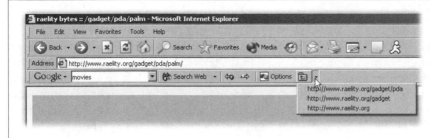

Figure 6-11:
*You can also navigate
through a site by clicking
the end of the URL in the
address bar (or by
pressing Ctrl+Tab, and
then the right arrow key),
and then deleting back
through the slashes until
you get to the page you
want to visit. Press Enter
to go there.*

burn out your eyeballs scrolling through the text. Instead, use the Highlight button to have Google block out your terms in hard-to-miss colors, as if it had hit them with an electronic highlighter pen. (Google highlights each word or quoted phrase in a different color, as shown in Figure 6-12.) The cool thing about this highlight feature is that you don't need to run a search to use it. Just type the words you want to find into the search box—but instead of hitting Enter, click the Highlight button. (To turn off the highlighting, click the button again.)

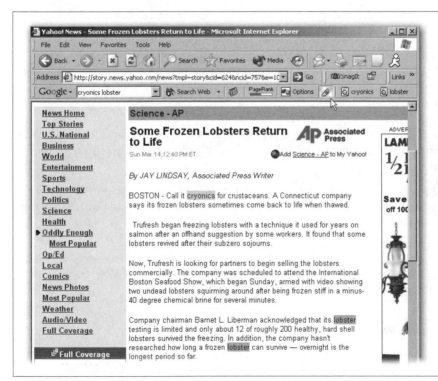

Figure 6-12:
*If you're using a friend's
computer, and he isn't
savvy enough to have
installed the toolbar, you
may still be able to
highlight your search
terms by using Google's
cache feature, explained
on page 26. Simply run a
Google search that
includes in its results the
page on which you want
to see the highlighted
terms. Click the Cached
link for that page, and
Google automatically
highlights your search
terms. (The possible
glitch here, though, is
that the cached page
may be outdated.)*

Word Find

Like the Highlight button, the Word Find buttons help you locate instances of a word or phrase on the current Web page. Instead of coloring them, however, these buttons, shown in Figure 6-13, *jump* to the terms. Also, like the Highlight button, you don't have to run a search to use the word buttons. Just type the words you want to find into the search box, but instead of hitting Enter, click the appropriate word button. Each time you click a button, you move to the next instance of that word or phrase. To go backwards, hold down Shift while clicking a button.

Figure 6-13:
The word-find buttons appear at the right end of the toolbar. Individual words get their own buttons, but if you want to search for two or more words together, like blue moon, put quotes around them.

In fact, the Word Find feature is really useful in *combination* with highlighting. If you first highlight your terms and then use Word Find to skip to them, they're even easier to find.

If you want to search for exact word matches only—say, *punk* but not *spunky*—press Ctrl when you click the *punk* button to have Google skip any words that contain *punk* along with other stuff.

Tip: If you've turned on the Word Find buttons, but you don't see them, they might have slipped off the edge of the screen (like the ones in Figure 6-6). Click the arrows on the right edge of the page to see the hidden buttons.

Search by Country

If you often use one of Google's internationally based search sites (page 58), you can add a toolbar button to run searches from the Google site of your favorite country. For example, if you do a lot of business in Brazil and you frequently want to search for pages from Brazilian sites, this button can save you a lot of clicking.

Warning: Unfortunately, when you add a country button, Google changes the interface language for *all* your results pages to match the country you've added–which means things like the cached link and all the buttons come out in Brazilian Portuguese. There's a workaround you can use to get back to an English interface, though, as described on page 48.

Setting up the button is a quick two-part process. First, open the Toolbar Options dialog box. At the bottom of the Search tab, pull down the "Use Google site" menu and pick a country. (For this example, say you picked Australia.) Second, under the "Add Google Search buttons to your Toolbar" area just above, turn on the "Search Australia" button that just appeared.

Now Google doesn't automatically restrict searches to the country you've chosen *unless* you click the country button you've just added. If you type in search terms and press Enter or Search Web, you get results from Google's regular site (which searches Web sites from anywhere in the world). But when you run a regular search, at the top of your results page, Google includes an option to run your search again and limit it to pages from the country you've specified—or pages in the language of that country (Figure 6-14).

Figure 6-14:
Use the country button to get results from sites in that country only. Or run a search as usual and then, at the top of the results page, select the country option to restrict your search. Press Enter or click Google Search to run your alternate search.

The workaround for getting your results back in English is simple: Head to Google's Preferences page and change your interface language to English, and then click Save Preferences (or Salvar Preferencias, if Google is speaking to you in Portuguese). The only problem with this solution is that your results pages now *omit* the option to run your search again on the alternate Google site. Still, the toolbar keeps your last search in the search box, so you can simply click the country button if you don't find what you want in a regular search.

WordTranslator

If English isn't your first language (or it is your first language and you're trying to learn a second one), Google Toolbar's WordTranslator feature beats the heck out of thumbing through a dictionary or leaping in and out of Google's Language Tools page (page 58) to look up words.

To turn on the translator, click the Options button on the Toolbar (page 176) and then, on the Browsing tab, turn on the checkbox for WordTranslator. Click the Translator Settings button and select the language you want to see onscreen when you point the mouse at an unfamiliar English word. Your tongue choices here include French, German, Spanish, Italian, Japanese, Korean, and both simplified and traditional Chinese.

WordTranslator doesn't exist as a Toolbar button—it just hitches along for the ride as you surf along and leaps into action when you hover the mouse over an unfamiliar word. Figure 6-15 shows you an example of WordTranslator at work.

Other Browsers with Google Features

Although Google makes its toolbar only for Firefox and Internet Explorer for Windows, several other browsers have noteworthy Google features.

Safari

The speedy Safari browser comes with Mac OS X, and it has a Google search box right on the main toolbar, as shown in Figure 6-16.

Note: If you have an earlier version of Mac OS X that doesn't include Safari, you can download the browser from *www.apple.com/downloads/macosx/apple/safari.html.* (The most recent versions of Mac OS X—Panther (10.3) and Tiger (10.4)—both include Safari.)

If you're still using Mac OS 9 and your inner geek is hankering for a little hacking, you can set Internet Explorer 5 to use Google as its search engine, allowing you to run Google searches from the Search Pane. Google doesn't provide directions, but it does semi-officially endorse the trick by pointing to the instructions at *www.visakopu.net/ie5google/.*

The Safari search box doesn't have all the features of the Google toolbar, but it does work beautifully for its essential purpose: running a Google search from anywhere on the Web. When you type in your terms and press Return, your Google results appear in the main browser window, just as with the Google toolbar.

Tip: If you've turned on *tabbed browsing* in Safari—which lets you open multiple Web pages within one browser window—you can open your Google search results in a new tab by pressing ⌘-Return after typing your search terms.

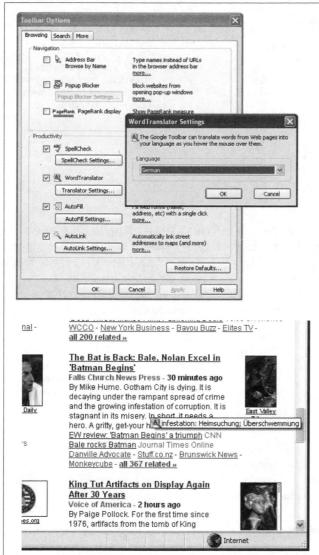

Figure 6-15:
Top: Click the Options button on the Toolbar to open up the Options box. To select a language to use with WordTranslator, turn on the WordTranslator checkbox and click the Translator Settings button so you can pick a language from the drop-down menu.

Bottom: With WordTranslator running as you browse, just pause your cursor over a word on a Web page to see it translated into your chosen language.

The minimalist Safari search box has a couple of cool tricks up its sleeve:

- **Search history.** The search box keeps a history of your recent searches; to get to them, click the magnifying glass on the left end of the box (it looks like a "Q"). When you select the search you want, Google runs that search again.

Note: You can clear the search history list (which you might want to do if you've been surfing, say, Gamblers Anonymous sites on your grandmother's Mac) by selecting the last line—Clear Recent Searches.

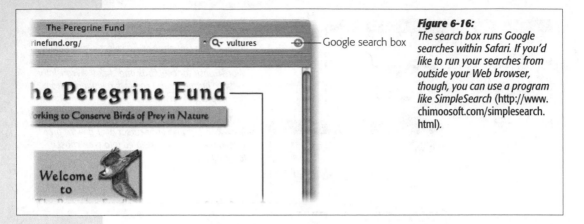

Figure 6-16:
The search box runs Google searches within Safari. If you'd like to run your searches from outside your Web browser, though, you can use a program like SimpleSearch (http://www.chimoosoft.com/simplesearch.html).

- **SnapBack.** After you've run a search and clicked through to one of your results pages, you can return directly to your Google search results without bushwhacking back through all the pages you've searched. Just click the SnapBack icon—the orange button with a white arrow at the right edge of the search box (Figure 6-17)—which takes you to the results page for the last search you ran. (It appears as a gray "x" when you're on a results page.)

Figure 6-17:
The cool thing about SnapBack is that it works no matter how far you've wandered away from your results, or even if you've typed new URLs into the address bar. At any time, just click the little orange arrow.

- **Sizability.** If you'd prefer a longer or shorter search box, you're in luck. Mouse over the little dot directly to the left of the box. When it becomes a two-headed arrow, you can drag the edge of the box left or right to resize it.

Two additional Safari features

Safari itself incorporates a couple of handy features that are part of the Google toolbar:

- **A pop-up blocker** that you can turn on by choosing Safari → Block Pop-Up Windows (or by pressing ⌘-K). The same process turns the blocker off.

- **AutoFill**, a button that automatically fills in forms on Web pages. You can turn on AutoFill by choosing Safari → Preferences → AutoFill and then selecting the place—such as your Address Book card—from which you'd like Safari to grab your personal information. Then, to add an AutoFill button to your toolbar, choose View → Customize Address Bar, and drag the Autofill button wherever you want on your toolbar.

Note: If you choose your Address Book card as a source for AutoFill info, you may have to set your card as Me. Do so by opening Address Book, selecting the card with your information, and then choosing Card → Make This My Card. (If this option is grayed out, the card is already set as Me.)

GEM IN THE ROUGH

A Nifty Toolbar Trick

You can turn your *address bar* into a blank Google search box. It's a great trick when you need to conserve every ounce of screen space and have to turn off the Google toolbar—but still want to run searches without visiting Google's home page. Head into the Toolbar Options dialog box, click the More tab, and turn on "Use Google as my default search engine in Internet Explorer."

That's it. You can now type search terms into your address bar, press Enter, and land on a page of Google search results. (It works whether or not you've got the Google toolbar open.)

This setting is useful even when the Google toolbar is visible. Here's why: The address bar comes set as a *Microsoft* search box. When you type a URL into Internet Explorer, the browser heads off and tries to find the page you've asked for. Normally, if it can't find the page, it takes you to the MSN (Microsoft Network) site and shows you search results for whatever you typed into the address bar. For example, if you enter *amazon*, it shows you a list of links for Amazon.com.

But if you've set Google as your search engine, when you accidentally type in a bogus URL, the browser takes you to *Google's* results for that URL. Microsoft's results tend to be loaded with more commercial links than Google's, so for many searchers, this setting is a good one to adjust.

Mozilla, Firefox, and Netscape

Like Goldilocks and the Three Browsers, Mac fans, Linux geeks, and PC people with an aversion to Microsoft all have other *free* options: Mozilla (*www.mozilla.org*), Netscape (*http://channels.netscape.com/ns/browsers/download.jsp*), and Firefox, which is a friendlier version of Mozilla (*http://mozilla.org/products/firefox/*). All three browsers are based on the same stable technology, known as Gecko.

They're all very fine programs, but perhaps the coolest thing about them is that you can download a feature for them called the Googlebar, shown in Figure 6-18. It emulates Google's official toolbar nicely, right down to the Search Site button and the highlighter feature (neither of which is available in Safari). If you've recently made the switch from a PC to the Mac and you're lamenting the loss of the Google toolbar, you could try one of these browsers.

Note: Mozilla, Firefox, and Netscape all include an option for tabbed browsing, a configuration that lets you open multiple Web pages within one browser window—a major screen-space conservation initiative. They block pop-ups, too, so the Googlebar doesn't have to.

Mozilla vs. Netscape

Mozilla 1.7.8 and Netscape 8.0—the latest versions of each, as of this writing—look similar and act nearly the same. The most obvious difference is that Mozilla installs with different themes. (A *theme* describes the way a program looks—things

---

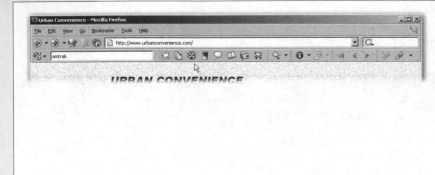

Figure 6-18:
The Googlebar is shown here in Firefox, though it is also available for Mozilla and Netscape. This picture shows a customized array of buttons. To choose which buttons appear on the Googlebar, right-click anywhere along it to bring up a menu of options.

like the colors and shape of the buttons, icons, and other interface elements.) But the two browsers are typically used by different types of people.

Mozilla is popular with programmers and other geek types because it comes with a seemingly infinite number of settings you can tweak, and because it always has a test version that's slightly more advanced than Netscape's latest version. Netscape, on the other hand, is owned by AOL. So while it comes with the same basic features Mozilla has, it includes AOL Instant Messenger, a shopping button, and a few other extras that make it appealing to civilians.

But Netscape also has a few notable problems. It harbors windows that crop up regularly, exhorting you to join the Netscape Network—an unnecessary distraction. And Netscape installs extra programs (like Rediscover AOL) and desktop icons, even if you don't ask for them.

On the bright side, AOL has made an effort to get Netscape up to speed in today's world; version 8.0 has self-configured settings that make it safer from the get-go, along with security features that warn you against spyware that might be trying to jack your system. The new version also comes with a Passcard Manager function that remembers your user names and passwords, just like AutoFill.

Note: If you already use at least Netscape 7.0 or 7.1 and you want to install the Googlebar, directions are on the next page.

Firefox

If Mozilla is too complicated and Netscape is too clogged up with AOL clutter, a third option, Firefox, might be juuuust right. Unlike Mozilla and Netscape, which come loaded with an email program, a Web page composer, chat tools, and tons of features that many people don't use, Firefox is a standalone browser that incorporates only the most popular tools and settings. Not only does this arrangement make Firefox easier for the average person to use, but it also means the program is speedier and takes up less room on your hard drive. (If you want a automatic weather report in your browser window, a built-in dictionary, or many other tasty features that let you do other things in your Web browser, Firefox offers dozens of *extensions*, otherwise known as add-ons, that you can easily install. For a list, check out *http://extensionroom.mozdev.org/main.php/Firefox*). The Autofill extension (*http://autofill.mozdev.org*) is a popular one for people who covet the Google Toolbar's time- and type-saving feature.

In addition to its lightweight configuration, Firefox has a sleek interface, state-of-the-tech security, pop-up blocking, tabbed browsing, and many other nifty features, including a built-in Google search box (which also lets you search for a term on the page you're currently viewing). For fancier features, you can add the Googlebar—or regular Google toolbar—to Firefox. And if you type a search term into the address bar, it automatically runs a Google I'm Feeling Lucky search.

Firefox, which suffers from far fewer security holes and exploitable issues than Microsoft's dominant Internet Explorer, saw an uptick in popularity when its first official version was released. The underlying technology is the same as Mozilla's, and there are a few problems, like the occasional misspelled menu item or a cookie setting that includes the observation, "Cookies are delicious delicacies," inserted by an engineer with a raging sense of humor.

Note: If you like the look and feel of Firefox, check out Mozilla's free email program, Thunderbird, at *www.mozilla.org/products/thunderbird/*. It's available for Mac OS X, Linux, and most Windows systems and comes with a Junk Mail filter to weed out annoying spam from your real messages.

For a nice set of answers to frequently asked questions about Firefox, see *www.mozilla.org/support/firefox/faq*. To download it, head over to *www.mozilla.org/products/firefox/*, choose your operating system, and let 'er rip.

Tip: In a hurry to get those Google results? Google itself helps you out by using a special feature called *prefetching* in recent versions of Firefox, Mozilla, and Netscape. Prefetching automatically load pages that turn up in search results, invisibly and in the background. That means that most of the page has already downloaded to your computer by the time you click its link. The downside? If you opt not to click on a prefetched page's link, you still have all its parts taking up a little piece of your hard drive space.

The Googlebar

The Googlebar works with Firefox, Mozilla, and newer versions of Netscape (7.0 or later). Installing it is a snap: Just visit *http://googlebar.mozdev.org/installation.html*, scroll down past the experimental version to the first version below that (currently 0.9.5), and click Install. Your browser handles the installation and then prompts you to restart the browser. That's it.

Tip: If the Googlebar doesn't appear after you install it and restart your browser, press Ctrl+F8 (⌘-F8 on a Mac), which turns the Googlebar on and off. Since Firefox has no menu item for turning the Googlebar on and off, this shortcut can be important.

You run a search from the Googlebar by typing your terms into the blank box and then pressing Enter; your browser shows you regular Google results as if you'd searched from the Google home page. If you have tabbed browsing set up (page 192), you can open a search in a new tab by pressing Ctrl (or, if you use a Mac, ⌘) when you press Enter or click on any button on the Googlebar.

If your first search seems to yield results in Spanish or some other language you didn't choose, your Googlebar installed itself with a twist. To fix it, click the button at the left edge of the toolbar, marked "G," to open a menu of choices for Google pages. Toward the bottom of the menu is a choice called "Gooblebar options," which opens a dialog box that lets you adjust settings on the Googlebar. Open the dialog box and then click the tab labeled "Google Sites." Change the first item, "Select international version of Google Search," to the United States (or wherever you'd like) and then click OK.

Note: On the "G" menu, the choice for Help takes you to a help page for the Googlebar, not to Google's help pages. To get to Google's help pages, you have to first hit the home page and then click the link for About Google, which takes you to a page with several help options.

To see a history of your searches, click the arrow on the right end of the search box, as shown in Figure 6-19, or click in the search box and press the down arrow on your keyboard.

Tip: The keyboard shortcut for jumping to the search box is Ctrl+F12 (on a Mac, ⌘-F12). Memorize this shortcut to save wear on your mouse and your wrist.

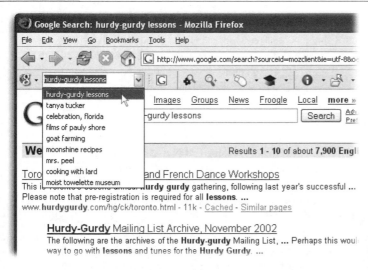

Figure 6-19:
You can choose how many search results show up in the Googlebar's history. On the far-left edge of the search box, click the "G" to bring up a menu, and then choose "Googlebar options." Click the Miscellaneous tab, and in the Save History section at the top, make sure "Preserve history across browser sessions" is turned on. Then use the "Maximum number of search terms kept in history" menu to pick how many searches the Googlebar saves. If you frequently rerun searches, consider storing a lot of them. But if you share your computer with other people and don't want them to know what you've been up to, you might want to clear your history with the option on the "G" menu—or turn off the history altogether.

In most respects, the Gooblebar works just like the regular old Google toolbar, and it includes nearly all the same features listed on page 179. For example, to search any of Google's special sections, like Images or the Directory, you type your terms and click the appropriate button (if you mouse over a button, a little box appears telling you what it does). You can choose which buttons appear on the Googlebar by right-clicking anywhere along it to bring up a contextual menu, as described in Figure 6-20.

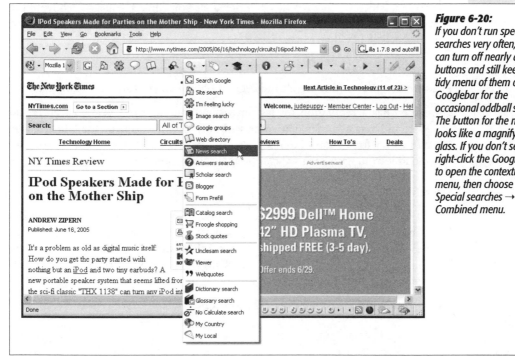

Figure 6-20:
If you don't run special searches very often, you can turn off nearly all the buttons and still keep a tidy menu of them on the Googlebar for the occasional oddball search. The button for the menu looks like a magnifying glass. If you don't see it, right-click the Googlebar to open the contextual menu, then choose Special searches → Combined menu.

The Googlebar has a few features that aren't on Google's own toolbar, including buttons for Catalog search (page 162), Google Answers (page 141), and computer and university searches (page 56). If you regularly search any of these offbeat areas, the Googlebar can save you precious clicks.

Tip: To make the search box smaller or bigger, drag the dotted line next to the right edge of the search box as far left or right as you'd like.

So what's missing from the Googlebar? A few buttons: PageRank, BlogThis!, Auto-Fill, the voting buttons, and the PopUp Blocker. If you really need those features, switch to Google's *own* toolbar—but keep in mind that you'll have to switch to a new browser, too, unless you're already using Firefox.

Two More Browsers Worth Mentioning

Truth be told, nearly everyone in the world uses Internet Explorer, and a handful of renegades use Safari or Mozilla and friends. An even smaller group of rebels uses other browsers, two of which have Google search features that make them worth a few paragraphs.

OmniWeb

OmniWeb, which works on Mac OS X only, lets you run a Google search from the address box. You can type directly into it, but you have to preface your search with the word *google*, like this:

```
google poker equipment
```

Press Return to run your search and get a Google listing of gambling supply sites.

OmniWeb has a reputation for fast browsing, and the latest version features ad blocking and versatile tabs that come with a thumbnail view of the tabbed page. It's free to try for 30 days (and $30 to buy after those 30 days are up). You can download it from *www.omnigroup.com/applications/omniweb.*

Opera

The Opera browser, which works on every major operating system in the world, has a built-in search bar with options for Google and a slew of other search engines. You can even search for video clips, MP3s, and other goodies—and Opera has tons of cool customization features. Unfortunately, the free version includes ads, and the paid version costs $39.

Still, if you're intrigued, you can download either version from *www.opera.com.*

More Cool Google Tools

The Google toolbar is great, but it's not the last word on useful ways to use Google. In fact, it may not even work with your browser. If you can't or don't want to use the toolbar, you can still avoid unnecessary trips to Google's home page by using browser buttons and sidebars instead. And bookmarklets, little buttons you can add to your browser, can help you perform a host of smart search tricks.

Google also has a bunch of other cool tools. The company has developed a search box for your desktop, for example, and a deskbar that lets you surf without even opening a browser.

Some of these offerings are still experimental, but Google lets you use them and offer feedback.

This chapter covers alternatives to the toolbar, the best of the new Google tools you can test-drive, and other often-neglected tips for Google efficiency—including keyboard shortcuts and secret mouse clicks. It also fills you in on Google Wireless, a special service that lets you use Google on the road using a mobile phone or palmtop with Internet access.

Alternative Search Boxes

A lot of people swear by the Google toolbar. But the Internet is about nothing if not choice, and some of these search tools offer nifty alternatives.

Browser Buttons

If you don't have the screen room for the Google toolbar (or one of its imitators), or if your browser of choice came out during the Carter administration and doesn't accommodate a search box, Google's browser buttons can be a good way to run searches without jumping to the home page.

The browser buttons, shown in Figure 7-1, are simply links that you can place on the same toolbar that holds your most frequently used bookmarks (also known as "favorites").

Figure 7-1:
Google's browser buttons sit right on your Links toolbar (called the Personal toolbar in Netscape and Mozilla). Obviously, if you don't normally keep a toolbar open for your bookmarks, these buttons don't save you any screen space.

The buttons come in two flavors, and you can install either or both of them:

- **Google Search** works two ways. You can highlight some text on a Web page and then click Google Search to search the Web for those words. Or, if you click the button *without* first selecting any text, a blank search box pops up where you can type any words you want to search for. (In Internet Explorer, the search box has the awkward moniker Explorer User Prompt, but it works the same.)

- **Google.com** simply delivers you to Google's home page.

The buttons work with pretty much any browser made in the last five years:

- **For Windows 95/98/NT/XP or Linux,** they work with Internet Explorer 4 and later, and Netscape 4 and later.

- **For the Mac,** they work with Internet Explorer 4 and later, and Netscape 4.5 and later.

Tip: Unofficially, the buttons also work with the Mozilla and Firefox browsers, because they use the same technology as Netscape. But Google won't say which *versions* of these browsers they work with. If you use Mozilla or Firefox and you want to know if the buttons will fly on your browser, just try installing the buttons as described below. The process takes two seconds, and if it doesn't work, you won't have done any damage.

If you click over to *www.google.com/options/buttons.html* and click Get Your Google Buttons Here, Google detects the kind of browser you're using and gives you appropriate instructions for installing the buttons—which takes less time than blinking an eye.

Tip: Google doesn't tell you this, but if you install the buttons all the way to one side of your Links or Personal toolbar, it's easier to hit them. You can always move them later by just dragging them elsewhere on the toolbar.

WORKAROUND WORKSHOP

Saying No to Toolbars, Browser Buttons, and the Google Home Page

If you don't want to add any superfluous tools to your browser, but you still want to run Google searches without dashing off to the home page every three seconds, there's an easy workaround—at least for some of your searches.

When you're visiting a Web page and you want to search a word on it, highlight that text, right-click to open a shortcut menu (Control-click on the Mac), and then choose Google Search (or Web Search). Your browser heads directly to the Google results page for the words you selected.

This trick works in Internet Explorer for Windows; Netscape, Mozilla, and Firefox (Windows and Mac); and Safari—if you have your browser set to use Google for such searches. (Unfortunately, it doesn't work in Internet Explorer for the Mac.)

Safari and Firefox already come equipped to let you use this secret handshake. Here's how to get it going in the other browsers:

Netscape and Mozilla both have the same setting you can change. Choose Edit → (on the Mac, Netscape/Mozilla → Preferences), and on the left side of the resulting window, find the word Navigator and then click the + (or flippy triangle) next to it to reveal a list of options. Choose Internet Search, and on the right side of the window, find the option for Default Search Engine, and then use the menu to choose Google. Click OK, and you're done.

In order to work the highlight/right-click trick in Internet Explorer for Windows, you have to install the Google toolbar (page 171). "But doesn't that defeat the whole purpose of this workaround?" you ask. Nope, because once you've got the toolbar installed, you can remove it from view (View → Toolbars → Google) and still use the right-click search technique.

Search Sidebars

In some browsers, you can open a sidebar, like the one shown in Figure 7-2, and run searches from there. When you click a link in the sidebar, the new page appears in the main window. A search sidebar is useful primarily because it can retain the list of results links—saving you the trouble of clicking back over to your results page when you want to explore more than one result.

Tip: If you use Internet Explorer for Mac, the search sidebar is also hugely useful as a substitute for the Google toolbar.

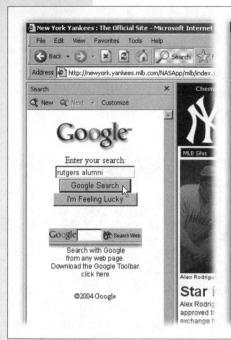 

Figure 7-2:
Left: The sidebar is a separate pane within your browser that lets you run Google searches without leaving the page you're on.

Right: Here, the results of the search appear in the sidebar only. You can also arrange it so that the results show up in the main window—which means you also get the full Google info for each page in the list. To clear the search box and results, click New in the sidebar (above the Google logo).

Internet Explorer, Netscape, and Mozilla all have search sidebars. Here's how they work.

Internet Explorer for Windows

The sidebar is somewhat superfluous in Internet Explorer for Windows, because the Google toolbar is more flexible and takes up less room. But if you want the listing of links, as shown in Figure 7-2, you need to use the sidebar—and you need to set it to display your results the way you want.

To open the search sidebar, choose View → Explorer Bar → Search, or on the Standard Buttons toolbar, click Search. To set Google to run sidebar searches and display results *in* the sidebar, you can use either of two methods: with or without the toolbar. Step 1 below gives you directions if you've already installed the toolbar. If you haven't installed it or don't want to, just follow the directions from step 2 on:

1. **Set Google as the search engine for Internet Explorer.**

   While installing the Google toolbar, the wizard asks if you want Google as the default search engine. Tell it you do.

   If you've *already* installed the toolbar, you can check or change the setting by opening the Toolbar Options dialog box (on the toolbar, click Options; or click the Google logo and then choose Options). Then on the More tab, turn on "Use Google as my default search engine in Internet Explorer."

> **Note:** If you're using the toolbar just so you can get the sidebar, you can, of course, turn *off* the toolbar at this point. Just right click anywhere along the Internet Explorer toolbars or choose View → Toolbars, and then click Google to remove the checkmark.

2. **Set Internet Explorer to display your results in the sidebar.**

   First, open the search sidebar by choosing View → Explorer Bar → Search. Then, in the sidebar, click New. That should open a blank Google search box for you.

   At this point, it's possible that the Google gods are smiling on you and everything will work just beautifully without any further action on your part. To see, first test out the sidebar with a search. If your results appear as a list of links in the sidebar, and that's what you want, you're in luck.

   If, however, the search results show up in the main window and that's not what you want, head over to *www.google.com/options/defaults.html* and scroll down to Make Google Your Default Search Engine. In the section for Internet Explorer, Google provides two links to downloads that change the way your results show up. The first link makes your results appear in the sidebar; the second link makes your results appear in the main window. (In Internet Explorer, you can't have it both ways—a list of links on the left and the full results listings on the right—unless you run the same search from the sidebar *and* the toolbar or main window.)

   Assuming you want your results to show up in the sidebar, click the first link. When asked if you want to save or open it, choose Open. Then, in the next two dialog boxes that appear, click Yes and OK, respectively.

3. **Close Internet Explorer and reopen it.**

   Run a search from the sidebar, and bask in glory as your results appear there.

Internet Explorer for Macintosh

Setting up a Google sidebar in Internet Explorer for the Mac is a big win because you can't get a Google toolbar for this browser. But the sidebar solution involves a twist, because the existing search sidebar doesn't let you use Google. Instead, you have to use the *Page Holder* sidebar, shown in Figure 7-3. The Page Holder feature anchors a single Web page—in this case the Google home page—in the browser's sidebar. When you click a link inside the sidebar, the new page opens in the browser's main window.

> **Note:** Actually, if you're in a geeky mood, you might be able to hack Internet Explorer for the Mac to run Google searches from the search sidebar; *www.visakopu.net/ie5google/* gives directions. But if you harbor no hackerish impulses, the Page Holder workaround is a good bet.

You can run Google searches from the Page Holder sidebar two different ways. If the page you hold in the sidebar is the Google home page (Figure 7-3, top), your results appear in the main window only. If the page you hold is a special search-box page from Google (Figure 7-3, bottom), however, your first page of results appears in the sidebar only, and it includes no details—though if you mouse over a link, a box appears and shows you the page snippet you'd see in a regular results listing.

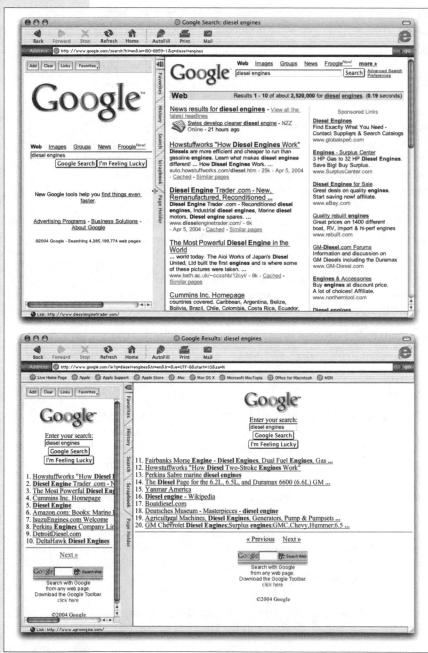

Figure 7-3:
Top: If you're holding the Google home page, you'll notice right away that it doesn't fit in the sidebar. You can, however, widen the sidebar. Mouse over the line just to the left of the sidebar tabs, until the cursor becomes a double-headed arrow. Then drag the line as far right as you want.

Bottom: You can do the same trick if you're holding the special Google search pane, but it fits reasonably in a narrower pane, too.

This Page Holder option, though, is helpful if you want to click through your first few results and view each page in the main window.

Here's how to set up Page Holder to run Google searches:

1. **Open Page Holder.**

   Internet Explorer calls the whole sidebar the *Explorer Bar,* and you can open it by pressing ⌘-T (or by choosing View → Explorer Bar). The bar has five tabs running along its right edge, and Page Holder is the bottom one. Click it to get the blank bar shown in Figure 7-4.

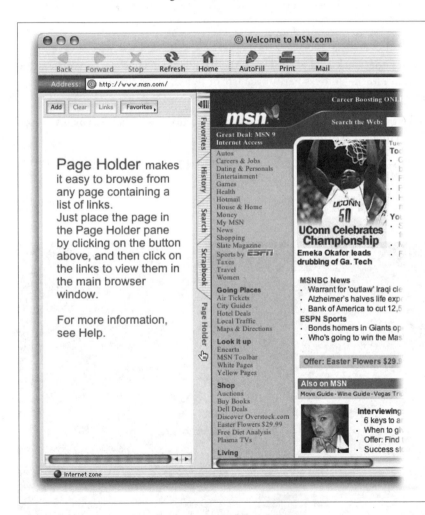

Figure 7-4:
Practically nobody knows how to use the Page Holder feature, but it's a great trick if you're wedded to Internet Explorer for the Mac.

2. **Open the page you want to preserve.**

   You have two choices here. You can hold the main Google home page by pointing your browser to *www.google.com.* (Searching from the home page opens your results in the main window only, as shown in Figure 7-3 at top.)

Or you can hold the special Google search pane, shown at bottom in Figure 7-3, by going to *www.google.com/ie.* (Searching from this search bar opens your first page of results in the sidebar only, as shown in Figure 7-3 at bottom. When you want to see results beyond the first ten, the sidebar gives you a Next link, but clicking it makes your results from 11 on appear in the *main* window. As in Internet Explorer for Windows, there's no way to run a search from the sidebar that displays your results in *both* windows.)

Note: You can create bookmarks within Page Holder for *any* page—and change it later, if you like. Just pick a page for now, and you can follow this procedure again to save the other.

---

3. **Add the open page to Page Holder.**

   You can either click Add at the top of the Page Holder window, or you can find the @ icon in the address bar, to the left of the URL, and drag it into the Page Holder pane.

4. **To save the page so you can easily return to it any time, click Favorites → Add to Page Holder Favorites.**

   Once you save it, the Google home page goes by the name Google; the search page goes by the name Google Results.

   That's it. You can now run a search from the sidebar *and* feel like you beat the system.

FOR MACINTOSH ONLY

The Google Service

In Mac OS X, every program has a feature called Services, which are extra, general-purpose tools that let you do things like send emails from within a program and add sticky notes. You can find these services in the Application menu—the menu that bears the name of whatever program you're using. The Services menu has a submenu with a list of options like Make New Sticky Note and Mail → Send to.

When you highlight some text in nearly any program, you can perform these Services on your selection. Thus, if you highlight a URL, and choose Application → Services → Make New Sticky Note, a new sticky with your URL appears.

The good news is that Search with Google (Shift-⌘-L) is also in the Services menu. The bad news is that Services don't work with all programs. In fact, they're mostly limited to applications that were written specifically for Mac OS X (known as *Cocoa* applications), which include programs like iChat, Safari, Mail, and TextEdit.

Quicker than using the Services menu, though, is running the Search in Google command from a program's *shortcut* menu. While typing in a Cocoa program, you can simply right-click (or Control-click) a selection of text and choose Search in Google. In a flash, your Web browser opens and performs the corresponding Google search.

Netscape and Mozilla (Mac, Windows, and Linux)

Netscape and Mozilla act pretty much the same when it comes to searching Google from a sidebar. You can use the existing Search sidebar and simply choose Google as your search engine (which works just like the sidebar for Internet Explorer for Windows shown in Figure 7-2). Or you can download a *special* sidebar from Google that lets you perform a Lucky search and reach Google's alternate collections (Images, Groups, Directory, and News). The special Google search is worth using only if you often look for things in the alternate collections—or if you're often Feeling Lucky.

With either sidebar, Mozilla and Netscape share the useful feature of listing links to your results in the sidebar *and* opening the full Google results page in the main window. This setup is handy when you want to take a gander at all the details in a results listing (main window) but then need only the links to surf around (sidebar).

To open the sidebar, choose View → Show/Hide → Sidebar (or My Sidebar, in Netscape). On Windows machines, you can also open and close the sidebar by pressing F9. If the sidebar has something other than a search box showing (like a history of your browsing), click the tab for Search (which might be at the bottom of the sidebar).

In addition to the blank search box, the Search tab includes a menu labeled "using" that lets you choose your favorite search engine. If you don't see Google on the list, choose Edit → Preferences (on the Mac, chose Mozilla [or Netscape] → Preferences); in the window that opens, click the plus sign (or flippy triangle) next to Navigator, and then choose Internet Search. At the top of the Internet Search page is a section for Default Search Engine. Use the "Search using" menu to pick Google, and then click OK. Voilà—you're now ready to run searches from the sidebar.

Tip: You can leave the Search sidebar open but actually run searches from the Google *toolbar.* The advantage of this system is that you get the search flexibility of the toolbar (page 171), but you wind up with a list of results links in the sidebar. It's the best of both worlds.

If you want to use the special Google-only sidebar, described above and shown in Figure 7-5, head over to *www.google.com/mozilla/google-search.html* and scroll down to "Install a new Google sidebar panel." When you click the link for your version of Netscape or Mozilla, the sidebar installs instantly, and you can begin using it right away.

Tip: Don't overlook the What's Related tab in the Mozilla and Netscape sidebar. Like the "Similar pages" link in a Google result, it shows a list of pages somehow related to the page you're currently viewing. Even better, the tab provides contact information for the site's owners (when available), so you can compliment (or insult) them about their Web design.

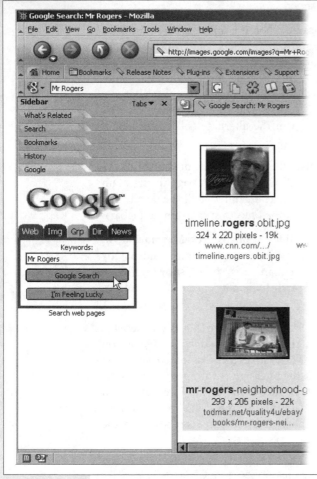

Figure 7-5:
*The Google sidebar is handy if you often search
Google Images, Groups, Directory, or News. Here,
the sidebar shows a search for Mister Rogers in
Google's image bank. A nice bonus of this sidebar
is that you can run Lucky Image searches—
meaning that Google takes you directly to the first
image, rather than showing you the entire list.*

Searching from the Address Bar

In Internet Explorer for Windows, and Netscape or Mozilla for any operating system, you can use your *address bar* (the place where URLs appear) as a blank Google search box. This trick is quite practical; since almost everyone keeps the address
bar visible, being able to search from it doesn't add any gunk to your browser
window.

Tip: In Firefox, running a search from the address bar takes you directly to Google's I'm Feeling Lucky
result for your keywords. For example, if you type in *auctions,* Firefox takes you to eBay.

Internet Explorer for Windows

In Internet Explorer, this system has a downside: Searches run slower than they do
using almost any other method. If you don't mind, here's how to set it up:

- If you have the Google toolbar installed, the box on page 195 explains how to set up your browser to let you search from the address bar instead.

- To search from the address bar *without* installing the toolbar, you have to set Google as your browser's default search engine. If you followed the directions on page 203 for setting up a Google search *sidebar*, you've already done this step. Try running a search from the address bar, and see if it's working.

If you haven't yet set your browser to use Google for searching, just click over to *www.google.com/options/defaults.html* and scroll down to Make Google Your Default Search Engine. In the section for Internet Explorer, Google provides two links to downloads that reset your browser; you can use either one. Click the link, and when it asks if you want to save or open it, choose Open. Then, in the next two dialog boxes that appear, click Yes and OK respectively. Close Internet Explorer and reopen it. You're now ready to search from the address bar.

Netscape and Mozilla (Mac, Windows, and Linux)

In Netscape and Mozilla, the address bar is actually called the *location bar*, and using it for searches is a snap. First, make sure Google is your default search engine. If you set the search sidebar to use Google, as described on page 203, you're all set. If not, just choose Edit → Preferences (on the Mac, Mozilla/Netscape → Preferences), and in the window that opens, click the plus sign (or flippy triangle) next to Navigator, and then choose Internet Search. At the top of the Internet Search page is a section for Default Search Engine. Use the "Search using" menu to pick Google, and then click OK. Now go ahead and type your keywords into the location bar and click Search (if you press Enter, the search doesn't happen).

Note: If you don't see the Search button on your toolbar in Mozilla, choose View → Show/Hide → Navigation Toolbar and make sure "Search button" is turned on. In Netscape, choose Edit → Preferences → Navigator (on the Mac, Netscape → Preferences → Navigator panel); at the bottom of the Navigator page, make sure the Search button is turned on.

If you don't want to go to the hassle of clicking Search every time you want some Google results, you can set your browser to understand a couple of letters typed into the location bar—like *gg*—as a sign that you want to run a Google search. For example, this:

```
gg "Cookie Monster"
```

could run a Google search for "Cookie Monster" and display the results in your main browser window. Here's how to set it up:

1. **Choose Bookmarks → Manage Bookmarks.**

   The Bookmark Manager snaps to attention.

2. **Choose File → New → Bookmark. (On the Mac, head to the main menu bar and choose File → New → Bookmark.)**

   A dialog box opens, and depending on the version of Netscape or Mozilla you're running, it either contains blank spaces for Name, Location, and Keyword, or for just Name and Location.

   Either way, for Name type in something like *Google Search,* and for Location type *http://www.google.com/search?q=%s.*

   If you have a field for keyword, type in the characters you want your browser to recognize as the sign to run a Google search. You can use anything you want, but it's a good idea to stick with something short and suggestive, like *gg.* Now click OK and close the Bookmark Manger.

   If you *don't* have a space for the keyword, type in the name and location, then click OK. Now choose Edit → Properties, and in the dialog box that opens, find the Keyword box. Type in *gg*—or whatever you'd like—and then click OK and close the Bookmark Manger.

3. **Run a search from the location bar by typing gg (or whatever) and your keywords.**

   Feel fancy.

You can also set up this location-bar trick to run Lucky searches, cache searches, and nearly anything else Google can do. For a few relevant Google URLs that you can cut and paste where you typed the URL in step 2 earlier, check out *www.google. com/mozilla/google-search.html.*

Bookmarklets

Google's browser buttons, described earlier in this chapter, are actually *bookmarklets*—tiny programs embedded in links that you store on your Favorites or Links toolbar. When you click one of them, it performs a certain task just like any button would. Bookmarklets are nifty because they add extra features to your browser, but take up virtually no room on your hard drive and are a snap to install.

For example, a bookmarklet can pop open a small window with a blank box that runs your search using Google, Yahoo, Dogpile, or any other search service out there. A bookmarklet can also add a liters-to-gallons conversion button to your toolbar, or a button that immediately tells you the number of days remaining in the year (good if your birthday is December 31).

Bookmarklets.com has a slew of handy tools, including a Google search box (*www. bookmarklets.com/tools/search/srchbook.phtml*). And SquareFree.com has a bunch of Google-specific tools at *http://squarefree.com/bookmarklets/seo.html.* To install any bookmarklet that catches your fancy, just drag it to your Links or Favorites toolbar.

Note: If you're the kind of JavaScript geek who thinks you might want to build your own bookmarklets, check out *www.webreference.com/js/column35/.* (If, on the other hand, you think JavaScript is a screenplay about coffee, stick with the prefab bookmarklets.)

SquareFree's bookmarklets include:

- **Google backlinks.** Replicates the *link* syntax (page 68) by showing pages linked to the current page. Keep in mind, though, that this trick works only if Google has given both the current page and the linked pages relatively high ranks. (If you want *every* page—regardless of popularity—try SquareFree's AllTheWeb backlinks bookmarklet, labeled "atw external backlinks.")

- **Google site search: all.** Gives you a list of all the pages on a single Web site. Most of the time, this is just a good way to count how many pages a site has, but on smaller sites, it may help you find things, too.

Tip: Many sites have related pages with varying URLs, like *www.conferences.oreilly.com* and *www.oreilly.com*. And most pages appear without your typing *www* first. Thus, if you want to see all the pages on a megasite like *oreilly.com*, leave out the *www* when you type the URL into the address bar; then, when you run the "all from site" bookmarklet, you also get listings from *conferences.oreilly.com, java.oreilly.com, perl.oreilly.com,* and a bunch of other geek-frequented sites.

- **Number google hits.** This bookmarklet numbers the individual listings on a Google results page, as shown in Figure 7-6. It's a quick way to find out how high a page ranks within a set of results, which is helpful for curiosity seekers and Webmasters checking out how their own pages fare on Google (page 212 has more on bookmarklets for Webmasters).

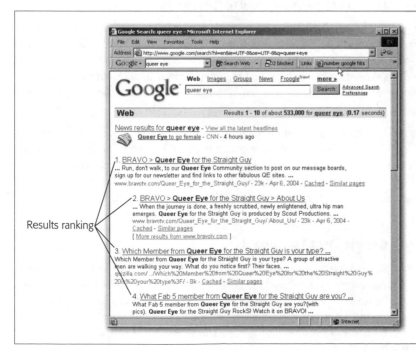

Figure 7-6:
To number your results, run a search and then click the bookmarklet. You have to repeat the process for each results page, but the bookmarklet accurately assesses which page of results you're on and begins with the correct number.

Google Desktop Search

If you've ever wished that Google could use its Web-searching superpowers to search the files on your *hard drive*, you might want to take a look at Google Desktop Search, another free program and a graduate of Google Labs (page 226).

Note: Mac mavens and Windows warriors using anything older than Windows 2000 with Service Pack 3 can skip this section. Google Desktop Search works only on Windows XP and Windows 2000 with the latest service pack installed.

But Mac OS X Tiger tamers have a little bit o' Google that's all their own: Google-themed Dashboard widgets. These playful little programs can do everything from streaming Internet radio to displaying the latest currency conversion rates. Among the ever-growing collection are widgets devoted to quickie Google Maps, Google Search, and even I'm Feeling Lucky results. You can fulfill all your widget whims at *www. apple.com/downloads/dashboard/*. (If you've got Tiger in your Mac, you don't need Google *Desktop* Search, as the system's Spotlight feature handles all your file search needs in a flash.)

With Google Desktop Search on the case, you can find all sorts of things buried on your computer, from Web pages you've seen to Word documents you've worked on to email messages you've sent or received. Google Search can also dig through conversations you had over AOL Instant Messenger and search for MP3 files based on the artist or album they came from. Desktop Search doesn't limit itself to looking for files by name or location, either—it can find files based on what's *inside* them, matching them up to the keywords or phrases you type into the Search box.

Say, for example, you dimly recall an email exchange a few years ago when you were passing roasted corn recipes and links to cooking sites back and forth with a friend—and you really want to find a message from that discussion again. All you have to do is type in *corn*, and Google Desktop Search looks high and low across your computer for any document, email message, or other file with the word "corn" inside (or in the title).

Desktop Search does this expert sleuthing by *indexing* the contents of your hard drive—scanning the contents of your documents and storing the information on its servers so it can quickly scan for matching results to your search terms. If you're nervous about having Google keep a copy of your info, check out their privacy info: *http://desktop.google.com/privacypolicy.html*. Still nervous? You may want to skip this Google goodie.

Installing Google Desktop Search

Windows 2000 and XP users can download a free copy of Google Desktop Search at *http://desktop.google.com*. When you first install the program, it takes some time to index all the files on your computers (Figure 7-7), but works quietly in the background so you don't have to stop what you're doing. You *will* need to close and re-open your email program after you install the program, though, so it can index your messages.

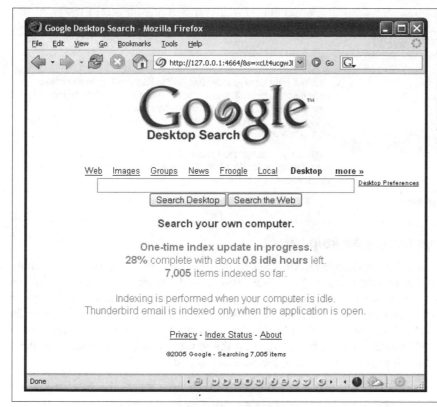

Figure 7-7:
After you first install the program, Google Desktop Search takes time to get to know your hard drive by making a record of its contents during the indexing procedure. The first indexing session is by far the slowest.

Google Desktop Search uses your computer's idle time to do its indexing and cache work, borrowing some processor power whenever the computer sits for more than 30 seconds without doing anything. The program can take anywhere between 15 minutes and several hours to index your whole drive, depending on the size of files, the number of files, and the time your PC has to spare. As you create and download new files later, Google Desktop Search makes note of them and adds them to the cache automatically.

Note: If you have any anti-spyware software like Webroot Spy Sweeper installed on your system, you may get an indignant warning about something trying to mess with your start-up programs. This alert is normal, as Google Desktop Search *does* install itself in your Startup folder.

Once your computer is fully indexed, you'll see a Desktop link above the Search box whenever you visit the Google home page; click that link to go searching through your computer's contents.

You can also use Desktop Search by entering keywords in the Desktop Search deskbar, down in the Windows taskbar area. As shown in Figure 7-8, the Search deskbar toggles back and forth so you can look for stuff on the desktop or on the Web from the same spot. If you select the More menu, you can switch to a groovy, ungrounded deskbar that hangs out on whatever part of your screen you want and floats around all your open windows.

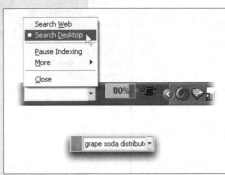

Figure 7-8:
Top: You can search your desktop (or the Web itself) from one of two convenient locations. If you like the grounded feeling of the taskbar, leave the Desktop Search box down where you can find it. Click the black triangle to see the menu of options. You can switch to a floating deskbar under the More menu.

Bottom: If you choose the floating desktop search bar, you can search your desktop or the Web from the wee window that floats about your open programs.

Using Google Desktop Search

You search with Google Desktop Search in the same way you search for anything else with a Google service: Type your terms into the Search box, and then hit the Enter key. When you search your desktop, however, you get results that show your highlighted terms along with the files' locations around your PC, so you can easily see what folder or drive the file lives in. (You may even find folders you forgot existed.) Google Desktop Search displays the results either by relevance or by date; click the link on the right side of the page to suit your fancy.

On the results page, there's an icon next to each item that tells you what kind of file it is. A musical note indicates it's a music file, an envelope means it's an email message, and so on. You'll also find familiar icons for Microsoft Office documents, Adobe PDF files, and America Online's little yellow running androgyne. Google Desktop Search displays thumbnail images of Web pages, digital photos, and other image files that wash up in the results, too, so you have a visual clue right there without opening the actual file. When you click a link on the results page, the file pops open.

Clicking the link for a Web page takes you right to it in your browser. If the current Web page is newer than the one you remember seeing in your surfing sessions, you can see an older version of the page by clicking the "cached" link in the last line of the result's description, as shown in Figure 7-9.

Clicking the title of a file—like a Word document or JPEG image—opens the most recent version of the file in the program you normally use to open such files. Old email messages show up on the results page with keywords highlighted within the text, and you have the option to open or reply to the original message in your regular email program with one click.

Tip: *If items show up in your desktop-search results that you'd rather not see at all, you can manually remove them from the Desktop Search cache. When you're on a page of results with items you don't want to see, click the Remove Items link at the top of the page next to the Search box. Turn on the checkboxes next to the results you don't want in the Desktop Search cache, and then click Remove Checked Items.*

Figure 7-9:
Not only do you get thumbnail images of Web pages and photos stored on your hard drive, but Desktop Search lets you go back in time to look at older cached versions of Web pages as well. The links at the top of the results page let you sort your results by type: emails, files, Web pages, or chats.

Setting the Desktop Search Preferences

You can fine-tune Google Desktop Search in its Preferences area (Figure 7-10), which you can get to by clicking the "Desktop Preferences" link next to the search box when you're using the program. Here, you can adjust seven different aspects of Desktop Search, including:

- **Search Types.** Tell Desktop Search what kinds of files you want to hunt for in your searches—and which you want to ignore. You can tell the program not to index AOL Instant Messenger chats, for example, if you don't want your online conversations with your buddies dredged up in the results page. You can also have the program not search for secure Web pages you may have used in the past, like ones where you had to fill out personal or confidential financial information.

- **Plug-ins.** Software developers have already taken a crack at enhancing Google Desktop Search with their own software *plug-ins*, little extras described in more detail in the box on page 220. You can add these features to the program to further its powers. Browse and install some of these helpful little tools here.

- **Don't Search These Items.** This preference lets you type in URLs or file paths to documents on your hard drive that you'd rather not have listed in your search results—like your tax forms or favorite online gambling sites.

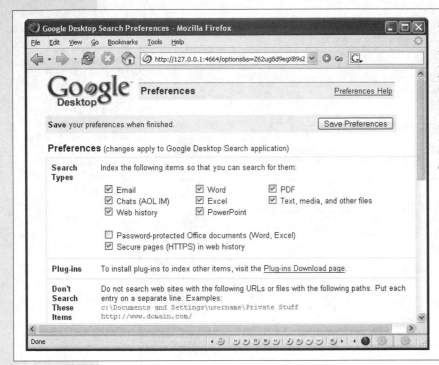

Figure 7-10:
*Tell Google Desktop
Search what kind of files
you do and don't want
indexed and cached in its
Desktop Preferences
area. You can do other
things here, too, like
adding plug-ins (page
220) and changing the
number of search results
per page.*

- **Search Box Display.** This is another place where you can opt for a floating or taskbar-anchored search box for your Desktop duties.

- **Number of Results.** If you hate clicking "Next Page" all the time as you wade through search results, you can change the number of results listed on a page from 10 to 20, 30, 50, or 100. Keep in mind that Desktop Search gets slower if you make the number higher that the original 10.

- **Google Integration.** If you get jumpy seeing pages with a mixture of your Desktop and Web results listed together, you can put a stop to it right here by turning off this box.

- **Help Us Improve.** Google would very much like it if you would allow anonymous reports to be sent from your computer to its headquarters, should you crash while using Desktop Search. If you're not willing to participate, you can turn off the crash reports here.

Note: Google Desktop Search is a complex and powerful program that has a deep and searchable Support area posted online for all to see. If you have a question, glitch, or problem with some part of the program, take a look at *http://desktop.google.com/support.* Answers to your questions may already be available.

A few words about privacy

Google's Desktop Search gives you the opportunity in the program's preference area to skip indexing certain types of documents and files. But many people (the ones not reading this book, for example) may not realize you can change this setting.

If you don't turn off certain kinds of searches, someone else could amble in, run a desktop search on your computer, and find all kinds of personal email messages and other documents you'd rather keep private. Or imagine if you used a public computer and didn't realize that Desktop Search was installed; it's possible someone could come along after you and call up personal email messages right out of the Desktop Search cache, no password needed at all.

Others may worry that Google uses the information it gleans from your computer's contents to serve up robot-generated advertising, like the text-only ads that can pepper the right side of Gmail messages (page 378). While you certainly see the text-based ads if you have Desktop Search set to mix in results from your computer alongside those from the Web at large, the company doesn't put ads on Desktop-only search results.

Google itself puts it this way: "We treat your privacy with the utmost respect. Google Desktop Search doesn't make your computer's content accessible to Google or anyone else. The application also offers privacy options such as not indexing password-protected Office files or secure (HTTPS) web pages."

If you want more specifics, Google's Desktop Search privacy policy is available to read online at *http://desktop.google.com/privacypolicy.html.*

If you're deeply worried about privacy in this increasingly indexed, connected, networked world of ours, either don't use Google Desktop Search on your computer or adjust its preferences to skip those private files and sites. And, if you're using someone else's computer, you can temporarily turn off Desktop Search while you use the machine, as the next section explains.

Note: Google Desktop Search is also available in an "enterprise" edition, meaning network and technology administrators can get a version that installs easily to all the connected PCs across the company network. That version is also free and is available at *http://desktop.google.com/enterprise/index.html.*

Disabling Google Desktop Search

If you like having Google Desktop Search around to help you track down *most* of your stuff, but don't want it to index *every little thing*, you can temporarily turn off the service—or shut it down altogether—without having to uninstall it from your computer. This can be helpful if, say, you want to pop over to a florist's Web site and order flowers for your beloved from the family computer without leaving a trail in the Desktop Search cache.

Plugging In to Desktop Search

Plug-ins are more powerful than most people think. In the case of Google Desktop Search, you can find plug-ins that let you index and search for file types not supported by the plain version of the program (the one that you get when you download it straight from the Web).

If you like Desktop Search but wish it could do things like find documents contained within *zip* archives, or index your Java source code files, you don't have to wish any longer. There's a page o' plug-ins posted right on the Google Desktop site at *http://desktop.google.com/plugins.html*.

There are dozens of plug-ins created by third-party developers here—most of them free. Among the offerings are plug-ins that add a Desktop Search bar to the Firefox browser window, one that lets you index other programs' chat logs, and a plug-in to search for information stored inside the text tags of AVI movie files.

If you're the type of person who writes your *own* programs, there are links to Google's software development kit here, too, along with a guide for developers. Sometimes, if you want something done right, you have to download the SDK and write out that code yourself.

To have Desktop Search stop indexing and caching everything in sight for the next 15 minutes, click the icon that looks like a rainbow pretzel in the Windows system tray, and then select Pause Indexing from the menu, as shown in Figure 7-11. (You can also get to this menu item by clicking the black triangle next to the anchored or floating deskbar on your screen.) When you get close to the end of the 15 minutes, a taskbar message balloon floats up and warns that you're down to your last minute before indexing and caching begin again.

Figure 7-11:
If you want to do some work without Google Desktop recording your every move, click its icon in the Windows system tray and select Pause Indexing for 15 minutes of unmonitored action.

If you get done with your secret mission before the 15 minutes are up, you can get Google Desktop indexing again by returning to the same taskbar menu and choosing "Resume Indexing." Need a bit more time? You can also select "Pause for 15 More Minutes."

Shutting down Google Desktop Search for the duration of your computer session is as easy as quitting any other program on your computer: just bop back to the taskbar menu and choose Exit. Quitting entirely out of Desktop Search means no indexing, caching, or searching the PC, however.

You can then turn Desktop Search back on in two different ways:

- Chose Start → Programs → Google Desktop Search → Google Desktop Search.

- Restart the computer; Google Desktop Search kicks back on when you reboot.

If you decide that you don't want Google Desktop Search in your life after all, uninstall the software by choosing Start → Programs → Google Desktop Search → Uninstall Google Desktop Search.

Google Deskbar

The Google deskbar, a search box that sits at the bottom of your Windows desktop, as shown in Figure 7-12, may not immediately appear useful. Why not just run searches from the toolbar in your browser?

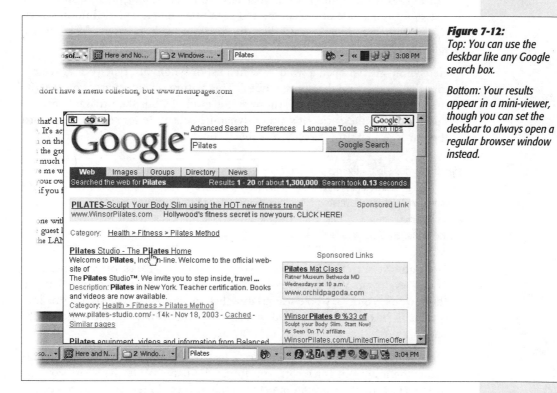

Figure 7-12:
Top: You can use the deskbar like any Google search box.

Bottom: Your results appear in a mini-viewer, though you can set the deskbar to always open a regular browser window instead.

It turns out there are *tons* of reasons to use the deskbar. Once you've tried it, you'll be hooked.

But before you read up on the many things the deskbar can do, you should know that it runs only in Windows 98, ME, 2000, and XP (though it runs in any Web browser on these systems). Unfortunately, if you're a foot soldier in the Linux or Mac armies, you can't add this weapon to your search arsenal.

Note: If you're a Linux or Mac jockey and you're wondering why Google discriminates against you all the time, understand this: According to Google, only about three percent of the computers used to reach Google are Macs, and a mere one percent are Linux machines. (For more fun facts, check *www.google. com/press/zeitgeist.html.*)

For the nearly 90 percent of computer users whose systems can run the deskbar, here's just a smattering of the excellent things you can use it for. And you can do all of it *without even opening your browser* (although you must be online):

- **Calculate things.** Like any blank Google search box, you can use the deskbar as a calculator (see page 38 for more on Google's calculator function).

- **Look up definitions.** The definition feature is particularly nice when you're reading a Web page and don't want to leave it in order to look something up. Type any term into the blank search box, press Ctrl+D, and a small window slides open with definitions. Alternatively, you can type *define:septentrion* (no spaces on either side of the colon) and then press Enter. The definition search works with individual words (like *thymine*) or with phrases (*"open source software"*).

- **Get synonyms.** To open a window with a list of synonyms, type your keywords into the deskbar and then press Ctrl+T. This feature is handy when you're writing an email and you need a synonym, for example, but the program you use doesn't have a thesaurus. It's also a dynamite substitute for the anemic Word thesaurus. And it's not directly available through any other Google search box.

Tip: If you don't install the deskbar, you can get synonyms with a little clicking around. You can run a regular Google search and then click the term as it appears in the blue bar above your results to get the Dictionary.com definition—where you can then click to get the term's thesaurus listing. Or, from the Google toolbar, you can type in your terms, click the arrow to the right of the Search Web button, and then choose Dictionary. When you land at the Dictionary.com page, switch to the thesaurus listing.

- **Do a quickie search.** When you're working in Word, Excel, or any other program—even your Web browser—and you want to look up something that you think won't require a whole search-and-click mission, just type your terms into the blank box, press Enter, and you're rewarded with a mini Google results page.

  For example, if you aren't properly caffeinated, and while working on a report about the history of Microsoft, you forget the name of its chairman, you can just type *Microsoft chairman* into the deskbar, press Enter, and you've got Bill Gates's name without having even to approach your browser.

- **Jump to a Web page.** Normally, when you're working in some program *other* than your browser and you want to open a Web page, you have to first open or click over to the browser, and then type the URL. Save yourself a whole click by typing a URL directly into the deskbar, which then opens your Web page in the full browser.

Installing the Deskbar

You can find the deskbar at *http://toolbar.google.com/deskbar/*. All you have to do to get it on your computer is click Download Google Deskbar and then choose

Open or Save. If you choose Open, an installation wizard opens directly. If you choose Save, the installer downloads to your hard drive, and then a dialog box pops up asking if you want to open the file; choose Open to bring up the installation wizard.

The wizard asks if you agree to Google's terms of use (say yes, or else you can't install the deskbar), and then it asks if you want to send feedback statistics to Google about the way you use the toolbar. The screen explains what information Google does and doesn't collect. Leaving the setting on (or not) is your choice—the deskbar works the same either way. Finally, it instructs you to right-click in your Windows taskbar (the band at the bottom of the screen) and choose Toolbars → Google Deskbar. That's it.

If you feel like it, you can make the deskbar wider or narrower. Just mouse over the vertical bar to the left of the search box, and when it becomes a two-headed arrow, drag it left or right. (If no two-headed arrow appears, right-click the taskbar and make sure "Lock the Taskbar" is turned off.) If you move the bar all the way left, it drops down and forms a whole new row on the taskbar, which gives your other buttons more breathing room on the regular taskbar.

Tip: Even better, you can move the application buttons below by dragging the bar to *their* left downward, giving these buttons space to spread out and making the deskbar more prominent (as in Figure 7-13). It's worth 60 seconds of your life to rearrange the taskbar elements until you find a system that work best for you.

Searching via the Deskbar

The most obvious way get to the deskbar is to click in it and start typing. But the *fastest* way to get there is via the keyboard shortcut: Ctrl+Alt+G. You can also search from the deskbar using any of the following methods:

- Highlight text in any program and drag it to the deskbar; the deskbar automatically runs the search.

- Put something on the clipboard (Ctrl+C to copy, or Ctrl+X to cut) and then press Ctrl+Alt+G. Your clipped text appears in the search box, but the deskbar doesn't automatically run a search; press Enter to trigger it.

- Type or drag a URL into the deskbar to launch a full browser window for that page.

Tip: When you place the cursor in the blank deskbar, you can press the up or down arrow to get an alphabetical history of searches you've performed there. Select one to run that search again.

In addition to running standard Google searches, the deskbar lets you do a bunch of other nifty stuff—like getting definitions and stock quotes—all from the arrow button on the right end of the search box, just to the right of the googly-eyed button. Figure 7-13 shows the menu you get when you click the arrow.

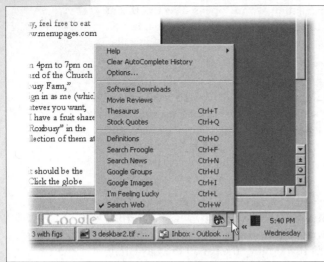

Figure 7-13:
You can use this button to get at movie reviews, software downloads, and a slew of Google's alternative searches, like News and Groups. But for the searches you perform regularly, the keyboard shortcuts are a lot faster.

Most of the time, when you perform a search using the deskbar, your results appear in what Google calls the *mini-viewer* (Figure 7-12, bottom).

Tip: Shift+F1 opens and closes the mini-viewer.

This small window is a big boon because it lets you run searches with your browser closed, which saves memory, screen space, and general clicking. You can surf around in the viewer as you would in a regular browser window; when you click outside the window, it slides shut.

Note: The deskbar actually *launches* your browser in two cases. First, if you type a URL into the search box and press Enter, the deskbar automatically opens the page in your browser. Second, if you want to see your mini-viewer results on the big screen, click the arrow in the upper-left corner of the mini-screen to pop open your browser.

Customizing the Deskbar

If you couldn't change a bunch of settings, most software would be about as much fun as a box of gray crayons. Happily, the Google Deskbar is flexible. For example, you can change the font size of the mini-viewer's display, add your own custom searches, and change the way the mini-viewer appears and disappears.

To reach the settings window shown in Figure 7-14, right-click the googly-eyed button on the right end of the deskbar, and then choose Google Deskbar Options.

Most of the options are self-explanatory, but here are a few you might not expect:

- **Turn the reporting feature on or off.** If you change your mind about whether you want to send Google information about how you use the deskbar (which you decided when you installed it), head to the General tab, where you can change the setting.

Figure 7-14:
The deskbar settings window has four tabs, each of which lets you adjust the behavior of a few settings.

- **Change the Google country site the deskbar uses for searches.** This is handy if you find yourself in Azerbaijan, for example, and you want to do as the Azerbaijanis do. On the General tab, choose *www.google.az* from the "Preferred Google site" menu.

- **Make the viewer stay open when you click outside it.** If you want to keep an eye on your results while you're working in another program, click the Mini-Viewer tab and then turn off "Automatically close mini-viewer when you leave it." (If you leave this setting on, the viewer will slide shut when you click out of it.)

- **Get the mini-viewer out of your sight.** If the mini-viewer annoys you and you'd prefer to view your deskbar results in a new browser window, open the Mini-Viewer tab and turn off "Display search results in mini-viewer."

- **View help, FAQs, privacy info, deskbar discussions, or links to places where you can tell Google what you think about the deskbar.** Click the About Google Deskbar tab, and then choose the link you want.

The Customized Searches tab sounds straightforward, but requires some explanation. Google has a handful of special search types already set up: stock quotes, a thesaurus, movie reviews, and software downloads. Each custom search runs your query on a particular Web site (movie reviews, for example, run your search on RottenTomatoes.com). Most specialized searches have a keyboard shortcut, too (Ctrl+T to search an online thesaurus, for instance), and they all get a listing in the deskbar menu (click the arrow on the right end of the search box).

Customized Searches lets you change the existing searches or add new ones. You might want to change one if, say, you prefer a stock-quote service other than Google's. Or you might want to add one if there's a site you search often (like AltaVista or your company's intranet), and you want to be able to reach it from the deskbar.

Here's the hard part: You have to know the URL for the search you want to add. Unfortunately, that doesn't mean the URL for the *site* in question but the *string that runs a search* on that site. For example, the stock-quote URL is *http://www.google. com/search?q=stocks:{1}*, and the movie-review URL is *http://www.rottentomatoes. com/search/movie.php?searchby=movies&search={1}*. Worse, Web sites all use different systems for creating that search URL. If you aren't a Webmaster and you don't know the search URL for a site you'd like to add, your only hope is to play around and try to hit on the right string.

Once you have the URL you need, head to Customize Searches, and click Edit to change an existing search or Add to create a new one. If you're editing a search, all you have to do is replace the existing URL and then click OK twice. If you're adding a new one, you need to name it and then add the URL. You can also try assigning a keyboard shortcut to your new search, but Google only gives you the option to use Ctrl plus one other key, and, frustratingly, most Ctrl+key combinations are already taken. Click OK twice to finish. To use your new search, type some keywords into the deskbar, click the arrow button on the right to get a menu of options, and then choose your special search from the list.

A Deskbar You Can Hack

Before the Google deskbar, there was Dave's Quick Search Deskbar. The two tools look and act remarkably alike, but Dave's has a handful of features Google's doesn't, and— geeks take note—Dave's is open source, so you can add your own features or tweak existing ones. (If hacking the tool appeals to you, bear in mind that its underlying code is in JavaScript and HTML, with a smidgen of C in the mix, too.)

Here are a few of the clever tricks Dave's deskbar performs:

- **It lets you run searches not just for Google,** but for 140 different Web sites, including Yahoo, Amazon, eBay, the Internet Movie Database (IMDB), and a herd of other search engines.

- **It has a wizard** that guides you through setting up your own custom searches. Dave suggests using a custom search for your company's intranet, although you can use one to automatically search any Web sites you'd like.

- **The blank search box isn't actually blank—** instead, it displays the date and time, so you can hide your system clock and save some valuable screen space.

Dave's deskbar works with Windows 95 or later and Internet Explorer 5.5 or later; you can't install it from any other browser. Check it out at *http://www.dqsd.net/*.

Experimental Google Tools

A lot of people think Google never changes. The home page has looked the same for several years, for example, and the results pages have maintained the same layout for about as long.

On the contrary, according to Google engineers, Google changes all the time. The way Google determines relevance (discussed on page 4) shifts from time to time, improving the quality of your results almost imperceptibly. In addition, Google is always trying out new ways to let you search for and glean information. The company's playground is called Google Labs (*http://labs.google.com/*), and the features on it sometimes become regular offerings.

Any feature posted on Google Labs is free for you to play with. You can even tell Google's engineers whether you like it or not, and why. Some of the toys are terrific (the Definitions search [page 38] is so great, it's now part of the regular site), and some are just kind of weird. For example, there's a voice search feature that lets you make a toll call to Google to tell it your search terms—but you have to go online to get your results, making it useful only when you're surfing on a cellphone (and even then it's limited; see *http://labs1.google.com/gvs.html* for more info). The ones that prove unpopular—or so popular they crash the Google servers—are sometimes discontinued without warning, so it's a good idea not to get too attached to anything you find in the Labs.

That said, the experimental tools can be useful, and if you like one of them, it's worth letting Google know if, say, RideFinder (page 65) saves your bacon one night when you really need to get to the airport on short notice. This section covers a couple of the handier search tools; other good ideas from the Labs are discussed elsewhere in the book (for example, News Alerts, a system that emails you when news breaks on topics you choose, is discussed in the "Google News" section on page 90).

Personalized Search

Google works hard to deliver highly relevant search results. But, of course, sometimes Google guesses wrong because what's relevant to Jane Searcher may not be relevant to you. To help it find pages that are more likely to be of interest to you, try Google's Personalized Web search.

Google Personalized (*http://labs.google.com/personalized*) lets you tell Google what topics generally interest you. Then, when you run a search, Google displays the regular results but gives you the choice of seeing them rearranged according to your preset preferences. Figure 7-15 has an example.

Note: To use Google Personalized, you can be on any operating system, but you need Internet Explorer 5 or later, Netscape 5 or later, Mozilla 1.4 or later, or Firefox .8 or later. Make sure you have both JavaScript and cookies turned on (check your browser settings). And run your search in English, from a browser set to use English.

To set your topics, head to *http://labs.google.com/personalized* and click Create Profile. Click any of the categories to get a list of subcategories you can designate (Figure 7-16).

Bonus Note: Personalized results appear on the first page of listings only, which means you're limited to ten just-for-you results.

Figure 7-15:
Top: When you run a search in Google Personalized, it first displays the same results you'd see by running a regular Google search. But in the upper-left corner of the screen, if you drag the slider to the right, Google brings to the top of the list any results that match your topics of interest.

Bottom: Here, the topic Publishing & Printing brought up the top two listings. You can tell which results are personalized because Google marks them with three colored balls.

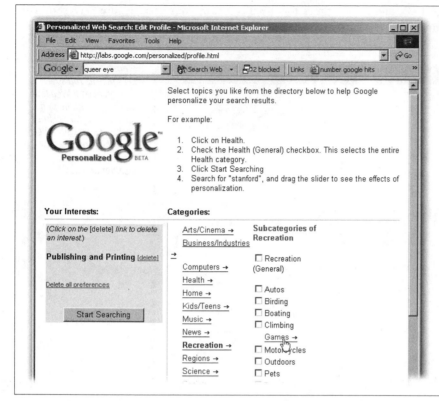

Figure 7-16:
*Turn on subcategories
that interest you. You can
select as many as you
want in every category
that intrigues you. If you
want to select an entire
category, click the
General choice (for
example, "Recreation
[General].")*

When you're done adding categories, click Start Searching. If you want to add or
delete categories at any time, just click Edit Profile from any Google Personalized
page. The list on the left lets you remove existing categories; the list on the right is
the same one you saw when you first set up your categories, and you can dive back
into it for additional choices.

Personalize Your Homepage

When Google first crashed the search engine party back in the 1998, many people
noticed how *plain* its home page was, especially in the era of Day-Glo background
colors, flashing banner ads, and the screeching jumble of links that adorned most
of the competition's portal pages. For many years, the simple white background
and search box remained just the way they'd always been whenever you hit up
Google for some information.

While it hasn't gone whole hog in tarting up the old home page, Google is experi-
menting with letting *you* add a few helpful elements yourself. With its Personalize
Your Homepage tool in Google Labs, you can customize the standard Google
search page to your liking by adding things like stock tickers, weather reports, and
news headlines from a variety of sources. You can also add helpful shortcuts, like a
preview of your Gmail Inbox (page 384), driving directions from Google Maps

(page 103), and movie times for the theaters in your area. Figure 7-17 shows an example of what a personalized Google page looks like.

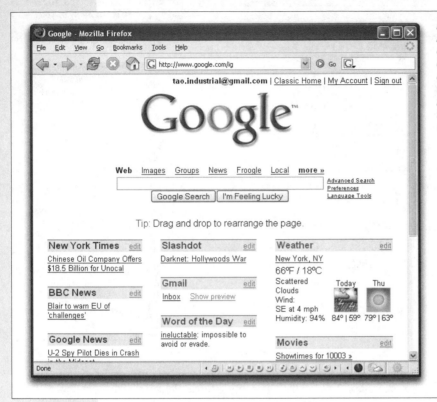

Figure 7-17:
Let's face it: You spend enough of your Web time on Google's home page, anyway, so you might as well jazz it up with other helpful information like the latest news and weather updates.

To personalize your page, you need just a few things, including a Google Account (you can use your Gmail, Google Groups, or Froogle Shopping List user name and password here) and the most up-to-date version of your favorite Web browser for Windows, Mac OS X, or Linux. Then you need to surf on over to *www.google.com/ig* and click the link in the upper-left corner marked Add Content.

The next screen lets you click various buttons to add content to your home page: a preview of your waiting Gmail messages, tidbits from Google News, Quotes of the Day, and so on. If you want the weather in your area, click the "edit" link in the Weather box and fill in your Zip code. When you've picked what you want, click the "close" button.

Tip: You can add headlines from *another* Web site to your Google home page, provided that other site has what's known as an *RSS feed*. (An RSS feed—like *feed://www.nytimes.com/services/xml/rss/nyt/ HomePage.xml*—provides a summary of all the headlines on a site.) If you know the address of an RSS feed for your favorite site, simply type it in the Create a Section box to add its headlines to your Google home page.

If you're not logged in to a Google service, you'll get pestered to sign in with your Google Account name and password. If you don't have an account, you're presented with a link to join up right there. Once you're signed up, signed in, and set to go, Google presents you with your customized creation.

You can rearrange the elements on the page by dragging and dropping them into an order that suits you. For example, if you always want the weather forecast and stock report right up front where you can see them, hover the mouse cursor over the section title until it turns into a cross, and then drag the weather box or stock section to the part of the page where you'd like to see it each time you visit Google.

You still have your beloved Google search box on the top half of the page now, but the lower half holds all your additions and customizations. (If you ever want to return to the plain-old Google home page, sans any of your decorations, click Classic Home in the upper-right corner.)

When you get the page *just so* and want to see it every time you're in Google mode, just paste its URL into the area of your browser's options or preferences where you tell it your home page.

Tip: Click the Edit link next to any section head on your personalized page to get in there and adjust your settings. You might need to temporarily tweak your settings if you're traveling, for example, and want the weather for your current location instead of the forecast for back home.

If you're on the road and away from your usual computer, you can still get to your custom page by popping over to *www.google.com/ig* and typing in your Google name and password. If you're using somebody else's computer, though, make sure you sign out of your Google account before you take off, since the next person who comes along to Google something will get an eyeful of your personalized page—including your stock tickers and Gmail message previews. Unless you feel like sharing with the rest of the class, then, click the Sign Out link at the top of the page before you leave.

My Search History

Have you ever spent some quality time with Google and found exactly what you were looking for—but then forgotten how you got there? Or moved to a different computer—in school, at a library, or at work—only to find your list of previous searches gone forever?

If either of these scenarios sounds frustrating and familiar, you may want to check out the My Search History experiment going on in Google Labs. With My Search History, Google keeps track of where you went and what you looked at. If you don't remember which keywords you used in a past search—but you know roughly when you did the query—you can find the searches you performed on a certain date and time.

My Search History is yet another Google service for which you need a user name and password, though. You can sign up by clicking the "Create a Google Account" link right on the page at *www.google.com/searchhistory*—or, if you have a previous Google account (Gmail, Froogle Shopping List, or Google Groups), you can simply log in with that.

Note: My Search History needs JavaScript enabled in order to work. This isn't a problem for most browsers created in the past five years or so, but you'll need at least Internet Explorer 4.0, Netscape 6, Opera 7, or Safari 1.2. Firefox and Mozilla should work like a charm.

Using your search history

In order for Google to track and store your Web wanderings, you need to be logged in to your Google account (if you don't see your email address in black at the top of the page, you're not signed in). If you're not logged in, click the Sign In link at the top of the Google home page.

After you've signed in, you can search with abandon, just like you normally do, but with the comforting knowledge that Google is quietly logging and compiling your searches as you go. (This is another one of those Google services that privacy advocates probably want to avoid.)

If you need to go back and look up something you saw earlier, click the Search History link at the top of the Google home page to see an organized list of all your searches—compiled by the keywords you originally used. As shown in Figure 7-18, the Search History displays the links to Web pages you visited during that search adventure, along with the date and time you visited. Click the links in the Search History list to revisit the sites. There's even a calendar on the right side that you can use to click back in time.

Note: If you don't see the Search History link at the top of the Google page, you probably need to log in to your account. Click the "Sign in" link at the top of the Google home page, or go to *www.google.com/ searchhistory*.

Thanks to your Google account creation, your search history is stored on a server somewhere in Googleland, which means you can get to it from different computers. Simply sign in to your Google account from the home page, and then click Search History to pop into your search past.

If you decide that you don't want to use the Search History after all, you can zap the whole thing. Sign in to your Google account by clicking the "Sign in" link on the home page (or at *www.google.com/searchhistory*). Click the My Account button at the top of the page. On the list of Google services on the next screen, click Delete Personalized Search to permanently discontinue the search.

Figure 7-18:
*Clicking the My Search
History link on the
Google home page takes
you back in time to
searches you've
previously run, with the
links you once clicked
through organized by
original keywords. The
calendar on the right side
of the page lets you jump
around by day of search.*

Note: Going through with this deletion has the side effect of deleting your *Personalized Search* preferences (page 227) as well. Unfortunately, there's no way to delete your Search History without also deleting your Personalized Search settings, and vice versa.

If you *do* go through with the deletion, however, you can always restart your Personalized Search and Search History by going to *www.google.com/accounts* and clicking Personalized Search (under Try New Services).

Removing specific searches from the history

There may be times when you don't want every little search you've ever made saved, like if you're shopping for a birthday present or pricing a surprise vacation, and don't want your spouse to find out.

Luckily, forgetting the past is just as easy as remembering it with My Search History. Click the link to go to your Search History page if you're not on it, and then click the "Remove items" link underneath the calendar. This puts you into a page-editing mode where you turn on the checkmarks next to items you'd rather not save, and use the Remove button at the top of the column to wipe them out with one click. If you're in a real house-cleaning mood, click All to select everything on your history page and then click the Remove button.

Tip: If you're doing some surreptitious searching and want to *temporarily* turn off the search tracking, click the Pause link in the blue bar towards the top of your Search History page. When you're ready to record again, return to the page and click Resume.

Google Suggest

In these times of repetitive stress injuries and carpal tunnel syndrome, anything that saves a few keystrokes is a helpful, healthy thing. Google Suggest (as its name, er, suggests), is a Google Labs creation that pays attention to the keywords you start to type and tries to finish them for you, too (Figure 7-19).

Figure 7-19:
Google Suggest tries to guess what you're typing as you type it and unfurls a list of possibilities based on the letters you've entered. For extra speed, leave the mouse behind and shoot up and down the list with the directional arrow keys on the keyboard. (There's a Japanese version as well.)

You can find the Google Suggest page at *www.google.com/webhp?complete=1&hl=en.* If you like it and want to make it your official Web browser starting page, cut and paste the URL into your browser's settings. (In Internet Explorer, choose Tools → Internet Options and then paste the address into the box in the Home Page area; most other Web browsers keep the settings in a similar place.)

Say you start by typing *rabb* in the search box. Google suggests everything from *rabbit* to *rabbie burns* to help you out. If you see your term on the list, tap the keyboard's down arrow key to select it, and then hit Enter to start the search.

Google Suggest uses an algorithm to anticipate the phrase you're typing, but says it doesn't use your personal searching history as part of the formula. Instead, it bases its predictions on the huge pile of data it gathers from everybody using Google, and uses the popularity of those other searches to whittle down its suggestions for you.

Note: To use Google Suggest, you must have JavaScript and cookies turned on in your browser's settings. And speaking of browsers, you need to be surfing on Internet Explorer 6.0 (or later) for Windows, or Safarai 1.2.2 (or later) for Mac OS X. You can also get by if you at least have Netscape 7.1, Firefox 0.8, Mozilla 1.4, or Opera 7.5.4 on your favorite operating system.

To work its suggestive magic, Google Suggest has to keep tabs on what you're typing as you type it. Privacy-minded individuals may get a little creeped out, as Google Suggest communicates with the mother ship before the keywords are even halfway entered, but the company claims it doesn't use your personal information for nefarious purposes without your consent. (You can read the company's privacy policy at *www.google.com/privacy.html.*)

Google Video

When Google first started tinkering around with video in 2005, there wasn't so much to look at—mainly screenshots and short text descriptions of the video pictured. The feature didn't get a lot of attention because most people expect their moving pictures to actually *move*.

Fast-forward to today, and Google Video is going like gangbusters. It's the company's online marketplace for selling digitized recordings of TV shows, music videos, movies, NBA basketball games, and (most important) *Rocky and Bullwinkle* cartoons, each for a few bucks.

But there's a lot of free, searchable stuff to see, too, from Super Bowl commercials to videos by future rock stars. Plus, Google offers everyone from indie filmmakers to regular camcorder-totin' folks an open invitation to submit their video productions to the site, no matter the running time. Who needs a movie studio to distribute your digital film when you've got Google?

Using Google Video

With Google Video, you can watch the goods right on the Web (via your browser), or through Google's own video-player software, or in certain cases, on a pocket media player like the Sony PlayStation Portable or Apple's video iPod.

Note: For some videos, Google lets you watch or buy them *only* through the Google Video Player (page 237). The player is a free, downloadable piece of software that, unfortunately for the Apple Corps, works only with Windows at the moment. (Check back periodically for a Mac version.)

To try out Google Video, head to *http://google.video.com.* When you land in Google's video emporium, you see a screen full of thumbnail images, each representing a particular clip or show. If you see an image with the familiar tape-deck Play triangle button in the corner, you can play the video right there; simply click the picture to jump to a page where the video starts automatically, running right in your Web browser with no extra effort from you. (If the video is for sale, a clip plays.) If you see an image that *doesn't* have the Play button, you can click the picture to get more options in that category.

When you click a thumbnail image and go to a video's page, the panel on the right side gives you information about where the video came from, when it was made, and the running time. Clickable buttons (Figure 7-20) tell you what exactly you can do with this video (besides just watching it through your browser):

- **Download** means the video is free and you can pipe your own copy of it down to your computer to play with the Google Video Player (see the next page) or, depending on the file, to your Mac, your video iPod, or your Sony PSP.

- **Day Pass** means you can pay a small fee to download the video and watch it with the Google Video Player anytime within 24 hours from your purchase—before the file stops working, sort of like a Blockbuster rental that goes *poof!*

- **Buy** means you can pay for it, download it, and keep it around on your PC to play. Prices to buy a show or get a day pass vary widely. Most TV reruns cost about $2 to buy, while some sporting events can cost around $15; day passes average about a buck or three. You need Windows and a Google Account (page 118) to buy video.

Figure 7-20:
After you click a video's thumbnail, Google takes you to a window where you can play that video onscreen and, in some cases, download it to the computer or potable device. Information about the video is listed on the right side of the screen.

Note: One thing to note on copy-protected shows you may buy from the Google Video Store: You have to be *online* to play them, so Google can check the playback and make sure everything's Copyright Kosher. This little sticking point really stinks if you want to watch your purchases off the grid on a plane, train, or bus.

Watching via your Web browser

If you want to watch free Google Video, your Web browser needs to meet a few specific system requirements. As far as operating systems go, Windows 2000 or later, and Mac OS X 10.3 (codenamed Panther) or later will get you into Google's screening room.

You have your choice of browsers, as long as they are *at least* Internet Explorer 5.0, Safari 1.0, or Firefox 1.1 You also need to add the Adobe Macromedia Flash player plug-in to your browser, available free at *www.adobe.com*. And lastly, for smooth playback that won't have you reaching for the Dramamine from all the jerky stop-startiness of the picture, you want a broadband Internet connection.

Watching with the Google Video Player

As mentioned earlier, some of the copy-protected video downloads you get from Google can be played *only* with the Google Video Player software. You may be prompted to download the player when you try to get a video, but you can also download it from a link at the top of the main Google Video page. The Google Video Player, for the moment, only works with Windows, and you need a PC with at least an Intel Pentium III 1-gigaherz processor (or its AMD equivalent), 128 megabytes of regular memory, and 16 megabytes of video memory.

With the Google Video Player, you can watch your vid in full-screen mode, skip over the boring stuff to get to the good parts, and browse the different scenes in the video with the built-in thumbnail pictures, sort of like DVD chapter-mark scenes.

Watching Google Video on portable devices

You can download some of the videos in the Google store to your computer and then shuttle them over to an Apple video iPod or Sony PSP for watching on the go. Look for a pop-up menu next to a video's Download button. If there's a portable version available, there'll be a "Sony PSP" or "Video iPod" option to select in the list (Figure 7-20).

Once you download the file to your computer, you can copy it to your portable player just like any other video clip you've added:

• For the iPod, add the file to the iTunes library and copy it to the iPod from there.

• For the PSP, rename the video file to MAQ*XXXX*.MP4 (where the *X*s are numbers from 0 to 9), and then copy the renamed file to the *MP_ROOT*\\ *101ANV01* folder on the PSP's Memory Stick.

If you're having trouble finding portable video in the first place, use the Search bar at the top of the page to seek out *video iPod* or *Sony PSP*.

Uploading your own video

Want to show or sell your own fabulous video works to the Google Video Store? Point your browser to *https://upload.video.google.com* and follow the instructions onscreen. If you want to charge people to see it, though, Google takes a cut.

If your submitted flick passes Google's inspection—which mostly means making sure you're not trying to post porn or somebody else's copyrighted stuff—your handicam work is posted and hosted online where millions of people could potentially see it. Take *that*, Hollywood establishment!

Tip: For further info on Google's Video store, visit *http://video.google.com/support*.

Google Web Accelerator

Even with broadband connections like DSL and cable modems, there's still a need for speed among many Web surfers. Google's Web Accelerator software—still in the beta testing stage as of this writing—aims to kick things up a notch; install it, and your Web pages download faster, courtesy of Google Labs technology.

Google relies on a number of different processes to pump those pages through the pipe faster. Google Web Accelerator has its own express lane into Google's servers, for example, and it stores its own copies of popular pages and makes them available more quickly. It can also prefetch (page 197) some pages to your PC ahead of time, anticipating that you'll click down a list of search results and want to see them.

In cases where not much on a Web page has changed since you looked at it last, Web Accelerator only grabs the *newest* stuff on the page and doesn't bother to make you wait for downloads of the parts you already have in your browser's cache. To squeeze more data into less bandwidth, the program compresses data before it sends it down to your computer, too.

Google Web Accelerator was designed with broadband connections in mind, however, so dial-up users with visions of shorter wait times will have to keep on waiting. The program was also created for use on Windows XP—or, at the very minimum, Windows 2000 with Service Pack 3 installed.

Note: Google Web Accelerator is optimized for Internet Explorer 5.5 and later, as well as Firefox 1.0 and later, but you can get it to work with other Windows Web browsers with a little finessing. Change your HTTP proxy settings to 127.0.0.1:9100 to accelerate Opera, Mozilla, or another browser.

Like a number of other Google services, this one has some privacy implications, because your Web surfing is no longer between you and the other site, but you, the

---

other site, and Google. If that bothers you, maybe you want to stay in the right lane on the Web.

Running Google Web Accelerator

Like many of its experimental products, Google Web Accelerator is in the beta testing stage as of this writing, so the software may still have a few bugs to work out. It lives at *http://webaccelerator.google.com*, and you can download it for free.

After you download and install the program, a little speedometer icon appears both at the top of your Web browser's window and down in your Windows system tray. When you go to a Web page that's Google-boosted, the speedometer spins around, and the amount of time you've just saved gets added to a running total, as shown at the top of the browser window in Figure 7-21. Click the number to see a chart of your time saved. (On this page, you can also click to reset the time-saved counter back to zero.)

Note: Security being security, Google Web Accelerator doesn't speed up encrypted pages with *https://* addresses, so your online banking, stock trading, and shopping won't be any faster.

If you click the speedometer icon itself (Figure 7-21), you get a menu of things to do with your Accelerator, including a preferences area that lets you tell the program the speed of your Internet connection, or instruct it to skip acceleration on specified sites. Your preferences for hauling down Web pages in advance are here (to prefetch or not to prefetch, for example [page 197]), as well as settings for your browser's history files and how frequently Google checks for new versions of pages already in its cache.

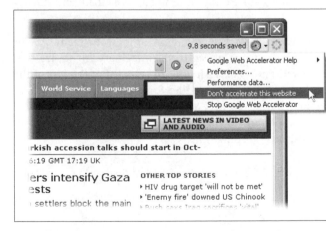

Figure 7-21:
With Google Web Accelerator installed, your browser gets a counter showing how much time you've saved since you hit the Accelerator (or hit the reset button). Click the speedometer icon to pull up the menu of Web Accelerator preferences and options.

For those pages you don't want to run through the Accelerator, there are a couple options. The Accelerator menu includes a "Don't accelerate this website" option, as well as an option to just turn off the acceleration altogether. If you opt to stop, the speedometer icon down in the system tray takes a break, and you can only restart the Accelerator from the icon on the browser window (unless you've booted the icon off your IE window; in that case, restore it to its rightful place by selecting it from the Toolbars menu).

Some people enjoy having pages popping up faster than before and will feel far more efficient as the time-saved counter continues to climb. If you decide, however, that Web Accelerator isn't doing all that much for you (or those privacy concerns are making you jumpy), you can uninstall Google Web Accelerator in the same place you go to uninstall other programs: Start → Control Panel → Add/ Remove Programs.

Google Sets

Google Sets is easily the experimental feature with the least revealing name. You half expect to hear Marv Albert yelling, "Google sets…he shoots…he scores!" But in fact, this feature performs a handy which-of-these-things-is-just-like-some-others search. For any set of related items you type, Google Sets tries to come up with a list of related search terms.

Here's how it works. Head over to *http://labs.google.com/sets*, shown in Figure 7-22. Fill in anywhere from one to five terms that all seem somehow related to you (try months of the year or soft-drink names, for example). Then press Enter or click Large Set or Small Set to find out what matches Google gives you.

Note: Sometimes, it takes a while—a full eight seconds or more—before Google pulls up Sets results.

Google Sets is quirky. If you search for *Yankees*, *Mets*, *Cardinals* and *Red Sox*, for example, it gives you a list of Major League Baseball teams—and a bunch of odd-ball teams, like the Skipjacks, plus a smattering of football, basketball, and hockey teams.

Still, Google Sets can be a nifty way to find related items or jog your memory. For example, if you can't remember the name of Big Bird's imaginary friend, try typing in *Big Bird*, *Oscar the Grouch*, and *Cookie Monster* to get a list of the rest of the Muppets (and people) on Sesame Street—including Snuffleupagus. Or if you're wondering who Seinfeld's neighbors were, try *Jerry*, *George*, and *Elaine*, to have Google finish the list with Kramer and Newman. To get a list of major cities, you need know only London, Paris, and Washington.

Tip: For more ideas, check the examples at the bottom of the Sets main page, and be sure to click through the link labeled "more."

Google Wireless

As the Zen maxim goes, "Wherever you go, there you are." Thankfully, so too is Google. Just because you've left your laptop at home doesn't mean you've forfeited

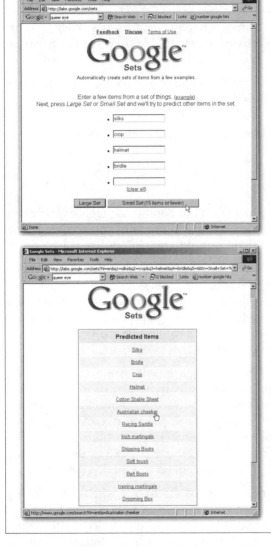

Figure 7-22:
Top: Type in anywhere from one to five terms. The more you give Google, the more focused your results.

Bottom: If you click one of the predicted results, Google runs a regular search for that term.

your basic right to Google—as long as you've got a cellphone or PDA purchased within the past few years with you.

Google Wireless (*www.google.com/wireless/guide.html*) provides mobile access to the full power of Google right from the PDA in your palm, the BlackBerry on your belt, or the cellphone in your pocket. Settle that "in like Flynn" versus "in like Flint" dinner-table argument without leaving your seat. Find quickie reviews and commentary on that Dustmeister 2000 vacuum *before* making the purchase. Figure out where you've seen that bit-part actor before without waiting for the credits at the end of the movie.

And beyond searching, you can actually *browse the Web* with a little help from Google. By squishing down those complex pages into something your cellphone can understand, Google brings any Web page you can get to from your desktop PC to your cellphone on the fly. This feature is hugely useful, as most Web pages are encoded in ways that make them otherwise inaccessible from the older wireless phones that don't have built-in browsers.

To get online out in the world you need two things: a phone or PDA capable of browsing the Web, and a data plan that lets you surf.

Tip: If you don't yet have a cellphone or wireless PDA, the box on the next page explains some choices you have for wireless Internet features.

Can Your Device Get Online?

The lion's share of today's mobile phones, PDAs, and other mobile devices are *Internet capable*, meaning they have technology built in to let you surf Web pages and read and send email. Different devices use different Internet-friendly technologies, however.

Some devices—like the palmOne Treo 650, Windows Mobile–based phones, and Sony Ericsson's P900 Smartphone—have a networking function that lets you reach the Internet over the same airwaves that carry your cellphone calls. This arrangement is similar to your home phone line, which can handle chatty phone calls or dial-up Internet connections with eqaul aplomb.

Other devices, like the Dell Axim X50, have built-in WiFi connectivity. *WiFi* is a system that lets you connect to the Internet wirelessly, via radio waves. In order to hop online with WiFi, though, you need to be near a unit, known as a *base station,* that broadcasts Internet signals. These days, your local airport, coffee shop, bookstore, and many McDonald's all have such base stations. Sometimes you can hook into WiFi hotspots for free; in other places, you have to pay a fee. Either way, using a WiFi-ready PDA is just like using a laptop to connect to a wireless network.

Finally, some handhelds use *Bluetooth,* a type of short-range wireless networking, to let you connect your PDA to a cellphone that has built-in data networking or to beam files to a printer over the airwaves. Bluetooth *itself* doesn't let you get online; rather, it links you with other devices that can connect to the Internet. So if you have a fancy handheld gizmo with Bluetooth features, you still need to find out if it has its own Internet connection, or if you need a cellphone that has built-in networking with which to connect.

If your gizmo has any of these features, consider yourself Internet-capable. If you have no idea what tricks your phone or PDA can do, check your cell carrier's Web site for information about your device.

Tip: If you're already a wireless subscriber and your phone doesn't do Internet, look into upgrade deals, which are often available after a certain period of time has passed on your contract. If you can't swing an upgrade deal, investigate buying a new phone from your provider or a cellphone retailer in your area.

Or pick up last season's model for a song on eBay. Just be sure that the phone you buy is compatible with your current phone service. Check your provider's site for a list of acceptable phones, or call their tech-support line and ask whether or not they support that "Snazphone 2003" you're about to bid on.

Choosing a Mobile Device

Choosing a mobile device—cellphone, PDA, or a combination—makes choosing the paint color for your house feel like a walk in the park. The choice can involve such complex considerations as how the phone feels in your hand and whether the PDA syncs up with your computer.

To make matters worse, you have a few choices when it comes to hitting the mobile Internet. Here are some considerations to weigh:

To get a high-speed connection, you need WiFi. WiFi is about as fast as you can go without plugging into a wall. The alternative—cellular Internet access—can be pokey, akin to your old 28.8 K modem, but newer devices can approach speeds about twice that of a 56 K dial-up modem. (In certain areas, *very* new services let you reach the speed of a slow DSL connection.)

Of course, to connect to the Internet using WiFi, you have to be within range of a wireless base station (usually about 200 feet). Any further away, and you don't get a connection.

To get Internet access in the greatest number of places, you need cellular. While cellular Internet connectivity has a long way to go before it can claim to be everywhere you want it to be, it does let you stay online from house to taxi to office in most urban areas. Bear in mind, though, that mobile Internet access isn't available everywhere telephone service is; you very well might find a place where your cellphone works quite nicely as a phone, but you can't get the Internet for love or money. Cellular data networks are improving, but it'll be a while before mobile Internet access is truly ubiquitous.

Hybrid means rarely having to say you're offline. You can have your wireless cake and eat it too with devices like souped-up cellphones that let you switch between WiFi and cellular Internet access.

In the meantime, if you don't mind carrying your body weight in gadgets, you can pair a WiFi laptop or PDA with an Internet-friendly cellphone, sharing connectivity in whatever form either device can find. For example, a PowerBook out of WiFi range of a coffee shop can hop on the Internet via Bluetooth connection to a Sony Ericsson T610 cellphone.

BlackBerry means never having to say you're offline. A *BlackBerry* is a high-speed wireless handheld device made by Research in Motion. It's designed to let you get your email, surf the Web, and organize your life. Most current models let you make calls, too.

Time was, people could use a BlackBerry only if they worked for a company that had set up a BlackBerry wireless network. But now individuals can get BlackBerries and matching wireless service from providers like T-Mobile, Verizon, and Cingular.

As you're trying to decide on a phone and a plan, ask your friends and coworkers for the provider with the best reputation in your area, and see what plans and free phones they offer. Amazon.com usually offers some amazing package deals on state-of-the-art phones, too—with service activation, of course.

Is Your Device Actually Online?

Just because your mobile device is *capable* of connecting to the Internet doesn't yet mean you can just jump online. Once you have the right kind of device, you still need the *service* that lets you connect wirelessly—just the way you can have a nice touch-tone phone, but you can't make any calls without a dial tone. You can usually reach wireless nirvana (the state of having the right device and the right service) by paying your cell service company a fee for Internet access.

Note: Actually, there's a big exception to this rule: If your PDA is WiFi-ready, you can use it anywhere you find a free or pay-for-use hotspot. No extra service needed.

Cell service providers, like Verizon and Sprint, sell *data plans*—that is, Internet access for cellphones and wireless PDAs—for an additional fee on top of your usual monthly calling plan. Depending on the provider, the fee for data plans can range from a flat rate of $15 to $85 per month. And some providers offer a per-megabyte package, similar in structure to your typical phone minute plan, in which you pre-pay for some amount of data and then pay extra for everything you use over that amount. Work with your cellular provider to select the right Internet access plan.

Tip: In the wireless world, extra minutes and megabytes can cost a small fortune. So if you go for the per-megabyte scheme, do as you would with a minutes-per-month voice plan and choose slightly more megabytes per month than you think you'll need. You can scale back if you find you're just not using the Internet as much as you thought you would, but at least you won't get stuck with the exorbitant extra charges.

Googling on the Fly

Once you've got your device and data plan lined up, you're ready to hit the Web. But the Web comes in two flavors on mobile devices. On newer "smart" phones, PDAs, and hiptops, you can get the regular, glorious Web—the one you're used to seeing on your desktop or laptop computer—via a small Web browser. On older and simpler phones, you may be limited to a text-only version of the Web called *WAP*, or Wireless Access Protocol, described in the box on page 248. Figure 7-23 illustrates the difference.

After you've sorted out your phone's Web proclivities, you can get Googling.

Googling by PDA, Hiptop, or Smartphone

If your mobile device of choice is a PDA or one of the smarter smartphones, surfing around works a lot like it does on your desktop or laptop computer. Here's how to run a Google search:

1. **Select Open, Enter Address, Go to URL, or the like from your browser's toolbar or menus, and enter Google's home page address: *www.google.com*.**

   If your small-screen browser just isn't up to the task of displaying full-sized Web pages in all their glory, try Google's scaled-down home page: *www.google.*

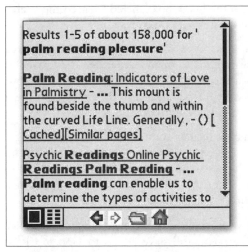

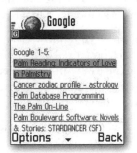

Figure 7-23:
Left: Google search results on a full-fledged wireless Web browser. As you can see, they look a lot like the results you'd see on your regular computer— just a lot smaller.

Right: Google search results on a WAP browser. Boring but serviceable.

com/palm. Never mind that it appears to be for Palm-branded devices; it works just as well on your Windows Mobile or BlackBerry handheld.

Note: Just visiting *http://google.com* (without the *www*) may, weirdly, take you to Google Canada. To avoid that quirk, just remember to type the full URL.

---

2. **Click Go or OK to get things rolling.**

Your browser springs into action, signified by a whirling globe, flowing progress bar, or a somewhat less dramatic "Connecting…" message. Depending on whether or not you were already online, you may also see various "Initializing," "Signing On," and "Established" messages along the way. It might take a few moments before you see the fresh, familiar face of Google (shown in Figure 7-24)—a tad more scrunched down than usual.

Figure 7-24:
Here you can see Google on a Handspring Treo 650. If you're on Google's PDA-optimized page, you can click the Full Google link to hop back to Google proper any time.

3. Write or type your search terms into the blank box labeled "Search the Web," and then click Google Search to send your query on its way.

Depending on your browser, you either type your search query right in the blank search box, or you tap the search box to open a separate little text-entry dialog box. If your browser opens a separate window where you type in your search terms, go ahead and enter your query; then tap OK or the equivalent button to return to the main browser window, and *then* tap Search.

You can run any search you would on a regular computer, and you've even got the full range of Google search syntax (see page 65) available to you. You might, however, find that those quotes, colons, parentheses, and minuses are tricky to type on your average mobile device. Sadly, the tech industry has yet to provide a solution for MPI (Mobile Punctuation Issues).

On mobile browsers, Google scales your results down a bit, leaving out the URL and page size for each (Figure 7-25). You still have access to Google's local cache of pages and a link to pages similar to a particular result, though. And you can alter your query and run it again from the Google search box at the bottom of every results page.

That's it! You can now surf the Web as you would normally.

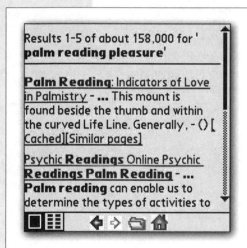

Figure 7-25:
Depending on your device, Google's PDA-optimized site may just give you 5 results per page, with a Next button at the bottom to let you move on to results 6 through 10, and so forth.

Googling by mobile phone

If your garden-variety mobile phone doesn't have a full-fledged Web browser, it almost certainly has a built-in WAP browser. WAP, described in gory detail in the box on page 248, is a simplified Web system, limited both in display and interactivity. When you use a WAP browser, you enter a world filled with almost nothing but 10 or 20 lines of text per screen. It's not pretty, but you've got the wealth, if not the Technicolor, of the Web right in your pocket.

FREQUENTLY ASKED QUESTION

Mouseless Navigation

My cellphone didn't come with a mouse. How do I navigate the Web?

The mechanics of choosing menu items, highlighting and selecting links, and entering text vary from device to device.

If your phone or PDA allows it, the simplest way to surf is using the up and down buttons, plus a third button (often called OK or Enter) for selecting or clicking.

If your gizmo has a joystick (middle picture) akin to the Ms. Pac-Man machine in your local museum, pushing it up and down should get you from textbox to button, and link to link. To select something, either press the joystick or look for a Select button.

Some gadgets have what's called a scroll key or D-Pad (right), a circular or D-shaped button or arrangement of buttons that serves as a joystick. Press the upper and lower edges or buttons to move about, the center to select.

Then there's the track wheel (left). As the name suggests, you scroll up and down by rotating a little wheel, either on the side or front of your phone. Push the wheel or a separate button to simulate a click. The big advantage of a scroll wheel? If your hand is shaped right, you can often scroll and click with only one hand, using the other for more important tasks—like, say, driving.

For newer phones that can support XHTML and can use the full Google Mobile offerings at *www.google.com*, however, things aren't so black-and-white, because you can search for Web words *and* pictures. That means if you really, really need to find that color photo of the ferret wearing bunny ears that you found when you were using Google Image Search on your laptop, you can find it on Google Mobile search as well by choosing an Images search and tapping in the keyword *ferret*. (Of course, loading pictures is much, much slower than loading text on a phone or palmtop.)

In addition to Images, Google's Mobile Search menu gives you the choice of Web (for your regular-old Web searches), Local, and Mobile Web (which are sites that have a version squished down and optimized especially for mobile phones). Yes, Google Local has now joined the company's portable offerings. As discussed back on page 62, you can skip the generalities of search results and go straight to local business listings and information. Skip ahead to page 259 for more information on using Google Local on your mobile phone.

Before you can even start Googling from your mobile phone, you first have to find the browser. This process, in and of itself, can take some thumbing around. Browsers are usually hidden in plain sight, cleverly disguised by a moniker like Web, Internet Services, Services, Downloads, WAP, or some branded version thereof (mMode Downloads or T-Zones, for example). If nothing's immediately obvious, look for an icon sporting your cellular provider's logo, or try menu items in turn. Still no luck? Dig out that cellphone manual and see if it offers any hints.

Once you've found that WAP browser, it works pretty much like any Web browser. Follow links by selecting and clicking them. Click the Back button to back up a page. Jump to a particular Web site by typing its address. And so on.

The big difference is in the way you "type" text on a cellular keypad, a painstaking process known as *texting*. If you're new to this technical torture, the box on page 251, "Texting Sure Ain't QWERTY," tells you how to master your cellphone's sorry excuse for a keyboard.

You can search Google on your cell in much the same way you'd do so on your regular computer: enter a query, click the Search button, browse through results, and click the link of anything that looks promising. Here's how it breaks down:

1. **Open your browser and type *www.google.com* in the URL box. Google should be able to figure out what mobile format your phone uses and automatically route you to the proper pages, but every once it a while, the auto-direct doesn't work. If you get nowhere with the basic URL, type in *www.google.com/xhtml*. If that gets you nothing (maybe you have an older phone), type in *wap.google. com/wml*, Google's WAP address, as shown in Figure 7-26. Then click "Go to" or the equivalent button to set the wheels in motion.**

   While the official Google Wireless URL is *http://www.google.com* on newer phones that support XHTML, and *http://wap.google.com/wml* on older models, you can shave off a few dozen keypresses by using just *google.com/xhtml* or *google.com/wml*. Even better, Google's set up *466453.com*—that's "google" without all the multi-tapping—to make it just a little easier on your fingers than

Figure 7-26:
You may need to select "Open URL," "Enter Address," or something similar from your browser's toolbar or menus before typing Google's address.

typing the whole URL the hard way. (You'd think they would have gone a tad further and assumed the */wml* part, but they didn't.)

Note: The *WML* in Google's WAP address stands for Wireless Markup Language, the lingua franca of WAP pages.

2. **Highlight the Google search box.**

   Use your cellphone's navigation buttons to highlight the Google search box. If you're not sure how to navigate on your phone, read the box, "Mouseless Navigation," on page 247 for a quick lesson.

3. **Put the cursor in the search box.**

   Before you can type anything into the search box, you need to put the cursor in place. Do so by clicking the center of the joystick, pushing inward on the scroll-wheel, or choosing Select from a nearby browser menu. On some browsers, this process opens a separate screen where you type in your query.

4. **Type in your search terms.**

   Figure 7-27 explains some subtleties.

Figure 7-27:
Type a Google query just as you would in your regular browser. Use the 0 button for a space and repeatedly press 1 to scroll through useful query syntax characters like quote marks, a minus sign, and a colon.

5. **Deselect the search box and click Search.**

   Hop out of the search box by clicking your joystick, scroll wheel, or choosing Done or the equivalent from a browser menu. Then highlight and click the

Search button to send your query on its way. Your WAP browser leaps into motion and whirs away, waiting for results.

Note: If you're a devotee of the I'm Feeling Lucky feature (page 22), you may note its conspicuous absence here. Unfortunately, there's no workaround, but you can take solace in the fact that arriving unluckily at the wrong page is a good way to blow both time and kilobits on a pokey, expensive cellular connection.

After a few moments, Google delivers the results (Figure 7-28).

Figure 7-28:
Left: Google Wireless gives you five results per screen, which is usually more than enough, thanks to Google's uncanny ability to find what you're after. Move to the next five results using the Next 5 link at the bottom of each result screen. (Although this phone appears to show seven results, it's actually just five—two of the lines are overflow. When you scroll down, your phone shows a visual indicator, like highlighting or a bullet, to show which lines are new listings.)

Right: Your WAP browser's "Options" or "Service options" or "More" menu holds some site-specific choices that might be useful to you. On Google's menu, you can find Next 5, which is a handy shortcut to the link on the bottom of the results screen.

6. **Highlight any result and click it to go to that page.**

Easy as pie, though sometimes as long as baking one if your cell network is slow. The extra-cool thing here is that while regular cellphones usually limit you to surfing Web pages that somebody has created specially for WAP browsers, Google actually lets you browse almost any normal Web page from your cellphone. The next section explains how.

Tip: You can use the *define* operator (page 38) on Google Mobile Search, too, just in case you need some word definitions right where you are.

WAP surfing

Most Web pages are not designed for the puny WAP browser on your mobile phone and are thus invisible when you're surfing on the cell. So how can you visit any of the results your Google searches turn up?

In truth, you don't actually leave Google and visit other sites at all. Instead, Google reads Web pages for you and scales them down to a form your mobile browser can

Texting Sure Ain't QWERTY

Whether you're a seventy-word-per-minute touch typist or a hunt-and-peck person, you're going to find texting a pokey chore. Rather than the array of letters, numbers, symbols, and Shift keys on your computer keyboard, everything you do on your cellphone is confined to twelve keys: 0–9, *, and #. Frankly, it's an annoying system to learn, although some folks actually become rather adept at it.

Look closely at your phone, and you'll notice each button also holds either a set of three to four alphabetic characters or obscure symbols not unlike those you'd expect to find on the UFO landing in your backyard. Like your regular phone, the 1 button is devoid of letters, while 2 holds ABC, 3 holds DEF, and so on through 9 (WXYZ).

When you're in Web-browsing mode on your phone, pressing a button once enters the first letter listed. Pressing the same button twice, quickly, gets you the second letter. The idea is that each time you press a button, you cycle through the letters listed on it. So, for example, when you're in Web browsing mode on your phone, you can press the 2 button once to type an A, press it twice in quick succession for B, and press it thrice for C. Four times nets you a 2. Keep going, and you'll make it back through A, B, C, and 2 again, on some phones encountering strange and wonderful foreign letters along the way.

Once you've typed a letter and are ready to enter the next, you may need to pause for about a second to let the phone know you're ready to input the next letter (as opposed to wanting to keep cycling through the letters on the button). In order to spell the word "google," for example, you type 4666666455533. Here's a tap-by-tap translation:

4 (gets you a "g")
pause (on some phones, to let the phone know you're ready to enter a new letter)

666 (tapping 6 three times quickly gets you an "o")
pause for the next letter
666 (another "o")
pause
4 (another "g")
pause
555 (gets you an "l")
pause
33 (gets you an "e")

When it comes to special characters like the "." and "/" common in Web addresses, you can usually turn to the 1 button (although some phones store their special characters in the "*" button). A period or dot is often a single tap of the 1 button, for example. The slash is often 15 taps. For those of you keeping score at home, that gives you 92714666 [pause] 6664555331222666 [pause] 611111111111111196555 for "wap.google.com/wml."

(Note that the texting equivalent of the Space bar is the 0 button, but you'll never use that in URLs.)

What of digits? Surely you don't need to type seventeen or so "1"s scrolling through all the symbols associated with the 1 button [.,-?!'@:;/( )] just to get back around to the *digit* 1 you wanted in the first place. Thankfully, all it takes is holding down the button for a second or so to jump right to the numeral. So instead of tapping through all the symbols to get to 1, just hold down the 1 key for a moment, and you're there.

Note that there are other more efficient input techniques such as *T9* ("Text on 9 keys") and other so-called predictive text systems, but they're not as useful for entering obscure words like those in Web addresses.

deal with—usually a neat 10 to 20 lines of text per page (Figure 7-29, top). This *proxy* service is simply Google acting on your behalf. You can see the proxy setup in this URL:

```
http://wmlproxy.google.com/wmltrans/h=en/g=/q=%22text+on+9+keys%22+-
discomfort/s=0/u=www.t9.com@2F/c=0
```

wmlproxy tells you Google is handling a wireless conversion for you, and the address *www.t9.com* is the actual URL you're visiting. All the rest is Google's way of keeping track of your original search.

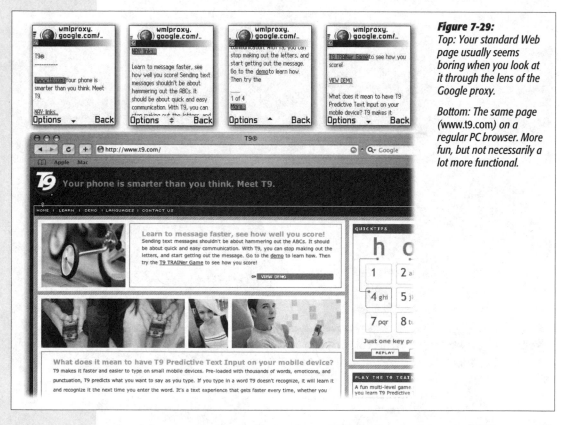

Figure 7-29:
Top: Your standard Web page usually seems boring when you look at it through the lens of the Google proxy.

Bottom: The same page (www.t9.com) on a regular PC browser. More fun, but not necessarily a lot more functional.

Google's proxy service goes beyond searching, letting you view any Web page at all. Here's how: On the Google Mobile home page, select the Search Options link and choose Go to URL. This link takes you to what appears to be the home page again, only instead of the search box, Google shows you a "Go to URL" box (Figure 7-30). Type in any URL you'd like to visit and then click Go to have Google show you the page in a form your phone can handle.

While the Google proxy is not a substitute for well-designed WAP sites targeted specifically at mobile jockeys, it does the terrific service of bringing you the entire Web on your WAP phone without a lick of work from individual site designers.

Figure 7-30:
When you follow a link from this page or any subsequent page, the Google proxy serves it to you, letting you reach every corner of the Web.

When Abbreviations Attack

Why are there two different addresses for mobilized Google search (www.google.com/xhtml and www.google.com/wml)? Is one better than the other, or does one have cooler stuff?

Both are mobile Web formats, but since XHTML (or WAP 2.0) is a newer standard, you get a bit more bang for your buck when it comes to browsing with the first URL. If you have a newer phone that supports the XHTML format, you can use Google to search for Web sites *and* images. (Whether or not you can actually see the images on a teeny-tiny phone screen depends on your hardware).

If you've got an older wireless phone that can only display WML pages, you can only use Google's Web search feature via the second URL—but WML can handle queries tapped in with Google Number Search, too (see below).

Luckily, though, if you just want to search on the go and don't care about all the WAP yap, just type in *www.google. com* and let Google figure out what kind of phone you have and which kind of mobile-Web pages to send your way.

WAP Search Options

Just as regular-old Google has some advanced features, Google's Wireless WAP service also has some rather useful search options, shown in Figure 7-31.

Figure 7-31:
Follow the Search Options link on the Google mobile home page to reach this menu of alternate ways to interact with the Google search engine.

Here's what you can do with Search Options:

- **Entire Web** lets you search the entire Web. Nothing mysterious here.

- **Number Entire Web** lets you search the entire Web using *Google Number Search*, a finger-saving system Google developed that lets you single-tap the keypad number associated with any of the letters it represents, rather than selecting a letter tap by tap. Use 0 for space and 1 for quotation marks. So with Google Number Search, you can tap out "google" as *466453*, rather than the more demanding *4666 666455533*.

Google Number Search is actually a clever twist on regular results. When you type in a string of numbers, Google figures out the possible words represented by that sequence, and then it shows you the most popular results that include those words. Because it's guessing about what you really want, the Number Search works well sometimes; other times, it feels like driving with your eyes closed.

Most of the time, its success depends on the complexity of your search terms. For example, *1839806606463053971*, "text on nine keys" as expressed in Google Number Search, comes up with different, yet no less relevant hits, than tapping out the phrase in full. Most people find texting easier, but Number Search is worth playing with if texting has burned out your thumbs.

• **Mobile Web** lets you search for pages designed specifically for wireless devices. For example, the BBC Mobile site (*www.bbc.co.uk/mobile*) lays out its links for painless navigation on a mobile keypad, and it divides its stories into logical, mobile-screen-sized bites. This option is handy when you want only fast-loading pages that are easy to cruise on your mobile keyboard.

Tip: If you're curious about the sorts of things you might find on the *Mobile Web* (that is, Web pages created for WAP browsers), but you're surfing on a regular computer, try adding *filetype:wml* to any Google search (pages in WML format are designed for wireless devices). You can convert WML pages, known as *cards,* to regular old HTML pages—just click the "View as HTML" link associated with any result.

• **Number Mobile Web** lets you search the Mobile Web using Google Number Search. For example, a simple *222* is a shortcut for BBCi, the BBC Interactive site.

• **Go to URL** gives you a jumping-off point to reach any Web address—WAP-specific or not—via Google's WAP proxy (page 252).

• **Language Options** lets you interact with Google in Français, Norsk, Svenska, and nine other languages. Similar to Google's Language Tools (page 58), Google Wireless's Language Options allow you to use Google in the language of your choice. It affects all the prompts, buttons, and messages from Google, but not the Web pages themselves.

• **Help** provides very limited online help—one page's worth—for some Google Wireless features. It's not that useful, so you may as well skip it.

Tip: If you're surfing on a cellphone, tapping or texting in the Google URL can take half a presidential administration. To avoid the slog every time you go to Google, save the URL in your bookmarks. Go to *google.com/wml* and then look around your browser toolbar or menus for something like "Add Bookmark" or "Add to Favorites." Your mobile browser should automatically name the bookmark for you, probably something like "Google." Bookmark not only Google but any other sites you visit on a regular basis to save yourself the hassle of retyping addresses again and again.

Google Mobile Local Search

Just as you can search for the businesses or restaurants in a specific town or Zip code with Google Local on your computer (page 62), you can also use the microscopic power of Google Local on your phone. Peck out *http://mobile.google.com/local* on your phone's browser, and you're ready to go Local.

Note: PDAs and phones that can handle the Google Mobile XHTML format can use Google Local Search on the go, but older WAP phones won't be able to display the maps and other images used by the service.

Google Local wants to know two things from you on the mobile version of the main screen. First, it wants to know *what* you're looking for. Then it wants to know *where* you're looking for it. Fill in the boxes with the appropriate information like, say, *burmese food* in *san diego* or *shoes* in *el paso* and then select the Google Search button.

Tip: If you know the Zip code of the burg you're searching, you can type that in the Where box instead of the town name.

You get back a list of local businesses that match, complete with addresses and phone numbers—and, best of all, a link to a tiny Google Map displaying the locations of the results, just like you get on the grown-up, deskbound version of Google Local. You can even adjust the view by zooming in and out of the wee maps.

As you can do with regular Google Local, you can also use Mobile Local to get yourself some driving direction to and from a place that turned up in your search results. Click the Driving Directions link at the top of your results page to bop to a fresh page where you can peck in starting and ending addresses. Now just navigate to and select the Get Directions button to get a list of instructions for getting between the two places.

Tip: If you find just the place you're looking for but don't have a pen handy to scribble down the number, fear not. You can call the number directly by selecting the number on screen and clicking your phone's equivalent of the Enter button. This assumes, of course, that your phone is one of those types that lets you make a call while you're wading around on the Web.

Froogle on the Road

If you're a fan of Google's Froogle feature (a product-search tool described in loving detail on page 159), you'll be glad to know you don't have to lug a laptop to the mall to compare prices of whisks on sale. Instead, try Froogle Wireless, which brings comparison shopping right to your phone or PDA.

Froogle Wireless—currently part of Google Labs—doesn't offer all the features of a regular Froogle search. You can't limit your search by price, group the results by store, or sort them in any way. And most limiting, the results from a Froogle Wireless search, like those shown in Figure 7-32, don't actually link anywhere.

Still, Froogle Wireless is a handy price-check tool when you're standing in the aisle at Circuit Cathedral, trying to figure out if $149 is a good deal for an extension cord.

Here's how to use it:

1. Tap *http://wml.froogle.com,* the Wireless Froogle address, into your mobile's browser.

   After a few moments, Froogle pops up on your tiny mobile screen.

2. Select the search box, type in your product terms, and then click Search. You can use the usual Froogle syntax (page 160).

   Google gives you a nice batch of results, shown in Figure 7-32. You can scroll through them as you would any Wireless Google results.

Figure 7-32:
$62.99 may be on the high side for a yogurt maker, but if the one in your hand is $75 and doesn't even make ice cream, you may want to make the purchase elsewhere—and buy some yogurt ingredients with the savings.

Google SMS

Images are impressive, but there's nothing like pure unadorned text for speed and efficiency. SMS, which stands for Short Message Service, is a communications system that combines the terse text of a telegram with the rapid response of an instant message. It's mostly used between mobile phones, where brevity is a necessary adaptation for using tiny phone keypads to peck out messages. Sending an SMS (sometimes called *texting*) from one phone to another is a popular activity with teenagers and businessfolk.

Google SMS lets you send messages to the Mighty Google itself on your wireless phone and get an answer back in a flash, right there on your phone's screen. You can get driving directions sent to your phone, look up local weather forecasts and movie listings, find nearby businesses, and look up dictionary definitions, among other things. To use the service, you'll need to have a wireless phone that can send and receive text messages and a service plan that allows for text messaging.

Tip: If you're just getting into text messaging, and you find some of the lingo looks more like a license plate than a decipherable sentence, check out the list of text-messaging abbreviations online at *www. webopedia.com/quick_ref/textmessageabbreviations.asp* to help crack the code.

Sending Out an SMS

To get Google SMS to text you back, you need to send it a question. You do so by starting the text-message application on your cellphone, typing in a query, and then sending the message to 46645, which spells out GOOGL on most phones. (If you're Googling merrily from the United Kingdom, though, dial 64664 instead—6GOOG, if you need something more alphabetical to remember.)

Driving directions

Let's say you're out driving around Los Angeles and you get lost on your way to the airport. You pull over in front of a movie theater and whip out your cell-phone. You start a text message and address it to 46645. In the message body, you type:

```
from 6925 hollywood blvd hollywood ca to lax
```

In about a minute or so, your phone will beep with a message back from Google SMS. In some cases, your phone will beep with *several* messages from Google SMS, as text messages can't have more than 160 characters and some service plans give you even fewer characters per message. When Google SMS sends you multiple messages in response to your query, they'll show up in your phone's message box numbered like this: 1/5, 2/5/, 3/5, and so on.

When you open up that first message, Google SMS informs you that Grauman's Chinese Theater, (where you are right now) is 17 miles from Los Angeles International Airport (LAX), and it should take you 15 steps in 22 minutes to get there. The steps are just like the directions you get from Google Maps (page 100), except they're text-only and use more abbreviations—*W* for west, *L* for left, *Cont.* for Continued, and so on. Remember, phone screens are tiny, and you only get a certain amount of text per SMS message.

Of course, tapping out a long address like the example above can be time-consuming, so Google SMS lets you send queries in different (and more important, *shorter*) formats. You can cut it down to city names, Zip codes, city and state, or even just airport codes like EWR (Newark Liberty International) or BOS (Boston's

---

Logan International). You just need to tell Google SMS where you're coming *from* and where you're going *to*.

For example, you can phrase your SMS queries as such:

```
47405 to ind
from nashville tn to memphis
to 570 second ave 10016 from 108 court st 11201
```

The above queries will get you directions (in order) from Bloomington, Indiana, to the Indianapolis International Airport; from Nashville to Memphis, Tennessee; and from Brooklyn to Manhattan.

Men, take note: No one will know you asked for directions if you just send Google a message.

Movie listings

Just as you can use Google from your regular computer to get movie schedules (page 44), you can also ask Google SMS to send the current listings right to your phone. In addition to listings, you can get information about a certain movie if you query its title, which could be helpful if you're out with the kids and can't remember if that wacky comedy is rated PG or PG-13.

To get movie information sent to your phone, send these types of queries to 46645:

- *bewitched pensacola fl* (shows you theaters playing *Bewitched* in Pensacola, Florida)

- *movie:movies 63101* (shows you a list of movies playing around St. Louis, Missouri)

- *movie:theaters palo alto* (shows you a list of theaters around Palo Alto, California and what's playing)

To get information about a movie, just tap its title into your phone and then send the message to Google SMS.

Tip: You can get help with Google SMS by simply sending the word *help* as a text message to 46645. If only getting help in other areas of life were so easy.

Weather forecasts

Getting a handful of Google weather updates sent to your phone uses many of the same search techniques you use to get Google weather information on your computer. Just start a new text message addressed to 46645 and type in *weather* followed by either the city and state name or the Zip code of the town you want to check. For example, just tap in *weather lubbock tx* to see how hot it's going to be in that part of Texas today or *weather 98101* to see if you'll see any sun in Seattle.

Tip: Google SMS can also handle temperature conversions from Fahrenheit to Celsius, or vice versa. Just send a message like *28 C in F* or *68 F in C* to get the translation to or from the metric system.

Local business listings

If you've wandered around Google Local (page 62), you've got a handle on how to find the nearest pizza joint or garage in the area. Those tricks work the same way on Google SMS. Just type what you're looking for (cleaners) and where you are, either by city and state or Zip code (*new haven ct* or *06501*), and fire the message off to Google SMS.

Q&A

Need some fast facts in a flash? Google SMS can answer many simple fact-based questions if you phrase them properly. To get the population of Canada, for example, send a text message with the query *canada population*, and get your answer back in a few seconds ("32,805,041" reports Google SMS, attributing the number to the CIA Fact Book).

For best results, remember to keep your queries grounded in fact, like *shakespeare's birthplace* or *capital of Bulgaria* or *who wrote moby-dick*. Figure 7-33 gives you a sample of what to expect when Google answers your question.

Product prices

Froogle (page 159) gets on the SMS train, too, and you can use the service to get current prices for products you're curious about. Use the query *price* followed by the item you're checking (*laser printer* or *hp laserjet 1012,* for example) to get a fistful of prices and stores sent back to your cellphone. You can also use the odd shortcut *f* instead of price (as in *f cd player*) or phrase the query as *cd player prices*. If you're looking for the price on a specific book or product, type in the book's ISBN number or the item's UPC number to find how much it costs elsewhere.

Phone book listings

You can text a query straight to Google SMS and get address and phone numbers for people who are publicly listed in the Google PhoneBook (page 39). There are a number of variations, including:

- The person's full name, city, and state (*john doe wheeling wv*)
- The full name and just the state (*john doe wv*)
- The full name and the telephone area code (*john doe 304*)
- The full name and the Zip code (*john doe 26003*)

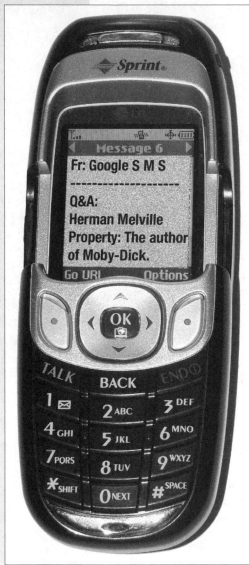

Figure 7-33:
Google can answer many popular questions in under a minute. Resist the urge to use it in class.

You may also get results with just the person's last name and either just the Zip code or the city and state. (If you know the phone number but need the *address*, type in the phone number and send it to Google SMS.)

Definitions

If you have an SMS-equipped cellphone, you'll never be caught flat without a dictionary. You can use the *define* operator (page 38) to look up word definitions on Google SMS, as in *define antediluvian*. Even better, you don't have to hunt and peck the word *define* out in your phone's tiny keypad; just type a *d* or a *D* followed by the word you want to look up and send the message off to 46645.

Tip: Google SMS is quite extensive and has its own 13-page section of Frequently Asked Questions posted at *www.google.com/sms/faq.html*.

Part Three:
Google for Webmasters

3

Becoming a Search Result

If it isn't in Google, it probably doesn't exist.

That statement may strike you as an exaggeration, but a lot of people act as if it were true. They run a quick Google search, and if they don't find what they're after right away, they're more likely to adjust their query than move on to another search engine. So if your site is listed on AltaVista, Yahoo, and every other search index on the planet, but Google doesn't know about it, chances are good that millions of people are going to miss it, too.

So if you've got a site and you want people to find it, you gotta get in Google; this chapter tells you how to go about it. And if you want to add a Google search to your own site, you can learn how to do that here, too. (This chapter assumes, however, that you already know your way around the back end of your Web site.)

Note: If you need information on building a Web site, running a Web server, or constructing Web pages, consult a book on Webmastering, like *Creating Web Sites: The Missing Manual* (*www.oreilly.com/ catalog/creatingwstmm/*). For guidance on Web site design, you might take a gander at *Learning Web Design* (*www.oreilly.com/catalog/learnWeb2/*).

If you want to try your hand at writing Google-based applications, you also need to learn about the Google *API* (*http://api.google.com/*)—which stands for Application Programming Interface, the programmer's way of talking to Google. For that, pick up a copy of Google Hacks (*www.oreilly.com/catalog/googlehks/*), the consummate guide to programming for Google.

Here's what you won't find in this chapter: tips on gaming the Google engine, interfering with the proper functioning of its index, or otherwise playing the Google ranking game unfairly. While Google tries its darndest to keep up with such attempts—and does a pretty good job of it—people have found some dirty tricks that pay off in the short run. If you came to this chapter looking for that sort of edge, you're going to be disappointed.

A sense of fairness ought to keep you playing straight. But if it doesn't, consider this: Google is known for ignoring or even removing from its database sites that try to trick the crawlers or interfere in the proper operation of the Google engine. Don't become one of those losers.

Reminder: Google adds sites to its index in two distinct steps (page 274). Crawling is the first, wherein the *Googlebot*—Google's robot (also known as a *spider* or *crawler*)—roams your site, culling text, hyperlinks, and so on. It then hands that stuff off to the Google indexer, which adds your pages to the Google index, assigning PageRank weights and making your goodies available to people searching the Web. Sometimes, there's a noticeable lag between the Googlebot's visit (that is, when Google knows your site exists) and the indexing (when Google knows what's on your site), so if a change on your site doesn't immediately appear in the Google index, just give it a few days.

Getting Your Site Ready for Google

If you want people—and Google—to notice your site, you've got to make it presentable. That means paying attention to visual, interactive, and technical details.

While Google doesn't give a hoot about color scheme or whether your humor site is actually funny, it does care about many of the same things your visitors do. If your site is difficult for Google to roam through and read, the search engine is unlikely to index it properly and show it in search results as you'd like.

Tip: As a Webmaster, it behooves you to keep up with the latest trends in search engines and how best to prepare your site for maximum indexing, impact, and, ultimately, visitors. (Geeks and other techno-wonks call this process *search engine optimization,* or SEO.)

Two fabulous resources for all things Webmaster- and search-engine-related are Search Engine Watch (*www.searchenginewatch.com*) and Webmaster World (*www.webmasterworld.com*).

The Fundamental Steps

Here's how you can win friends and influence Google.

Don't hide indoors

Google tracks only what is actually on the Web and readily accessible. Just because your site is on a *server* (a networked computer that holds the files that make up a Web site) doesn't mean other people can see it. If you trap your site behind a corporate firewall, at the end of a DSL or cable-modem link that doesn't allow traffic to your home server, or make it unreachable in any other way to the general public, Google will never find it. It may sound obvious, but many a fledgling Webmaster has missed this point.

If you set up your site at work and you can't reach it from outside your corporate network, chances are your company doesn't like its employees running Web sites from its computers and has set up their system to prevent it. Check with your IT department about their policy and where best to put your site on their system.

If you've set up your site at home, make sure your Internet service provider lets you run a server over their network. Many don't, so it's important to ask. But they may well provide some space for your site on *their* servers. In fact, many individuals' sites actually live on their ISP's servers.

Appear stable

Google—and your visitors—are likely to be put off by complex URLs that are hard to decode and differentiate from one another. For instance, nobody but you and your server knows what to make of *http://www.example.com/products.cgi?cat=autoparts&partnum=6502.*

Humans like easily readable, memorable addresses. But Google has its own logic for avoiding complicated URLs. The problem, as Google sees it, is that complex addresses often point to *dynamic* pages—those that your site has created temporarily, in response to a query. And a dynamic page suggests to Google that your site may have a large database underlying it—one for which it would take Google's spiders eons to discern all the possible ways people could view the data.

Tip: You can spot dynamic pages easily: they include a "?" in the URL.

For example, say your site sells hosiery, and it's connected to your huge database containing descriptions and prices for thousands of pairs of socks and leggings. When somebody searches your Web site for *blue children's stockings*, your site might generate a page just for that person, showing the eight items that match the query. If Google catches a whiff of this setup, it flees in terror, assuming that to properly track your site, it would need to index thousands or millions of pages, many of which might show the same things in a different order.

The most well-known system for creating dynamic pages is called *CGI*, which stands for Common Gateway Interface and is the "Look at me, I'm building Web pages on the fly" of file types. CGI scripts are bits of programming code you can set to build Web pages on request out of databases and other bits and bobs. If you're using CGI scripts, Google may not properly index your site—which is what's happening if Google seems to know about all of your site except for the parts served up by a CGI script. If the situation is dire enough (that is, Google is ignoring you altogether), you might want to consider reconfiguring your system.

Warning: Other dynamic pages that Google may consider too hot to handle include those built with templating systems like PHP, JSP, and ASP, and those named after programming languages like Perl (*.pl*), and Python (*.py*), to name a few.

Because it knows what it's getting, Google is more comfortable with sites consisting of pages that you always have up (known as *static* pages). URLs with endings like *.html* and *.htm* indicate stability and are thus Google-friendly.

Alternatively, you can try massaging your Web site application or content management system so that it produces clear and simple URLs rather than a litany of session variables strung together like so many Christmas lights. Why use *http://www.example.com/products.cgi?cat=autoparts&partnum=6502*, for example, when *http://www.example.com/autoparts/6502.html* will do?

Provide a clear path into your site

Google, like everyone else, hates wasting time on superfluous pages. The most serious offender is the *splash page,* those annoying intro pages that you sometimes have to view or click through before you get to a site's real home page. Splash pages typically feature Flash animations that can suck important minutes out of your day, but offer nary a real link to anything. Google—and many visitors—take a dim view of splash pages. Do everyone a favor and skip them. You can show off your graphic sensibility and your Flash skills on *real* pages in your site.

Identify yourself clearly and concisely

Your friendly, homey design touches and inviting color scheme draw people in by the ton. But they don't mean a thing to poor color-blind and design-sense-deprived Google. All the Google robots and spiders have to go by are the *metadata*—the details you embed in your Web pages' HTML code, like the title (<title> Hosiery R Us</title>, for example).

Google may interpret your metadata hierarchically when it's trying to decide how relevant your page is to a particular search. For example, if you have a first-order heading like <h1>Socks</h1> followed by a word set off in italics, like <i>plaid</i>, Google might consider the word in the heading more important than the word in italics. Which is just what you want—if somebody is looking for *socks*. But if your site is primarily about plaid items, and you want people searching for *plaid* to find you near the top of their results, you probably ought to make the word "plaid" a heading and not just an italicized comment.

Here are more tricks to help Google read between the lines, and therefore index your site appropriately:

- **Title your pages properly.** Nothing says "half-baked" quite like a site where all the pages have the same title, an utterly meaningless title, or no title at all. Title or subtitle different sections of your site appropriately. Take the 11 seconds to add <title>Al's Auto Parts: Support</title> to your HTML code.

Tip: Watch out for the dreaded "New Page" title that some Web page software automatically slaps onto any new HTML page. Microsoft FrontPage, for instance, automatically dubs your new pages serially as *New Page 1, New Page 2,* and so on—which is definitely not what you want to see in your Google results.

- **Provide *meta* tags.** *meta* tags are bits of detail about your site that you can embed in HTML tags. The cool thing is, they're invisible to your visitors but useful to Web robots. Google doesn't say how much attention it pays to *meta* tags, but it can't hurt to add them, and they might just be useful to another search engine, too. Useful options include a description (as in, <meta name="description" content="A blog about computers, politics, and the punk rock underworld." />), some keywords (for example, <meta name="keywords" content="fenders, hoses, wiper blades" />), and perhaps even who's put it together (<meta name="author" content="Jonny Slick" />). Figure 8-1 shows some possible meta tags.

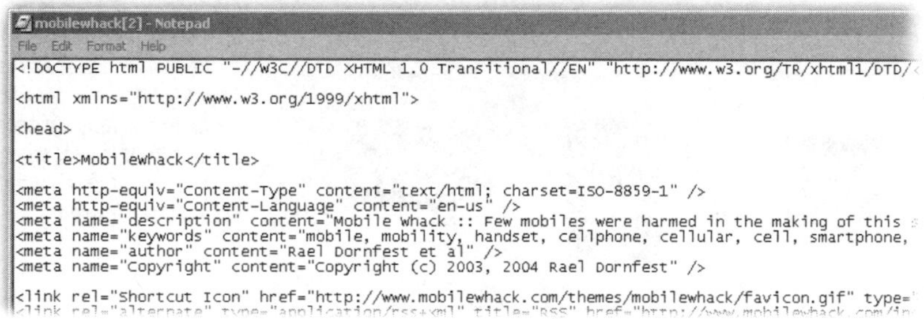

```
mobilewhack[2] - Notepad
File  Edit  Format  Help
<!DOCTYPE html PUBLIC "-//W3C//DTD XHTML 1.0 Transitional//EN" "http://www.w3.org/TR/xhtml1/DTD/
<html xmlns="http://www.w3.org/1999/xhtml">
<head>
<title>Mobilewhack</title>
<meta http-equiv="Content-Type" content="text/html; charset=ISO-8859-1" />
<meta http-equiv="Content-Language" content="en-us" />
<meta name="description" content="Mobile whack :: Few mobiles were harmed in the making of this
<meta name="keywords" content="mobile, mobility, handset, cellphone, cellular, cell, smartphone,
<meta name="author" content="Rael Dornfest et al" />
<meta name="Copyright" content="Copyright (c) 2003, 2004 Rael Dornfest" />
<link rel="Shortcut Icon" href="http://www.mobilewhack.com/themes/mobilewhack/favicon.gif" type=
<link rel="alternate" type="application/rss+xml" title="RSS" href="http://www.mobilewhack.com/in
```

Figure 8-1:
You can see the source code for most pages by right-clicking them (Control-clicking on a Mac) and choosing View Page Source or View Source.

Tip: There is some evidence that excessive keywords are off-putting to search engines—especially if they're repetitive and obvious, like "free, free, free, sale, sale, sale, Viagra, Viagra, Viagra…". When it comes to keywords, focus and frugality are your friends.

- **Augment your pictures with *alt tags*.** Ever wonder how Google Images (page 82) knows what's a photo of your Aunt Sarah on her 101st birthday and what's a snap of your summer holiday in Spain? Mostly, Google takes hints from nearby text. But what if your nearby text mentions Aunt Sarah *and* ugly Uncle Phil? You can help ensure that Google understands and properly indexes your pictures by giving them descriptive titles in *alt*—or "alternative" information—tags.

Tagging pictures is particularly important because most image-editing software automatically names pictures things like *camera_1.jpg* or *set55_02.tif*, which never helps anyone—Google or human—figure out that you're really offering a lovely photo of Monarch butterflies migrating or a diagram of the food chain. And if you've renamed those pictures *butterfly.jpg* and *diagram.tif*, you haven't helped much, either. But when you associate an *alt* tag with a picture, you can give explicit details, like this: <img src="butterfly.jpg" alt="Monarch butterflies migrating over Kansas" />). The *alt* tag then appears as your picture loads on your Web page—and with your picture in Google Images—helping everyone find your meticulous migration study. Figure 8-2 shows you how the *alt* tag looks in a Google Images search.

Figure 8-2:
An image search for soup cans. Most of these pictures have alt *tags, which are the names that identify the images as something to do with soup cans or Andy Warhol. But on the top row, the rightmost picture has no alt tag, and it doesn't appear to contain any soup cans. In fact, it's a picture of a museum that once had an exhibit called "From Soup Cans to Nuts: Prints by Andy Warhol." Google found that reference near the photo of the museum and assumed that's what the picture showed.*

Don't fence yourself in with an overabundance of frames

Frames—pieces of Web pages you can designate to appear independently, like a scrolling column that moves while the navigation bar stays put—are confusing to robots and people alike. Use them sparingly, if you must use them at all, and label them clearly (for example, <frame src="menu.html" name="menubar"> and <frame src="home.html" name="content">). You should also provide a <noframes> option just in case the spider—or, indeed, your visitor's browser—doesn't know what to do with frames.

Tip: Danny Sullivan's excellent article, "Search Engines and Frames" (*www.searchenginewatch.com/Webmasters/article.php/2167901*), provides much-needed advice on keeping your frames search-engine friendly.

Find and fix broken links

Google's spiders, like nearly all Web site visitors, have zero interest in guessing where this or that link *should* have taken them. In fact, spiders have nothing but links to go on to find the rest of your site; don't stop them short with a broken link. Before you publish a new article or add any new links within your site, preview the content in your browser and make sure that any links you've embedded do in fact point where they're supposed to.

While you're at it, do your pals downstream a favor and make sure your outbound links (your links to other Web sites) are still valid. Remember: The next downstream site the Google spider doesn't find could be your own.

Let Google in

Make sure you aren't fencing Google out with *robots.txt* files (notes telling robots that they can't look at all or part of your site) or *meta rules* (notes telling robots that they can't perform certain behaviors on a particular page, like indexing it, caching it, or following links to other pages). For an introduction to the art of letting robots in and keeping them out, read the box on page 275 and "Hiding from Google" on page 282.

Tip: For even more loving detail on making your Web site inviting to Google, be sure to take a stroll through Brett Tabke's Search Engine Optimization Template (*www.clickmojo.com/more/122_0_1_0_M/*). Brett is the proprietor of WebmasterWorld.com and knows an awful lot about search engine optimization.

That should do it. With your virtual tie tied and shoes shined, it's high time you introduced yourself to Google and the Web.

Getting Google's Attention

You can get into Google's index two ways, and both are worth pursuing. First, you can simply wave your arms and tell Google you want to be part of its index. Second, you can link to other sites—and have them link to yours—so that when Google crawls the Web and follows links from one site to another, it automatically discovers yours.

Tip: For a refresher on the difference between being crawled and getting indexed, take a gander at the discussion at the beginning of the chapter.

Introduce Yourself to Google

Virtually speaking, you can just walk over to Google and say, "Hello." Simply visit the "Add your URL to Google" page at *www.google.com/addurl.html,* type your site's Web address into the URL field, and click Add URL (see Figure 8-3). You only need introduce Google to your home page; it'll use your links to find the rest of the site you've linked to and made available for public consumption. Once Google knows about your site, it sends out the Googlebot for a look—anywhere from one day to a couple of weeks after you sign up.

Google doesn't make any promises about when your site is likely to appear in search results, though it usually takes between 24 hours and a week. Google also doesn't give any guarantee that they'll actually *add* your site to their index. And, unfortunately, you have no way to tell whether Google has indexed your site or whether it's rejected you without actually performing the crawl. If you submitted a

---

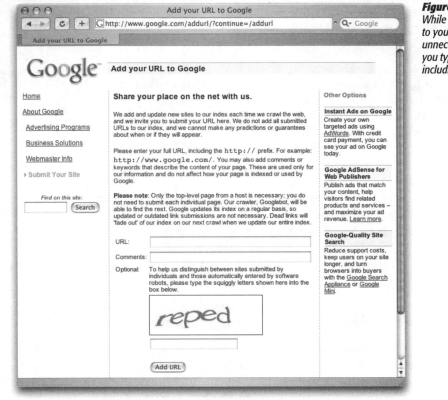

Figure 8-3:
*While adding a comment
to your submission is
unnecessary, it's vital that
you type in a proper URL,
including the http:// bit.*

URL a couple of weeks ago and Google doesn't seem to know anything about you, check out the guidelines and rules for Webmasters at *www.google.com/webmasters/ guidelines.html,* and then resubmit your site.

Tip: Google suggests listing your site with Yahoo (*http://docs.yahoo.com/info/suggest/*) and the Open Directory Project (*http://www.dmoz.org,* page 281). Once you're in either Yahoo or the Open Directory, Google should find and index your site in six to eight weeks. It's a belt-and-suspenders step worth taking.

Link Up I

The other route into Google is via links. When Google's spiders crawl the Web, they check old pages for new text, pictures, and links—and then they follow the new links, looking for new pages to add to Google's index. So a great way to get into Google is to have other sites already in the index link to yours.

If you've got a friend, business associate, neighbor, or peer with a Web site or Weblog (page 188) already known to Google, see if he's up for linking to yours. If he goes for it, he's essentially introducing your site to Google by association. (You can return the favor by linking back to his site, thereby increasing his PageRank rating.)

Link Up II

Sites on just about every subject are itching for news and events of interest to their readers. And if you have something whiz-bang interesting or Earth-shatteringly important on your site, you can try to catch the eye of a site you think should know you—who might then link to your site.

On sites that you'd like to link to you, look for "Suggest a Link" or "Submit a Story" features. Write up a meaty-though-modest description, fill in the form as directed, and suggest they take a gander at something in particular on your site. If they go for it, you're that much closer to being in the Google database.

Tip: It is considered tacky to actually ask another site, "Please link to me," or "If I link to you, will you link to me?"(otherwise called a link exchange). Simply let other sites know about something that is probably of interest to them and let the links fall where they may.

Does Google Know You're There?

You've done everything in your power to get Google's attention. Now, how do you know when the Googlebot (*www.google.com/bot.html*), Google's Web-crawling robot, has come calling? Of course, if your site starts appearing in Google results, you can rest easy knowing Google is hip to you.

Otherwise, it's not particularly obvious when the Googlebot arrives, investigates, and leaves your site. With a little simple research, however, you can figure out what parts of your site Google is and isn't finding.

The place to look is your Web site's *logs,* which keep a record of comings and goings from your site—*requests* and *responses* in Webmaster vernacular. They make for an entertaining read, in a geeky way, and are worth getting familiar with.

Web server logs are simple text files, as shown in Figure 8-4, and you can read them by using a simple text editor or Unix command-line tools. You can also peruse them through a log-analysis tool, a desktop application, an administrative tool, or a Web-based service.

If you know where your logs are kept and you have access to them (some Web site administrators keep them off-limits), go ahead and take a look. If not, contact your local server administrator or Internet Service Provider and ask them where you can find the logs.

Once you've opened the logs, you can find traces of the Googlebot. A typical visit follows these steps:

Note: The only bits that concern you are those in bold in the examples, following the word "GET."

• **First, the Googlebot knocks and sees if it's welcome.** When it hits your site, the first thing the Googlebot does is request your site's *robots.txt* file to see if it even

---

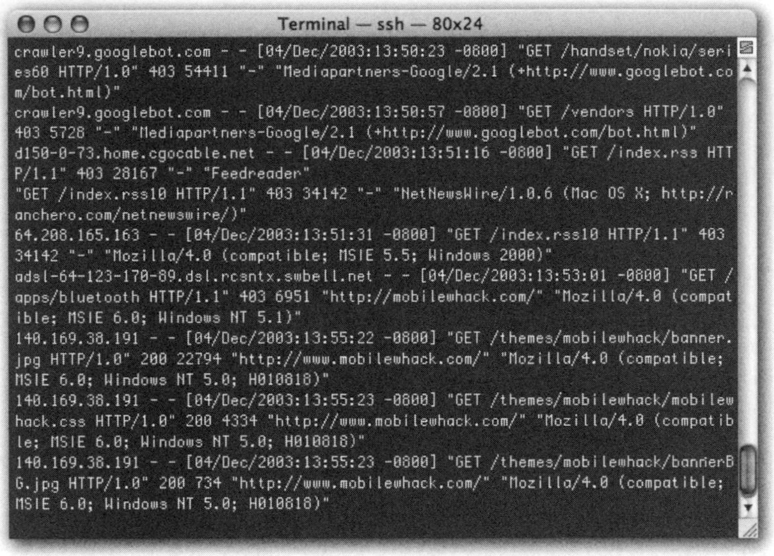

Figure 8-4:
Here's a piece of a raw server log from Mobilewhack.com. The first two requests are from the Googlebot, which is looking for access to the site's sections on Nokia's series 60 phones and vendors. The rest of the requests are from other entities on the Web (things like browsers and other search engines' bots).

has permission to come in and take a look around. (Read more about *robots.txt* in the box "Robot Rules of the Road" on page 284.) The request looks something like this:

```
208.201.239.21 - - [19/Feb/2004:19:16:05 -0800] "GET /robots.txt HTTP/1.1"
200 199 "-" "Googlebot/2.1 (+http://www.googlebot.com/bot.html)"
```

Here's what you're looking at: The first set of numbers is your site's IP address. The stuff in the brackets is the date and time of the Googlebot's request. The actual request is the **/robots.txt** part. **HTTP/1.1** is the version of HTTP in use (HTTP is the language Web browsers and servers speak); **200** is the status code for that request (200 says the request was successful; 404 means it failed); and **199** is the number of bytes transferred. The dash in quotes tells you there's no login necessary for people (or bots) to access the site. And everything else is the *user-agent identification* (that is, the Googlebot's cyber-credentials).

If the Googlebot finds a *robots.txt* file, it reads it and follows any rules that tell it where not to go. If it can't find *robots.txt*, the Googlebot assumes it has permission to index your site in its entirety.

- **Next, the Googlebot requests the *index pages* for your site's directories.** As you know, you build Web sites out of pages that you store in folders, called *directories*. And you nest directories within each other, much the way you store files on your hard drive. Usually, you put an index page (*index.html* or *index.htm,* for example) into each directory, which acts as the home page for that directory.

For example, your site may contain the directory *www.yoursite.com/products*. When a robot asks your server for a directory (*/products*) rather than a specific

Web page (*/products/cheddar.html*), your server shows it the directory's index. In Web server parlance, this request for the index is /, (say "slash"), and it's simply the Web way of asking for a list of the contents of the directory following the slash. Put another way, the slash is like asking, "What's in this room?" In the server log, the request looks like this:

```
208.201.239.21 - - [19/Feb/2004:18:46:46 -0800] "GET /products HTTP/1.1" 200
5719 "-" "Googlebot/2.1 (+http://www.googlebot.com/bot.html)"
```

and the / after the word GET tells your server to "offer up the index page for this directory." In this case, the Googlebot is asking for the index page for the products directory. If the request specified no directory and looked like this— "GET / HTTP/1.1"—that would mean the Googlebot was knocking at your site's front door, asking to see the contents of the main directory for the whole place. (By extension, the request **GET /products** is like asking to look in, say, the cupboard.)

• **Next, the Googlebot follows all the links and image tags on the index pages.** When you hit a Web page, your browser follows HTML image tags to find, download, and display any pictures on that page. The Googlebot does the same thing. Similarly, just as you follow hyperlinks to move between pages on a site or between sites, so does the Googlebot. As it goes, the Googlebot gleans text and underlying HTML from your pages and reports the info back to the Google indexer, which adds it to the master list.

Note: In your server logs, you should see a lot of requests from the Googlebot, one after another, as it asks to crawl each page. The requests should all look a lot like the one above for the */products* directory. For example, when the Googlebot requests the contents of a page called *tshirts*, it'll look something like this:

```
208.201.239.21 - - [19/Feb/2004:18:58:15 -0800] "GET /tshirts/ HTTP/1.1" 200
6358 "-" "Googlebot/2.1 (+http://www.googlebot.com/bot.html)".
```

FREQUENTLY ASKED QUESTION

The Importance of Index Pages

What happens if I don't put index pages in every directory?

If you blow off an index page, your server can respond in either of two ways when a browser or robot requests the missing URL. It can automatically generate a generic-looking page with a list of links to the pages in that directory. Or it can deny the request and show an error page. Neither option is one that visitors like, and an error can stop the Googlebot cold. So it's a good idea to create index pages for every directory.

Still, on a large site, you're bound to forget one or two of them. The solution is to create an *ErrorDocument* directive, which serves up a special page every time somebody asks for an index that's missing. The special page can contain links to other pages on your site, possibly preventing people—and the Googlebot—from giving up in a huff. For more info on ErrorDocument, check out *http://hoohoo.ncsa.uiuc.edu/docs/setup/srm/ErrorDocument.html*.

- **The Googlebot conducts this process throughout your site.** It follows working links until it hits something it's seen before or something with no link, like an image. When the bot's done with your site, it heads off to other sites you've linked to.

Don't be too concerned if the Googlebot has come and gone, but your site isn't yet showing up in Google results. It takes some time for Google to index, store, and make available to the search engine everything it's found.

Even so, some material may not make it into the index at all, particularly if the Googlebot found duplicate text or encountered a glitch. For example, a stray *robots.txt* file in the wrong place could have sent the Googlebot packing. Or some part of your site might not be linked to anything else within your site, rendering it invisible to the Googlebot.

If your logs reveal that the Googlebot has come calling, but after a week or two your site still isn't coming up in search results, recheck your logs, *robots.txt* files, and your site itself for anything that might have thrown Google off.

Note: The only way to tell Google that your site is not in its index is to submit or resubmit your URL.

POWER USERS' CLINIC

Adding Some Flavor

Don't you just hate it when you're using a search box on a Web site devoted to all things reptilian, and a search for "snake" brings up sites devoted to plumbers' tools and drain-cleaning services? To help Webmasters get listed in search results that actually pertain to their topic, Google has come up with a little recipe it calls "Site-Flavored Search."

To give your Web site a taste of Site-Flavored Google search, head to *labs.google.com/personalized/siteflavored*. On this page, you can type in your site's URL and have Google analyze its content and create a *profile*. This may make it sound like your Web site is looking to date other Web sites—and in a way, it kind of is, because you want to have it find other sites with similar interests.

After you click the Get Profile button on the page, Google scans your site and tries to categorize it under a number of general labels—*www.nasa.gov* is profiled as a "Technology" site, for example—based on the kind of information Google finds. If you think Google is off the mark and has misunderstood your site, you can adjust, tinker, and fine-tune the profile. If you have a Web site about music, you can label it

as Music and even add on some deeper descriptions under the Music tag, like R&B or Hip Hop.

Once you complete the site profiling, click the button at the top of the page to generate a chunk of HTML that you can paste into your own Web page's code. This Google-generated code creates a special Site-Flavored Search box on your site, complete with a Custom Search button. Now, when people use this special search box on your site, they'll get results similar in flavor to your own site, meaning people searching for Prince should have a better chance of getting results about the prolific pop star rather than a member of the royal family.

Google Site-Flavored Search is still in the beta stage, and to use it, you need to have at least Netscape 5, Internet Explorer 5, or Mozilla 1.4, and have JavaScript enabled. And although Google eventually gets around to adding tons of languages, for now, all your flavored searches need to be in English.

Adding this code to your web site will create a search box that looks like this:

Google™ Site-Flavored ꞵᴇᴛᴀ [   ] [Custom Search]

Rising in Google Results

The Googlebot has found your site, you and Google are becoming fast friends, and your site has just entered the PageRank popularity contest. How do you become a rising search engine star, reaching one of the coveted top spots on the first page of search results?

The secret to pleasing Google turns out to be rather straightforward: please your visitors. Happy visitors lead to inbound links, because when people like a site, they link to it from their own sites. And when there are links, Google rankings follow. That's it.

UP TO SPEED

The Importance of PageRank

PageRank is Google's algorithm for determining the ranking of Web pages. It was formulated by Google founders Sergey Brin and Larry Page and has been used ever since—in concert with a plethora of other calculations and corrections—as the juice behind Google.

Put succinctly, the rank of a page is determined by the number of pages that point to it. The PageRank algorithm rates pages on a scale from 0 to 10, scoring everything from as-yet-unheard-of Web pages to the likes of Amazon, Google, and Yahoo. Despite its name, however, PageRank is more of a *score* than a rank. Google doesn't have a single hierarchy of pages, and many pages share the same value.

In addition, a page's rank exists outside of any particular Google search. Put another way, Google ignores PageRank when it's searching, using it instead to decide the order in which it *displays* the results of that search. So when you run a search, Google looks through its various indexes of keywords and phrases, and first builds a list of results from pages that match your criteria. Then Google uses the PageRank of each of these pages to help decide what order to offer them in.

You can find out your site's PageRank on the Google toolbar (page 171). First, make sure you've got the PageRank display turned on. To do so, open the Toolbar Options dialog box by clicking the Options button and then the Options tab, where you can find the PageRank display choice; to turn it on, you must have the Advanced Features enabled (page 181). Then go to a page on your site and mouse over the PageRank bar to display a little box telling you the rank.

If you're interested in more of the intricate details of PageRank, Mark Horrell's "The PageRank Algorithm" (*www.markhorrell.com/seo/pagerank.html*) is worth a read.

Here are some suggestions for pleasing your visitors:

- **Keep things fresh, focused, and fascinating.** Outdated material can be a real turn-off, while nothing keeps visitors coming back like fresh, hot-off-the-keyboard prose and links.

Note: Some search engine experts believe that Google indexes rapidly changing sites more often than those updated only every now and then.

So take the time to update your site when appropriate. And when you've got fresh reading material available, make it immediately obvious by maintaining a What's New page, adding new items to the top of the home page, or listing the latest additions in a sidebar. You can't expect your visitors to remember what they read last time and hunt around for the new stuff.

Also, provide new links whenever you can. While some Web sites believe that every link provided to other Web sites offers another reason for visitors to leave, in practice the opposite is true. If your site is a rich resource for what's happening on the Web, your readers will come to see you as a trusted friend, putting you on their virtual speed-dial and visiting more frequently.

- **Be responsive.** Keep a watchful eye on your server logs to learn what's popular. If you discover certain sections of your site or particular articles draw the most visitors, consider filling out those parts of your site with more stories. If you find that a lot of people are coming to you through certain search engine queries, you have some great hints about what they're looking for and whether they're finding it on your site. And if you know they're searching on your site itself and *not* finding what they want, respond to their wishes by providing just what they were looking for. Figure 8-5 shows you a typical log file.

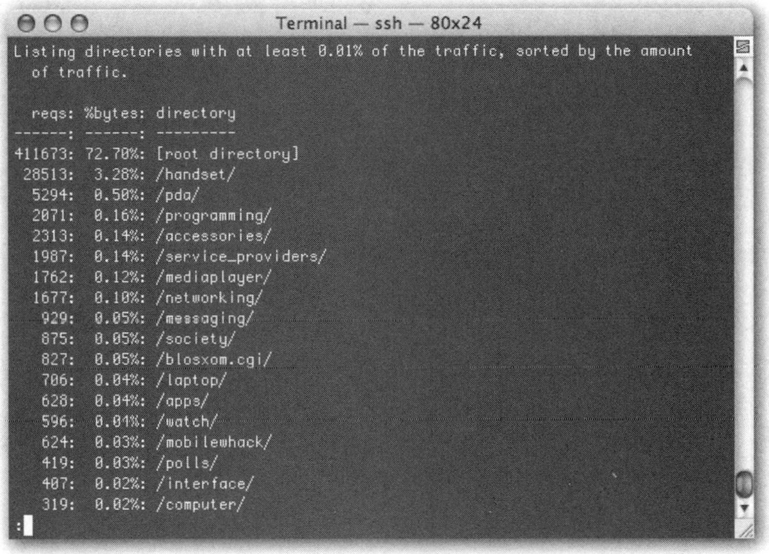

Figure 8-5:
Server logs can look like anything from a text-only listing to a fancy report provided by your ISP or by Google (page 273). In this plain-Jane log, the column on the left shows the number of visits over time, and the column on the right shows the section of the Web site people visited. (The middle column, percentage of bytes transferred, is mostly useless because the volume depends on what's on that page. A page with lots of pictures is going to transfer a higher percentage than a text-only page.) This log tells you that the home page ("root") of this site gets the most traffic, followed by the "handset" section.

Tip: Visitors who find your site through a search engine usually carry a record of their query with them to your site. Most log-analysis tools make note of these search terms, including them in any generated reports. Thus, if you know the right place to look, you can usually figure out *what people were searching for* when they came to your site. Chapter 10 is all about Google Analytics, a free tool for analyzing your Web site traffic.

- **Give each page, article, or product its own permanent URL.** When people want to send their best friend the URL for your page about family eggplant recipes, they really hate adding: "Click on the third link down in the What's New section, below the picture of Barney." They may hate it so much that they stop bothering with your site at all.

There are two ways you can make your site harder for people to use. First, if you put a lot of articles on one page, you force people to say, "It's the fifth story on the page." It also forces you to keep the article in that slot if you want people to find it. Second, using frames for whole pages causes your visitors to see the same URL in their address bar no matter what page of your site they're on—which means they can't send friends a link without also providing a roadmap to find the page in question. (That's yet another excellent reason to eschew frames.)

So make things simple for your visitors *and* Google: Every time you create a page on your site, link to it from at least one other page—and, if possible, don't change the page's name.

- **Let them share.** Go a step better and let visitors hang a hat on your site through forums, feedback forms, and customization. Read the feedback channels on a regular basis and become an active participant in discussions of your site.

- **Plain and simple wins the race.** Keep your Web pages as lightweight as possible. Just because you're at the end of a high-speed broadband connection doesn't mean your visitors are. In fact, many Web surfers still poke along at 56 K, not to mention those visiting from their cellphones and PDAs—who often have *very* slow connections.

- **Don't annoy your visitors.** Nothing screams "Go Away" like in-your-face Flash animations, ads strewn all over the place, pages that link to nothing, and dopey gimmicks. It's all right to have a long article span multiple linked pages, but be fair about how much content is on each page, and avoid click-through pages set up solely for advertising impressions. While you're at it, provide a Print view for those who want a story all on one page for a manageable print job, as shown in Figure 8-6.

Keep busy trying to please your visitors, and don't spend time trying to fool Google. The Google folks are smart, and they have set up all manner of checks and balances to make sure the sites they index are on the up-and-up. Indeed, Google considers the following practices unfair—so much so that if they discover you engaging in them, the Googlebot may stop visiting and including you in the index. (Google doesn't say how long it'll keep you out in the cold, but anecdotal evidence suggests the icy treatment may be permanent.)

- **Don't misrepresent your site to Google by feeding different content to the Googlebot than you do your regular human visitors.** This trick is known among Webmasters as *cloaking*. It entails manipulating your site in response to *User-Agent identifiers*, which are signatures associated with every request from a Web browser or robot to view a site. Some sites use this identifier to show different content to a bot (User-Agent: Googlebot) than to your garden-variety Web browser (User-Agent: Internet Explorer). It's a nasty business, and a good way to draw Google's ire.

Figure 8-6:
Top: The Web-friendly
version of a story may
span several Web pages.

Bottom: A printer-friendly
view, by contrast, keeps
the entire article on one
page and is all but bereft
of advertising. The
printer-friendly version is
also a good format for
emailing a story to a
friend or transferring to a
PDA.

- **Stay away from HTML shenanigans intended to confuse the Googlebot.** These tricks include giving your page multiple titles, embedding inaccurate keywords, stuffing your page with repetitive keywords, and so forth.

- **Steer well clear of so-called link farms and link-exchanges that exist solely to boost your Google ranking.** They're an investment in trouble.

WORD TO THE WISE

List Yourself Elsewhere

While Google is the champion of search engines, people will find you most readily if you're listed everywhere: on Web directories, on other search engines, and on other sites *related* to yours. (If your site sells specialty knitting needles, for example, you want knitting resource sites to include you.)

First and foremost, be sure to get yourself into the two granddaddies of directories, the Open Directory Project (*www.dmoz.org*), which is the directory behind the Google Directory (page 107), and Yahoo (*www.yahoo.com*). Not only do these directories help people find you when they're browsing the listings, but they increase your chances of being spotted and indexed by Google in a timely manner.

Oodles of other search engines live on the Web. AltaVista, HotBot, and Ask Jeeves are among the most popular. Introduce yourself to each by finding and filling out their respective URL-submission forms. You can also use a service that

goes around listing you anywhere and everywhere you'd like to be found. These services, which can be a good timesaver, range from free to rather costly, depending on breadth and depth of features. You can find a nice selection of such listing services at *http://directory.google.com/Top/Computers/ Internet/Web_Design_and_Development/Promotion/.*

For sites you want to exchange links with that *aren't* directories or other types of search engines, choose wisely. Linking randomly so that lots of other sites will link to you can *decrease* your PageRank (because PageRank evaluates the quality of sites linking to you). On the other hand, exchanging links with rich sources of information is actually useful to readers *and* beneficial to your PageRank.

In short, list yourself only on good, clean, well-known, legitimate sites—both general and specific to your topic of interest—where you think it'll do some good. Then stop.

Getting Rid of Google

Some Webmasters, for whatever reasons, prefer their sites remain word-of-mouth affairs and shy away from the Google limelight. The most effective way to keep some or all of your content out of Google is making sure it never gets in the Google index in the first place. This is quite a trick. A stray link from a nosy-parker to otherwise undiscovered material can leave you exposed in no time flat—the moment the Googlebot finds it, that is.

Hiding from the Whole World

If you don't want *anyone* finding all or a portion of your site, simply failing to mention it or hiding some of it behind obscure URLs won't do the trick. Assume that if it's publicly accessible, someone, sometime will stumble across it. To keep your site from falling into the hands of strollers-by:

- **Don't put it online in the first place.** If your site is meant for coworkers' or household-members' eyes only, place it behind a firewall configured to disallow incoming requests to your Web server.

- **Lock it up tight.** Protect your site from prying eyes by limiting access to visitors coming from particular IP addresses or to those supplying the correct user name and password.

Hiding from Google

If, on the other hand, you just don't want *Google* to find, crawl, and index your site or portions thereof, no problem. You can set up specific *rules*, which are instructions that the Googlebot follows:

- **Invoke the Robot Exclusion rule.** The Googlebot, like any well-behaved robot, obeys any explicit request placed in your *robots.txt* file not to roam your site, keep out of some particular corners, or keep its mitts off files of particular types. Learn more about robots in the box on page 284.

- **Add a *robots* meta tag.** You can tag *individual* pages as "hands-off" to robots by adding a *meta* tag (page 269) to the pages themselves.

Tip: If you want to block the Googlebot from a whole *directory*, use a *robots.txt* file (page 284).

— To keep Google from indexing a page, add the following to the <head> section of your Web page:

```
<meta name="googlebot" content="noindex">
```

Tip: Many robots ignore the *robots* meta tag, but the Googlebot actually does pay attention. You can, nevertheless, try to warn off other robots by replacing *googlebot* in the meta tag with *robots.* The Googlebot respects either.

— You may want to keep *part* of your site out of the Google index. For example, you'd probably rather people visit your product database *directly* than have them view outdated information on Google. To have the Googlebot index your home page but not follow any of its links to the rest of your site, therefore, use:

```
<meta name="googlebot" content="nofollow">
```

Tip: If you want to block the Googlebot from a single page or a couple of pages only, add the *noindex* meta tag to those particular pages, like this: *<meta name="googlebot" content="noindex">*. Be sure to put the meta tag between the opening <head> and closing </head> tags.

— You can also control whether or not Google search results display snippets of text from your pages along with their titles. This option is handy if, say, you've built up a nice community of visitors who participate regularly in ongoing discussions on your site. To prevent their wisdom from being taken out of context, use:

```
<meta name="googlebot" content="nosnippet">
```

— When it indexes your site, Google caches (page 26) full copies of your pages on its servers. When your site appears in a list of Google search results, the searcher can look up pages in Google's cache, rather than on your actual site. The cache may be outdated, as it's simply a snapshot of a page *at the time Google indexed it*. If you'd prefer people visit your site directly, use:

```
<meta name="googlebot" content="nocache">
```

You can combine any number of these properties in your *robots* meta tags by listing them, one after the other, separated by commas. For example, to prevent both caching and snippet gathering, add the following to your Web page:

```
<meta name="googlebot" content="nocache, nosnippet">
```

Tip: For more of the nitty-gritty details on the *robots* meta tag, visit the official "HTML Author's Guide to the Robots meta tag" at *www.robotstxt.org/wc/meta-user.html*.

If you've invoked the Robot Exclusion rule or added a *robots* meta tag *after* Google has already found pieces of your site, it may take days or weeks before Google incorporates the changes into its behavior. If time is of the essence and you'd like Google to pay attention to your changes as soon as possible, you can remove your entire site or parts of it from Google and request a reindexing. Read on.

Removing Yourself from Google

What do you do when you've made it into Google, only to discover that your site includes a few things you'd hoped the search engine wouldn't find—like pictures you uploaded during the height of your bachelorette party?

You can, of course, take the drastic step of shutting down your site entirely. This prevents anyone from actually getting to your site. Yet the results themselves—and, more likely than not, cached copies of your pages—already exist in Google's index. So you've ineffectually closed the proverbial barn door after the horse has already left hoofprints in the neighbor's vegetable garden.

For better and for worse, the Web has an incredible memory: that which is spoken online can never really be unspoken. You can, however, use the same methods described in the previous section to actually remove ill-indexed booty from Google.

Once you've invoked the Robot Exclusion rule, peppered appropriate pages with *robots* meta tags, and taken offline the content you didn't want online in the first place, you're ready to request that Google immediately remove the material from its index.

Warning: Requesting your content be removed from the Google index does not put a stop to the Googlebot's visits; the next time it stumbles across your site, it dutifully roams and re-indexes. Thus, it is vital that you take the steps mentioned in "Hiding from Google" on page 282 to stop the Googlebot from indexing your site *before* you bother to request that Google remove material from its current index. Going about all this in the wrong order is simply a waste of time.

Here's how to get Google to clean your site out of its index:

1. **Visit Google's URL Removal page.**

   Point your Web browser to *http://services.google.com/urlconsole/controller*.

2. **Establish a Google account.**

   In the form provided, type your email address and a password (make one up), and click Create Account.

UP TO SPEED

Robot Rules of the Road

Robots, by and large, keep to the rules of the road. They're supposed to identify themselves properly, be respectful of the sites they visit, and do their best to represent fairly the sites they're indexing.

The primary method for controlling robot access to your site is the *Robot Exclusion Standard* (*www.robotstxt.org/wc/norobots.html*). This standard is an agreed-upon method for stating where robots are (or are not) allowed to roam on your site. Think of it as a virtual garland of garlic to ward off unwanted nightly visitors.

You usually hear the Robot Exclusion Standard mentioned as *robots.txt*, a reference to the rather simple way in which it's implemented. As a Webmaster, you simply place a plain text file—that's what the *.txt* bit is all about—in the root directory of your Web site. Name it *robots.txt* to have it read by any well-behaved robot visiting your site before it moves on to seek out and index your content.

The contents of the *robots.txt* file are just as simple. The first line states which robot you're talking to; you can single out a particular robot (such as Googlebot) or use a * (wildcard character) to speak to any and every robot. Subsequent lines state which directories, files, and file types the robot should skip.

Here are some examples:

- To keep the Googlebot out entirely, your *robots.txt* should read:

  User-agent: Googlebot

  Disallow: /

This code means, "Any robot with the name (**User-agent**) Googlebot should keep its mitts off of everything, including and beyond the root (/) of my site."

- To keep the Googlebot out of just your forums, your *robots.txt* should read:

  User-agent: Googlebot

  Disallow: /forums

Translation: "Googlebot, keep out of anything inside my site's **/forums** directory."

- Perhaps you're more than happy for the Googlebot to read and index your prose but you're adamant about your images staying out of Google Images (page 82). You can simply disallow indexing of particular file types like so:

  User-agent: Googlebot

  Disallow: /*.gif

  Disallow: /*.jpg

  Disallow: /*.png

Translation: "Googlebot, don't look at any GIF, JPG, or PNG images anywhere on my site."

- To apply these rules to *any* rule-obeying robot, simply replace the User-agent name with a *, meaning "any robot":

  User-agent: *

  Disallow: /

You can add any number of lines in the file for any folder or page within your site. You need to add another User-agent line only to define rules for a different robot.

If you already have a Google account, type your email address and password into the "Already have an account?" form and click Login. Skip to step 4.

3. **Check your email.**

In just a few minutes, you should receive email from Google containing a link to follow. Click the link or paste the URL into your Web browser. You arrive back at Google's URL Removal Options page, logged in and ready to remove your content.

4. **Tell Google whether you want to remove a whole site, a section of a site, or just a page (Figure 8-7).**

Google has no way of verifying that you are indeed the owner of the pages you say you want removed. After all, if your site is *www.roadrunner.com*, Google can't tell whether the request for removal is coming from a legitimate Webmaster or from Wile E. Coyote. Google thus lets you simply *request* that it nix pages. Meantime, the Googlebot checks the site in question for a *robots.txt* file (which would tell Google that it isn't welcome on that site), or for embedded *robots* meta tags (which would tell it to ignore specific pages). This system prevents people from shutting each other's sites out of Google, because Google rejects the request if it finds no robots rules or tags. Again, this process means you must implement those robot rules *before* you send Google on a mission to your site.

You can also remove an outdated link, although Google will most likely do so automatically the next time it tries to follow that link and can't.

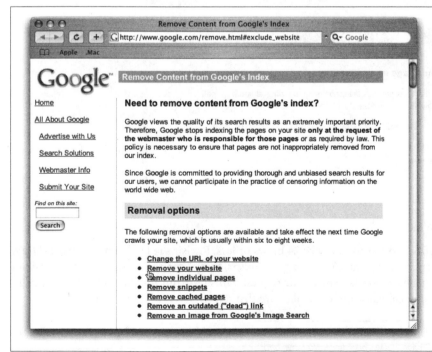

Figure 8-7:
Google lets you remove your entire site, sets of directories or pages, individual pages, or images from its index. If you remove a directory, everything within it will disappear from Google's index. Simply click the link associated with the pages you wish Google to remove.

5. Indicate the URL for the offending content.

Type in the URL for your *robots.txt* file, or for the URL of the page you wish
removed (Figure 8-8).

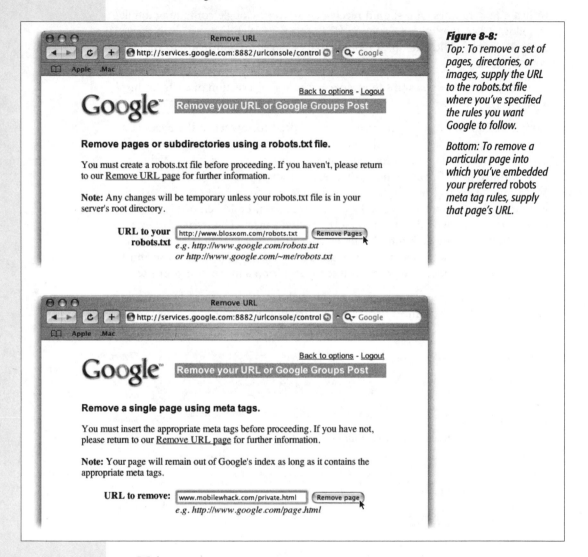

Figure 8-8:
*Top: To remove a set of
pages, directories, or
images, supply the URL
to the robots.txt file
where you've specified
the rules you want
Google to follow.*

*Bottom: To remove a
particular page into
which you've embedded
your preferred robots
meta tag rules, supply
that page's URL.*

6. Wait.

Your request should take 24 hours or less. Revisit the URL removal page (*http://
services.google.com/urlconsole/controller*) every so often to take a gander at your
queued requests; when your request vanishes from the Status list on that page,
run a Google search to make sure that it's removed what you wanted.

Tip: For more detail on removing your site from Google, visit the "Remove Content from Google's
Index" page at *www.google.com/remove.html*.

Adding Google Searches to Your Site

No doubt you've noticed Google search boxes on sites ranging from Uncle Ralph's Fishing Cornucopia to mega-destinations like Amazon.com. You, too, can add a so-called *Google box* to your site, providing visitors with a handy shortcut for searching the whole Web. But even better, you can add a Google box that also lets people search *your site*—saving you the considerable trouble of implementing a local site search yourself and instead tapping the power of Google for your own pages. Figure 8-9 shows you an example.

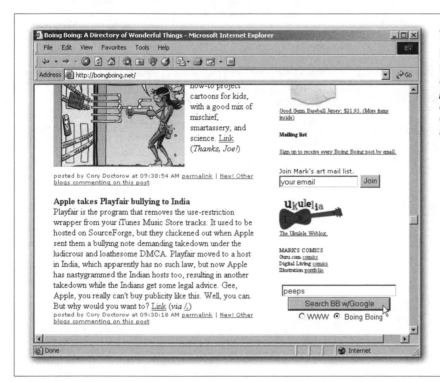

Figure 8-9:
The GoogleBox on www.
boingboing.net *lets
visitors search simply by
typing in their terms and
picking whether they'd
like Google to scour the
entire Web or just the
BoingBoing site.*

Adding a Box for Searching the Web

You can add Google's free WebSearch box to your site by simply pasting some HTML into your Web pages. Here's how: Point your Web browser to *www.google. com/searchcode.html*. Decide whether you want to add a full-fledged Google Web-Search box to your site or whether you'd prefer to keep things a little tamer with their SafeSearch box (page 77)—worth considering if you run a religious site, a children's site, or a religious children's site. Highlight the HTML code in either the Web search or SafeSearch box, copy it, and paste it into the HTML code for your Web page. Save your page as you usually do and take a look at it in your Web browser. You should now have your very own Google search box right on your site.

Adding a Box for Searching Your Site

You can turn the Google spotlight on your own site. SiteSearch (*www.google.com/searchcode.html#both*) is Google's free search feature for *your* Web site. It's as simple to deploy as the copy-and-paste Google box described above. Figure 8-10 shows you how.

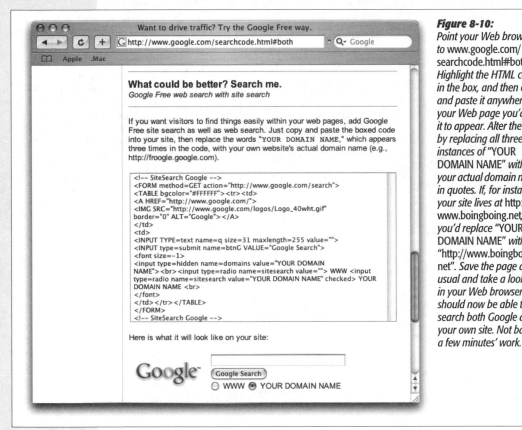

Figure 8-10:
Point your Web browser to www.google.com/searchcode.html#both. Highlight the HTML code in the box, and then copy and paste it anywhere in your Web page you'd like it to appear. Alter the code by replacing all three instances of "YOUR DOMAIN NAME" with your actual domain name, in quotes. If, for instance, your site lives at http://www.boingboing.net, you'd replace "YOUR DOMAIN NAME" with "http://www.boingboing.net". Save the page as usual and take a look at it in your Web browser. You should now be able to search both Google and your own site. Not bad for a few minutes' work.

Customizing the SiteSearch box

There's nothing wrong with the classic look and feel of a Google results page. But with just a dollop of work, you can make Google's SiteSearch look as if it were built into your site rather than bolted on.

Point your browser to *www.google.com/services/free.html*, sign up for an account, and follow the simple wizard-like directions to customize the background, text, and link colors on your Google results page. While you don't end up with anything that looks enormously different from the standard Google results page, you can differentiate yourself a tad, as shown in Figure 8-11.

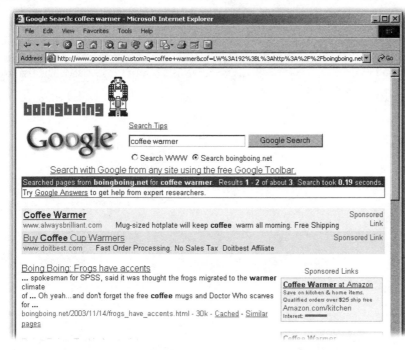

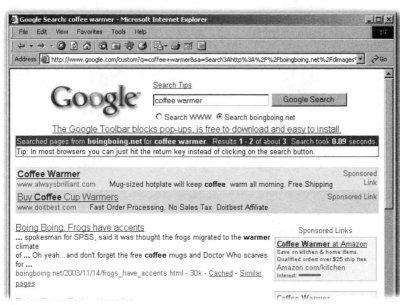

Figure 8-11:
A branded results page (top) doesn't look all that different from the unbranded version (bottom), but having your logo appear does at least remind your visitors—who are now at Google.com—where they were just before their search.

Note: Google offers more search options for your site, at a price. For instance, their Silver/Gold Search (*www.google.com/services/silver_gold.html*) provides top-notch features like the ability to further customize results pages and run your own ads. It costs a minimum monthly fee of U.S. $599, plus additional click-through fees. Their Custom WebSearch (*www.google.com/services/custom.html*) is for portal sites issuing four million or more queries per year—with commensurate fees. Learn all about Google Business Solutions at *www.google.com/services/*.

Making Money with Google

You've mastered searching with Google, you've gotten your site in Google's index, and you have a healthy PageRank. So how do you pay the bills? Unless your site makes a profit on donations from visitors who just love your wacky sense of humor, consider trying Google's advertising programs: AdWords and AdSense.

AdWords lets you buy spots among the *sponsored links*—the ads you see on many Google results pages. *AdSense* lets you *sell* advertising space on your own site for other people's ads. Both programs, shown in Figure 9-1, draw from the same pool of about 150,000 advertisers—everyone from 16-year-old babysitters selling hand-knit cellphone pouches to Fortune 500 companies selling cellphone service.

AdWords and AdSense are both easy to get started with, but neither is intuitive. This chapter provides an introduction to the programs, explaining how they work, when to use them, and how to get the most out of them.

Note: If this chapter doesn't answer a question you have about Google's ad programs, check the Google help pages for AdSense (*https://google.com/adsense/online-help*) and AdWords (*https://adwords. google.com/select/index.html*), which are pretty thorough and generally good. This chapter points out some of the more useful help pages.

Google AdSense

AdSense is a great program, though Google has given it a confusing name. If they'd called it Ad*Space*, you'd know right away what it's about: selling advertising space on your Web site. Despite the nomenclature issue, AdSense (*www.google.com/adsense*) has become popular with bloggers and other people who run noncommercial sites.

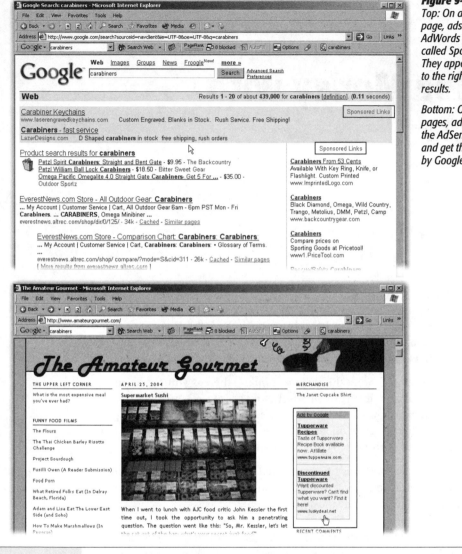

Figure 9-1:
Top: On a Google results page, ads from the AdWords program are called Sponsored Links. They appear above and to the right of the regular results.

Bottom: On other Web pages, ads come from the AdSense program and get the label, "Ads by Google."

You sign up, carve out some space on your pages for the ads (Figure 9-2), paste a few lines of code from Google into the HTML for your site, and let Google fill in your pages with color-coordinated ads. When somebody clicks one of the ads, Google pays you a fee (the amount varies, and the company doesn't disclose its payments).

Note: AdSense can be tricky for e-commerce sites because you can't fully control which ads appear on your site, and you wouldn't want to run ads for your competitors' merchandise right next to your own displays. You can, however, filter out *some* ads. Page 310 tells you more.

Figure 9-2:
In each ad, the first line is a title, followed by a few short lines of description, and finally the advertiser's main URL. All the text in the ad is hyperlinked to the advertiser's choice of URL, so if someone clicks an ad, she may wind up on a specific product page rather than on the advertiser's home page.

Tool Pouches
Quality tool pouches & accessories from brands like Bucket Boss.
www.duluthtrading.com

Though you can't decide which ads appear on your site, Google does a very nice job of assessing your pages and supplying ads that might interest your visitors. For example, if you run a site about the history of window treatments, Google is likely to dish up ads for vintage blinds and specialty curtain rods. That kind of relevance is important, because Google doesn't pay you when somebody sees an ad on your site—it pays you when somebody *clicks* an ad, so you want Google to fill your space with blurbs likely to interest your readers.

Note: Participating in AdSense doesn't have any effect on your site's rank in Google search results.

The $64,000 question is, of course, how much can you make? The exact answer is: it depends. If your site gets tons of visitors, and you focus on a narrow topic, there's a good chance Google will serve up ads that appeal to a lot of people hitting your site. For example, if you run a popular site devoted to mobile gadgetry, you might make enough to buy a new device every few months. If your site gets sporadic traffic or, more important, if it's not clearly *about* something, it may be hard for Google to supply highly relevant ads, and you might make enough to cover a box of paper clips every so often.

Tip: If you fall into the second category, consider Amazon's Associates program, which lets you place ads on your site for specific items sold at Amazon. When somebody clicks and buys the item in the ad, Amazon pays you a referral fee. From any page on Amazon, look for a link to Sell Your Stuff, and then look for links to the Associates program.

The beauty of AdSense, however, is that it's free—absolutely gratis—to join and run, so you may as well give it a whirl. And the program automatically tailors itself to your site over time, supplying more relevant ads as it gets to know you better or as you change your content. It can take a few months before Google hits the sweet spot with ads that your readers love, but the only thing you have to do is set it up and watch it go to work.

Warning: Don't try to game AdSense. It probably won't surprise you a whit to learn that people have set up sites primarily to showcase ads and draw lots of clicks (and make buckets of money). When Google finds out about these sites—and it often does—it blocks the ads immediately. But dirty play makes the whole system weaker, and it harms not only Google but the people who pay for clicks, too. Don't be part of that damage.

Know Your Audience

How does Google know what ads will interest my audience?

Google's AdSense engine—as with everything Google—is rather sophisticated. Rather than simply serving up random ads from its advertiser base, Google works hard to make sure the ads your visitors see are likely to pique their interest.

From the day you start offering ads, the AdSense robot visits on a regular basis, reading through your pages with ads (for more on robots, see page 284). The robot takes a look at the words you use, the frequency with which you use them, even some of your page structure and formatting (for example, bigger fonts usually signify something important). Then Google uses all this info to figure out which ads your readers will warm to.

Even better, Google takes the language of your site and the location of your visitors into account, serving up language-specific, location-targeted ads for maximum impact. So a visitor from France—or a person browsing the Internet from her Frenchified computer—may see AdWords in French (shown here) or from French companies, while your U.S. visitors see theirs in English, Germans in German, and so forth. (The box on page 323 explains how Google knows where your visitors are from.)

Bottom line: Google may know more about your audience than you do. Use AdSense to work that knowledge to your advantage.

Ads by Google

Golf
Trouvez et achetez vêtements et chaussures par catégorie !
www.eBay.fr

Trueplane putting trainer
Copy the pros and apply the latest science to improve your putting
www.trueplane.com

Les USA
Découvrez les tarifs négociés par Cercle des Vacances
billetsdiscount.com

Golf
1,3 millions de produits attractifs Toutes les grandes marques.
http://shopping.lycos.fr

Signing Up for Google AdSense

Setting up an account takes two minutes, plus two or three days: You fill out an application, and then you wait to get accepted. Google does not allow just any online riffraff into the program. Personal sites, for example, are usually a no-go. So if your blog is about you and your cat, Google may reject your application. On the other hand, if you run a popular feline couture blog, you've got a good shot at getting in—and winding up with ads for kitty clothing. In addition, Google places some technical restrictions on the sites it accepts. For instance, it's not fond of pages that require passwords or those with text and pictures that rarely change. And your site must be primarily in English, French, German, Italian, Dutch, Portuguese, Japanese, or Spanish. Before you try to sign up, take a look at the AdSense policies and make sure your site qualifies: *https://www.google.com/adsense/policies.*

Note: When you sign up for AdSense, you have to give Google a U.S. tax ID, like a Social Security number or taxpayer identification number. For more information about tax IDs and why Google needs them, see *https://google.com/adsense/faq#tax.*

When you're ready to sign up:

1. **Head over to *www.google.com/adsense*.**

   Press Click Here to Apply. Google takes you to a page that lets you log in if you already have an account or sign up if you don't.

2. **Create an account.**

   Even if you want to put AdSense ads on 285 different sites, you need only one account, because you can paste your AdSense HTML code on any page of yours that meets the Google guidelines.

   If you're new to Google advertising, use the form on the right side of the page to create a Google AdSense account. Simply enter your email address and make up a password you'll use for subsequent visits.

Tip: Google insists that you use a combination of letters and numbers in your password.

   If you already have a Google AdWords account, use the form on the left part of the page to add AdSense.

   Click Continue.

3. **Provide contact information.**

   Fill in the Account Information form with your contact information, Web site address, and language. Even if you plan to run ads on more than one site, you need to fill in only one site for now.

4. **Choose the type of AdSense that you want to use.**

   Google gives you the option of ordinary AdSense (called "AdSense for content") and a search-based feature called "AdSense for search." So far, this chapter has focused on the most popular choice, which is AdSense for content. With AdSense for search, you provide a Google search box on your page that visitors can use to search the rest of the Web using Google's famous search engine. The neat part is that when Google shows promotional links alongside the search results, they're treated like ads on your Web site. That means you get paid if a visitor clicks any of the sponsored links. You may as well choose both AdSense programs since you can decide later what you actually want to add to your Web site.

Warning: If you want to post ads on a site that doesn't fit under Google's policies, it may seem like you can slide in a legit site here and then later post ads to your noncompliant site. But if Google finds you've added ads to an inappropriate site—and, remember, in order to supply relevant ads, it will crawl your sites regularly—the company may block ads from *all* your sites.

Click Submit. The final page shows a summary of all the information you supplied.

Click Continue to finish the process.

5. **Wait.**

While Google reviews your application, you can dream about upgrading your daily coffee to a large mocha latte with all your AdSense loot. A day or two after signing up, you should receive an email confirmation that your account is ready.

Note: If you don't hear from Google in a timely manner—say five days or so to be on the safe side—let them know using the Contact Us form at *https://www.google.com/adsense/contact*. Even if they reject your application, you might not hear from them, so it's best to be proactive.

You might also take a second look at the Google AdSense Policies page (*https://google.com/adsense/policies*) in case there's something about your site that might disqualify you.

---

6. **Log in.**

When you get the confirmation email, head back to *www.google.com/adsense* and log in using your email address and the password you created in step 2. (The next section gives you the skinny on logging in.)

That's all there is to signing up for a Google AdSense account.

Logging in to Your AdSense Account

Before you can do anything with AdSense, you need to head back to *www.google.com/adsense* and log in. Once you do, you'll see the central Google AdSense page (see Figure 9-3).

Figure 9-3:
The AdSense page is divided into several tabs. Initially, you begin at the Reports tab, where you can survey a day-by-day breakdown of the money you've made.

The AdSense page has five central sections, which are represented by tabs at the top of the page. These sections include:

• **Reports.** This tab helps you assess the performance of your AdSense ads. You'll see a summary of the money you've made today and over the last week. For more information, jump ahead to page 306.

- **AdSense for Content.** This is your starting point for generating AdSense ads—it's where you specify the type of ad you want and get the HTML code you need to insert into your Web pages. You also have access to some advanced features here, such as filtering out ads from specific Web sites (page 311).

- **AdSense for Search.** Using this tab, you can generate the HTML for a Google search box that you can place on your Web pages. When a visitor performs a search through this Google box, they may see some relevant ads, and if they click one, you'll get the usual commission.

- **Referrals.** Looking for another way to net some cash? Google pays you up to $100 for referring new customers their way. See page 310 for the full scoop.

- **My Account.** This tab lets you update most of the information you supplied when you registered. This includes details like your mailing address and tax information.

Now on to the fun part—building your ads.

Building Your AdSense Ads and Adding Them to Your Pages

Building your AdSense ads is easier than you might imagine: select an ad layout, choose a color palette, optionally choose an alternate ad, and then paste some JavaScript code from Google into your Web pages' HTML. That's it.

Note: These steps supply the basic process for creating ads. If you want to place different ads on different pages—perhaps using various color schemes or shapes, depending on your pages' layout, or using different channels (page 302)—you need to go back through to rebuild the ads and then place them on the appropriate pages.

---

1. **Log in and click the "AdSense for Content" tab.**

   This tab includes four separate pages, whose links are shown just under the row of tabs. These sections are: "Ad layout code," "Ad colors," "Channels," and "Competitive Ad Filter." Right now you're in the "Ad layout code" section (shown in Figure 9-4), but you can use the other links to define custom colors and custom channels, or to block out URLs you don't want to use in your ads, as you'll see.

2. **Choose the type of ad you want to create—either an ad unit or a link unit.**

   An *ad unit* is a group of one or more ads, complete with descriptive text or (optionally) images. When a visitor clicks an ad, he winds up at the advertiser's Web site (and you get paid). If you're used to seeing AdSense ads on Web pages, ad units are what you've probably seen most of in the past.

   A *link unit* is a slim box of links with no descriptive text. The title of the box is "Ads by Google" and the links are one or two word entries, like Digital Cameras or Consumer Electronics. If a visitor clicks one of these links, Google serves up a new page that's filled with ads for that topic. If the visitor then clicks one of these ads, you get paid.

Figure 9-4:
As you make changes to the various settings, Google automatically adjusts the code in the window at the bottom of the screen. When you're done choosing options, you have some nifty, customized code that you can paste right into your Web pages.

3. **Choose the exact type of ad (from the list box next to the "Ad unit" or "Link unit" option).**

If you're creating an ad unit, you can choose whether you want to use text or image ads. Generally, image ads stand out more than text ads. However, you need to balance two conflicting goals: the desire to make money by attracting clicks with eye-catching ads, and the desire to minimize the distraction on your Web page by choosing ad types that are less obtrusive.

If you're creating a link unit, you're limited to choosing how many links appear in the box.

4. **Select the ad layout.**

AdSense provides a nice selection of ad styles, from single-ad buttons at 125×125 pixels, to five-ad skyscrapers measuring 160×600 pixels (a *pixel* is the smallest dot you can place on a computer screen, and it's a common measurement in Web pages). To see the examples in Figure 9-5, click "View samples" or head to *https://google.com/adsense/adformats.*

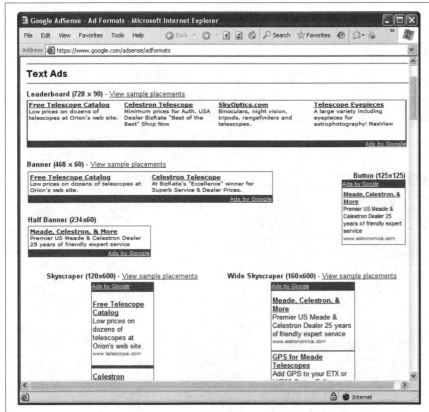

Figure 9-5:
Google provides a bunch of sample ad formats. How to choose? On your site, is there anywhere an ad might fill in some empty space or even draw the page together—especially above the fold (the first screen your visitors see without scrolling down). Where might your readers' eyes end up? Use these observations to guide your decisions.

When you choose an ad layout, start small. Don't crowd your page with a skyscraper or rectangle just to get the most ads possible on your site. The ads should never dominate your pages, or you'll risk turning off your visitors.

Once you've decided on a shape and size, head back to the layout page, open the layout menu, and select your preference.

5. **Choose a color palette.**

The ads on your site can incorporate up to five colors: one each for the background, border, title, text, and URL. To take the guesswork out of color coordination, AdSense provides a nice selection of color palettes, everything from Peach Melba to Swamp Green. Figure 9-6 explains how to choose them.

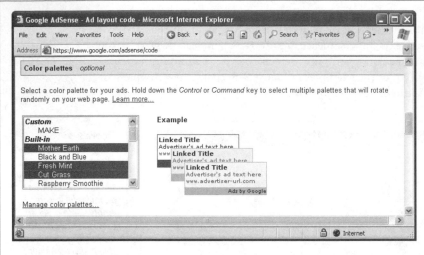

Figure 9-6:
Use the pop-up menu to find existing color palettes and select the ones that sound intriguing. The sample ad just to the right of the palette list changes to reflect your selection, giving you a live preview of what your ads could look like. If you can't settle on one, you can choose up to four palettes, and Google will rotate them on your site. To select multiple palettes, Ctrl+click (⌘-click) them. (In this example, three color palettes are selected.)

Custom Color Palettes

If none of the built-in color palettes work with your exquisite site design, you can create your own. Under the built-in palettes, click the "Manage color palettes" link. Google takes you to a page that lets you control the color of every aspect of your ad: the border, background, title, ad text, and URL.

Google provides a chart of *Web safe colors*, the 216 colors that look the same on nearly every browser, no matter the operating system. Each color has a six-character code, known as a *hex code*; if you mouse over the grid, Google displays the codes, as shown here, at bottom right.

Above the grid, Google provides a menu of the existing palettes and suggests that you choose one as a starting point. Click Reset or choose another palette at any time to wipe out your changes and start from scratch.

To start picking your own colors, select one of the ad elements below the color grid. For example, choose Title, and then click any color from the rainbow of available choices. Google incorporates the change immediately, both in the sample ad on the left and in the numerical color code to the right of the word "Title." Do the same for each ad element you want to change.

When you're satisfied with your ad, type a name for your custom color palette in the "Palette name" box at the bottom of the screen and then click Save. Your newly minted palette appears both in the "Custom palettes" list to the right and in the "Choose a palette" menu above.

You're allowed up to a hundred custom color palettes, so you have lots of room to fiddle. Should you wish to delete a particularly abominable creation, select it in the Custom palettes list and click Delete.

Once you're done, click "Save and get code," which takes you back to the Ad layout screen. When you return to the layout process, be sure to choose your custom palette from the "Color palette" list; Google doesn't do it for you automatically.

6. **Provide an alternate ad if you want to.**

If Google can't provide targeted ads for your page—either because they haven't indexed your page yet and so don't know what's appropriate, they have nothing suitable on hand, or AdSense has simply hiccuped—it serves up a public service advertisement instead, as shown in Figure 9-7.

Figure 9-7:
Google's alternate ads are usually from organizations like the Red Cross, ASPCA, or some other nonprofit.

If you'd rather not waste good page real estate on nontargeted advertising, you can provide an alternate ad or picture of your own to replace the public service announcement. You have a few choices for the substitute:

• **Static image.** You can supply a GIF or JPG. Click Alternate URL, and then enter the link to your picture. The URL might look something like this:

```
http://www.yoursite.com/images/alternate.gif
```

- **Ads from another company.** If you're part of another advertising network, like DoubleClick, you can drop in an ad from that service. Check with the other company for the code or the URL that points to their ads. Then click Alternate URL and enter it.

- **Block of color.** If you want just a block of color, click "Color code." If you know the hex code of the color that matches your page background, type it in. To pick it out of a color lineup, click the "Choose a color" link, pick a color out of the choices you're offered, and click the "Save and get code" button to copy it back to your ad page.

Note: If your alternate image or ad is larger than your selected AdSense ad format, Google just crops it.

7. **Add channels, if you wish.**

Channels are Google's name for tags that you can add to any of your Web pages, letting you track pages separately and compare their performance in your AdSense reports. Channels are useful when, for example, you want to find out whether your index pages or your archive pages draw more click-throughs over time. Channels are also good for determining whether your tower ads work better than your *leaderboards* (horizontal ad panels), or whether a contrasting color palette gets more attention than one that blends in.

To create a couple of channels, click the "Manage channels" link, which takes you to the page shown in Figure 9-8.

Reminder: If you want to place different channels on different pages—which is really the point—you must go through the whole process of creating ads for every page, or group of pages, you assign a channel to.

8. **Tell Google if your page has frames.**

If you use frames to lay out your pages, you have to let Google's crawlers know which frame to look at when they come by seeking clues about your pages so that AdSense can serve up relevant ads. To alert them, simply turn on the"Ad will be placed on a framed page" checkbox.

Note: For the whole thing to work, you must place your ad layout code in the same frame as your main text—that's the only way Google can decide which ads are appropriate for your site.

9. **Copy the code from the box labeled "Your AdSense code."**

When you're done choosing all the settings, the box at the bottom of the page reflects your choices of color palette, ad layout, and so forth. Highlight all of the code in the box and copy it by typing Ctrl+C (⌘-C).

Tip: If you're not quite ready to paste the AdSense code into your Web page, paste it somewhere else for safekeeping—Notepad on Windows, and TextEdit or Stickies on Mac are good choices.

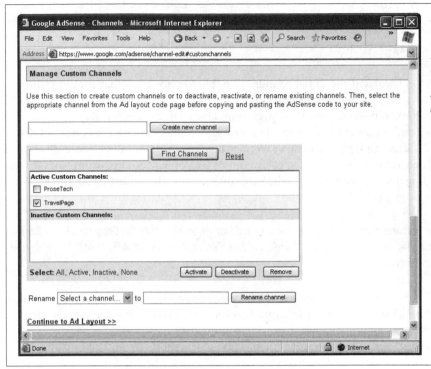

Figure 9-8:
Creating a custom channel is easy—just type in a name, click "Create new channel," select your channel, and then click Activate. Repeat the process to add as many channels as you want. When you're done, click "Continue to Ad Layout" to get back to the ad creation page.

10. **Edit your Web pages.**

With ad code in hand, it's time to head on over to your Web site for a quick paste. Use whatever editing tools you usually do; the only stipulation is that you need to get to the HTML source view because the code from Google uses HTML to connect to your site's code.

Tip: Google prefers pages with lots of text rather than lots of pictures, because it can better assess what kind of ads will be interesting to your visitors.

Open the Web page or pages on which you'd like to display the ads you just set up. Paste in the code you copied during the last step—Google asks that you don't make any changes to it—then save your pages as you usually do.

Warning: Google has been known to cut off sites where it has detected altered code.

---

11. **Take a look.**

View your Web pages in a browser, which automatically sends a message to Google, telling its robot to come on by at its earliest convenience. While you're there, assess your ads. If they don't seem to fit in with the rest of your décor, play around with ad placement and, if necessary, go back and rebuild the ad, choosing a different color palette and/or layout.

Tip: If you want to see how your ads look before they go live, you can check them on a test server that's online. But keep in mind that if the server is connected to the Internet, Google can see your pages, so it can—and will—index them.

Don't worry if the initial rounds are public service ads—that should change in anywhere from a few minutes to 48 hours or so as the AdSense bot visits and figures out what your Web page is all about. If, after a few days, the ads still haven't become more targeted to your site, chances are you're either not giving AdSense enough material to work with (your page is rather spare of text) or their robot is barred at the gates (you've got some robot exclusion rules forbidding it entry; see page 284). Be sure you're letting the AdSense robot in and providing it enough to chew on.

Tip: For more help, including instructions on blocking robots *other* than the Googlebot, check the Troubleshooting Tips section of the "Google AdSense Technical Implementation Guide" at *https://www. google.com/adsense/faq-tech*.

If you ever want to alter your contact information, visit the My Account tab (or *https://google.com/adsense/account*), which has links across the top that let you change your mailing address, login information (email address, display language, and email preferences), and tax information (if you need help with this one, Google provides a wizard on the right side of the screen).

Note: The display language is the language in which Google speaks to you on your account pages. The way ads appear on your *site* is a different matter. To decide which ads to show and what language they should be in, AdSense checks where your visitors are from—based on information it can glean from their computers' Internet connections—before it serves up ads. Thus, it may serve different, regionally targeted ads to people from Iran and from Mexico, and it might show ads in different languages. Most of the time, this system (called *geotargeting*) is very cool. The only hitch is that you can't always see the ads other people see on your site, because *your* location determines the ads Google shows you, too.

Adding a Google Search Box to Your Pages

Nothing beats Web page ads for making quick money on a popular site. But if you're restless (and looking for another way to scrape in the Web revenue), you can use Google's "AdSense for search" promotional program. Here's how it works: you add a Google search box to a Web page, which lets visitors launch their Google queries right from your site. However, if these visitors click any ads in the search results, you pocket the earnings, just as though you placed the ad directly on your site.

Here's how to set it up:

1. **Log in to your AdSense account, and click the "AdSense for Search" tab.**

   This shows the "AdSense for Search" page (Figure 9-9).

Figure 9-9:
The "Adsense for Search" page is a lot like the "AdSense for Content" page. It asks you a series of questions and gives you a block of HTML you can copy into your Web page at the end. Unlike the ads, the search HTML doesn't use JavaScript—it's just an ordinary HTML table.

2. **Select the language and country of your Web site.**

    The standard options are English and United States. As you probably know, Google has country-specific pages that can tweak search results, providing them in different languages or giving priority to local sites.

3. **Choose Google Search (if you want visitors to be able to explore the whole Web, including your site) or Google SiteSearch (if you want them to be confined to just searching the pages on your site).**

Google SiteSearch is an innovative idea—it's a search box for searching just *your site*. For example, if you have dozens of pages of travel stories, a visitor could home in on the page she wants by typing *"funny story about rubber chicken in Peru"* into a SiteSearch box. However, there's one catch. SiteSearch still uses Google's standard, centralized catalog of Web pages; it just limits the search to the pages from your site. But if Google doesn't have the page in its catalog (either because you just created it or because Google doesn't know your site exists), SiteSearch won't find it.

If you want to provide both options (Google Search and Google SiteSearch), just follow these instructions twice to create two different text boxes. But be careful you don't wind up confusing your visitors.

4. **If you want to filter out profanity and sexual content from search results, choose the SafeSearch option.**

SafeSearch is useful in two situations. First, it's de rigueur for sites that provide children's content. Second, it's handy if your Web site deals in a topic that shares some keywords with adult-only sites. For example, if you're creating a breast-cancer awareness page, you don't want searches for *"breast exam"* to dig up the wrong goods.

5. **Tailor the appearance of the Google search box.**

You can tweak the background color, width, and placement of the logo and search button.

6. **Choose any optional features you want.**

Turn on the "Open search results in a new browser window" checkbox if you want a new page to pop up with the results of the visitor's search. This is usually annoying to Web surfers, but handy if you want to make sure your Web site sticks around on the visitor's desktop.

Choose a style palette for the search results page. This way, the search results can blend in with the color scheme used for the rest of your Web site. Style palettes are almost the same as the color palettes discussed with ad creation (page 299), except they also allow you to add a custom logo.

Choose a channel if you want to track the ad dollars you make from this search box. See page 302 for more information about channels.

7. **The text box at the bottom of the page now has your complete, customized search engine box.**

You can copy this with a quick Ctrl+C (⌘-C) and paste it into any Web page.

Getting Paid

Thirty days or so after the end of each month, you'll receive a check in the mail for your Google AdSense revenue. But Google pays only when you've reached $100 in revenue or more; anything under gets carried through from month to month until it reaches the $100 mark. The only exception to this rule is a new year, upon which AdSense clears its books and sends you a check for all outstanding earnings.

Note: AdSense offers payment by check or electronic funds transfer (EFT), which deposits the money directly to your bank. At the time of this writing, EFT is available in 16 countries and is ready to go once you supply some information about your bank (see *https://www.google.com/support/adsense/bin/answer.py?answer=15918* for more details).

Monitoring Your Performance

It's easy to get obsessed and spend all your time wondering how your AdSense ads are faring. Did all your hard work buy you a cup of coffee this morning? Perhaps a bagel, too?

To help your find out, AdSense offers three reports. To see them, start by clicking the Reports tab or surfing directly to *https://google.com/adsense/reports*. Under the Reports tab, you'll see three links: Overview, Advanced Reports - Ad Performance, and Advanced Reports - Search Performance. The Overview section (Figure 9-10) provides an at-a-glance look at your ad performance, and it's a perfect place to start.

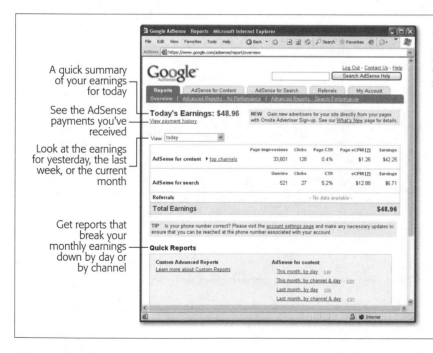

A quick summary of your earnings for today

See the AdSense payments you've received

Look at the earnings for yesterday, the last week, or the current month

Get reports that break your monthly earnings down by day or by channel

Figure 9-10:
The Overview report gives you most of the information you need, at a glance.

Advanced performance report

The Performance reports let you dig into the details of how your ads have performed over the course of time. To view the Performance report, choose either the

Advanced Reports - Ad Performance or Advanced Reports - Search Performance link, depending on whether you want to track the progress of your ordinary ad units or sponsored Google searches (page 297).

To fine-tune your report, simply pick a date range to see your progress over time (it shows you today's info if you don't specify another range), decide if you want to see info about your channels, and then click Display Report. Google fills in the chart at the bottom of the page (Figure 9-11).

Tip: You can sort the report by any of its five fields by clicking the column heading.

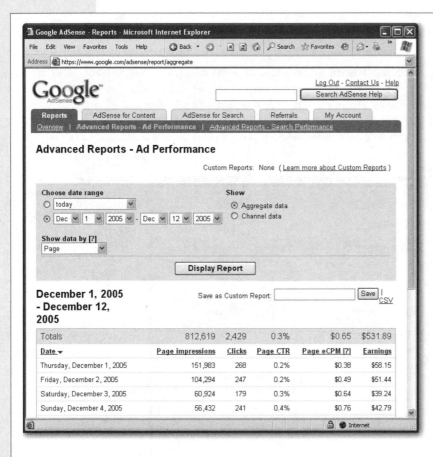

Figure 9-11:
The basic Performance report provides some valuable data (which Google normally updates hourly) on how many people are seeing your pages and clicking through the ads. From left to right, the report shows the date, number of impressions (how many times the ads have been displayed by a browser somewhere), how many times your visitors have clicked the ads, the click-through rate (clicks divided by page impressions, multiplied by 100 to give you a percentage), the cost-per-1000 impressions (the value you'd expect if your ads were served 1000 times based on the click-through rate you're receiving now), and your earnings (for the current day, the earnings may be partial). If you added channels to your pages (page 302), use the "Channel data" menu to get a similar report showing how your separate channels are faring.

In the marketplace of clicks that Google has created, some clicks are worth more than others, based on the price advertisers are willing to pay for them. So while your number of clicks might be exactly the same from day to day, and the click-through rate (page 315) might be similar, your earnings will typically fluctuate depending on which ads your visitors clicked and what they were worth at the time—things that Google doesn't tell you. On your report, it simply says that, for example, one day six clicks are worth $2.31 while another day they net you a mere $0.69. To learn more about the value of clicks, see page 317.

Despite this mushiness in your earnings information, you can still use the report to see what you've earned and whether you're making more money over time (which you should be, as Google gets to know your pages better and serves more relevant ads, and as more people flock to your site). And if you've set up channels, you can also see whether one page of ads is earning you more money than another.

Note: There's one other option on the Performance report page—the "Show data by" list. When you use the standard value (Page), the chart indicates how many times a surfer visits one of your ad-adorned pages. But if you use Individual Ad Unit, the chart instead calculates each ad unit served out as a distinct impression. That means if you have one page with four ad units on it, Google counts four impressions for every one visit.

Payment History

The payment report is the poster child for simplicity. To see it, click the "Payment history" link in the Reports tab. Google shows you how much it sent you and when (Figure 9-12).

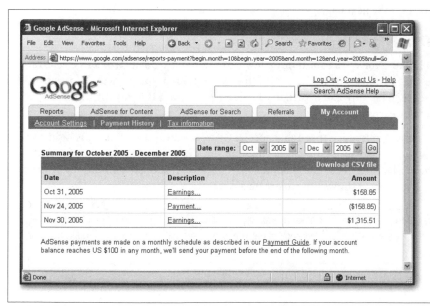

Figure 9-12:
Click the Earnings link to see how much of your total came from AdSense for Content and how much is thanks to AdSense for Search. Click the corresponding Payment link to see when and how the payment was made. (This is what you'll need to check out if for some reason you don't receive a payment.) This sample report shows one payment (made on November 24) and a sizable current amount still to be paid out.

Honing Your Ads

The sheer simplicity of AdSense's copy-and-paste ad code means you can change the ads' look at will. And shaking things up a little can make a huge difference in the number of people noticing and clicking your ads. It's therefore worth playing with your ads every so often. Change their color scheme (for example, if you have complementary colors, try contrasting colors). Or fiddle with the layout or placement on your Web page. Then leave things alone for a few days. You may find a nice change in your click-through rate—and earnings.

Tip: Use channels (page 302) to keep track of how your changes are affecting individual pages or sections of your site.

If you find that AdSense is using your site to advertise products or services from a competing company, or you just don't like a particular advertiser's wares, you can block ads from up to 200 URLs. Under the AdSense for Content tab, click Competitive Ad Filter (or head to *https://google.com/adsense/filter*), and then click Edit to open a box where you can type in any URLs you want to nix. Add just one URL per line, and when you're done, click "Save changes."

The tricky thing here is that you can block URLs on a domain-wide basis (if you block *www.example.com*, Google won't show anything from that site, including *www.example.com/rubber_duckies* and *www.example.com/rubber_duckies/ornamental,* for example), but when you do so, you *really* reduce the number of potential ad matches for your pages and thus your potential earnings. In fact, it's easy to do more harm than good by blocking ads, and you should filter URLs with great care—even those from your direct competitors. For tips on blocking *pages* rather than whole *sites*, see the box on the next page.

Referrals

Still looking for ways to fish out a few extra dollars? Google provides a referral feature that promises to net you $100 for every person you convince to sign up for AdSense. The only catch is that you don't get your $100 payout until the person you refer earns *her* first $100.

Google referrals work through a special referral button that you must add to your Web site. When someone clicks this link, he's prompted to sign up for AdSense. (Obviously, if he clicks the link and then back out, you get nothing for your trouble.) Figure 9-13 shows how to create a referral.

Note: Google may also offer other referral opportunities through the referral tab. Currently, there's an offer that nets you $1.00 for every copy of the Firefox browser that's downloaded through a link on your site.

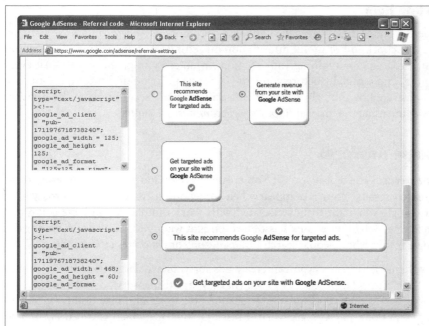

Figure 9-13:
To create a referral, click the Referral tab. Scroll down the page until you find a referral button that best suits your site (on the right). Select it, and then copy the provided code (on the left). Now all you need to do is paste this code onto a Web page, in much the same way that you added the Google AdSense ads.

Blocking the Right URLs

If blocking a whole site seems too drastic, you may want to block ads associated only with a specific *page* on a competitor's site. For example, you sell macramé mousepads, and you want to block the mousepad pages on *www.staples.com*. The hard part is figuring out which pages a competitor has associated with his ads. Although ads have URLs on their last line, you can't always tell by looking at an ad where it's going to take you, because they can have destination URLs built into their code, and that's invisible to viewers (the destination itself is known as a *landing page*).

You can, of course, click an ad to find out where it takes you. But Google asks that you don't click them because that artificially ratchets up the click-through rate. Here's the way around the problem.

Right-click an ad title, and from the menu that appears, select Copy Shortcut or Copy Link Location (on a Mac, Control-click the title and then select Copy Link to Clipboard). Then paste the link into a text editor like Notepad or TextEdit. The part you want to extract is between 'adurl=' and '&'. For example, if the URL looks like this:

```
http://pagead2.googlesyndication.com/
pagead/adclick?sa=l&ai=ACY8BJ9HbAtdwhOJ_
Os_6ZudAKm-2FI7Oa-YAA34tB4jAEOK9BAAkwqQAD
IAmWAAA3d3du4Wew92cO5yYv1GAzADM4JTNw8FchN
3XhJ2ZuNGAAA&num=2&adurl=http://www.house
ofstyle.com/hstyle/dept.asp%3Fs%255Fid%3DO
%26dept%255Fid%3D540%26dp%255Fid%3D%26dl%2
55Fid%3D&client=ca-nypost_300x250
```

the part you want is:

```
http://www.houseofstyle.com/hstyle/dept.
asp%3Fs%255Fid%3DO%26dept%255Fid%3D540%26
dp%255Fid%3D%26dl%255Fid%3D
```

Cut this section and paste it into the URL Filter form to prevent the ad for this page from showing up on your site.

This system isn't perfect because competitors can change their landing pages at any time (and some Webmasters change them daily). In addition, you can't see the ads that Google is showing people from other parts of the world (page 304), so you can't cover all your bases. *C'est la guerre.*

Getting Help

Google's online help pages for AdSense (*https://www.google.com/adsense/online-help*) are chock-full of useful information on setting up shop, getting the most out of the program, maintaining your account, troubleshooting, and so on. Visit every so often, and especially before you write in for help. If you do have a question that isn't answered by the help pages or is specific to your account, drop the AdSense crew a line using the form at *https://google.com/adsense/contact*.

Google AdWords

The AdWords concept is simple: You create ads that Google shows alongside regular search results. Your ads appear when somebody searches for keywords you've told Google you want to be associated with. For example, if you have a site that sells SpongeBob SquarePants scissors, you might want your ad to appear alongside Google results when people search for *SpongeBob* or *children's office supplies.*

As with any advertising, you can create ads for your whole site (kiddie office supplies), for particular products you sell (Barney tape dispensers), or even for ideas (a comparison of political candidates' education policies). But unlike traditional advertising, you don't pay Google when it *displays* your ad (which is called an *impression*); instead you pay only when somebody *clicks* your ad (more on that later).

The true beauty of AdWords is that the sponsored links are every bit as relevant as the regular results. If somebody searches Google for *Volvo safety*, Google displays—alongside the Volvo safety reports and crash tests—Car Safety ads from Carfax.com and Volvo Auctions from CheapCarFinder.com. If somebody searches Google for your keywords, you *know* they're looking for whatever you're advertising. AdWords can thus be a great choice when you want to direct your ads to a narrow audience. (In fact, advertising gurus think of AdWords as a form of *direct marketing*, which means your message is delivered individually to each potential customer.)

AdWords may also be a good choice when you have just a few dollars for reaching your audience. You can advertise on Google for as little as $1.50 a month. Google charges just $5 to sign up for AdWords, and after that, you can set a budget as low as five cents per day. It costs more to send five snail-mail letters a month.

The confusing part about AdWords is that Google doesn't charge a set price for ads. Instead, the company lets you *bid* on the *keywords* that you want to trigger your ads. If you bid higher than everyone else who's bid on the same keyword, your ad is likely to appear near the top of the sponsored links.

For example, if you set a maximum bid of 35 cents for the word *stapler*, and the next highest bid is 23 cents, Google gives your ad priority among the sponsored links it serves up when somebody searches for *stapler*. Even better, Google charges you only a *penny* more than the second-highest bidder, so you may never even have to pay the full 35 cents you bid. If you bid less than the highest bid, Google still lets you play; it just doesn't show your ad as often as other people's. "Understanding the Costs" on page 315 tells you more about how pricing and payment work.

Note: When deciding who gets top billing among the sponsored links, Google factors in bids *and* how many people click through each ad, giving preference to the more effective ads. You can't, therefore, buy the top spot outright. But you might be able to sneak up on a competitor with deeper pockets. Page 315 tells you more.

If that all sounds appealing, it should: Google has designed a seductively smart system, and joining takes just a few minutes. But make no mistake: AdWords is a demanding way to advertise on the Web. This chapter explains the challenges, but first you need to get your head around Google's advertising terminology.

Note: AdWords changes pretty regularly, which makes writing a book about the program like trying to nail Jell-O to a tree. This chapter covers all the features that exist at the time of this writing.

> **UP TO SPEED**
>
> ## Direct Marketing: The Bigger Picture
>
> Direct marketing—which includes junk mail like catalogs and charity appeals, plus telemarketing calls and spam—is a distinct type of advertising. It's a cousin to mass marketing, which includes billboards, TV commercials, and magazine ads—all of which advertisers hope will influence consumers in a general way. Direct marketing, on the other hand, allows an advertiser to carefully choose who sees an ad and to gauge whether the ad led to a sale or other desired activity—like signing up for future mailings. Unsurprisingly, direct marketers tend to be obsessed with measures like return on investment, which help them decide whether the sales generated by an ad justify the amount they spent on it.
>
> AdWords is very much a direct marketing tool. And your competition may include not just a savvy Webmaster or two, but teams of marketing experts who know direct campaign angles inside out and work full-time to massage AdWords. That's important to remember, because when you run a campaign, you have to pay close attention to your competition to make sure your ads are getting the positioning and clicks that make the program worth doing in the first place.
>
> Think of joining AdWords as a way of running a direct marketing campaign rather than a way of appearing on Google, and you'll be in the right mind-set.

Understanding AdWords Terminology

Google tries hard to make AdWords perfectly understandable, even to the advertising neophyte. Yet for all the PDF guides and multimedia tutorials Google offers (*https://adwords.google.com/select/library*), the concepts can get rather confusing, rather fast.

It's useful to remember that the AdWords universe is a hierarchy. It begins with keywords, which are connected to ads, which are connected to Ad Groups, which are connected to campaigns, which are connected to accounts, which are connected to the anklebone:

- **Keywords** are the magic words that trigger Google to show your ads when people (read: potential customers) search for the terms. If, for instance, you're selling a new line of floral shirts and you choose *Hawaiian shirts* as keywords, Google displays your ads when people search for—what else?—Hawaiian shirts.

Google lets you decide whether you also want people searching for *leisurewear* or *Hawaiian cruises* or other inexact matches to see your ad. To give you flexibility, Google offers four types of keywords: broad match, phrase match, exact match, and negative keyword. The box on page 327 explains the differences and how to set them.

Tip: AdWords provides a helpful Keyword Suggestion Tool (*https://adwords.google.com/select/main?cmd=KeywordSandbox*) to guide you beyond the obvious choices for your products and services. Page 324 tells you all about it.

Once you pick your keywords, you associate them with an ad, described next.

- **An ad** appears on a Google search results page as a sponsored link (page 31) or on an associated Web site, via AdSense (page 291), under the legend "Ads by Google." Figure 9-14 has an example.

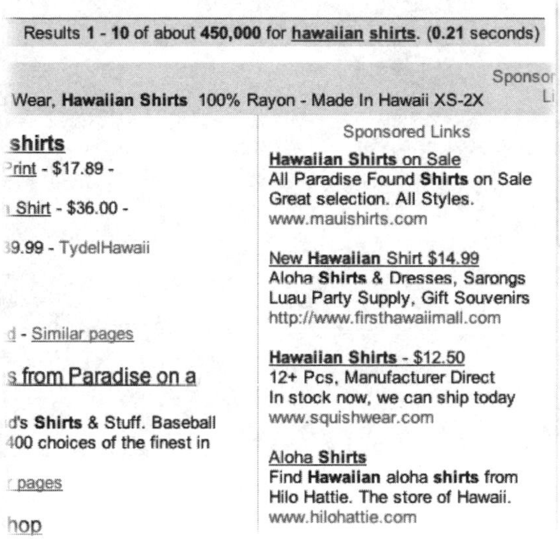

Figure 9-14:
As the top ad shows, a single ad consists of a headline ("Hawaiian Shirts on Sale"), two short lines of description ("All Paradise Found Shirts on Sale," "Great selection. All styles."), and a URL ("www.mauishirts.com").

One or more ads make up an Ad Group.

- **An Ad Group** is a collection of ads taken out by one advertiser that all target the same keywords. For example, you might have three or four variations on the "Hip Hip Hawaii" ad or separate yet similar ads ("Boffo Bermudas," for example) that you've associated with the same *Hawaiian shirts* keywords. You may think of this as your Clothing Ad Group.

An Ad Group is part of a campaign.

• **A campaign** is a collection of Ad Groups. How you slice a campaign is really up to you. For Hiphawaiian.com, it might be spring vs. summer, men's vs. women's, clothing made of cotton vs. clothing made of shells.

Note: You figure out your budget per *campaign* (see below).

And any number of campaigns make up your one account.

• **AdWords accounts** are unlike any other advertising account you may have come across, because Google has gone out of its way to make this program flexible. Your minimum cost is $1.50 per month. You can run ads for as short or as long a time as you like. And you can run as many or as few campaigns, Ad Groups, and ads as you wish, targeting any keywords that are in some way related to your line of products or services. The Fruit of the Month Club is a bigger commitment.

Note: If you're looking to sell just one small widget, and you plan on having just one ad, you still need to set up an Ad Group and campaign to hold that ad.

Understanding the Costs

Upon signing up for AdWords, you owe Google a whopping $5 activation fee. That's it. You don't owe anything else for another 30 days, and you get to tell Google in advance how much you're willing to spend for the month. Even more amazing: No matter how many times Google shows your ads to prospective clickers, you don't spend a penny unless people *actually click through* to your site.

Here's how it works. You choose the *cost-per-click* that you're willing to pay for your keywords. Then you choose an average daily amount you're willing to pay for all your keywords. Google cleverly displays your ads often enough so that your *click-throughs* (the number of people who see your ad and then actually click it) multiplied by your costs-per-click equals your daily budget.

Note: Some days, your click-through rate might produce costs lower than your daily budget, and some days it might generate higher costs, but over the course of 30 days, it usually evens out. If it doesn't, and your costs run higher than the monthly budget you set, Google gives you a credit for the overcharge. For example, if your daily budget is $10, your actual costs might fluctuate between $9 and $11 per day. But if the actual cost exceeds your monthly budget, you still pay Google no more than $300 for 30 days.

Fortunately, you don't have to bid for keywords in the dark. After you've chosen your keywords, Google suggests a maximum cost-per-click based on what other advertisers have agreed to pay for those terms. Other people's bids are important, because the price you're willing to pay helps determine whether your ad appears above or below your competitors' ads and how often it shows up. For example, you could tell Google you're willing to pay 50 cents for the keyword *Hawaiian*. If your nearest competitor is willing to pay only 40 cents, Google actually *lowers* your price to 41 cents and gives your ad some priority when it displays them.

So why not pay just enough to keep your ad in the top spot? Because you can't. When it ranks sponsored links, Google also looks at ads' click-through rates, bumping up the ads with the highest rates. As a result, you can't simply bid higher than everyone else to ensure the top spot. In fact, if your click-through rate is higher than your competitors', you could wind up in the top spot with a lower bid. (This scheme sounds counterintuitive, but it's actually very much in keeping with Google's philosophy of delivering results based on popularity.)

See "Signing Up" on page 320 for some tips for balancing your costs with your ads' exposure.

AdWords charges your credit or debit card every 30 days after your first click comes through. For acceptable cards by country, see *https://adwords.google.com/ select/pay_options.html*.

Note: If you think you'll be spending at least $7,500 a month for three months or more, Google may provide you with a line of credit and bill you monthly. For more info, see *https://adwords.google.com/ select/pricing.html#billing5.*

Before You Sign Up

Before you even consider shelling out valuable advertising dollars, you should consider two things: Is AdWords even necessary for your business, and is it worthwhile? If you decide to go for it, you need to do some market research to figure out the keywords that might work for you.

Is it necessary?

You might just have all the free, targeted advertising you need in regular Google search results. And as good as AdWords are, nothing beats a great ranking when it comes to click-throughs. (For proof, ask your friends if they ever read or click the sponsored links—you'll be amazed to find that most people ignore them completely.)

Run a few Google searches using keywords or phrases you'd *hope* (not *expect*) would turn up your site in results. Make note of those in which you appear above the fold—typically the first five results or so. If you're consistently showing up near the top, consider putting that ad cash elsewhere (toward other keywords, for example, or other marketing outlets entirely).

If you're making it into the top ten results, but not the top five, think about whether pumping those advertising dollars into a bigger and better site might net you some more attention and links—perhaps enough to raise you a result or two in the regular rankings. $5,000 or $10,000 can buy a lot more in the way of site improvements than AdWords ads.

Is it worthwhile?

The biggest mistake people make before joining AdWords is not figuring out how much clicks are worth to them. That's like wandering into a car dealership knowing you need a new auto but having *no idea* how much you can afford. Before you know it, you're driving out in a nice convertible that costs more per month than your salary.

Fortunately, there are a few fairly simple calculations you can use to figure out how much you can sanely spend on AdWords, or whether the costs are even worthwhile for your business.

The first step is to figure out how much you're willing to spend for every sale. For example, if you sell fur-covered, roof-mounted ski racks for $3,000 a pop, and your *gross margin* (the amount you make after factoring in your costs) is $1,500, you might be willing to pay $200 or more to make a sale. If you sell fur-covered mountain bike seats for $250, you may be willing to spend only about $30 for a sale. (Unfortunately, there's no general rule of thumb for determining your maximum *cost-per-sale*; it's a business decision you have to make independent of AdWords.)

Once you've determined a maximum cost-per-sale, you need to get your head around a *conversion rate*, the percentage of people who click your ad and then actually buy a furry item. Conversion rates can vary from campaign to campaign, but industry experts say that a rate of one percent is fairly common. You read that right: Only one out of every hundred people who click through to your site is likely to actually spend money.

With your maximum cost-per-sale and an estimated conversion rate, you're ready to do some math.

Note: Weirdly, you do this math *before* you have a clue as to how many people will see your ad or what your click-through rate will be. That stuff comes later.

Here's the magic equation: Simply multiply your max cost-per-sale by the conversion rate. The answer equals the most you should pay for a single click. For example, if you decide that the most you can afford to pay for a sale is $10, and you assume that one percent of people who click your ad will wind up buying your product, then the most you can afford to pay for a click is a dime ($10 × 1% = $0.10). If your conversion rate is a stellar two percent, you can afford 20 cents.

If you're advertising a bunch of products with a range of prices, or if you want to find out how different conversion rates affect your cost-per-click (or if you hate math), you can create a spreadsheet like the one in Figure 9-15 to let you see at a glance the most you can afford to bid per keyword for any particular campaign.

Note: To make it easier for those of you keeping score at home, the spreadsheets shown in Figures 9-15 and 9-16 are available on the "Missing CD" page at *www.missingmanuals.com*. Simply download them and plug in your own numbers.

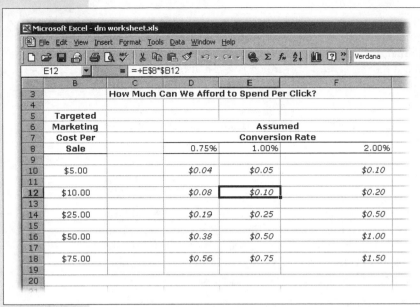

Figure 9-15:
A chart like this helps you play around with different costs-per-sale and a range of possible conversion rates. Here, the maximum costs-per-click shown in columns D, E, and F, comes from multiplying column B (different possible costs-per-sale) by the percentages in row 8 (different possible conversion rates).

Once you've determined your max cost-per-click, you can start figuring out how much AdWords might cost you every day, and how many sales you can expect to get for your daily budget. The charts in Figure 9-16 guide you through the process.

If you estimate a one-percent click-through rate, a one-percent conversion rate, and 35 cents per keyword, you'll probably get a ballpark guess on what AdWords might cost—and earn—you. And all of this math may very well lead you to the point of deciding AdWords is simply too expensive or will likely yield too few sales to work for your site. But if you're still intrigued, you can find out whether Google is actually selling keywords at a price you can afford and how many impressions you can expect to get for those keywords. Simply sign up for AdWords and play with the Traffic Estimator—a tool for guesstimating just those factors (page 325)—without spending a dime.

The market research

If you decide to increase your visibility with AdWords, take the time now to do some market research:

- **Mix and match your keywords and phrases to learn which searches your competitors are associated with.** Bear in mind that you'll have to pay more for popular keywords, and in many cases, you'll do better if you differentiate yourself with very specific keywords and effective, targeted ads. For example, if you have a small bookstore in Boise, Idaho, you can associate yourself with your locale (page 321) and a specialty, like first-edition Jane Austen books. If all you have to say is "We also have books," no ad will help you compete against giants like BarnesandNoble.com or BooksAMillion.com.

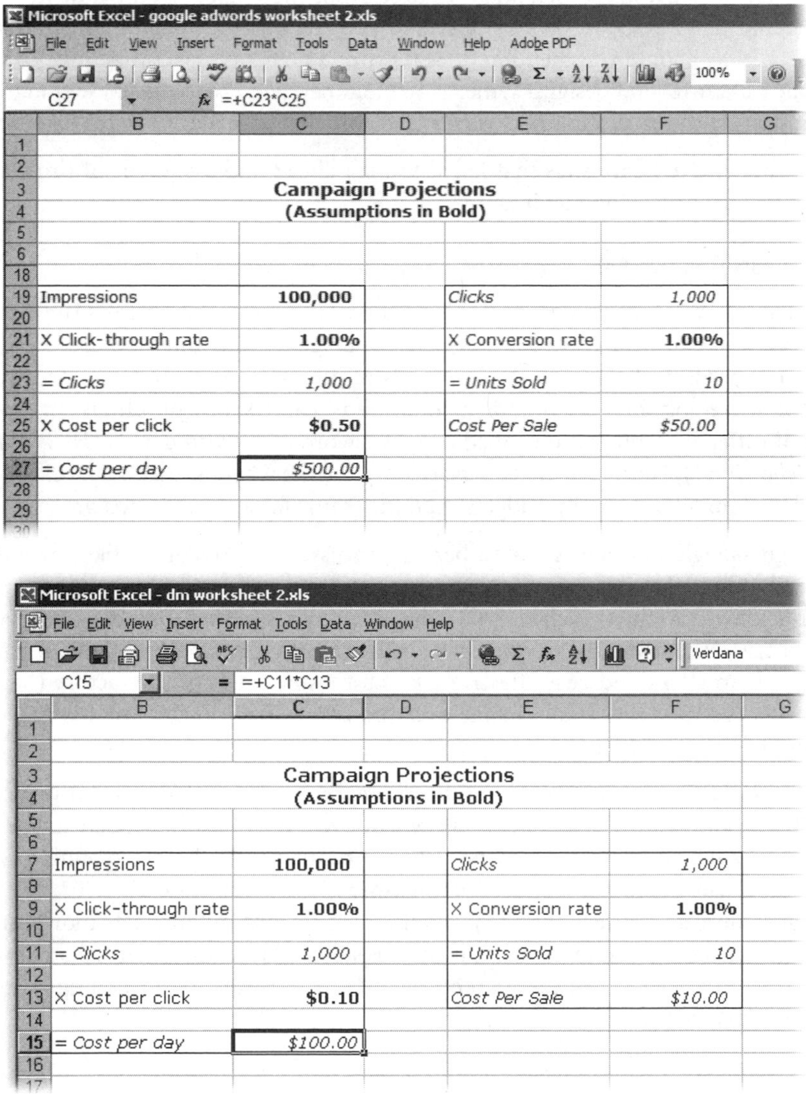

Figure 9-16:
Top left: This chart shows you how much AdWords will cost you per day if you get 100,000 impressions at a click-through rate of one percent and a cost-per-click of 50 cents.

Top right: This chart shows you how many sales you can expect to make based on the clicks you'll get multiplied by the conversion rate. The cost-per-sale is the total cost from the chart on the left divided by the units sold.

Bottom left and right: The same formulas, but with a different cost-per-click. You can also play with the impressions, the click-through rate, and the conversion rate to find different winning scenarios.

Tip: Your keywords might bring up ads unrelated to your products and services. For example, if you sell video camera parts, your keywords might pull up ads for video-rental services. Even if those advertisers aren't your competitors, you'll still be competing with them for people's attention. Accordingly, plan ads that will help distinguish your offerings from the rest of the crowd. Think, too, about finding less obvious keywords that might have fewer advertisers—and lower costs.

- **Put yourself in the shoes of your potential customers when you think about what your ad might look like.** What are they looking for? What enticing words might draw their attention from the search results and direct their eyeballs (and mice) to your ad? What would differentiate your ad from those above and below it? You certainly don't want to be just one of many advertisers sporting a "Hawaiian Shirts" title. Should you mention price (is your $39.95 pricing competitive)? Discount? Hard-to-find designs? Other matching merchandise? Keep these things in mind, and be prepared to tweak your ads to come up with the most effective copy.

The Web is littered with sites that failed to plan ahead and lost scads of time and money to AdWords. Don't let it happen to you.

A Few Final Words of Warning

To run an AdWords campaign that makes you more money than it costs (or draws enough readers to justify the costs, if that's your goal), you must be prepared to spend a good deal of time, maybe hundreds of hours, honing your ads. And you must be incredibly organized and methodical as you try out hundreds or thousands of different combinations of ad copy, keywords, keyword details (*Hello Kitty* vs. *"Hello Kitty"*), landing pages (the place on your site where somebody goes when they click your ad), and daily budgets. And that's just for a *small* campaign.

Although Google automates a number of processes in AdWords (like lowering high bids for clicks to a penny above your competitors'), you have to manually juggle a lot of variables, each of which has many possibilities. Furthermore, you have to try perhaps dozens of strategies to figure out what combinations of variables leads to clicks and cost-effective ads. Moreover, some of the factors (like a keyword's cost-per-click) can change over the course of a single day. It's not for the faint of time or patience.

In addition, while you can spend as little as five cents a day *in theory*, and you can definitely set your own daily budget, *in practice* you may find it difficult to spend within your limits and still reach potential customers. Small-scale spending was easier when Google first introduced its cost-per-click system in early 2002. But as more and more advertisers join the program, the keyword bidding gets more competitive, and costs go up incrementally. As a result, today many potential advertisers are nearly priced out of the market (page 317 offers tips on how to figure out whether AdWords is worth it for you).

All that said, AdWords is a great Web marketing tool for a lot of advertisers, and it may be for you, too.

Signing Up

You join AdWords by creating an Ad Group to hold your first ad, writing the ad itself, and choosing your keywords.

Tip: As you go through the process of signing up, don't use your browser's Back button to return to previous pages. Doing so can cancel your session. Instead, use the links Google provides to navigate between the pages.

---

1. **Go to the Google AdWords home page:** *http://adwords.google.com.*

   To get things rolling, click "Sign Up Now: Click to begin."

---

2. Pick target languages, countries, and particular regions.

Not only are your ads specific to the keywords folks are searching for, but you can also decide who sees them based on the language people search Google in, and their country or region (Figure 9-17).

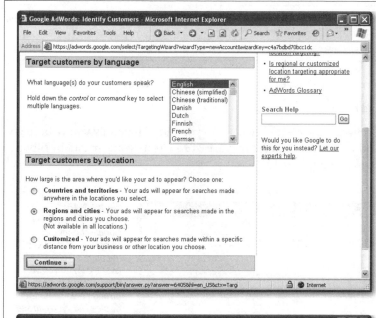

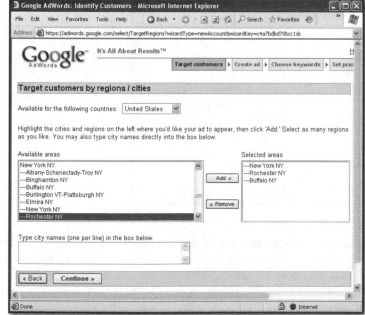

Figure 9-17:
Top: First, you choose a combination of languages; Ctrl+click (⌘-click) to select more than one in a list. You should also decide what level of location-specific targeting you want to use. When you've picked your settings, click Continue.

Bottom: If you choose regional targeting, Google takes you to this page. Choose the country you want to target, and then choose as many specific areas as you want. After you select an area, click the add button. (You can remove a region from your list by highlighting it and then clicking Remove.) If you want to focus in even closer, you can type in a list of city names (one per line) in the text box at the bottom.

Google provides regions for many countries, and these regions may correspond to states and metropolitan areas (in the U.S.), provinces (in Canada), and so on. If you *want* to reach people in a limited geographic area, regional targeting can bring down your cost-per-click substantially, because many fewer sites tend to compete for keywords in smaller physical areas.

Tip: The language and countries you choose don't have to be native matches. For example, you can allow French speakers from Canada but not from France. For that matter, you can target the French speakers from Australia or anywhere else you know they're wild about Hawaiian shirts.

When you're ready to move on, click the Continue button.

3. **Fill in the ad form.**

   It's time to inject those creative juices into your ad. (Hopefully you've been giving it some thought, as suggested on page 313.) Create your first ad by filling in the form shown in Figure 9-18.

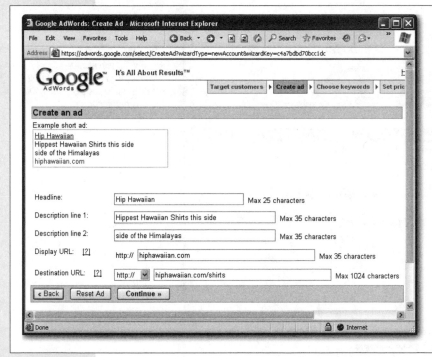

Figure 9-18:
As you fill in each line, Google changes the sample ad at the top of the page to reflect your choices. When you've filled in everything up through the line for the display URL, you can see what your ad will look like when it appears in Google results.

The first thing your audience sees (or summarily ignores) is your ad's headline, so make it stand out with a phrase that's enticing and novel, yet explanatory. And do it all in 25 or fewer characters. Similarly, Google gives you only 2 lines of 35 characters apiece for your description, so every letter counts. If you can, focus on products or services you offer that distinguish you from your competitors.

FREQUENTLY ASKED QUESTION

How Good Is Google's Geographical Location?

How does Google know where somebody is?

Google relies on the *Internet Protocol*, or IP, address of incoming Google queries to determine where the searcher actually is on the planet. Although generally invisible to you, an IP address—which is a unique number assigned to every computer connected to the Internet—usually includes clues about where a computer is physically located, helping other computers determine where it is.

Google claims an accuracy of near 99 percent in its guesses about where your potential customers are actually sitting. However, there are some quirks you need to be aware of. Most people connect to the Internet through an Internet Service Provider (ISP). (The notable exceptions are people that are surfing from a large company, or a large educational or government institution.) In this case, it's the IP address of the ISP's computers that determines the regional information Google sees.

Here's the problem: ISPs often pool together large amounts of traffic. So although the regional information Google gets is generally accurate, it doesn't necessarily match the person who's sitting at the other end of the browser. The country and region Google sees is almost always the same as the Web surfer's, but the city may not match exactly. Thus, be aware that if you create extremely targeted ads, they may not always appear in front of your target audience.

For example, if you're sure Hawaiian shirts are more popular among French speakers, serve your ads only to people searching Google in French. If you notice a predilection for Hawaiian shirts among residents of northern California, and you suspect a latent desire for beachwear in Cedar Rapids, Iowa, target your ads at people searching Google from those locales only.

Tip: Consider keeping your character count below rather than right at the maximum for each line of your ad. Your ad may appear on associate sites as part of the AdSense program (page 291), and sometimes Webmasters for associate sites scale their ad space improperly, or their sites may behave oddly on some browsers, both of which can cut off wider ads.

Google recommends making your ads available to their AdSense network for widest exposure. In fact, when you sign up for AdWords, Google *automatically* puts your ads in the pool for its whole distribution network. But you can choose to have your ads show up in Google results only. For directions on setting your distribution preferences, see page 331.

Google gives you two slots for URLs. First is your *display* URL, which is the one that appears in your ad. It should be short and sweet—again, no more than 35 characters—and for advertising purposes, it ought to represent your whole site, so your home page URL is probably best.

Tip: If people can reach your site without typing in *www*, leave that part out to help keep your ad trim.

The *destination* URL is the page people actually go to when they click your ad (no matter where in your ad people click, they go to the same page), so you can bring customers to just the right page for the product or service you're advertising. Here you've got 1,024 characters, and the URL doesn't appear in the ad itself, so link to as wide or deep a page on your site as you'd like.

Click Continue to move to the keywords page. At this point, Google checks your ad for inappropriate language. For example, if you inadvertently leave out the "r" in *Shirts*, Google rejects your ad.

4. **On the "Choose keywords" page, type your keywords.**

You should already have thought of these, tried them out earlier, and honed 'em (page 314). Once you've got your list, type each keyword or phrase on its own line. Start with some obvious choices for your products or services (*Hawaiian shirts*). Then widen the circle to include synonyms (*Hawaiian clothing*), misspellings (*Hawaiin shirts, Hawaiian shorts, Hawaiin shorts*), singular or plural forms (*Hawaiian shirt*), associated phrases (*leisurewear*), and so on. You can always add keywords, so consider starting with just a few to test the waters. Later on, you can play with the mix as you learn what's working and what's not.

Note: You can have as many keywords as you'd like for each ad. Each line (that is, each query), however, has a ten-word maximum, just as Google limits all searches to ten words (page 23).

As you go, you also need to tell Google how you want it to deal with your ads when somebody searches for your keywords. You have four match choices, described in the box on page 327, each of which has punctuation you can use to indicate your choice:

- For broad matches, use no punctuation.

- For phrase matches, put your phrase in quotes.

- For exact matches, put your phrase in brackets.

- For negative keywords, put a minus sign or dash before the word or phrase you want to ignore.

Tip: Google has a pretty good multimedia tutorial on AdWords keywords at *https://services.google.com/ marketing/stats/tutorial_redirect.*

It can be tedious coming up with all the keyword combinations you want to use. For help thinking of similar keywords and phrases, give the Keyword Tool a whirl (Figure 9-19). A similar version of the tool is available for you to use at any time at *https://adwords.google.com/select/KeywordSandbox.*

When you've finished setting your keywords, click Continue.

5. **Set your currency and your daily budget.**

AdWords suggests a daily budget, but if it's more than you can afford, you can change the "Daily budget" number. (Remember that your *monthly* expenditure equals no more than 30 days times your daily budget.)

No matter your daily budget, Google tries to show your ad evenly throughout each day. The lower your daily budget, however, the less often Google shows your ads. Unfortunately, Google doesn't provide an estimate of how a lower

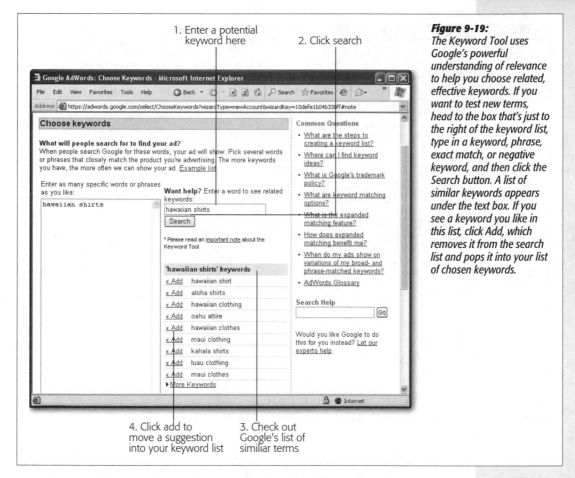

1. Enter a potential keyword here

2. Click search

Figure 9-19:
The Keyword Tool uses Google's powerful understanding of relevance to help you choose related, effective keywords. If you want to test new terms, head to the box that's just to the right of the keyword list, type in a keyword, phrase, exact match, or negative keyword, and then click the Search button. A list of similar keywords appears under the text box. If you see a keyword you like in this list, click Add, which removes it from the search list and pops it into your list of chosen keywords.

4. Click add to move a suggestion into your keyword list

3. Check out Google's list of similiar terms

daily budget might affect your exposure, so you have to simply try out an amount you can afford and keep an eye on your reports (page 334) to see what happens.

6. **Choose your maximum cost-per-click.**

Remember, when you bid on keywords, you're actually agreeing to pay Google anywhere from five cents to $50 for each person who clicks through your ads. But you don't have to guess at the marketplace for your keywords, because Google automatically suggests a maximum cost-per-click, based on what existing advertisers are already paying for your keywords. To find out how that suggestion will play out, click View Traffic Estimator, and check out Figure 9-20.

The Traffic Estimator is a terrifically handy predictor of the number of clicks you can expect for each of your keywords, your average cost-per-click and cost per day, and what position your ad is likely to reach (1.0 is the highest, 2.0 is second, and so on). At the top is your total cost per day. If it's more than you're prepared to pay, you can delete keywords, reduce the maximum cost-per-click you're willing to pay, or limit your target languages and countries. Conversely, if

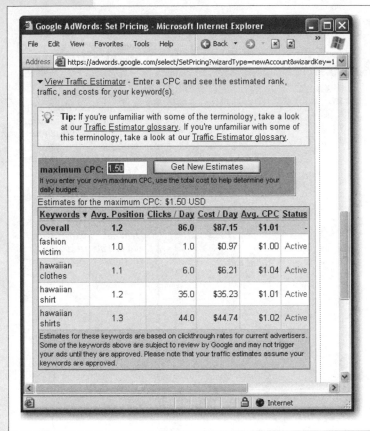

Figure 9-20:
The Traffic Estimator suggests a maximum cost-per-click for all the keywords in your Ad Group. (If your local currency is not U.S. dollars, choose another from the currency list.) If you want to set the cost-per-click for each keyword individually, you can do so after your account is established (page 325).

you want more exposure and you have a bigger budget, you can add keywords, increase your maximum cost-per-click, or expand your target language and countries. After you've changed any of those factors, click Get New Estimates (above the Traffic Estimator) to find out how your new scenario will work.

As you work with the Traffic Estimator, use its numbers to refine the projections spreadsheet you created before you signed up (page 317). The reality check of the Traffic Estimator, combined with your own calculations on cost-per-sale, units sold, and daily budget, may lead you to reconsider whether AdWords is worth your precious time and money. If the numbers don't look good but you're still itching to try it, you can always run a campaign for a few hours or a few days to see how things really play out.

Tip: If the Traffic Estimator is giving you bad news about your keywords—either they cost too much, or the exposure is too skimpy, or both—and you want to tweak your terms to see how that affects your bottom line, click "Edit your keyword list" under the Traffic Estimator, which takes you back to the "Choose keywords" page (step 4 above).

When you're satisfied you've set your costs properly, click the Continue button.

The Four Types of Keywords

When you choose your keywords (page 314), Google gives you four options for how it treats them. You signal each option with specific punctuation, described below. (Google ignores capitalization in keywords.)

Broad match. When you opt for a broad match—which you do simply by typing in your keywords with no punctuation—Google displays your ad not only when people search for your keywords but also when they look for synonyms, plurals, and related phrases—even if they don't appear in your keywords list. (Google calls these related terms *expanded matches*.)

While broad matching might seem like a good way to go, you should actually avoid it if you want your ads seen by the people most likely to find your products and services interesting. Broad matching might put your ad in front of people looking for tangentially related products (such as surfboards and scuba gear), but those people are less likely to net you a sale than people specifically looking for what you have on offer (Hawaiian shirts).

In addition, broad matching is potentially the most costly choice because the more keywords that match yours, the more likely it is that someone else has chosen the same ones, driving up the cost-per-click (page 315). If you go for broad matching, consider picking unusual keywords so as to have the least overlap with other advertisers.

Of course, broad matching is a good choice if you simply want the maximum number of people to *see* your ad, or perhaps if you're hoping that once people click through, they'll read your site rather than buy things from it.

Phrase match. When you run a regular Google search, putting a phrase in quotes (*"Hawaiian shirts"*) helps you find pages that contain that phrase and not just pages that have the word "Hawaiian" *or* "shirts." In AdWords, a phrase match works the same way. Put quotes around a phrase in your keywords, and Google displays your ad only when people search for that phrase. If somebody searches

for a phrase that *includes* yours—like *"Hawaiian shirts and pants,"* or *"colorful Hawaiian shirts"*—Google shows them your ad, too. Phrase match is a good choice if you want to advertise something for which *interested* people are likely to search for your terms as a phrase, and people looking for other things might search for the words separately. "Hawaiian shirts" could be a good candidate because you don't want to draw people searching for, say, *Hawaiian volcanoes*, or *Brooks Brothers shirts*.

Exact match. An exact match is a variation on the phrase match, except that Google doesn't show your ad if somebody's search includes anything other than exact phrase you've specified. For example, if you've chosen exact match for your line of shirts—which you do by enclosing your phrase in square brackets like this: *[Hawaiian shirts]*—Google doesn't show your ad to somebody searching for *"petite Hawaiian shirts."* This option cuts out a lot of searchers, but it can be a good choice if you really want to draw only the most focused searchers.

Negative keyword. A negative keyword tells Google to suppress your ad if somebody's search includes a particular term. For example, you might use a negative keyword to avoid showing your ad when somebody searches for *"ugly Hawaiian shirts."* Prefix a negative keyword with a dash or minus sign, like this: *"Hawaiian shirts" -ugly -cheesy*. You can also negate phrases, like this: *"Hawaiian shirts" -"hippo pattern."*

You can't put a negative keyword on its own line; it has to go along with a broad match or phrase match. Putting a negative keyword on its own line would be telling Google, "Show my ad if somebody doesn't surf for ugly," which would make your ad appear in *every* search that didn't include *ugly*. Fortunately, after you've set up your ads, you can add negative keywords to your whole *campaign*; page 333 tells you how.

7. **Confirm your choices.**

   Google gives you a final look at your ad, daily budget, and keywords. To back up and take another whack or three at any of these numbers, click the Back button (at the bottom of the page).

   When you're comfortable with your ad (and its cost), click the Continue to Sign Up button. Finally: It's time to sign up for an AdWords account.

8. **Use an existing account or create a new AdWords account.**

   If you have an existing Google account (one that you use for Gmail, for example), you can use that as your AdWords account as well. Click the "Sign in to AdWords with your Google Account" option, and supply your email and password.

   If you don't have a Google account or if you want to keep it separate from your AdWords account, click "Create a new Google Account to be your login to AdWords" instead. Fill in the AdWords sign-up form, providing an email address and making up a password. Be sure you choose an email address that is actually up and running, as Google sends a confirmation email to that address, and you need to retrieve it to finalize your account.

   Either way, you click the Create AdWords Account button to seal the deal.

9. **Check your email, verify it, and log in.**

   An email message from Google AdWords soon lands in your inbox. Click the hyperlink in it to go to the page where you complete the AdWords sign-up process. Log in using your email address and password.

10. **Set up billing.**

    After you've logged in, click the My Account tab and then Billing Preferences to get to the page where you can set up your billing options (Figure 9-21). Google deploys your first Ad Group and the associated ads the moment you provide your billing details.

    That's it. Now you can start wondering how your ads are faring. The next section tells you how to find out.

Note: AdWords' terms and conditions don't permit the publication of certain information about individual accounts. To meet that requirement, the illustrations throughout the rest of this chapter have been digitally altered.

Managing AdWords

After you've set up an account, the name of the game is tweaking. And lots of it. To reach your sales goals, you'll have to try many combinations of keywords, keyword

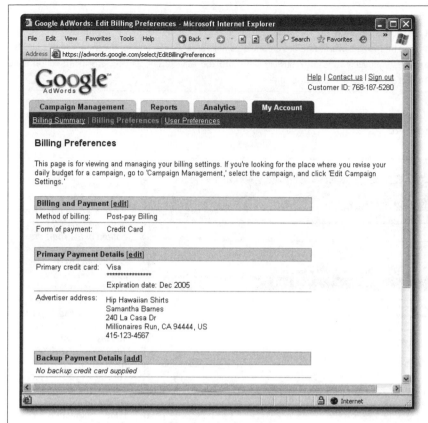

Figure 9-21:
Provide AdWords with your credit card number, contact information, and primary business type— Business to Business, or Business to Consumer— and subtype. Click Save Changes, and you're off to the races. Google charges your card the $5.00 sign-up fee, and any ads you've set up begin appearing immediately alongside appropriate Google search results. If you want to change any of these details later, just return to this page.

matches, ad copy, landing pages, costs-per-click, and daily budget. And to be successful, you have to treat it like science. When you do an experiment, you can't change everything at once. In fact, you can only learn what's working if you change one factor at a time. There's no way around it: AdWords is high maintenance. Fortunately, Google offers a slew of tools to help you assess the performance of every detail in your campaigns.

Note: Google offers some useful optimization and adjustment tips at *https://adwords.google.com/ select/tips.html.*

When you're logged in to your AdWords account, the Campaign Management tab is your command center. The tab has three pages: Campaign Summary, a nifty way to view your account; Tools, which lets you adjust the keywords across all your campaigns (described on page 333); and Conversion Tracking, an optional system for determining the effectiveness of your ads (see the box "Tracking Conversions" on page 333).

Tip: You can search through all your campaigns, Ad Groups, ad text, and keywords by using the Search box at the top right of every Campaign Management tool screen. It's handy when you have a lot of ads, and you can't remember which one has an outdated link to, say, your "Shirt of the Month" page. It's also useful if you've suddenly run out of flowery shirts and you want to find all your ads that mention floral patterns and change them to advertise stripes.

The Campaign Summary page, Figure 9-22, is where you'll do most of your clicking around.

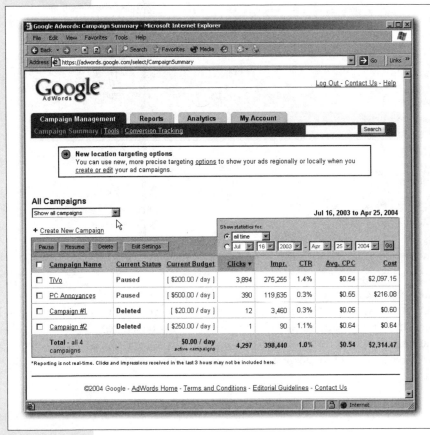

Figure 9-22:
The grid columns are self-explanatory, except the cost, which is the cost to you so far. At the very bottom of the chart are totals for all your campaigns. To sort the information by clicks, cost, or any other column, click the blue column heading. You can adjust the chart to show you just a set of campaigns (use the menu in the top-left corner), or you can pick a different time period to review (in the middle, under "Show statistics for," choose a date range, and then click Go to update the display), which is useful when, for example, you want to find out whether your click-throughs are seasonal.

As you know, a campaign contains one or more Ad Groups. For each campaign, Google gives you a summary of its status, letting you take various actions.

Note: To apply an action to a particular campaign, turn on its associated checkbox and then click the appropriate action button. For example, to pause the first campaign on your list, click its checkbox and then click Pause. Select multiple campaigns by turning on multiple checkboxes. Select them all by turning on the checkbox to the left of the Campaign Name heading.

- **Create New Campaign.** Use this link to create a campaign for your nifty new line of Hawaiian footwear. Google takes you back to step 2 on page 321.

- **Pause.** Perhaps your campaign has been too successful and you're plumb out of Hawaiian shirts, or you've decided to take a different tack for June, focusing on an overstock of Bermuda shorts instead. Pause a campaign at any time to suspend the appearance of its ads alongside Google results.

- **Resume.** Your supplier has managed to come up with a few more gross of shirts; you can safely resume your campaign now that you've got merchandise to sell.

- **Delete.** Campaign just not working at all? Time to try something different. While you can just Pause a campaign, if you're sure you won't ever want it again, simply delete it.

- **Edit Settings.** You can alter any of the options you set when you created your account or the current campaign, including campaign name, daily budget, a time period for displaying the ads, language and country, and which Web sites Google displays your ads on. If you don't want your ads to appear on sites in the AdSense network (page 291), here's the place to change that setting.

- **Visit the Ad Groups in a campaign.** Click the blue name of an ad campaign to zoom in on it and work with the Ad Groups within it, discussed next.

Managing your Ad Groups

An Ad Group consists of one or more ads. When you're on the Campaign Summary page, clicking a campaign name shows the Ad Groups within that campaign (Figure 9-23) and lets you take action on the groups. You can do most of the same things you could do at the campaign level (create new groups, pause, resume, and delete them), but you can also do a few extra things.

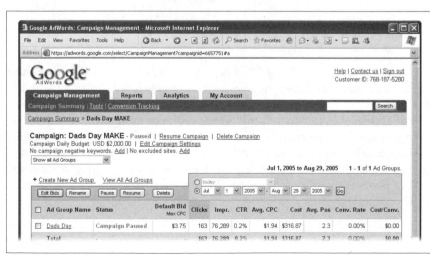

Figure 9-23:
The Ad Groups report looks just like the Campaign Summary, but it shows you statistics for your individual Ad Groups and lets you perform actions on them.

• **Edit Bids.** Change your mind about how much you're prepared to pay for each click for *all the ads in a group*? Raise or lower your maximum cost-per-click at any time.

• **Rename.** Perhaps you're combining your Bermuda shorts with your entire line of pants; rename the "Bermudas" Ad Group to "Pants."

• **Visit the ads in an Ad Group.** Click the blue name of an Ad Group to zoom in and fiddle about with the ads themselves, discussed below.

Managing your ads and keywords

Click an Ad Group for an overview of its keywords and the ads triggered by these keywords, shown at the bottom of the Web page (Figure 9-24).

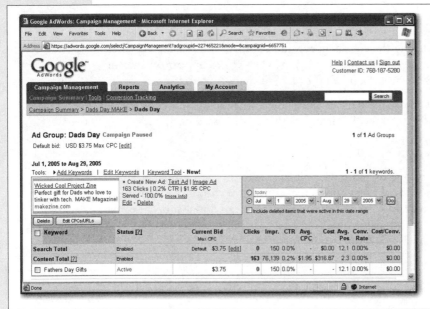

Figure 9-24:
This page is where you manage the keywords associated with an Ad Group. The lines at the top, Search Total and Content Total, tell you the difference between people who see your ads in Google results and people who see them on other sites via AdSense, respectively. Below that is a breakdown of how each of your keywords is performing.

Here you can create a new ad or delete a keyword that just isn't coming up enough or seems to be attracting the wrong crowd. You can also jump to Edit CPCs/URLs page, where you can also edit your cost-per-clicks for each individual *keyword*, a level of specificity you couldn't reach during setup. For example, if you're willing to pay more for *"vintage Hawaiian shirts"* because that's your specialty and you really want to draw people looking for them, you can bump up your cost-per-click when people search for that phrase. If people searching for *"newfangled Hawaiian shirts"* are potential customers but not as likely to buy, you can pay less per click for them.

On the Edit CPCs/URLs page you can also tailor the URLs associated with individual keywords so that your landing pages are different depending on what people

Tracking Conversions

You've got a bunch of ads out there, and people are clicking through. But wouldn't it be nice to tie particular ads to actual sales, sign-ups, and other actions on your site? Google AdWords Conversion Tracking (*https://adwords.google.com/select/convtracking*) is just the ticket.

For any page that you consider a conversion—say, the "Checkout" page of your shopping cart, confirmation of a service subscription, or sign-up for an email newsletter—you can embed in it a bit of Google-supplied JavaScript code that sends a message back to the Google AdWords conversion tracker each time the page loads, noting which ad brought the person to your site. (The tool doesn't track your visitors; it tracks the ads they've clicked through and the conversions you've achieved as a result.)

In an AdWords report, the conversion rate is the number of conversions divided by the number of tracked ad clicks. The cost-per-conversion is the total ad cost divided by the number of conversions. This information can help you learn that the ad in which you tout "cheap shirts" is earning you $.75 per click, on average, while the ad in which you stipulate "$35 Hawaiian shirts" is earning you nearly $15 per click, on average. You can also use the conversion rate to learn things like whether ads with your company name are more effective than ads that give a product name, too.

Google gives you two types of conversion tracking. *Basic Conversion Tracking* simply tracks conversions—how often people who click through your ads actually buy something, sign up, or otherwise do whatever you consider a conversion—and requires nothing more on your end than mixing some JavaScript into your page's HTML code.

Customized Conversion Tracking lets you specify conversion types (purchases/sales, leads, sign-ups, and basic page views) and throws in values, too ($25.95 for that Large Floral Print Hawaiian shirt, for example) for particular conversions, so that Google can do the conversion math for you. For customized tracking, you have to take a few steps before pasting some JavaScript into your HTML.

Both types of conversion tracking are free, and Google provides a rather nice multimedia Conversion Tracking Tutorial (*https://services.google.com/tutorial/cvt/cvt.html*) that takes you through every step of the process, from setup to reporting.

are searching for. For example, perhaps you want people searching for *Hawaiian* to click through to your general store (*www.hiphawaiian.com*), but you want people looking for *"Hawaiian shirts"* to go straight to the right section of your site (*www. hiphawaiian/clothing/shirts*). Again, associating individual keywords with specific links to your site is a level of detail you couldn't achieve when you set up the ads.

You can take your keyword management to yet another level. From the Campaign Management tab, click Tools to get a page that's packed full of AdWords goodness. You'll see three groups of links. The first group is Optimize Your Ads, which brings the following features together:

- **Keyword Tool.** Here you can build a master list of keywords for use in various campaigns with the familiar Keyword Tool (which you first used on page 324). As its name implies, the tool suggests keywords related to the ones you've already picked, helping you refine your targeting.

- **Edit Campaign Negative Keywords.** Use this option to define negative keywords (page 324) that will apply to an entire campaign, rather than just one Ad Group.

- **Site Exclusion.** Use this option to define sites on which your ads should never appear.

- **Traffic Estimator.** This brings you back to the familiar Traffic Estimator (page 325), which is useful for budgeting out keywords and campaigns.

The second group is named Analyze Your Ad Performance. Here, you can explore and analyze how your ads are working. Your options include:

- **Ads Diagnostic Tool.** This is a nifty tool that lets you try out a sample Google search and see if it pulls up any of your ads. You can choose to try your virtual search for different Google-controlled sites (like *www.google.com*, *www.google.ca*, *froogle.google.com*, and so on) and you can choose the language and region settings that you want to use for the search. Once you've configured these details, just supply the keywords and click Continue. Google tells you if any of your ads fit the bill.

- **Disapproved Ads.** If one or more of your ads were rejected by Google, click here to find out what they were and why Google didn't like them.

- **Conversion Tracking.** Brings you to the handy Conversion Tracking tool (page 333), where you can see how many visitor ad clicks lead to the ultimate goal you have in mind (for example, a sale).

- **My Change history.** Review the changes that you've made to your account over the last three months.

Finally, the Modify Your Campaigns section of links has a few tools that are useful when you have several campaigns going. You can search for ads throughout all your campaigns and then choose to tweak their Max CPC value (click "Find and Edit Max CPCs"), text ("Find and Edit Ad Text"), or keywords ("Find and Edit Ad Keywords"). Finally, use "Copy or Move Keywords and Ad Text" to shuffle ads and keywords from one campaign to another, which is useful when you need to create new campaigns that have some similarities to old ones.

Reporting

AdWords reports are basically the spreadsheets in the Campaign Management tab, but you can't take any actions from the reports (read: muck something up). Reports are thus good for people like coworkers who need "look but don't touch" access to your campaigns, and they let you create crowd-pleasing graphs. Reports are also good for letting you get a bird's-eye view of your campaigns without losing detail. For example, you can see how a keyword is performing across several campaigns, including the number of impressions it's drawing, the clicks, conversion rate, and more. Perhaps the best feature of the reporting tools is that you can have Google email you any report daily, weekly, or monthly, which lets you keep an eye on things without having to remember to go look.

The Reports tab has two links: Report Center, which shows all the reports you've created so far (and lets you review them with a single click), and Create Report, which lets you build a new report. Here's how you can create a report:

1. **In the Reports tab, click Create Report.**

   The Create Report page appears (Figure 9-25).

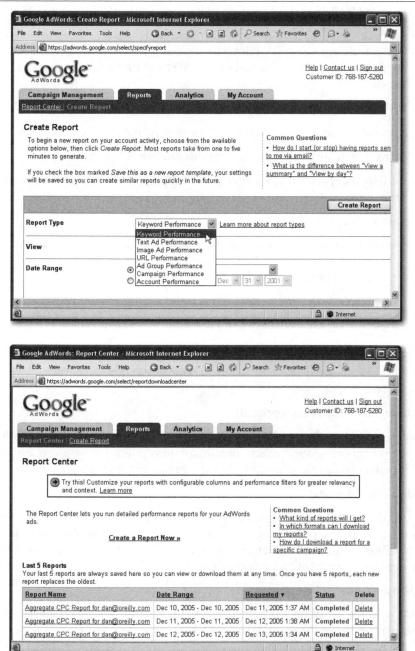

Figure 9-25:

Top: To create a new report, click Create Report. The first step is to choose one of several handy report types.

Bottom: From the Report Center page, you can review the reports you've generated in the past.

2. **Select the Report Type.**

In the Report Type box, Google provides a number of handy prefab report options. They include:

- **Keyword Report.** See how your individual keywords and phrases are faring.

- **Ad Text Report.** Check how slight alterations to the titles and descriptions of your ads change your click-through rates. For example, find out if the headline "Hawaii Five-Whoa" garners a higher rate than the headline "Hawaiian Punch."

- **URL Report.** Keep track of the landing pages you've embedded in your ads.

- **Account Report.** Get an overview of how your AdWords account is doing.

- **Campaign Report.** Compare your various campaigns against one another.

- **Ad Group Report.** Compare your Ad Groups and their associated keywords against one another.

3. **Choose a view.**

The view determines how detailed the chart is. You can choose Summary, Daily, Monthly, Quarterly, or Yearly, depending on whether you want to look at the big picture or hone in on daily fluctuations.

4. **Change the date range (optional).**

Reports cover the last seven days if you don't change the date range.

5. **Choose a specific campaign or ad group (optional).**

If you don't make a selection here, the report includes data from all your campaigns.

6. **Add or remove columns (optional).**

Google provides a lengthy list of columns for every report type. Based on the type you choose, Google selects certain columns. However, you can add or remove individual columns—just add a checkmark next to the ones you want.

7. **Add a filter (optional).**

If you don't want to see everything, you can limit your report with a filter. For example, if you're performing a keyword report, you could show only keywords that resulted in a minimum 10 clicks, cost more than a certain amount, or were served a minimum number of times.

8. **Choose a name for your report.**

This is the name that the report will have on the Report Center page. By default, this name matches the report type (as in Account Report or Keyword Report). If you've applied more settings, you should customize it to be something more meaningful.

9. **If you want to reuse your report, choose "Save this as a new report template."**

   This choice lets you create a new report based on this report in this future. You can also use the scheduling options (described in step 10).

10. **Set scheduling options (optional).**

    Complex reports can take some time to generate, so you might want to schedule them so the information is ready when you want it. You can configure a report to run automatically on a daily, weekly, or monthly basis. Even better, if you switch on this option (by selecting "Schedule this report to run automatically"), you can also have the report emailed to you (select "Whenever the report runs, send email to" and fill in an email address) so you get the results without needing to log in to AdWords.

11. **Click Create Report.**

    There's a short delay while Google generates the report. Once it's finished, the page refreshes. Click the "View data" link to continue on to your report. (Figure 9-26 shows you the Keyword Report, which is one of the handiest.)

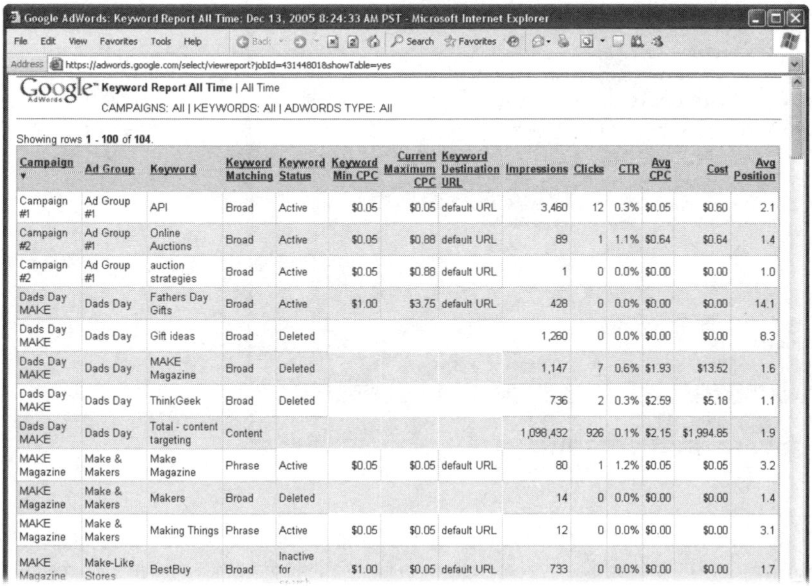

Campaign ▼	Ad Group	Keyword	Keyword Matching	Keyword Status	Keyword Min CPC	Current Maximum CPC	Keyword Destination URL	Impressions	Clicks	CTR	Avg CPC	Cost	Avg Position
Campaign #1	Ad Group #1	API	Broad	Active	$0.05	$0.05	default URL	3,460	12	0.3%	$0.05	$0.60	2.1
Campaign #2	Ad Group #1	Online Auctions	Broad	Active	$0.05	$0.88	default URL	89	1	1.1%	$0.64	$0.64	1.4
Campaign #2	Ad Group #1	auction strategies	Broad	Active	$0.05	$0.88	default URL	1	0	0.0%	$0.00	$0.00	1.0
Dads Day MAKE	Dads Day	Fathers Day Gifts	Broad	Active	$1.00	$3.75	default URL	428	0	0.0%	$0.00	$0.00	14.1
Dads Day MAKE	Dads Day	Gift ideas	Broad	Deleted				1,260	0	0.0%	$0.00	$0.00	8.3
Dads Day MAKE	Dads Day	MAKE Magazine	Broad	Deleted				1,147	7	0.6%	$1.93	$13.52	1.6
Dads Day MAKE	Dads Day	ThinkGeek	Broad	Deleted				736	2	0.3%	$2.59	$5.18	1.1
Dads Day MAKE	Dads Day	Total - content targeting	Content					1,098,432	926	0.1%	$2.15	$1,994.85	1.9
MAKE Magazine	Make & Makers	Make Magazine	Phrase	Active	$0.05	$0.05	default URL	80	1	1.2%	$0.05	$0.05	3.2
MAKE Magazine	Make & Makers	Makers	Broad	Deleted				14	0	0.0%	$0.00	$0.00	1.4
MAKE Magazine	Make & Makers	Making Things	Phrase	Active	$0.05	$0.05	default URL	12	0	0.0%	$0.00	$0.00	3.1
MAKE Magazine	Make-Like Stores	BestBuy	Broad	Inactive for	$1.00	$0.05	default URL	733	0	0.0%	$0.00	$0.00	1.7

Figure 9-26: *Using Google's reporting tools, you can create a Keyword Report like this—and you can control what you see in each column. For example, under Keyword Matching, you can choose Broad, Phrase, Exact, Content, or Any Type. You can also add a graph and display conversion statistics (see the box "Tracking Conversions" on page 333). In general, the AdWords reports all look similar to the Keyword Report.*

Tip: You can view reports right there in your browser by choosing "View data" once the report is generated. But if you want to view them in your favorite spreadsheet or database application—so you can create your own charts or compare data with another marketing campaign—you can download the data in a format that other programs can read, known as *comma-separated values,* or .csv (in this format, you get just the columns of data, separated by commas, which most database and spreadsheet programs can easily import). Text and XML downloads are also available—just click the appropriate link in the Download Report section.

Billing

Under the My Account tab, you can get a billing summary, or alter your billing preferences (such as which credit card Google charges) or user preferences (such as your contact information). Mostly, you'll ignore the preference pages and check out the billing summary, shown in Figure 9-27, which lets you track pending charges and payments you've made on your AdWords account.

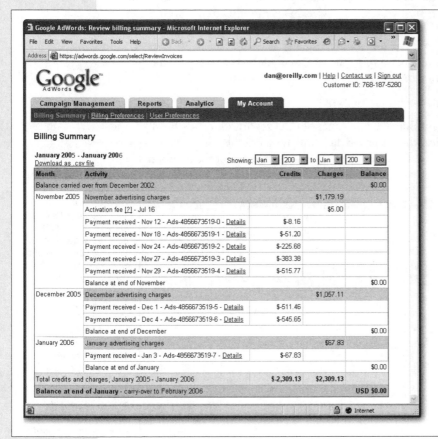

Figure 9-27:
On each line, if you click Details, Google displays a sub-report for that time period, showing how many clicks you received per campaign, the average cost-per-click, and how much you actually paid.

Tip: If you want to view the billing information in your own spreadsheet or accounting program, click "Download as .csv file" to have Google convert the data into a format that other programs can read.

The billing summary is a handy way to check your charges and credits, but most of the time, you can use the campaign summary pages and your reports to keep track of what's happening in your AdWords world.

Note: If Google mistakenly charged you more for your ads than you were prepared to pay, an *overdelivery* credit shows up on your billing summary.

Getting Help

You can view AdWords online help two ways: at *https://adwords.google.com/select/index.html*, which includes links to pages about what an AdWords campaign can do for you, and at *https://adwords.google.com/support,* which focuses on FAQs and running a campaign. From this page, you can also search for specific terms or look them up in a glossary.

If you can't find what you need, use the contact form at *https://adwords.google.com/support/bin/request.py* to ask a question.

Google Analytics

In order to create a flourishing Web site, you need to get inside the minds of your visitors. First, you need to know *what* they're doing. Are they staying for hours browsing your ample catalogue of Elvis memorabilia, or are they surfing away after a few seconds? Are they browsing each and every page in your scandalous life story or heading straight to a particularly juicy document? Are they returning regularly to check for new developments, or have they forgotten all about you?

Once you know what visitors are doing, you need to discover *why*. Ordinary Web sites fail for a variety of reasons. For example, a gargantuan Java applet could be choking the underpowered browsers of your visitors. Or maybe your Web site's navigation menu makes it too hard to find the pages visitors want. Only after you've finished this Sherlockian exercise of deduction can you build a more popular Web site or craft a more successful ad campaign.

In the past, Webmasters had a hard time getting this sort of information. You were struck with essentially two choices: using limited hit counters and the underpowered reporting features provided by most Web hosting companies, or digging up some serious cash for a more sophisticated software tool that analyzes Web server logs.

But now Google has sailed to the rescue. In 2005, Google purchased Urchin, one of the premium Web tracking companies, and transformed it into Google Analytics. A few months later, they abolished its hefty $500/month price tag and made it free for everyone. In this chapter, you'll learn how to use the high-powered Google Analytics service to track your visitors and summarize their habits in detailed reports.

Note: Technically, Google Analytics users that don't have an AdWords account (page 312) are limited to analyzing sites that receive no more than five million page views per month. If your Web site exceeds this threshold, congratulations! Why not celebrate by spending $5 to open a new AdWords account, which nets you a lifetime of unlimited page views?

How Google Analytics Works

Google Analytics is refreshingly simple. Unlike other log-analysis tools, Google Analytics doesn't ask you to provide server logs or other low-level information. Instead, Google Analytics tracks all the information you need *on its own*. It stores this information indefinitely and lets you analyze it anytime with a range of snazzy Web reports.

In order to use Google Analytics, you need to add a small snippet of JavaScript code to every Web page in your Web site (unless you have specific pages that you don't want to track). The code tracks each visitor using a cookie (page 47).

Once you've got the JavaScript code in place, everything works seamlessly. When a visitor heads to a page in your site, their browser sends a record of the request to Google's army of monster Web servers, which store it for later analysis. The visitor doesn't see the Google Analytics stuff. Figure 10-1 shows you how it works.

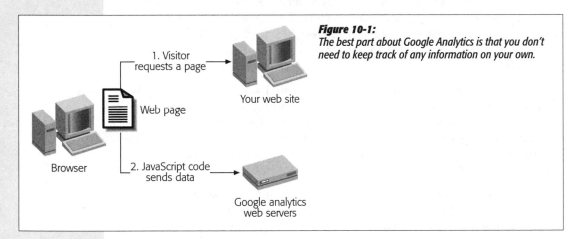

Figure 10-1:
The best part about Google Analytics is that you don't need to keep track of any information on your own.

1. Visitor requests a page

Web page

Your web site

Browser

2. JavaScript code sends data

Google analytics web servers

Using this system, Google Analytics is able to get two kinds of information:

- **Information about your visitors' browsers.** Whenever a browser requests a page, it supplies a basic set of information. This information includes the type of browser, the features it supports, and the IP address of the computer it's connecting through. (An *IP address* is a numeric code that identifies a computer on a network.) These details don't include the information you really want—for example, there's no way to find out personal details like names and addresses. However, Google can use the browser information to infer some additional details. For example, using the IP address, it can make an educated guess about a visitor's geographic location.

- **Visitor tracking.** Thanks to its cookie-based tracking system, Google Analytics can determine more interesting information about a visitor's surfing patterns. Ordinarily, if a surfer requests two separate Web pages from the same site, there's no way to establish whether those requests came from the same person. However, with the cookie in place, Google can uniquely identify each visitor. As a result, when visitors click links and move from page to page, Google can determine their navigation path, the amount of time they spend on each page, and whether they return later.

Google Analytics wouldn't be nearly as useful if it were up to you to make sense of all this information. But as you'll see, Google not only tracks these details, it also provides reports that help you figure out what the data really means. You generate the reports through a handy Web interface, and you can also print your reports or download the data for use in another program.

Setting Up Google Analytics

To get set up with Google Analytics, you have to take three steps. First, you create an account. Next, you add the tracking code to every page in your site. Finally, you wait—and within 24 hours, Google will have enough information to provide detailed reports.

Note: At the time of this writing, Google Analytics is experiencing growing pains due to high demand. As a result, the sign-in process may be restricted from time to time. If you can't create a Google Analytics account, check back later, or add yourself to the waiting list.

Signing Up

Signing up for Google Analytics is easy:

1. Head over to *www.google.com/analytics* and click the sign-up link.

   The sign-up process takes you through a few short steps. Here's the information you need to supply:

   - The email address and password you want to use.

Note: Google Analytics is one of many services that are accessible through a single Google Account. That means that you can use Google Analytics with the same account you use for services like Gmail and Google Groups. (Google AdSense and Google AdWords require dedicated accounts, because they need additional information like financial details.)

   - The Web site you want to track. A Google Analytics account can track up to 50 Web sites, but for now start with just one.

• Whether or not your Web site uses frames.

• The types of reports you want to see. Use the default settings, which include all the Google Analytics reports. The box "How Reports Are Organized" (page 349) has more about the report categories in Google Analytics.

2. **Copy the tracking code.**

When you finish the sign-in process, Google gives you a box with the Java-Script code you need to start tracking visits (see Figure 10-2). The next section tells you how to add it to your pages.

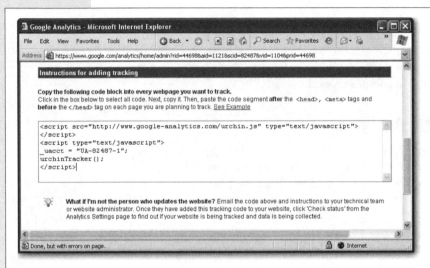

Figure 10-2:
The Google Analytics code is lean and concise, requiring just six lines. Select it all and copy it to the clipboard. (You can do this in most browsers by right-clicking the selected text and choosing Copy.)

Setting Up Your Site for Tracking

Once you've created your Google Analytics account, you're ready to add the Java-Script code to every Web page you want to track.

Tip: For best results, copy the tracking code to every Web page in your site. The only exception is in a frames-based site. If you have a frames-based site, don't copy the tracking code to the pages used for navigation bars, headers, and other noncontent regions.

The tracking code looks like this:

```
<script src="http://www.google-analytics.com/urchin.js" type="text/
javascript">
</script>
<script type="text/javascript">
_uacct = "UA-02487-1";
urchinTracker();
</script>
```

Frames and Google Analytics

If your Web site uses frames, make sure you place the Java-Script tracking code in every content page. You don't need to place the tracking code in other frames, like a navigation bar or title section. You can if you want, but there's generally no point in recording requests for these elements, because they're shown automatically.

You should also place the tracking code in the frameset page (the page that actually splits the window into multiple panes).

That's because this is the page the visitor requests first, and if you don't capture the first request you'll lose valuable information about how a visitor arrived at your site.

For example, imagine your site includes the page *index.html*, which is a frameset that splits the window into two panes. The top pane (*header.html*) shows a header bar, and the bottom pane (*main.html*) shows some content. You should add tracking code to *main.html* and *index.html*.

The first two lines define a link to the file *www.google-analytics.com/urchin.js*. This file is packed full of customized tracking code.

Tip: Curious JavaScript gurus can request this file in their browsers, save a local copy, and take a closer look.

The rest of the code defines a script that runs automatically when the page is processed. This script contains exactly two lines. The first line sets the tracking identifier (_uacct), which identifies your Web site. The second line calls the urchinTracker( ) JavaScript function (one of the ingredients in the *urchin.js* file) to create the cookie and send the tracking information to Google's Web servers.

Note: If your Web pages include their own custom JavaScript functions, they could conflict with Google Analytics—but it's extremely unlikely. Aside from the urchinTracker( ) function, all the other function names in the *urchin.js* file start with _u or __u. So unless you're in the habit of using cryptic function names like __utmVisitorCode( ), you won't have a problem.

When adding the script code to a Web page, you place it inside the <head> section at the beginning of your page, after any <meta> tags. Here's an example that shows where it fits in a typical Web page:

```
<html>

<head>
  <meta http-equiv="Content-Language" content="en-us">
  <meta http-equiv="Content-Type" content="text/html; charset=windows-1252">
  <title>Welcome</title>
  <!-- Put the analytics code here. -->
</head>

<body>
```

```
    <!-- The page content goes here. -->
</body>


</html>
```

Once you've changed all the pages, make sure to upload them to your Web server. Only then can Google Analytics start tracking visits.

Tip: You can also use Google Analytics with many blog sites, as long as you're able to edit the actual HTML. For example, a blogging tool like Blogger (*www.blogger.com*) lets you edit the template that's used for blog entries. Add the Google Analytics code to this template, and you'll have the same Web tracking a full-blown Web site enjoys.

TROUBLESHOOTING MOMENT

Help! I've Misplaced the Tracking Code

Google provides the tracking code at the end of the sign-in process. Your block of script code will look identical to the example on page 344, aside from the _uacct value, which is unique for every Web site that's registered with Google Analytics.

If you misplace the ever-important tracking code, you can get it back. Just follow these steps:

1. Head to *www.google.com/analytics* and log in. You'll start off at the Analytics Settings page.

2. Next to your Web site profile, click Edit. This takes you to the Profile Settings page.

3. Click the Check Status link (shown here). This loads the Tracking Status page.

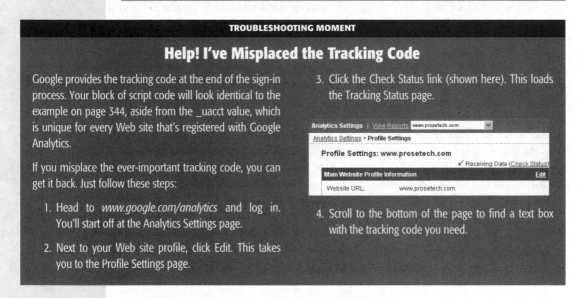

4. Scroll to the bottom of the page to find a text box with the tracking code you need.

A Snapshot of Your Web Traffic

Now that you're a registered Google Analytics user, you can log in to read reports and check the status of the whole operation. If you haven't already done so, now's the time to head to *www.google.com/analytics*.

When you first log in, you'll see the Analytics Settings page shown in Figure 10-3. Using this page, you can add new Web sites that you want to track and configure the existing ones. You can also get a little guidance from a list of help topics that appears on the right.

To determine whether your Web site's tracking code is working, check the Status column in the Website Profiles list. Here's how to interpret different statuses you might see:

- **Receiving Data** indicates that all's well. Your visitors are surfing under the watchful eye of Google Analytics.

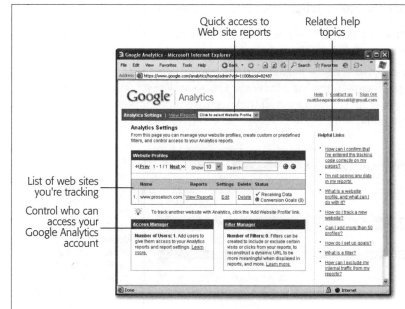

Figure 10-3:
This sample account has one configured Web site (in the Website Profiles section). You can use the View Reports link to start reviewing reports, the Edit link to change the information you supplied for your Web site, and the Delete link to remove the profile altogether. You'll explore other details, like Conversion Goals (page 364), the Access Manager (see the box on page 356), and the Filter Manager (page 360), later in this chapter.

- **Waiting For Data** indicates the JavaScript code is running on your Web pages, but the information isn't available for reporting yet. Usually, you'll see this for the first 6 to 12 hours after you set up a new Web site.

- **Unknown** indicates that Google isn't collecting any information. This could be because you need to wait for visitors to hit your site, or it could suggest you haven't inserted the correct JavaScript tracking code. To double check the code, follow the steps in the "Help! I've Misplaced the Tracking Code" box on page 346.

The Executive Overview

By now, you're probably itching to get your hands on a Google Analytics report and see what's going down in your corner of the Web. The best way to start out with the Google Analytics reports is to try the *executive dashboard*. It shows four snapshots that summarize what's taken place at your Web site over the last week.

Note: *Dashboards* are Google Analytics pages that show one or more reports. Typically, dashboards focus on summary information, while reports offer views of more specific data. Overall, Google Analytics offers many more reports than dashboards.

Here's how to get to the executive dashboard:

1. **If you aren't signed in yet, surf to *www.google.com/analytics* and sign in.**

   The Analytics Settings page appears, with a list of all your Web site profiles.

2. **Click the View Reports link next to the Web site you want to track.**

   The reporting page appears. Unless you've changed the standard settings, you'll always start out at the executive dashboard (Figure 10-4).

   If you *have* changed the default settings, you can get to the executive dashboard using the menu on the left. Under the Dashboard heading, in the View list box, choose Executive. This shows all the executive reports. Now click the Executive Overview link.

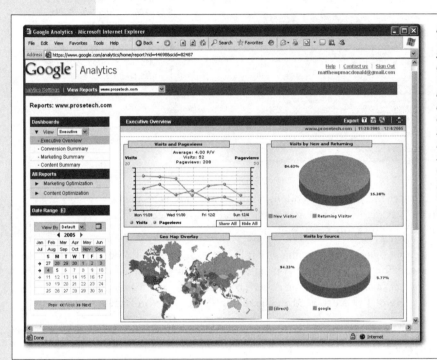

Figure 10-4:
The executive dashboard splits the page into four charts that detail your Web site's vital signs. The menu on the left lets you browse to new dashboards (the top section) or specific reports (the middle section). You can also adjust the date range you're working with (in the bottom section), as described on page 353.

> **Note:** All Google's reports use Macromedia Flash, a popular browser plug-in that supports interactive and animated content. Most people have Flash installed, but if you don't, you can download what you need at *www.macromedia.com/go/getflashplayer*.

The information that appears in the executive dashboard can be a little overwhelming. To give you a better sense of what's going on, the following sections break it down one chart at a time.

> **Note:** Mac fans who use Apple's Safari browser have reported problems viewing Google Analytics reports. If you suffer from the same headaches, Google recommends adjusting the text size (from the browser's menu) after the reports have loaded. If this doesn't solve the problem, you'll need to use a Mozilla-based browser like Netscape or Firefox (page 195), which are the only Mac browsers Google officially supports (at least for now).

How Reports Are Organized

Google Analytics is stuffed full of detailed, dense reports. But the creators of Google Analytics realized that certain reports would naturally appeal to specific sorts of people. For example, marketers and Webmasters can both benefit from reviewing Web site activity, but they are interested in different details.

With that distinction in mind, Google separated its dashboards into three basic categories: Executive, Marketer, and Webmaster. You can choose an option from the drop-down View list box in the Dashboards section of the menu. Depending on the category you choose, you'll see a different set of links:

• **The Executive view** displays high-level summary information with a bit of everything. It's the type of no-nonsense details that are usually presented to the head honchos. You'll see the overall Web site traffic, the conversion rate for specific goals (page 364), and the marketing effectiveness. The other categories drill down into more detail.

• **The Marketer view** shows statistics about marketing campaigns. This is where you'll spend the most time if you want to evaluate whether your Web site is meeting its financial targets. Most usefully, you can evaluate the success of paid placements and the return on investment of various Google AdWords keywords. This section is the best place to go if you want to plan your Web site budget.

• **The Webmaster view** shows the details needed for the people who create the Web site content. It details information about the capabilities of visitors' browsers, operating systems, and computers. It also highlights the most and least successful pages, and it lets you analyze navigation patterns. This section is the best place to go if you want to tweak your Web site to optimize it for visitors.

The View category only changes the list of options in the Dashboards section of the menu. It doesn't affect the All Reports section (the portion of the menu just underneath the Dashboards section), which always lists the full range of reports.

Visits and Pageviews

The Visits and Pageviews chart (top left of the Executive Overview) shows the day-by-day popularity of your Web site over the last week. The yellow line shows the rise or fall of *pageviews*—a raw record of the number of pages your site has served out. The blue line compares the number of *visits*—a count of how many different people surfed through your site.

In other words, if an eager shopper visits your Banana Painting e-commerce store, checks out several enticing products, and completes a purchase, Google Analytics records close to a dozen pageviews, but only a single visit. The number of pageviews is always more than the number of visits—after all, each visit includes at least one pageview.

Like many of the charts in Google Analytics, the Visits and Pageviews chart is packed with information (see Figure 10-5). You can study the daily trend lines, or refer to the summary at the top of the chart for the total number of visits and pageviews over the week.

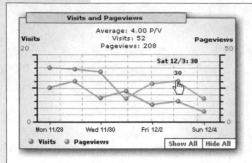

Figure 10-5:
To get the specific value for a data point, click it. For example, this chart clearly indicates a modest 30 pageviews occurred on Sat 12/3. To see all data points, click the Show All button in the bottom-right corner of the chart.

Tip: The summary at the top of the chart includes the P/V average, which is the average number of pageviews made in one visit.

Be aware that the pageview and visit lines use different scales. In the example in Figure 10-5, visits are scaled from 0 to 20 using the axis on the left, while pageviews are tracked from 0 to 50 on the axis on the right. Google adjusts the scale so the lines for visits and pageviews are as close as possible, which lets you see when trends change.

Here are some of the details you can study in the Visits and Pageviews chart:

- **Check the overall uptrend or downtrend of pageviews.** This indicates whether your Web site is becoming more or less popular. But remember, daily trends aren't as significant as weekly or monthly ones. See page 353 for information about how to adjust the date range for a chart.

- **Check for day-of-the-week patterns.** For example, visitors might spend more time at your Celebrity Gossip site on the weekend.

- **Check the correlation between visits and pageviews.** Usually, these two factors are related. As visits increase, pageviews should increase proportionately. If these trends don't line up, there could be a more interesting shift taking place in your site. For example, if visits remain the same while pageviews trend up, that means the average visitor is surfing through more pages. Of course, be aware that there's still a healthy gap between discovering a relationship and interpreting it. For example, visitors might be surfing through more pages because you've expanded your Web site with new and gripping information, or because you've introduced a whizzy new navigation system that's forcing your visitors to hunt around for the content they want.

Tip: Before you speculate, make sure you're dealing with large numbers. If your Web site receives a fairly small amount of traffic (dozens of visits instead of hundreds or thousands), these trends aren't as revealing. They're probably just a natural fluctuation of the numbers.

Geo Map Overlay

The Geo Map Overlay chart (at the bottom left of the executive overview) gives a fascinating look at where your visitors are located on the globe. Google adds a small circle next to every location where a visitor resides, using slightly larger circles for areas that funneled a particularly large amount of traffic your way. In order to take a look at the city-by-city details, you need to hover your mouse over individual data points, as shown in Figure 10-6. You can also right-click and choose to zoom in for a closer look.

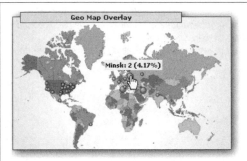

Figure 10-6:
This chart shows that two visitors connected to your Web site from Minsk, which represents 4.17% of the total traffic for that week.

There's no way to use the Geo Map Overlay to pick out other differences between visitors from different geographic locations. For example, you can't use this chart to determine whether the visitors in Minsk favor certain pages or are more likely to make return visits when compared to the surfers in Tehran. However, Google Analytics does provide other, more specific reports that can ferret out these details, as you'll see on page 369.

FREQUENTLY ASKED QUESTION

Does Google Really Know Where I Live?

How accurate is the location data Google supplies?

Being able to determine the location of your visitors is a powerful tool. After all, if you know your Graceland Vacation site is absurdly popular in Japan, you might consider accepting payments in Yen, translating a few pages, or adding some new pictures. But Google's geographic locating service isn't perfect. In fact, there are several weaknesses:

- The location service is based on the ISP (Internet Service Provider), not the actual visitor. In many cases, the ISP is located in a different location than the visitor's own computer.

- The location service examines the information registered with the IP address. This registration information could be incorrect.

- ISPs economize by pooling their traffic together and dumping it onto the Internet at a central location. That means even if the visitor and Web surfer are located in a specific city, the computer that connects these surfers to the Internet might be somewhere else.

As a general rule of thumb, the geographic information that Google uses is likely to be close to reality, but not exact. It's highly likely that the country is correct, but the specific city may not match that of the actual visitor.

Visits by New and Returning

The Visits by New and Returning chart (top-right corner of the Executive Overview) compares the number of visitors who arrived for the first time with those who returned for a repeat visit. This information tells you whether your site is winning wide popularity or languishing in the surf-and-forget dustbin of history. Figure 10-7 shows a close-up.

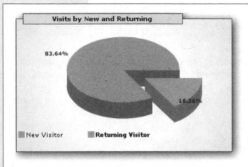

Figure 10-7:
In all the Google Analytics pie charts, you can click part of the legend to pull out a slice. This example shows the result of clicking the Returning Visitor heading. You can also click the pie slice itself to hide or show the percentage value, which is useful if overcrowding is preventing you from seeing what's most important.

Note: Remember, Google identifies return visitors based on the presence of a cookie on their computer. However, there are some types of repeat visitors that Google won't correctly identify. For example, if a repeat visitor uses a different computer, a different browser, or logs in to their computer with a different user name, they'll appear to be a new visitor. For these reasons, the number of repeat visitors may be slightly underreported.

Visits by Source

The Visits by Source chart (bottom-right corner of the Executive Overview) identifies how visitors are getting to your Web site. In Web marketing jargon, this list shows you the *top referrers*—other Web sites that link to yours and send visitors your way.

Google creates a separate pie slice for each *domain*. (A domain is the first part of the Web site address, as in *www.amazon.com*.) For example, if there are several pages on the Web site *www.partyfavors.com* that all lead to your site, Google will create a single slice that represents the cumulative traffic from all the links. There are also three pie slices with special meanings:

- **google** indicates a visitor who comes to your site through a Google search or ad.

- **(direct)** indicates a visitor that types your URL directly into their browser or uses a bookmark to make a return visit.

- **(other)** indicates a contribution that's too small to show. For example, a typical Visits by Source chart will show your top five referrers and group all the others into a single (other) pie slice.

Figure 10-8 shows a closer look.

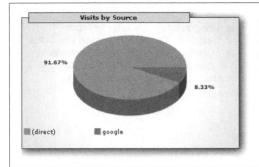

Figure 10-8:
Over the past week, visitors found this Web site in one of two ways—by entering the URL directly or searching in Google. To get more traffic, it makes sense to consider sharing links with other Web sites.

All in all, the Visits by Source chart is great tool for quickly identifying your most successful Web partnerships and judging the success of your search engine optimization. For example, if you're in the habit of posting blog comments, newsgroup messages, or articles on other Web sites, you can gauge the success of your strategy: Do visitors who read your content follow the trail to your own Web site?

Changing the Date Range

Ordinarily, all the charts and reports in Google Analytics are based on the past week's data. But if you've collected data for a longer period of time, you might want to broaden your perspective. Or, if you're really curious about a sudden spike in traffic or an unexpected decline, you might want to home in on a certain day.

The secret to changing the date range is the calendar at the bottom left of the report page. Here's what you can do:

- To see a single day's data, click that day. If the day isn't in the current year, use the arrow links at the top of the calendar to move to another year.

- To see an entire week, click the arrow next to the week.

- To see an entire month, click the month heading at the top of the calendar.

- To see an entire year, click the year heading (above the month headings).

- To choose a custom date range, click the calendar icon next to the View By list and follow the instructions in Figure 10-9.

Once you make your selection, there's a short delay while Google updates all of the charts to include only the data you've chosen.

Tip: If you select a single day, the Visits and Pageviews chart shows an hourly traffic log.

Exporting the Data

Google Analytics has enough tools for many long nights of caffeine-fueled Web analysis. However, you aren't locked into the Google Analytics interface. If you've thought of another way you'd like to present your data, or if you just need to

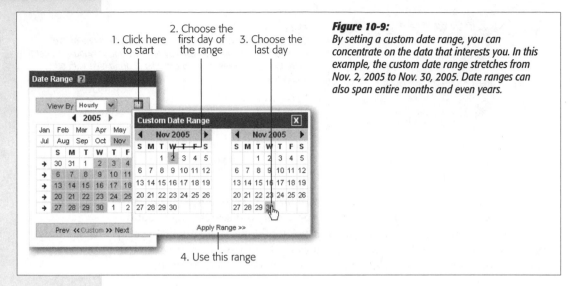

1. Click here to start
2. Choose the first day of the range
3. Choose the last day

Figure 10-9:
By setting a custom date range, you can concentrate on the data that interests you. In this example, the custom date range stretches from Nov. 2, 2005 to Nov. 30, 2005. Date ranges can also span entire months and even years.

4. Use this range

import those record-breaking numbers into a PowerPoint presentation, you'll be happy to hear that Google makes it easy. All you need to do is look for the export and printing icons at the top right of the report or dashboard box (Figure 10-10). A single click can get your data in a plain text, XML, or an Excel file.

Note: At the time of this writing, the Excel feature is a little quirky. If you run into trouble, use the text export option instead.

Printing a Report

As with any Web page, you can send the current Google Analytics dashboard to the printer with the Print command in your Web browser. However, before you do, look for the Standard/Print View icon (which looks like a printer) at the top right of the report or dashboard box. When you click this button, Google clears the menu bar and header information out of the way, so that the page shows only your report data. You can then use the browser's Print command to create a more attractive printout.

When you're finished, click the Standard/Print View icon again to get back to the normal view.

Assessing Your Site

So far, you've seen only one of the dashboards in Google Analytics—the Executive Overview. The Executive Overview shows your Web site's vital signs, but not much more. If you want to answer demanding questions about your Web site and discover its strengths, weaknesses, and quirks, you'll need to dig into the mountains of statistics with more focused reports.

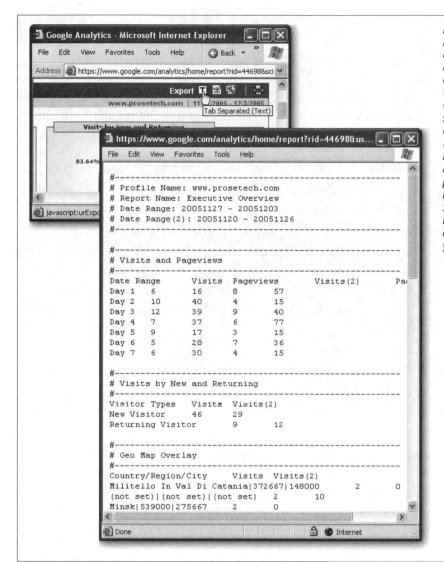

Figure 10-10:
In this example, the full contents of the executive dashboard are being exported to plain text. When you use this option, Google Analytics separates the values in each column using tabs. (Tab-separated files can be imported into virtually any spreadsheet program.) However, you'll need to use the File → Save command in your browser to save the exported text to a file on your computer.

There's no way that this chapter can walk you through every one of the dozens of Google Analytics reports. (And even if it could, you'd have trouble keeping awake for the entire tour.) However, before you've finished this chapter, you'll see many of the most useful reports—and you'll learn your way around the surprisingly powerful charting tools.

Your Most (and Least) Popular Pages

As every Webmaster knows, all pages aren't created equal. Some might command tremendous interest while others languish ignored. However, it's not enough to simply determine which pages your visitors view the most. That's because visitors often browse a site once they reach it. For example, the page of Member Photos on

Letting Other People Use Your Account

Managing a Web site is rarely a one-person job. If you have other friends or colleagues who work with you on the same Web site, you can add them to your Google Analytics account. Once you do, they'll be able to log in to Google Analytics and generate their own reports. The only requirement is that every person you add must have a Google account (page 118).

Here's how you do it:

1. If you aren't already at the Analytics Settings page, click the Analytics Settings link in the top-right corner of the current page.

2. Click the Access Manager link. You'll see a list of all the people who can use your account. (Initially, this only includes you.)

3. Click the Add User link.

4. Fill in the person's first name, last name, and email address.

5. Choose the access type. "View reports only" limits the person to reading reports, while "Account administrator" gives the person the ability to change account settings and add or remove other users.

6. Choose your Web site from the profile list and then click Add.

7. Click Finish.

The newly registered user has the ability to see all the same reports you do. If this exposes too much information, you can follow a slightly more involved set of steps to provide more limited access.

The trick is to create a new Web site profile for your Web site. (You can create new profiles from the Analytics Settings page.) When you create a Web site profile, Google gives you the choice to limit it to certain types of reports. Choose only the types of reports that you want other people to see. Now, when you add new users, you can give them access to the more limited profile, rather than the full Web site profile.

your International Nudist site might be attracting large volumes of visitors who then stick around to check out your personalized coffee cups, clothing, and memorabilia. A good reporting tool shows you where visitors *enter* your site, so you know what pages are the important attention-getters that lure traffic.

Fortunately, Google Analytics excels at figuring out exactly these sorts of details. To see a summary that profiles the Web page activity of your entire site, head to Dashboards section of the menu and then click the Content Summary link. (The Content Summary link is visible only if you've selected Executive or Webmaster in the View box at the top of the menu.)

Content Summary brings together three top-five lists (see Figure 10-11). They include:

- **Top 5 Entrances.** These are the pages that visitors surf to first. Typically, your default page (like index.htm) tops the list, because that comes up when surfers head straight to the site without requesting a specific page. However, the rest of the list indicates other popular entry points. For example, a page that's linked to on another site or a page that's often returned by a search engine can creep up the list.

- **Top 5 Exits.** These are pages that mark the end of a visit. Be on the watch for pages that really shouldn't make this list. For example, if you find visitors are

Figure 10-11:
As with most reports in Google Analytics, the tables in the Content Summary pack in a lot of extra information. One important detail is the percentage change from the previous period, which lets you spot pages that are waning or increasing in popularity.

Content Summary							Export
						www.prosetech.com | 11/1/2005 - 11/30/2005	
Top 5 Entrances		**Entrances**	**%±**	**Bounces**	**%±**	**Bounce Rate**	**%±**
1.	/prosetech/BooksNET.htm	83	↑118%	23	↑156%	27.71%	↑17%
2.	/prosetech/CreatingWebSitesLinks.htm	4	↑100%	3	↑200%	75.00%	↑50%
3.	/prosetech/BegASP.NET2.0inC.htm	2	↑100%	1	↑100%	50.00%	↑100%
4.	/prosetech/ProASP.NET2.0inC.htm	1	—0%	1	—0%	100.00%	—0%
5.	/prosetech/Pro.NET2.0WindowsFormsIn	1	—0%	1	↑100%	100.00%	↑100%
Top 5 Exits		**Exits**	**%±**	**Pageviews**	**%±**	**% Exit**	**%±**
1.	/prosetech/BooksNET.htm	49	↑158%	207	↑196%	23.67%	↓-13%
2.	/prosetech/Classes.htm	12	↑200%	93	↑365%	12.90%	↓-35%
3.	/prosetech/About.htm	8	↑167%	64	↑237%	12.50%	↓-21%
4.	/prosetech/ProASP.NET2.0inC.htm	5	—0%	17	↑113%	29.41%	↓-53%
5.	/prosetech/BookOfVB.NET.htm	4	↑100%	8	↑167%	50.00%	↓-25%
Top 5 Content		**Visits**	**%±**	**Pageviews**	**%±**	**Avg Time**	**%±**
1.	/prosetech/BooksNET.htm	84	↑115%	207	↑196%	00:01:02	↓-4%
2.	/prosetech/Classes.htm	37	↑131%	93	↑365%	00:00:40	↓-75%
3.	/prosetech/About.htm	31	↑158%	64	↑237%	00:00:46	↓-65%
4.	/prosetech/ProASP.NET2.0inC.htm	15	↑88%	17	↑113%	00:00:46	↑29%
5.	/prosetech/BooksWeb.htm	11	↑267%	16	↑300%	00:00:06	↓-9%

deserting in droves when they get to the checkout page of your e-commerce shop, maybe there's an unexpected obstacle in place (like a surprise shipping charge).

Tip: If a particular page is head and shoulders above the rest in the Top 5 Exits list, check to make sure it doesn't suffer from weak content, isn't unnecessarily large, and doesn't require an uncommon browser feature. All of these characteristics could drive away timid surfers.

- **Top 5 Contents.** This is a no-nonsense list of the most popular pages on your site. Use it to determine what content is commanding the most interest once visitors arrive at your site.

As you can see in Figure 10-11, the Content Summary has highlights about a site. The Top 5 Entrances table points out that for this sample site, most visitors arrive through the *BooksNET.htm* page (which is the default page for the Web site). Seventeen percent leave without viewing anything more, while those who continue are most likely to request the Classes.htm page (which comes in a solid second in the Top 5 Content list). Both *BooksNET.htm* and *Classes.htm* are common exit points. But the most interesting statistic may be the percentage change values in the Top 5 Content table, which show that *Classes.htm* and *BooksWeb.htm* have 300 percent increases in traffic when compared to the previous period.

The Top 5 Content table also includes an Average Time column that details how long a surfer looks at a page before surfing on. This can help you determine whether a popular page is truly successful. For example, a page that tops the list for pageviews but has an extremely short time value is attracting visitors, but not keeping them. Maybe the content is overly long, complicated, poorly formatted, or just doesn't deliver what it promises.

The Top 5 Exits table includes the total exit count (the number of times this page marked the end of a visit) and an exit percentage (the percentage chance that once this page is requested, the visitor won't continue any farther). These numbers can point out potential problems. For example, an exit rate of 50 percent indicates that half of the people who reach this page don't stick around, which is a very ominous sign.

Finally, the Top 5 Entrances table includes the number of bounces. A *bounce* occurs when a visitor views only one page—in other words, they surf into your site through a specific page and then depart without browsing any further. Bounces are keenly important to Web masters, because they indicate lost potential visitors. If you can identify why a particular page has a large bounce rate, and keep a visitor interested enough to check out a few more pages, you'll increase the popularity of your site.

GEM IN THE ROUGH

Comparing Dates

As you learned on page 353, you aren't limited to looking at statistics one week at a time. You can also set a custom date range. Of course, this makes the percentage change values much less useful–or does it?

It turns out that Google Analytics has an almost hidden feature that lets you compare any two date ranges of your choice. To choose the first date range, configure the calendar in the bottom-right corner, as described earlier (page 353). To choose the second date range (the one used for the purpose of comparison), click the double calendar icon in the Date Range bar (shown here). Another calendar appears underneath the first one. You use this calendar to set the second date range.

Keep in mind that you should compare date ranges of a similar length. Obviously, if you compare a week's worth of traffic to a single day, the week will have much higher pageview numbers.

More Content Performance Reports

The Content Summary is a great place to start, but there are more statistics in store in the expansive All Reports section of the menu (which you can find underneath the Dashboards section). Click Content Optimization, and then click the Content Performance subgroup. The reports you'll see include:

- **Top Content.** Similar to the Top 5 Contents table, but it includes *all* the pages that visitors accessed, not just the best five. This report also presents the information in a bar chart or pie chart and lets you use more analysis tools, like cross-segmenting (page 363).

- **Content Drilldown.** Similar to Top Content, but this report assigns a dollar value to pages based on the likelihood that a visitor will continue to complete a goal after viewing this page. Goals are explained on page 364.

- **Content by Titles.** Similar to the Top 5 Contents page, but this report identifies each page by its title (the information in the <title> tag in the actual HTML) rather than the page's URL. This means that if you have more than one page with the same title, their combined information appears as one entry in this table.

- **Page Query Terms.** Show the most commonly used query terms for any page.

Note: *Query terms* are used to transmit information from page to page in a Web application. They're the dynamic portion of the URL. For example, in the URL *http://www.mysite.com/quote.htm?prodID=321* the query term is prodID=321.

- **Depth of Visit.** Shows the number of pages that visitors view in a typical visit (see Figure 10-12).

- **Length of Visit.** Shows the amount of time that visitors spend in a typical visit (see Figure 10-12).

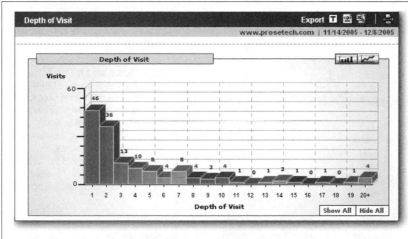

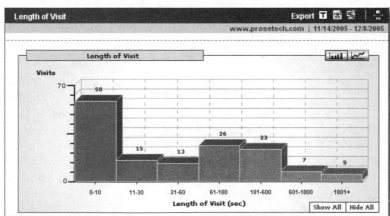

Figure 10-12:
Top: In the "Depth of Visit" chart, longer bars indicate more people. The bar at the far left represents a visit of exactly one page— which is far and away the most common visit depth, with 46 visitors leaving that quickly. By contrast, the bar at the far right of the chart indicates that 4 visitors surfed 20 pages or more in one go.

Bottom: The "Length of Visit" chart tells a similar story: 58 visitors were out in less than 10 seconds (a definite negative sign), while 5 lingered for half an hour or more.

You'll also find more reports of interest in the Navigational Analysis subgroup of the menu, which is just underneath the Content Optimization section. Look for the Entrance Bounce Rates and Top Exit Points reports. These are very similar to the Top 5 Entrances and Top 5 Exits tables you saw in the Content Summary, but they're expanded to feature all the entrance and exit pages (not just the top five items).

Fine-Tuning a Chart

The slick charting features in Google Analytics conceal quite a few features. You can pull out pieces of a pie (page 352), and show or hide individual data points (page 362). However, there are several additional ways that you can interact with a chart to filter out information or focus on just the numbers that interest you.

Before going any further, orient yourself with Figure 10-13, which shows the chart for the indispensable Top Content report. The Top Content report gives a detailed ranking of every page on your site based on the number of visits it receives. To get to the Top Content Report, under the All Reports section of the menu, click to expand the Content Optimization group, then click Content Performance, and finally click Top Content.

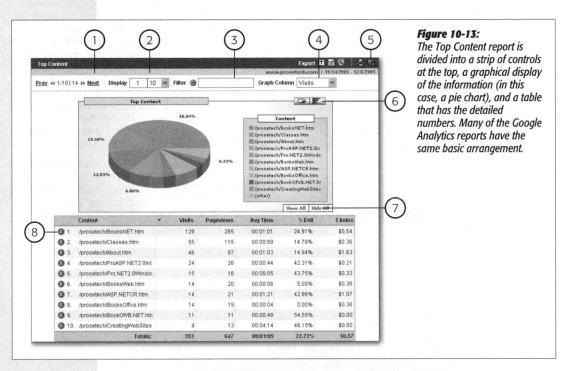

Figure 10-13:
The Top Content report is divided into a strip of controls at the top, a graphical display of the information (in this case, a pie chart), and a table that has the detailed numbers. Many of the Google Analytics reports have the same basic arrangement.

Here's a guide that walks you through the different parts of the report (the numbers in the list correspond to the numbers in Figure 10-13):

1. **Prev/Next links.** You can't always cram everything into sight at once. In this example, there are 14 pages to consider, but only 10 are shown at a time. To see the next segment of data, click the Next button. (In this example, the chart would display the pages ranked 11th through 14th.)

2. **Display Count.** You can use the Display boxes to choose exactly what segment of information you want to see. The first box is the number of the first segment that you want shown. (It's initially 1, which represents the first item in the results.) For example, if you want to disregard the top two pages, set this to 3.

   The second box is the number of items that are shown at once. (It's initially 10.) You have only a few preset options, which include 10, 25, 50, 100, and 500. However, this selection affects only the data table under the chart, not the chart itself. (Google Analytics just can't cram more than 10 slices into a pie chart or 10 bars into a bar chart.)

Tip: When changing the Display or Filter settings, your page may not update itself automatically. Press the Enter key to trigger a refresh with your new settings.

---

3. **Filter Expression.** You can use a filter expression to show or hide specific items. This gets a little tricky, because technically filters use *regular expressions*, a ridiculously powerful and complex pattern-matching language. But you can use the Filter box to match simple snippets of text, as shown in Figure 10-14.

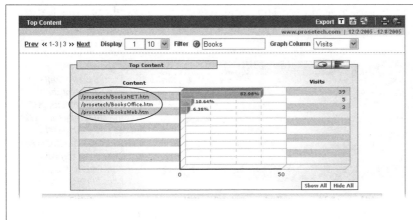

Figure 10-14:
By adding a filter of "Books", you can limit this chart to the three pages that contain that word, including BooksNET. htm, BooksOffice.html, and BooksWeb.htm. This is an inclusive filter; it chooses the pages that Google should include in the report. You can also create an exclusive filter that hides certain pages. Just click the plus (+) symbol next to the Filter box, so that it changes into a minus (–) sign.

4. **Graph Column.** The chart displays information from a single column from the table below. In the Top Contents report, for example, the chart shows the number of unique visits. However, you can choose to chart any of the other columns in the table, including pageviews and the average time spend viewing the page. Just select the column name from the Graph Column box.

5. **Export and Printing.** These icons let you export the data in the report table, as described on page 353.

---

6. **Chart Type.** Depending on the type of report, you may have the option of displaying the data as a pie chart, line chart, or bar chart. Just click the appropriate icon to have Google generate the matching chart.

7. **Show or Hide Data Points.** You can use these buttons to quickly show or hide the specific data values next to every slice (in a pie chart), bar (in a bar chart), or point (in a line chart). This trick is a great way to see all the numbers in your chart at a glance.

8. **Drill Down.** Ready to get more information about a specific segment of your chart? You can click the red double arrow to launch a more detailed analysis. The following section explains how this feature works.

Drill-Down Analysis

Sometimes, you might want to get more info about a value in your chart. For example, once you know the top performing page, you might want to see how its performance has changed over the reporting period. Or maybe you want to get a breakdown of how its popularity varies for visitors in different geographic locations or using different browsers. You can answer these sorts of questions with the drill-down feature.

To start, just click the red double arrow next to the data you want to explore. A pop-up menu appears with three options: Data Over Time, To-date Lifetime Value, and Cross Segment Performance:

• **Data Over Time** shows the fluctuations in a data item over your reporting period. For example, in the Top Contents report, you could use this feature to track down pages that are changing in popularity (see Figure 10-15).

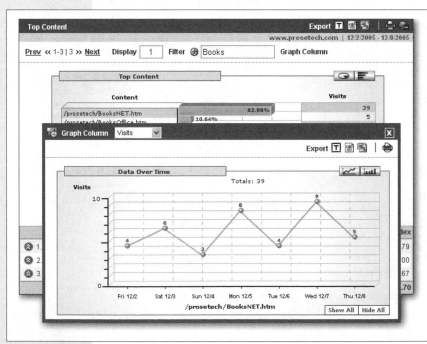

Figure 10-15:
From the Top Contents chart, it's clear that BooksNET.htm topped the popularity chart with 39 visits. But only by looking at the Data Over Time chart can you see how visits to this page have fluctuated over the course of the week.

- **To-date Lifetime Value** is an option Google uses with goal tracking (discussed on page 364). It shows whether the visitors who surfed to this page also completed one of your goals. If you've assigned a dollar value to your goal, this table uses that number to calculate an average value for every visitor in this category.

- **Cross Segment Performance** allows you to take the category you've selected and split it into several subcategories, which are technically known as *segments* (see Figure 10-16). For example, you could take a popular page from the Top Contents chart and take a look at how its popularity varies based on other factors (like the visitor's home city). This approach is great for ferreting out hidden relationships in the data. For example, it could show you that your Origami Magic page is particularly popular with surfers from Switzerland. However, there are so many different ways that you can cross-segment the same information that you could easily spend a long jail term cross-segmenting your data.

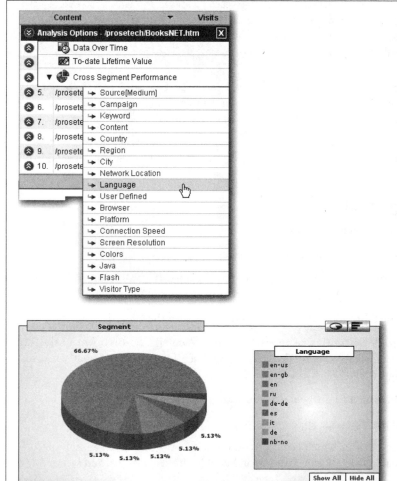

Figure 10-16:
Top: You can choose from a list of options to create a Cross Segment Performance chart. This example uses Language to subdivide the traffic to BooksNET.htm based on the language information supplied by the browser.

Bottom: The results show that 67 percent of the requesters of this page had U.S English configured in the browsers, although languages from Russian to Italian also figure into the list. To make sense of these results, you might want to compare these language percentages with the language percentages of the whole Web site.

Goal Tracking

Some pages in your Web site have a special significance because visitors don't reach them unless they complete a specific process. For example, after visitors make a purchase from your store, they see an order confirmation page. After making a donation to your charity, they're sent to a thank-you page. After signing up for your Elvis Lives! newsletter, they see a welcome page.

These pages are particularly important, because they indicate that a transaction has taken place. For example, if you're creating an e-commerce site, you're keenly interested in how many users place orders. Google Analytics includes a *goal tracking* feature that lets you distinguish these pages and measure your success.

Note: Of course, any e-commerce site worth its salt has other ways of tracking information like the number of orders placed. For example, you could count the number of order records in your database. But by tracking this information with Google Analytics, you open your site to a great many more analysis options. For example, you could combine the order information with other statistics that Google Analytics collects to answer more questions, like how many pages does a purchaser browse through before performing an order, where do they enter your site, and how long do they spend reading each page?

To perform goal tracking, you define a Web page URL as a *goal*. When a visitor reaches a goal page, it's called a *conversion*. In marketing speak, a conversion is the shining moment when an anonymous visitor is transformed into a customer.

Google keeps track of how many people reach your goal pages. Every Web site can have up to four goals—if you want more, you'll need to create additional profiles for your Web site (see the box on page 356).

Creating a Goal

Here's how you define a goal:

1. **Navigate to the Analytics Settings page.**

   This is the first page you see when you log in. If you're currently viewing a report, click the Analytics Settings link in the top-right corner of the page.

2. **Click the Edit link in the Settings column next to the Web site you want to use.**

   The Profile Settings page appears for your Web site. Scroll down to the "Conversion Goals and Funnel" section. You'll see four goal slots that you can use (see Figure 10-17).

3. **Click Edit next to the goal slot you want to use.**

   A Goal Settings page appears where you can configure the goal.

   It doesn't matter which goal slot you use. However, it makes sense to place your first goal in the first slot, your second goal in the second slot, and so on.

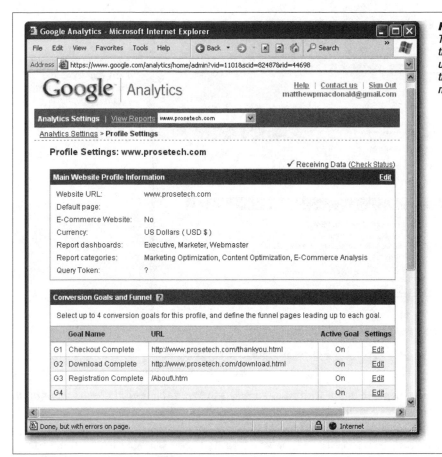

Figure 10-17:
This Web site defines three goals. The first two use full URLs, while the third defines a partial match.

4. **Enter a URL for the goal (see Figure 10-18).**

When supplying a URL, you have two options. Your first option is to supply the whole URL, starting with http://. For example, a URL in this form is *http:// www.mysite.com/ThankYou.htm.*

Your second option is to supply part of the URL (usually the page name). In this case, Google matches any URL that contains that text. However, life isn't quite as easy as it should be. When you match a portion of a URL, Google actually interprets your text as a full-fledged *regular expression*. (For die-hard programmers with hours of extra time, that means you can use extra pattern-matching features.) Unfortunately, there are certain characters that have a special meaning in the regular-expression world (namely: * + - ? ( ) . [ ] | ^ $ \). If you use any of these characters in your URL, you need to precede it with a backward slash (\). For example, instead of specifying the page */About.html*, you must use */About\.html*, because the period is considered a special character. This URL matches any request for a page named About.html, anywhere on your site. If you leave off the initial slash and specify *About\.html* you might also

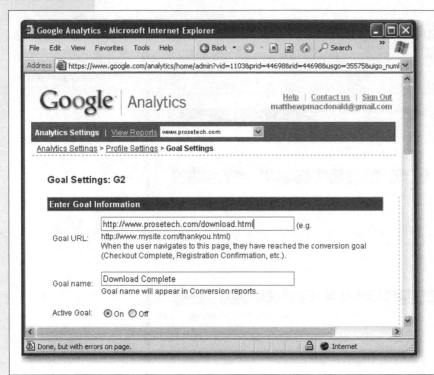

Figure 10-18:
The URL is the most important piece of information for a goal. In a very real sense, the URL is the goal. You can use any page, but typically you'll use a page to which you want to drive traffic.

match pages that end with *About.html*, as in *WhatAbout.html*, *Roundabout.html*, and *HowzAbout.html*.

Tip: Although you can't delete a goal, you can edit it and set a blank URL, which has the same effect.

---

5. **Enter a goal name.**

   You can use any name you want. *Registration Complete*, *Checkout*, or *Signup* are good choices. The goal name is used to identify the goal in your reports.

6. **If you don't want to use the goal right away, set the Active Goal setting to Off.**

   You can also change the Active Goal setting of an existing goal to temporarily turn it off and to switch it back on.

7. **If desired, add funnel pages.**

   A funnel consists of one or more pages that lead up to the goal. For example, if a visitor must travel through *http://www.mysite.com/SignUp.htm* to get to *http://www.mysite.com/ThankYou.htm*, the page *http://www.mysite.com/SignUp.htm* is a funnel. Because a transaction like signing up or making an order can require several steps and take place over multiple pages, you can define a list of pages for your funnel, in order from first to last.

The value of a funnel is that some reports (like the Defined Funnel Navigation report) let you see how many visitors reach your funnel but don't continue through it to the goal. In turn, that can help you identify and remove last-minute obstacles that are preventing people from reaching your goal.

8. **If desired, set the "Case sensitive" checkbox.**

When you select the "Case sensitive" checkbox, Google matches the URL only if the capitalization that's used by the page making the request matches the capitalization you used in step 4. Usually, you won't want this option, because it's unnecessarily strict and could cause you to miss conversions.

9. **Choose the Match type.**

If you entered a full URL in step 4, choose Head Match or Exact Match. An Exact Match succeeds only if the URL the visitor requests matches the goal URL *exactly*. On the other hand, a Head Match allows Web side code to tack on some extra information at the end of the URL, in the form of query arguments (see page 359). That means a URL like *http://www.mysite.com/TheGoalPage.htm?language=en* matches the goal URL *http://www.mysite.com/TheGoalPage.htm*. In general, this difference matters only if you use server-side code in your Web pages that inserts query arguments into a URL. For basic Web sites, there is no difference between Head Match and Exact Match.

If you entered a partial URL in step 4, choose Regular Expression Match. This matches part off the URL using regular-expression pattern-matching magic (page 365).

10. **If desired, assign a monetary goal value.**

The goal value is used to assign dollar values to various report statistics. Although it's impossible to give an exact value, here are some guidelines:

• If you're selling a product, enter the *average value* of a transaction.

- If the value is based on other actions (such as whether or not the visitor clicks an ad), multiply the *probability* of the action by its value. For example, if 10 percent of visitors click an ad after reaching your goal page, and the ad click is worth $2.00, your goal value is $2*0.1=0.20.

11. **Click Save Changes.**

You can't create reports with goal information just yet. Instead, you'll need to wait 24 hours until Google Analytics has collected the next round of information, complete with conversion statistics.

Note: Goals are not retroactive. For example, imagine you create a goal for the page *Register.cgi*. Any subsequent requests for this page are counted as conversions. However, any requests for *Register.cgi* that happened in the past aren't counted, and they won't show up as conversions in your reports.

POWER USERS' CLINIC

Using Dynamic URLs

In many Web applications, the same URL is used for several different stages of a transaction. For example, an e-commerce store might have a page called *CheckOut.aspx* that contains the code for processing an order. When the visitor confirms the order, the *CheckOut.aspx* page can display a thank you message, without redirecting the user to another URL. So how can Google track these conversions?

There are two options. First, you could alter your Web application so that a redirect *does* take place at the end of an order. However, this approach results in extra work, and it could slow down the performance of your page. A better choice is to use a virtual URL—that is, a URL that doesn't really exist but is used solely for the purpose of goal tracking.

Here's how it works. First, you create a goal using this imaginary URL (say, *http://www.mysite.com/CheckOutGoalComplete*). Now, you can fake a call to this URL by adding a snippet of Java-Script code to your Web page that calls the urchinTracker() function. Here's what this code needs to look like:

```
urchinTracker("/CheckOutGoalComplete");
```

The end result is that Google registers a request for this virtual page, even though it never actually occurred. The trick is to make sure that you only call the urchinTracker() function once the goal is complete.

Reporting with Goals

There are several reports that let you see goal information:

- **From the Dashboards section of the menu, you can select Conversion Summary (if the View is Executive or Marketer).** This option shows the percentage of visits that result in a conversion.

- **From the All Reports section of the menu, you can select Content Optimization and then Goals & Funnel Process.** This option gives you the choice of several goal-tracking reports, including ones that show the number of conversions (Goal Tracking), the percentage of conversions per visit (Goal Conversion), and the number of visitors who start the process toward a goal but stop before they reach the final URL (Defined Funnel Navigation and Defined Funnel Abandonment).

All goal reports show multiple charts, one for each goal you've defined. Figure 10-19 shows one of the charts from a sample Goal Conversion report.

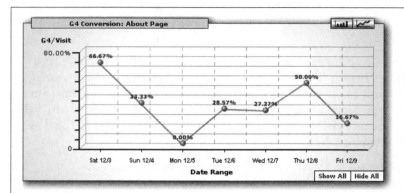

Figure 10-19:
This chart tracks the percentage of visitors that met a goal (reading the about page) over a period of one week. The goal rate starts off at 67 percent (meaning most visitors completed the goal), declines rapidly, and then climbs up modestly.

Understanding Your Visitors

A large part of success in any Web site is getting inside the minds of your visitors. Why did they come? Why did they leave? What were they thinking when they spent 48 minutes reading your Hawaiian T-Shirt picture page?

In this section, you'll learn about the reports that help you ferret out important details about your visitors.

Where They Live and Who They Are

In the Marketing Optimization section of the menu, there are two subgroups that are useful for tracking visitors: Visitor Segment Performance and Unique Visitor Tracking.

Visitor Segment Performance provides a wealth of information about what Web site visitors are coming from, where they live, and what service provider they're using. All of these reports include the same information: the number of visits, the pages per visit, and the conversion rate for your goals. The reports include:

- **New vs. Returning.** Compares new and return visitors.

- **Referring Source.** Compares visitors based on how they arrived at the Web site (directly by typing in the URL, through a search engine, or from a link in a specific site).

- **Geo Location.** Compares visitors based on the countries they live in. You can also cross-segment the table (page 363) to compare regions or cities inside a specific country.

- **Geo Map Overlay.** Gives you a geographic map like the one shown on the Executive Overview (page 347). However, this chart adds filtering capability, and if you click a visitor location in the map, a pop-up window appears with the number of visits, the pages per visit, and the conversion rate for your goals.

- **Language.** Compares visitors based on their language. Remember, the language is set in the browser—there's no guarantee that's the preferred language of the visitor.

- **Domains.** Compares visitors based on domain name, the short computer name that's linked to their IP address (like verizon.net). Remember, the domain name is determined by the computer that connects the surfer to the Internet. Surfers inside a large company may be able to connect to the Internet directly. Other people need to travel through an ISP (Internet Service Provider). The domain name is determined by that ISP.

- **Network Location.** Similar to the Domain report, except this report shows the company name of the computer that connects the Web surfer to the Internet, which is based on the company or ISP. Figure 10-20 shows an example.

Note: The Domains and Network Location reports aren't terribly interesting for ordinary people, because they show only information about the ISP. However, these charts are useful if you want to find out if your Web site is popular with any large institutions, like specific schools or companies.

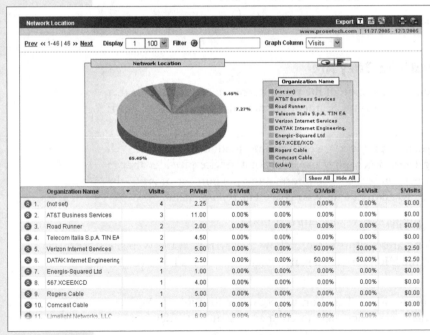

Figure 10-20:
The pie chart isn't terribly useful at showing the breakdown of different network locations because there are too many—it groups most of the data into a single slice labeled "other." However, the data table tells a more interesting story. Searching through it indicates that visitors are arriving from companies like General Electric and schools like Belarusian State University.

New and Returning Visitors

The Unique Visitor Tracking section contains reports that make use of Google's cookie-tracking system. By checking for the existence of the tracking cookie,

Google can tell when a new visitor hits your site. (In the marketing world, the number of visits is more important the total number of page requests. That's because each visitor is a real, distinct person—and therefore a potential customer.)

There are a dizzying number of ways to explore this visitor information. Here are the reports Google provides:

- **Daily Visitors.** This report includes two charts. The first shows the number of visitors day by day, and the second shows the number of new visitors over the same time period.

- **Visits & Pageview Tracking.** This report includes three charts. They show the number of visits, the number of pageviews, and the average number of pageviews per visit over the reporting period.

- **Goal Conversion Tracking.** Shows conversion rates over time.

- **Absolute Unique Visitors.** Compares new and returning visitors with a simple pie chart.

- **Visitor Loyalty.** Shows the number of repeat visits (Figure 10-21).

- **Visitor Recency.** Shows the amount of time in between visits for repeat visitors (Figure 10-21).

Browser Capabilities

So far, this chapter has focused squarely on content-oriented questions. But there's a whole other set of considerations when crafting a Web site—browser support. Even the most winning content fails if you rely on browser gimmicks and plug-ins that only display correctly on specific browsers. As a rule of thumb, if in doubt, keep it simple.

Of course, top-notch Web sites need to distinguish themselves somehow. Skilled Webmasters have ways to introduce new frills that enhance the experience for certain browsers without preventing older browers from using the page. An example is Amazon, which recently introduced a few snazzy pop-up menus. Browsers that lack the required level of JavaScript and DHTML support don't get the pop-up menus but still let visitors click through to the pages they want the long way.

In other words, the best design advice for any site is to make sure it's usable by everyone—and then consider adding features that benefit newer browsers. But before you start working, you need to be sure that the features you're adding will benefit a large-enough portion of visitors. (Otherwise, why bother?) That means you need to determine which browsers are accessing your site and what features they support.

Google Analytics has a set of reports dedicated to summarizing the browser support of visitors. To see these reports, in the All Reports section of the menu, click the Content Optimization group. Then click Web Design Parameters.

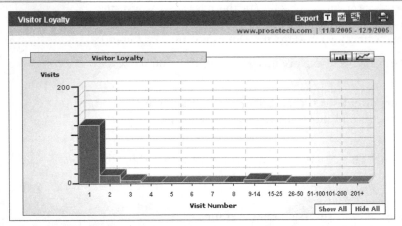

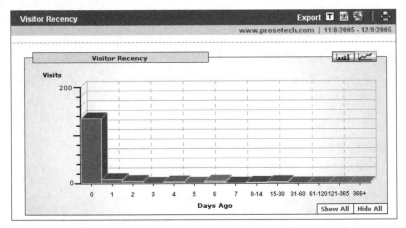

Figure 10-21:
Both the Visitor Loyalty (top) and Visitor Recency (bottom) chart use a similar arrangement: they split visitors into several categories (represented by bars) along the x-axis. The taller the bar, the more visitors in the category. Both charts show that most visitors (over 100) have made only one visit.

GEM IN THE ROUGH

How to Configure the Visit Timeout

Google has to use some common sense to tell the difference between a return visit and a single, long visit. As a rule of thumb, if more than 30 minutes elapse in between page requests, Google assumes a new visit has started. If you don't like the 30-minute rule, you can make the timeout period longer or shorter by setting the _utimeout variable in the Google JavaScript code. In other words, if you have this tracking code in your Web pages:

```
<script type="text/javascript">
_uacct = "UA-02487-1";
 urchinTracker();
</script>
```

You simply need to insert this line in bold:

```
<script type="text/javascript">
_uacct = "UA-02487-1";
var _utimeout="1800";
 urchinTracker();
</script>
```

The _utimeout variable specifies a value in seconds, so 1800 seconds is 30 minutes. Make sure you keep the lines of code in the order shown above, so that you set the variable before you start the tracking process.

The reports you can use include:

- **Browser Versions.** Separates browsers based on brand, such as Internet Explorer, Firefox, Opera, and Netscape.

- **Platform Versions.** Compares different operating systems, like Windows and Mac.

- **Browser & Platform Combos.** Splits the traffic into detailed groups based on browser brand, browser version number, and exact operating system. For example, one group might be Internet Explorer 6.0 - Windows XP. Figure 10-22 shows an example.

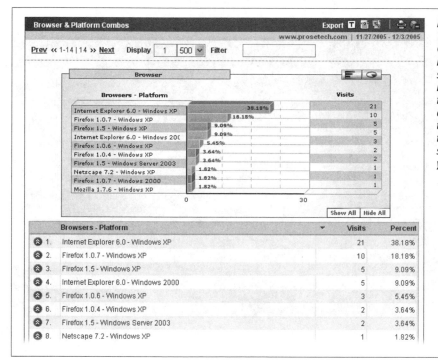

Figure 10-22:
The Browser & Platform Combos is an indispensable tool. You should note every Web browser that contributes five percent of your traffic or more. Then you can test your Web site with that browser to make sure it appears the way you intended.

- **Screen Resolutions.** Separates visitors based on screen resolution. For example, a screen resolution of 1024×768 pixels provides more space than a screen resolution of 800×600. (A *pixel* is the smallest dot a computer screen shows.) If your visitors have large screens, they can tolerate wider pages.

- **Screen Colors.** Separates visitors based on color support. However, most Web surfers have high-enough color support these days that you rarely need to worry about this information, and it almost never makes sense to design pages with limited color sets.

- **Languages.** Splits visitors according to the language information that's configured by their browser. For example, "ru" represents the Russian language.

- **Java Enabled.** Divides visitors into two groups: those that have Java enabled and those that don't. Java can be used to embed standalone applets in Web pages.

- **Flash Version.** Divides visitors into groups based on the version of Macromedia Flash that they support. Flash is often used to show dynamic content, like animation, movies, and annoying advertisements.

- **Connection Speed.** Separates visitors based on the speed of their Internet connection. The faster the connection, the more likely a visitor is to tolerate large, graphics-intensive pages, download big files, and sample rich content like movies.

POWER USERS' CLINIC

Analytics and AdWords

As you've seen, Google Analytics has a staggering number of reports to sort through. In this chapter, you've dealt with reports that rate the pages in your site, track goals, and reveal detailed information about your visitors. However, there's one set of reports that you haven't touched—the marketing reports that work with Google AdWords (Chapter 9).

If you have a Google AdWords account, you can use the reports in the Marketing Campaign Results and Search Engine Marketing to assess whether your Google ads are driving the traffic that you want. You can explore whether visitors that arrive through an ad stay to read more (or go on to complete a goal), and what keywords have the best conversion rates. If you've assigned a dollar value to your goals, you can even start to calculate the return on investment—in other words, for every $1 of Googe AdWords expenditure, how much money is your site making?

To get help on this subject (and many more Google Analytics feature), check out the help pages at *http://www.google.com/support/analytics*. And to learn the craft of Web site marketing, and brush up on strategies for luring in traffic and increasing your conversion rate, check out Google's Conversion University at *http://www.google.com/analytics/conversionuniversity.html*. It's a great tricks-of-the-trade resource with guidelines for Web capitalists everywhere.

4

Part Four: Gmail

Chapter 11: Gmail

Gmail

When Google unveiled Gmail, its free Web-based email service, on April 1, 2004, and announced that each user could have an entire *gigabyte* of space for mail and attachments, many people assumed it was a nerdy April Fool's joke. (A gigabyte is so large, it needs its own box to explain how big it is; see page 379.) Most free Webmail services at the time parceled out only 2, 4, or maybe 10 *megabytes* of mailspace (a megabyte is about a thousand times smaller than a gigabyte). With those services, when your inbox filled up with spam, your incoming messages started bouncing back like toddlers on a trampoline.

Google wasn't joking about the gigabyte. As with the other Webmail services, it lets you check your mail and send messages from just about any computer, anywhere on the planet, that has a Web browser and an Internet connection. But with Gmail, you have room to *receive and save* all your messages, too—two and a half times over, now that Google has upgraded its accounts to store two gigabytes instead of one.

Note: Several other Webmail services have scrambled to improve their own offerings since Gmail got up and running. Hotmail accounts now offer 250 megabytes of room for mail, and Yahoo upped its free mailbox capacity to one gigabyte per person in an attempt to match Gmail—but it tries to wheedle $20 a year from you for the two-gigabyte account. Gmailers now get 2.5 gigs free.

In addition to giving you two and a half gigabytes of server space to pile up your electronic epistles, Google has included some other features with Gmail that make it stand out from your average Webmail service. For one, your new Gmail account can handle file attachments up to 10 megabytes in size, which means if your spouse goes nuts with the digital camera and emails you a half-dozen high-resolution photos of the new beagle puppy attached to a single message, they should land in your Gmail Inbox just fine. Most other email services have smaller attachment limits, which means those pics are likely to bounce back.

Size is not the only thing that matters in Gmail. The service has a number of other cool features, including:

- **Rich text.** Instead of boring, plain text, you can use different fonts and colors—not to mention bullet points and highlighting—in messages. Learn how to art up your mail on page 390.

- **Multiple languages.** Display the Gmail interface in any of 13 different languages, including French, German, Italian, Dutch, Spanish, Portuguese, Russian, Korean, Japanese, simplified or traditional Chinese, and two flavors of English: U.S. or U.K. There are instructions for changing your Gmail language on page 422.

- **Google your Gmail.** If you think any email service created by the world's largest search engine would be super-speedy, you'd be right. The Gmail search (page 408) pops up matching messages quickly and accurately, and does the same when you're looking for someone within your Gmail Contacts address book.

- **Contacts importing.** Speaking of contacts, you know that huge list of email addresses in your Yahoo or Outlook Express address book? You can bring the gang along when you make the jump to Gmail with just a couple of clicks (page 416).

- **Gmail everywhere.** People read email in all kinds of ways, including on portable devices like BlackBerry handhelds, downloaded with software like Outlook Express, and forwarded from other email programs. Gmail is flexible enough to follow you anywhere and into nearly any email program you want to use (page 423).

So how does Google expect to make money from offering all of these features and services with Gmail? The same way ABC can afford to bring you new episodes of *Alias* every Wednesday night: advertising. Gmail displays ads alongside your email messages.

Despite the fact that Gmail is free, noncompulsory, and useful, it drew a lot of criticism early on for displaying advertising. "But ads show up everywhere on the Web these days," you say. "Why would anyone care about these ads in particular?" The thing that freaked people out was that Gmail ads were *related* to your email messages, making it seem as if Google employees were sifting through your Inbox, matching ads to your personal life.

For example, if you received an email from your mother about your great-uncle's funeral, the ads along the side might be for hearse services. While some people found those ads useful or simply ignorable, others thought they were a breach of privacy.

In fact, Google uses a sophisticated software system to look for keywords and slot in potentially relevant ads; no humans at Google read your Gmail to make sure you're getting the right ads. Once the world got used to that idea, the controversy over Gmail died down, and people got on with the project of creating and storing a massive amount of email.

Note: Gmail is a free service: You can't pay a fee in order to prevent those ads from appearing. If ad intrusion, however robotic, still squicks you out, perhaps Gmail is not the service for you.

(Incidentally, the ads in Gmail come from the same pool as those in AdSense and AdWords, as described in Chapter 9.)

This chapter takes a look at the ins and outs of Gmail, from setting up your account and composing messages to keeping track of that 528-message round-robin mail chat you have going with your buddies about the Philadelphia Eagles. As you'll see on the following pages, Webmail—especially two and a half gigabytes of it—can be incredibly liberating.

Note: Gmail works on most, but not all, Web browsers and operating systems. Although you can still read mail on, say, Internet Explorer creaking along on an arthritic Mac OS 9 system, you'll need a Gmail-approved browser to fully use all of the service's features.

Minimum versions of Windows Web browsers that fully support the Gmail service include Microsoft Internet Explorer 5.5, Netscape 7.1, Mozilla 1.4 and Firefox 0.8. Mac OS X and Linux fans can get by with Firefox 0.8, Netscape 7.1 and Mozilla 1.4, and the Mac folks also have the option of using Apple's Safari 1.2.1 browser for their Gmailing.

UP TO SPEED

Big Gigs for Your Mail Rig

When Google announced that the first Gmail account holders would get an entire gigabyte's worth of space on the company's servers, people who understand the business of bits and bytes were deeply impressed. Everyone else simply asked, "Will it be enough to hold all responses from the new online personal ad I just posted?"

The short answer, fortunately, is yes.

The long answer involves a quick trip to Geek World. A *bit* is the smallest unit of data a computer can understand. Eight bits make up a *byte*, which is how much space it takes to store one character of text, like a B or a 2. A *kilobyte* is 1,024 bytes of data, and a *megabyte* is approximately a million bytes of data. To put things in perspective, you could fit the complete works of Shakespeare in five megabytes.

A *gigabyte*, however, is approximately 1,000 megabytes, or one *billion* bytes of data. (For those of you who thrive on specificity, it's exactly 1,073,741,824 bytes.) Of course, adding text styling, pictures, and other decorations to your messages will make them take up more room, but the *two and a half* gigabytes you now get with Gmail will still let you write the complete works of Shakespeare a hundred times over—plus let you collect thousands of responses to your personal ad, with pictures. (More than 400 images from a 5-megapixel camera can fit in a gigabyte's worth of space.)

You can monitor just how big a bite you're taking out of your Gmail gigs by casting your eyes downward next time you're tooling around in your Inbox: Google helpfully lists the percentage of your allotted space you're using up and the current size of your mailbox right at the bottom of the browser window.

Welcome to Gmail

You can find Gmail at *http://gmail.google.com*. Like Google's own practical-yet-minimalist approach to Web-page design, the Gmail home page (Figure 11-1) is stark compared to its Webmail competitors, with no loudly colored boxes or strobing banner ads. The Gmail page is just a discreet logo on a white background with a few lines of text and an account sign-in box off to the right.

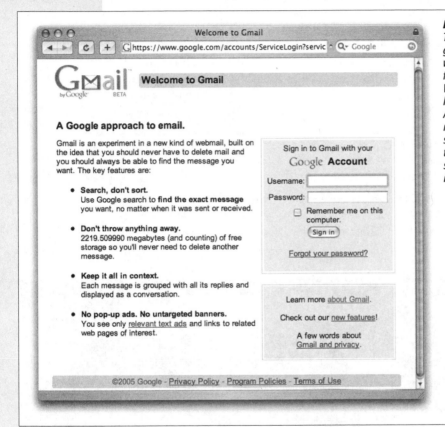

Figure 11-1:
The Gmail home page gives you a list of reasons why Gmail is different from all those other Webmail services on the left side of the screen. After the first few visits, most people ignore that stuff and proceed directly to the box on the right side of the screen to log into their Gmail accounts.

One thing other Webmail services have that Gmail currently *doesn't* have is a Sign Up button. When the company first rolled Gmail out of the Google Garage, they made it invitation-only for a few select people. Then Google gave those people a few invitations that they could pass along to friends to create new Gmail accounts. You couldn't just go to the Gmail page and sign yourself up—someone you know had to personally extend an invitation to you.

When they first appeared, Gmail invitations were a hot commodity because they were so rare. Holders of extra invites were hawking the coveted accounts for $60 to $125 on eBay. Google eventually became much more generous and gave five or six sharable invitations to everyone with an account. Over time, the company upped the allotment to 100 invites—and the allotment replenishes all the time.

Google claims all of this exclusive invitation business was because Gmail was still in *beta*, the software testing stage when the program mostly works and is available for the public to try, even though there are still a few glitches. By controlling the number of people who had accounts, the company could test, monitor, and maintain the Gmail service without worrying about a mad crush of new email fanatics stampeding its Gmail servers all at once and crashing them all to pieces.

A year after its introduction, Gmail remains invitation-only. If you don't have an account, however, read on.

Getting a Gmail Account

Before you try anything else, check the Gmail home page (*http://gmail.google.com*). As of this writing, the service was still invitation-only, but by the time you're reading, Google might have made it free for all.

If you find yourself stuck behind the virtual velvet rope of Club Gmail, fear not. Gmail invitations are easy to come by these days. First, ask anyone you know, or anyone who has sent you email from a Gmail account, if she can spare an invite. With a steady 100 invitations at their disposal, most Gmailers have extras to dispense.

Note: You can tell if somebody has emailed you from a Gmail account because the part of his e-address *after* the @ symbol will be *gmail.com,* like this: *generousfriend@gmail.com.*

If you don't personally know a Gmailer who'll invite you onboard, fire up Google itself and search for *Gmail invitations*, which should generate results with plenty of sites that dispense spare Gmail accounts, like the Gmail Invite Spooler (*http://isnoop.net/gmail*).

No matter where your Gmail invitation comes from, you'll need an existing email address to receive the invite. Once you've persuaded someone to send the Gmail invite to you, you'll get a message like the one in Figure 11-2.

When you use the Web link from the Gmail invite, you land on an account setup page that looks pretty much like any other. The page has a form where you type in the email address, name, language, and password you'd like to use for your Gmail account. Click the "check availability!" button (as shown in Figure 11-3) to see if your desired account name is available.

If it's not, you'll have to type in something else until you come up with a unique Gmail address. Be sure to pick an address you like, because you can't change it without getting another invite and making yourself a whole new account. Luckily, the one thing you *don't* have to type in on the account-creation page is a credit card number.

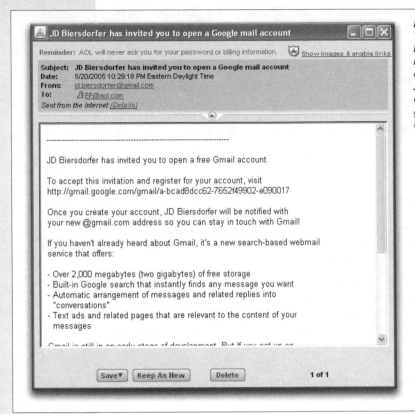

Figure 11-2:
Your ticket into Gmail comes in the form of a Gmail invitation message sent by a friend or other keeper of Gmail Invites. Just click the supplied Web link or paste it into your browser to get to the Gmail account-creation page.

Tip: If you're the giving sort of person, check along the left side of the Gmail window for the "Invite a friend to Gmail" box, which you can use to bequeath a mail account to up to 100 of your closest friends. To send the invitation, type in your buddy's current email address and then click the Send Invite button to send out an invitation message just like the one you got when you signed up for Gmail. What comes around can indeed go around, courtesy of the Internet. (You can even use this trick to send an invite to your *own* alternate email address, thereby creating a new Gmail account.)

Once you've invited someone onboard the good ship Gmail, you won't have to work too hard to keep in touch. If the person accepts your Gmail invitation and creates an account, Gmail sends you a message letting you know your friend has joined up and displays the email address that she chose. Gmail even puts this new address in your own Contacts list so you have no excuse not to write.

As soon as you've created your new Gmail account, Google whisks you away to a Welcome screen highlighting all the latest and greatest features of the service. If you want to get right to the part where you actually get to send email to people, look for a link that says "I'm ready—show me my account." Click that link and you're off to your brand new Gmail Inbox.

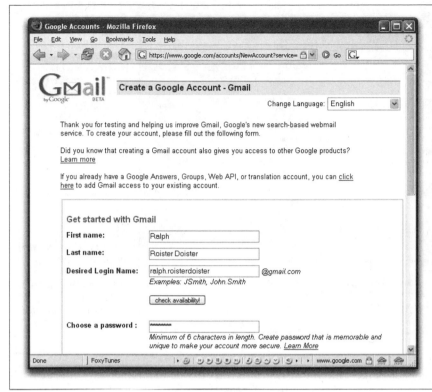

Tip: The greeting message that lands in your Inbox as soon as you sign up has a couple of worthwhile links, especially if you're new to the concept of Web-based email. The Gmail Tour link offers up an animated demo of Gmail in action, for example, and the Getting Started link quickly points out the unique and helpful features the service offers.

A Peek in the Gmail Window

When you first open Gmail, you may notice that it looks slightly different from other Web-based email services, as you can see in Figure 11-4. For one thing, there's a Search box right on top of the window that lets you type in keywords and track down a particular message in your vast, two-and-a-half-gigabyte mailbox.

After that, the top of the Gmail window has a series of buttons and links for various features and aspects of the service, including the Settings for your account (page 423), a Help area, a place to create a mail filter (page 406), and buttons to archive mail (page 402) and report spam (page 400).

The controls for creating new messages, as well as those for the other sections of your Gmailbox (like your Inbox, Sent Mail, Spam, and Trash areas), appear along

Figure 11-4:
The typical Gmail Inbox has everything laid out neatly for you. Links to your collection of mailboxes, contacts, message labels, and Gmail invites are along the left side of the window. Past and present messages are front and center. Multiple sender names mean you're having a conversation with more than one person, and the number in parentheses corresponds to the number of messages in the conversation. Messages can be tagged with labels (like "Books") or starred for importance, and the bold subject lines mean the note is unread.

the left side of the window. Just click the link to bop to another part of your mailbox. For example, if you want to see messages you've sent, click the Sent Mail link, and you'll find yourself wading around in copies of messages you've already fired off to people. To get back to your Inbox, just click the Inbox link.

The left side of the main window also contains a link to your Gmail contacts—the address book for all your correspondents, described in detail on page 413—as well as the controls for making *labels* for your messages (page 405), a simple system that lets you group them under headings.

If you have messages in your Inbox (and there should be at least one: the welcome note from Google), Gmail shows you 50 of them at a time, with the most recently received at the top. To see older messages, click the links in the upper-right or bottom-right corner of the window to jump to the previous 50 messages or the very oldest 50. Unlike most conventional mail programs, you can't sort your Inbox by sender or oldest-message-first, but Gmail does let you search for messages with specific criteria (page 408), which gives you a similar way of viewing things.

From your Inbox, you can click any message to open not only that individual message, but also any messages you sent or received that are part of that particular exchange. When an email program clumps together all the messages in one discussion, it's often called *threading*, though Gmail calls these clumps *conversations* (page 397). Once you get used to them, conversations are a great way to keep on

NOTE FROM THE LAWYERS

The Good, the Bad, and the Legal

If you're curious about the information Google collects about you, or what your rights as a Gmail user might be—or if you're just fighting a losing battle with insomnia—Google has some reading material for you in the form of lengthy legal documents known as the Privacy Policy and the Terms of Service Agreement.

The Privacy Policy (*http://gmail.google.com/gmail/help/ privacy.html*) is the one that people worried about issues of personal information are probably the most concerned about. Even though Gmail is a free service, you do have to pony up a few pieces of personal information when you sign up for a Gmail account, like another email address you can be reached at and, in theory, your actual name (some people use pseudonyms). The company's servers then store, send, and collect your mail for you in exchange for sprinkling a few advertising links alongside the right margin of your message window.

Although the truly concerned will read the privacy policy in full, the bullet points are as follows: Google states that it won't "rent, sell, or share information" about you for marketing purposes without your permission, and explains that

no humans are sifting through your correspondence looking for opportunities to stick in advertisements for prickly-heat rash cream. The privacy policy also discusses other topics, like the company's use of cookie files to identify your computer when you log in to a Google site or service.

On the flip side of the responsibility coin, the Terms of Use document at *http://gmail.google.com/gmail/help/terms_ of_use.html* explains what Google expects from *you* when you sign up for a Gmail account—and states the rules you must abide by to keep your account.

Thanks to the Children's Online Privacy Protection Act of 1998, you have to be over the age of 13 to hold your own Gmail account, and you must acknowledge that you accept the presence of advertising links Google places in your messages. Then there are the No-Nos: no sending spam, no impersonating other users, no distributing viruses or pornography or bootleg music, no pyramid schemes, no hassling other users, and no hacking the Gmail service.

Google also reserves the right to periodically update both of these policy pages, so the next time you're bored, just aim your browser back at the aforementioned pages.

top of your email because you don't have to hop all over your Inbox to remember who said what to whom and when.

Note: It's a good thing that threading is a cool feature, because Gmail gives you no way to turn it off.

When you've opened a message (Figure 11-5), the edges of the Gmail window look pretty much the same as in the Inbox view, but the right side of the window now contains the controls for printing your messages and expanding or collapsing conversations (page 397). The aforementioned ad links also show up on this side of the window. (The ad links are very subdued, with no flash-dancing windows or colored boxes popping up at you as you try to read your mail.) As advertising goes, it's almost *tasteful*, and if you're deep in electronic conversation, you might forget that the ad links are even there.

Now that you've had a little time to get used to the look of Gmail, it's time to start sending out mail like a power user. The next section tells you how.

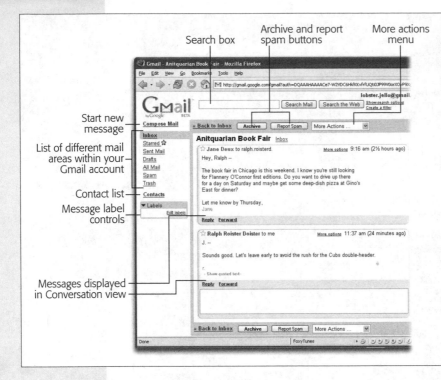

Search box

Archive and report
spam buttons

More actions
menu

Start new
message

List of different mail
areas within your
Gmail account

Contact list

Message label
controls

Messages displayed
in Conversation view

Figure 11-5:
*An open Gmail message
with an exchange
between two people. The
left side of the mailbox
window has all your
controls for creating a
message or moving and
organizing existing ones.
The Sponsored Links on
the right side (not shown
here) pick up keywords in
the message, particularly
"Chicago" and "pizza"–
two great tastes that go
great together. Even
Google's adbot recognizes
the fact.*

Tip: If one of the ads Google has sprinkled in your message happens to catch your eye, all you have to do is click its link to get whisked into a new browser window that opens over your Inbox. Once you've satisfied your curiosity or helped the gross national product by buying something from the sponsor, you can switch back and continue your mail chores.

Composing and Sending Messages

Webmail programs are simple affairs: You sign onto your account, type in the address of the person you want to contact, compose your message, and hit the Send button to fling the note out to its Internet destination. Gmail lets you go with that basic process, but you can also call on its free-styling and spell-checking tools to make sure your message is spiffy and spelled properly.

To create and send a Gmail message, first sign into your account (page 381), and then:

1. **In the upper-left corner of the screen, just under the Gmail logo, click the Compose Mail link.**

   This link takes you to a new blank message form in the middle of the screen, complete with address field and message body ready for you to fill in. If you want to isolate a message from the browser window, either for aesthetic reasons or so you can start a message and come back to it later, you can also start a new message in its own window by holding down the Shift key when you click Compose Mail. If you get a warning like the one in Figure 11-6, check your Web browser's settings for pop-up blocking (on a PC, try looking under Tools → Options or Tools → Pop-up Blocker; on a Mac, try Browser Name → Preferences).

Figure 11-6:
Gmail gets cranky if it tries to open a new message window for you but window-squasher software smacks it down. You can usually allow pop-up windows from a specific site by adding its URL to a list of exceptions; in this case, when you find the list, type in http://gmail.google.com.

If you already have a full-screen message form open, you can isolate it from the *rest* of the browser and pop it open in its own window, as shown in Figure 11-7, by clicking the "New window" link next to the little blue-arrow icon on the right side of the browser window.

Figure 11-7:
If you don't want to be distracted by the other links and elements on the Gmail screen, click the "New window" link next to the saucy blue-arrow icon to open a message in its own private little window.

(This same blue-arrow icon appears by itself at the top of the screen when you click Compose Message and start a fresh message, giving you the option to finish the note in its own private window should you need to return to your Inbox for more pressing matters.) This trick helps you isolate the different features of Gmail in different windows (composing and reading email, for example), much like an email program on your hard drive would.

2. **In the To field, type in the email addresses of your intended recipients. In the Subject field, type in your message intentions.**

   If you're sending the message to multiple addresses, type a comma after each address. Once you've used Gmail for a while and have some frequently used addresses in your Contacts list (page 413), the program will pop up a list of similar addresses as you type, in an attempt to auto-complete your friends' email addresses. If you see the person you're trying to reach, scroll down to that address and then press Enter. (If you *don't* see the person you're trying to reach, just ignore the pop-up menu.)

Tip: Gmail includes address lines for people you want to Carbon Copy (Cc) as well as people you want to Blind Carbon Copy (Bcc) on your message. Everyone can see who's been carbon-copied on a message, but sticking an address in the Bcc: field hides it from the rest of the recipients.

If you're sending out a large group email, (you can send a Gmail message to 100 people at a time) and don't want to reveal who is on the list, address the message to your own account and put everyone else in the Bcc field. None of your recipients will be able to see who else got the message—an arrangement that both protects their privacy *and* keeps them from having to scroll through a list of 100 email addresses at the top of their message.

FREQUENTLY ASKED QUESTION

A Views Review

I see the choice of Standard or HTML view at the bottom of my Gmail window. What's the difference?

As mentioned in the Note on page 379, Gmail works best on Web browsers that fully support it, like Microsoft Internet Explorer 5.5 for Windows, Safari 1.2.1 for Mac OS X, and so on.

Gmail's Standard view lets you take advantage of all the advanced JavaScript technology under the hood in modern Web browsers. By using Gmail on a supported browser, you can do things like forward your Gmail to other accounts, create filters for your incoming messages, and have email addresses automatically complete themselves when you start typing them. There's also a spell checker and a bunch of keyboard shortcuts you can use when you're using the Standard view.

If you're not using a supported Web browser (say you're still limping along in Internet Explorer 4.0 on a Jurassic Windows box), then Gmail automatically kicks you into what it calls "HTML view." With HMTL view, you can read and send messages from your Gmail account, but that's about it. There's no spell checker or any of the fancy mail-management features offered in Standard view.

If you log in to your account and find yourself in HTML view and want to use some of the advanced features, you can try to force Gmail to move you back to Standard view. Just head to the address bar, type *http://gmail.google.com/gmail?nocheckbrowser* and then press Enter to see if you can get back to Standard view. If the browser you're using is too old to cooperate, though, you'll be stuck in the HTML View.

3. **Write your message.**

   If you're just dashing off a quick note, plain text will do. But Gmail gives you the option of dressing up your message with rich-text formatting, too (page 390).

   If you don't have time to finish your message, click the Save Draft button to store a copy of the unfinished work in the Drafts area until you can pick it up again. If you decide to call the whole thing off, click Discard.

4. **Check your spelling.**

   Weed out unfortunate typos and keyboard slips in your message by clicking the Check Spelling link that appears in the upper-right corner just above the message window. Gmail highlights in yellow any suspect words (Figure 11-8). Click the highlighted words to see a list of suggestions for what you *meant* to type. Select a correction for each flagged word, and then click the Recheck link until Gmail tells you it doesn't see any misspellings. Click Done.

Figure 11-8:
After you click the Check Spelling link, it transforms itself into Recheck. Once you fix your errors, click Recheck to have Gmail check the message again, just in case you accidentally re-misspelled a word.

5. **Click Send.**

   When you're satisfied with your message, click Send to release it to the wilds of the Internet. Gmail flashes a small yellow box on the screen informing you that your message has been sent.

Of course, sending a simple message in plain text is easy enough, but if you want to add pizzazz to your e-postal efforts, you can do that, too. Read on for the skinny.

Formatting a Message with Rich Text

As you may have noticed, not everybody on Earth uses the same word-processing software or email program. Choice is good, but when you and a correspondent use different software, formatting in *the same document* or email message can vary wildly or looked completely scrambled on one of your machines. *Plain text* is pretty much a universal format because it includes no formatting at all, but it's dull.

Fortunately, the world has *rich text,* too. The term has nothing to do with the economic status or dairy quotient of your message; instead, it refers to a format that lets you add type styles like bold and italic to your otherwise plain text.

Rich text is the next most common format after plain text, which means lots of computers can read it readily. Even better, it gives you juicy options for text styling. You can make certain words in your message bold or italic, underline them for even more emphasis ("Honey, don't forget to bring home <u>MiLk</u> tonight"), change the size of your fonts for dramatic effect, change your fonts to a prettier typeface, create bulleted lists, and much more.

Note: Rich-text formatting isn't available if you're using Gmail in HTML view (page 29).

To create a message with rich-text formatting, click Compose Mail and then click the "Rich formatting" link above the message window. A toolbar like the one in Figure 11-9 immediately pops up with a variety of text-enhancing options.

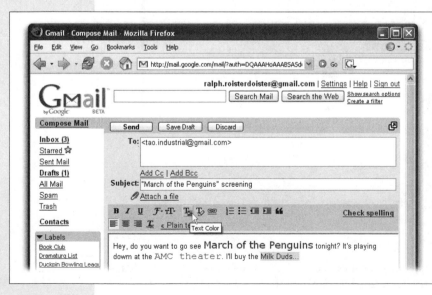

Figure 11-9:
If you don't know the meaning of a symbol in the toolbar, just move over it to reveal a yellow label for that icon. The icon of a T next to what looks like a Rubik's Cube is the button for font colors. The T with "x" next to it removes formatting from your selected text.

To apply text styling to a message you've just whipped up, select the words you'd like to style by highlighting them with the cursor, and then click the icon for the type of style you want to use: B for bold, I for italic, and so on. You can use the text-alignment controls toward the other end of the toolbar to center your text lines on screen.

Tip: When the toolbar is open, you can use many familiar keyboard shortcuts for formatting, like Ctrl+B for bold and Ctrl+I for italic.

You can start a message in plain text and switch to rich formatting in the middle of typing. If you start the message in rich formatting and decide to go back to plain text for the whole thing (when you realize your recipient has an ancient email program that can't display rich text properly), you can switch back to plain text (on the Rich Text toolbar, click the "Plain text" link). Gmail gives you a warning that you'll lose all your rich-text formatting, but you probably knew that was going to happen.

Adding File Attachments to Messages

If a picture is worth a thousand words, just think of all the typing you'd save by attaching photos and other image files to your Gmessages. You can add several kinds of file attachments to your mail, including JPEG photos, Word and Excel documents, MP3 songs, and other popular file types. Each Gmail message and attachment can be up to 10 megabytes in size, which is quite a generous amount compared to what other mail services allow you to send. You can fit about three average pop-song MP3 files or six average-size digital photos in 10 megabytes of space; Word documents can range in size from a few kilobytes to The File That Ate Cleveland, depending on what you've got inside, so check the file's size before attaching it to your message.

WORKAROUND WORKSHOP

The Files You Can't Send

Gmail won't let you attach and send *executable files* (usually small programs that end with the *.exe* extension), because executable files can contain viruses or other malicious code that wreak havoc and wreck both your computer and your day. It's this sort of nasty code that has made the Internet such a contagiously dangerous place for a computer that has no antivirus software installed.

In addition, the Gmail servers scan all incoming attachments and block executable files, even if they are enclosed in a compressed file format like *.zip, .tar,* or *.gz.* Google also blocks any *incoming* messages with *.exe* files attached and bounces them right back to where they came from.

Since most people rarely, if ever, need to exchange executable files for legitimate reasons, this limitation shouldn't be a problem for you. If you *do* want to send an *.exe* file, however, consider burning it to a CD and snail-mailing it to its destination, or posting it on a Web site.

To attach a file to your Gmail message-in-progress, look below the message's Subject line for the "Attach a file" link next to the little paper clip icon. Click it to open up a new box on the message form with a handy Browse button right next to it, as shown in Figure 11-10.

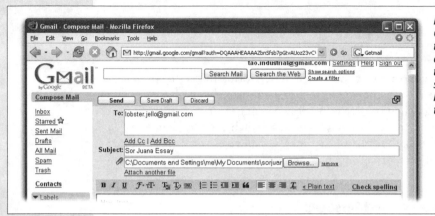

Figure 11-10:
Click the Browse button to navigate through your computer until you find the file you want to send—or, if you already know the file path, just type it in.

Click the Browse button and navigate through your hard drive until you find the file you want to attach. Once you locate the file, select it and then click Open. Gmail jumps back to the message window, where a *file path* (a cryptic string of names and slashes in Computerese that points to the file's location on your system) appears next to the paper clip icon, signifying that your file is attached to the message. If you need to attach another file to the same message, click the "Attach another file" link and repeat the process.

If you change your mind about sending a file, click the "remove" link on the other side of the Browse button to knock the attachment off the message.

When you've got your message written and your attachments lined up, click Send.

Using Picasa to Send Photos by Gmail

Picasa is an intuitive and powerful photo-management program, and there are two really great things about it. First, it's free to download at *www.picasa.com*. Second, Google owns it, so it works seamlessly with Gmail.

"Why," you wonder, "do I need a whole 'nother photo program when I just read that whole section about attaching files directly in Gmail?" The truth is, you *don't* need Picasa to send picture attachments in Gmail, but it makes managing your whole digital photo collection and sharing pics via email a lot easier. (And it does some other really cool stuff, too.)

Note: Picasa works only with Windows 2000 and XP, so Mac OS X enthusiasts may want to bop over to page 427, where's there's a discussion of using your Gmail account with standard email programs like Apple Mail, Eudora, and Entourage. Once you can send and receive your Gmail messages through your regular mail program, you can use Apple's iPhoto software to manage and manipulate the photos you want to email.

Composing and
Sending Messages

When you first install Picasa, the program scans your system and displays a
thumbnail image of every single photo lurking in the deepest, darkest corners of
your computer, as shown in Figure 11-11.

Figure 11-11:
*Google's free Picasa
program seeks out and
shows you every photo
scattered around your
system. In addition to
organizing your
collection, you can also
perform basic touch-up
tasks like fixing red eye
and adjusting the color in
your pictures. For a good
tutorial on all Picasa's
features, check out http://
picasa.google.com/
support/.*

One of the things that makes Picasa worth its wait in download time is the program's ability to instantly resize and attach photos to messages. This is a huge
boon, because digital cameras usually take photos at higher *resolutions* than you'd
want for sending and viewing them in email (that is, the pictures have a ton of
information per square inch, making them really hefty). All that extra digital data
becomes a burden when you attach a wad—or even just one full-size photo—to an
email, creating a monster message that might choke your recipient's email server
or clog up his system if he's on a dial-up connection. And even if the message
doesn't die in transit, the time it takes to download could make your correspondents want to kill *you*.

Picasa comes to the rescue by quickly downsizing a copy of each photo you want to
send before attaching it to an outgoing message for you.

Once you've downloaded and installed Picasa—and let it round up all your photos—attaching a picture to a Gmail message is easy. In Picasa, find the photo you
want to send, click it once to select it (Ctrl-click to select multiple pics), and then
click the Email button at the bottom of the Picasa window.

Picasa presents a box asking you to pick the email program you'd like to use to
send the photos. You have your choice of your PC's default email program (Outlook Express, Outlook, Mozilla Thunderbird, Eudora, whatever), your Gmail

account, or Picasa'a own mail program. Select your Gmail account if that's the one
you want to use. If this is your initial voyage into emailing with Picasa, you'll be
asked to type in your account name and password.

After you supply the information, Picasa pops up a message window in which you
can address and type in a note to your recipient. As shown in Figure 11-12, the
window also displays a small thumbnail version of the photo(s) you're sending and
lists the file size of the attachment Picasa has created. When you're done with the
message, just click the Send button to blast off your picture mail.

Figure 11-12:
*Digital photos can be ginormous files to send.
Picasa saves the day by automatically shrinking
them down so they still look good—but won't take
forever to download on the receiving end.*

Creating a Signature File

You can have Gmail add a *signature file* to the bottom of each and every message
you send. A signature file is usually your full name and contact information—like
an electronic business card pasted to the tail end of your message—but some people prefer to put stirring historical quotes, classic lines from *The Simpsons, King of
the Hill* jokes, or other bits of text-based whimsy at the end of a message. It's all up
to you.

To create a signature file in your Gmail account, click the Settings link at the top of
the Gmail window. In the Mail Settings area, you can change all sorts of things
about how Gmail looks and feels, but for now, click the General tab and then scroll

down to the Signature area, which is at the bottom of the General tab. Click the button next to the empty text box (Figure 11-13), and then type in the information you'd like to include in all your messages.

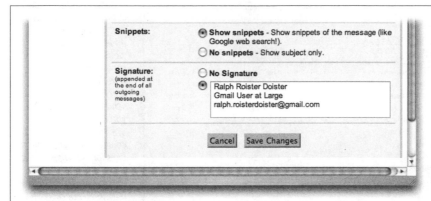

Figure 11-13:
Even though any email recipient will get your e-address in your message headers, it's not a bad idea to include your address in the signature file anyway. Putting it at the bottom of every message simply makes it easier for people to find.

When you've got it just the way you want it, click the Save Changes button at the bottom of the window. The next time you click Compose Mail, your blank message form will pop up with your signature file attached, complete with a little separator line between where the message text ends and the signature file begins. Just type your message above it.

If you decide you don't want to use the signature file for that particular message, simply delete it from the bottom before you click the Send button. If you tire of having a signature file altogether, return to Settings → General, and then click the button next to No Signature before clicking the Save Changes button.

Receiving and Reading Gmail

Once you've sent off a few messages from your new Gmail account, you won't have to wait long for people to start writing you back. And when the messages start flooding your Inbox, Gmail includes plenty of tools to help you organize and keep track of them—even those lengthy back-and-forth electronic conversations you have over the course of days or weeks.

Checking Your Gmail

As soon as you sign in to your Gmail account, all your new messages appear in bold at the top of your Inbox. You can tell how many new ones have arrived by looking at the number in parentheses next to the Inbox link on the left side of the screen (Figure 11-14).

If you're in the middle of message ping-pong with someone and want to see if they've written you back while you've been writing messages to other people, head to the top of the Inbox window, and then click the Refresh link to the right of the More Actions menu; this link tells Gmail to check for and display any fresh messages.

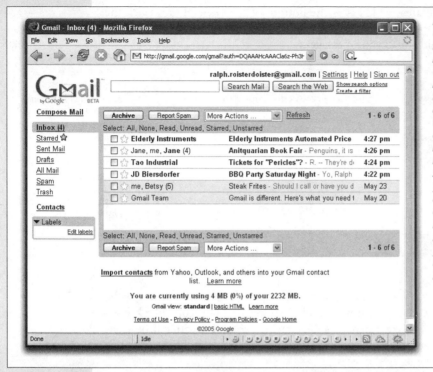

Figure 11-14:
Gmail helpfully tells you the number of new messages in your Inbox. Unread messages appear in bold, and messages that are part of back-and-forth exchanges, which Gmail calls conversations (see the next page), have a number next to the sender's name that tells you how many messages are part of the conversation. The subject lines for messages you've read and conversations you're caught up on have a light-blue background in the Inbox.

POWER USERS' CLINIC

The Gmail Notifier

Want to know when you've got new mail, even if you're not logged in to your Gmail account? Just download the free Gmail Notifier, a vigilant little helper for Windows 2000 and XP that checks for new messages every two minutes. (Mac fans can skip to the last paragraph of this box.)

When you get new mail, the Notifier lets you know with an icon in your system tray (the area in the lower-right corner of your screen). It can even give you an audio alert that mail is waiting. The Notifier can also preview a sliver of text from up to 30 unread messages.

Nab a copy of Gmail Notifier at *http://toolbar.google.com/gmail-helper/*.

If you use a Mac, check out Gee!, a free tool for Mac OS X Tiger that sits perched in your Mac's menu bar. Gee! keeps tabs on your Gmail and lets you know when new messages have arrived. You can find it at *www.apple.com/downloads.macosx/email_chat/gee.html*.

Reading Your Gmail Messages

At first glance, the Gmail Inbox looks like any other emailbox: stacks of messages with the sender's name, the message subject and the date it was sent all piled on top of each other. After you use Gmail for a few days, though, you may notice a few unique things about the service.

Conversation View

When it's not spam, email can be a form of dialogue between you and a friend or
group of friends. Google has taken this idea to heart and makes it an integral part
of the Gmail system, which it calls Conversation View. People familiar with electronic mailing lists, message-board posts, Slashdot article responses, and other digital discussions call these ongoing messages on the same topic *threads*. Gmail calls
them *conversations*. Once you get used to it, this feature is handy—which is a good
thing, because you can't turn it off.

With conversations, Gmail clusters together all messages with the same Subject
line. The clusters appear anytime you see a message that has related messages
attached to it, most commonly in your Inbox and when you open a message.

When you're on your Inbox page, you can tell you have a conversation going
because a message line has a number after it in parentheses, which you can see in
Figure 11-14. This number indicates how many messages have been passed in the
conversation and who was in on it for easy reference. When you click a conversation, Gmail opens it as a clump, shown in Figure 11-15.

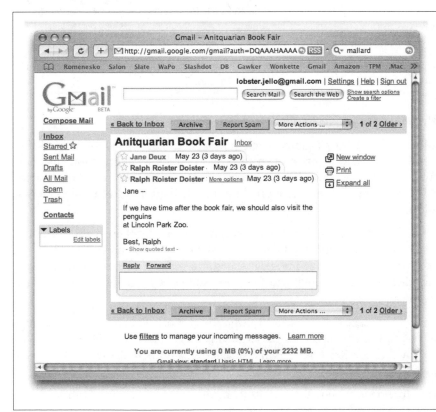

Figure 11-15:
*In the open Conversation
View, Gmail places
earlier messages—those
you've already read and
replied to—at the top of
the clump, and it places
the newest messages at
the bottom, ready to
read.*

Tip: If you have extremely chatty pals, you may notice that Gmail doesn't show the entire text of long messages. If you find any of these truncated notes, click the "More options" link next to the sender's name, and then click the link for Show Original to get the full story on your screen.

To see what you or a correspondent said in a prior message in the conversation, click one of the previous emails to expand the view and read it right there without having to burrow back though your Inbox looking for it. You can also click the Expand/Collapse All link on the right side of the window to open or close all the previous messages in one fell swoop. If you want to read the conversation in a new window, click the "New window" link (also on the right side of the Gmail screen).

To continue the conversation, you can hit Reply right there as you read the most recent message in the exchange and have all the previous messages right in front of you as you make plans, argue a point, or wheedle a raise. Once you're done reviewing prior messages, click the Expand/Collapse All link to collapse them back.

Note: Most people get tons of email a day, but you can tell Gmail to let you know which messages in the Inbox were addressed just to you *personally*, and which ones were addressed to a group that happens to include you. The Gmail Personal Level Indicator arrows point the way: A single > arrow means the message was sent to a group, and a double arrow (>>) means the message was sent only to you.

To turn on the arrows, click the Settings link at the top of the Inbox page and click the radio button to turn on Personal Level Indicators. Messages from Internet mailing lists won't get the arrow treatment, but the rest of your mail will soon be divided between the We and the Me.

Replying to messages, forwarding messages, and more options

Just like mail in other programs, Gmail messages can be replied to, forwarded on to another recipient, or pried open to reveal all sorts of information (like what email program your sender happens to be using). The first two commands, Reply and Forward, are conveniently located right at the bottom of your open message window.

Want to write your buddy right back and say you *do* want those extra jazz festival tickets he's got? Just click the Reply link and dash off your note; his address will already be in the To field. If a message slides into your Inbox that you want to pass along, click the Forward link and fill in the addresses of the people you want to share the message with.

If you get a message that was sent to a whole bunch of folks, and you want to reply to the whole team at once, click the "More options" link next to the sender's name and then click the Reply All link that magically appears underneath the message header.

This "More options" box lives up to its billing and provides you with additional actions to take with the open message on your screen. You can trash the message directly, report a suspected phishing scam (page 402), print the message for posterity, or add the sender to your Contacts list. If you're an inquisitive soul (or just bored) and like to look at message headers to see all the servers that this piece of mail visited on its way to you, or what email program was used to send the message, click the Show Original link. This action springs open a plain text version of the message, complete with full header information and other geeky goodness.

Tip: *You often get a link to send a Gmail invite directly to your correspondent when you're reading a message from the person.*

Downloading file attachments

In Gmail, you can receive file attachments up to 10 megabytes in size. In your Inbox, you can tell a message has an attachment, because on the right end of the message line, Gmail displays a paper clip. If you open a message with a JPEG picture attachment, you see a small thumbnail of the image, along with links to view the picture at full size right there on the screen, or to download it to your hard drive (Figure 11-16). (Some picture-file types like TIFF aren't as forthcoming as Internet-friendly JPEG files, though, so you may just see a file icon next to the View and Download links.) If you get a word processing document or other non-picture file, you just get the option to download the attachment to your hard drive. (The exception to receiving attachments is executable files, discussed in the box on page 391.)

Figure 11-16:
When you receive a photo or other file attachment along with a message, you can download it to your hard drive by clicking the Download link next to the thumbnail image. When you click Download, you get the generic Windows dialog box asking if you want to open the file or save it to your hard disk. If you choose to save the file to your disk, your browser dumps a copy of the file to your preferred spot for downloaded files.

Note: If you use Google's Picasa photo-management software (page 392), you can easily keep track of all the digital images people send you after you download the pictures to your hard drive, because Picasa automatically displays any new photo files it finds on your hard drive.

Once you see a photo in Picasa, you just need to click its thumbnail image once to see what its name is and what folder it lives in on your computer. Double-click the thumbnail image to call up a toolbox of photo-editing options like cropping and contrast controls.

FREQUENTLY ASKED QUESTION

Cleaning Out the Cache Closet

I sometimes have trouble downloading my Gmail attachments. I know we get 10 megabytes of space for each message, so what's the deal?

Your Web browser spends every surfing session downloading the little bits and pieces that make up a Web page, including text and images. It places all of these parts in a folder called the *cache*, a temporary storage space that speeds up surfing because it holds elements of Web sites on your computer—which means you don't have to download all the parts again every time you visit a site.

If you spend hours on the Web every day, however, your cache folder can start to get large and unwieldy, which can have a couple of repercussions for Gmailing. It can make using Gmail unbearably slow, and it can also prevent you from successfully downloading attachments that come in with your messages.

Fortunately, you can clear out the cache, removing the old Web site detritus and giving you room to move around and download.

Before you clear out the cache, log out of your Gmail account and close any other browser windows.

To dump the cache in Internet Explorer for Windows, choose Tools → Internet Options → General. Then, under Temporary Internet Files, click the Delete Files button, and turn on the checkbox next to "Delete all offline content" before clicking OK.

To clear the cache in the Firefox browser, choose Tools → Options → Privacy. Click Cache, and then click the Clear button before clicking OK.

Cache-chucking is even easier in Apple's Safari browser for Mac OS X. Just choose Safari → Empty Cache, or press ⌘-Option-E.

Spam, Spam, Spam, Spam

Cheap Rolexes! Quality software at a fraction of the retail price! Enhancements for body parts you may not even have! Spam is a fact of life for anyone who has had an email account for more than 20 minutes. Fortunately, email software and service providers, including Gmail, are fighting back with filters that help block junk mail—or at least reroute it away from your Inbox and into its own festering holding pen (or the Trash).

Gmail automatically bounces as much spam as it can into your Spam box. But it needs your help in identifying incoming junk mail that slips through to your Inbox. When you see a message that's obviously unwanted garbage mail, select it by turning on the checkbox next to the sender's name, and then click the Report

Spam button at the top of the mailbox window (Figure 11-17). That feature lets you smack the spam right out of your Inbox and into your Spam bin—while also giving the Gmail system the information it needs to block similar messages from slithering into your Inbox the next time around.

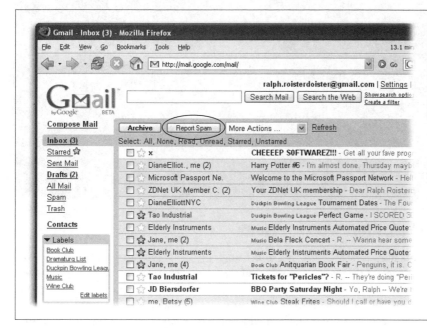

Figure 11-17:
When you report spam, you help Google get smarter by building up its database of spammers, which makes it easier for Gmail to recognize—and nix—junk mail when it next sees it.

Note: If you get fooled into opening a junk message that has a camouflaged subject line, the Report Spam button is still conveniently available at the top of the open message window.

If you suspect a message you actually *want* landed in your Spam box, click the Spam link on the left side of the mailbox window to see which messages wound up in there. If Gmail has gotten too aggressive and tagged a legitimate message as spam, you can rectify the situation by turning on the checkbox next to its header and clicking the Not Spam button at the top of the window. Doing so moves the message back into your Inbox *and* puts the sender back in your Gmail good graces by adding him or her to your Contacts list to ensure express delivery into your Inbox.

Note: After 30 days, Gmail automatically deletes messages left in the Spam box.

Of course, if you peek in your Gmail Spam box and see that all of it's total dreck, there's something deeply satisfying about clicking Select: All and then whamming the mouse button down on the glorious Delete Forever button.

Catching Phish

A rising percentage of spam messages are also *phishing* scams—forged, fraudulent messages that often disguise themselves as customer service notes from banks, Internet service providers, and e-commerce sites. These messages attempt to get you to type in your password, credit card information or Social Security number to a bogus Web site so the perp can steal your money or identity.

If you suspect a message in your Inbox might be a scam, click the More Options link next to the sender's name to open up a list of choices, and then click "Report phishing."

So how do you know a phish in the first place? Mail from banks or sites that you don't have an account with is a big

tip-off, as is any message that asks you to click a link to a Web site and divulge personal information. In addition, phishing messages commonly have lots of little mistakes, like misspelled words, oddly phrased sentences, and poor grammar.

If you get a message from someone claiming to be from the account management department of PayPal, eBay, America Online, or any other large institution you actually use, report it. If you're worried about your account, call the company's customer service number (almost always posted on its Web site) and check in.

Gmail Mailbox Management

After you use Gmail for a while and things begin to pile up in your Inbox, you might get sick of thrashing around in all the messages trying to find a specific piece of email or a collected conversation. Lucky for you, Gmail gives you plenty of ways to organize, sort, and store your mail so you can find what you want, when you want it. In addition to making your Inbox less of a jungle, the things you can do— like tagging messages with different labels, creating filters to perform specific actions on incoming mail, and archiving old conversations—help the search tool within Gmail find the messages you want with greater precision.

Archiving Messages

Let's face it—you can store a heckuva lotta messages in two and a half gigabytes of space. That's good because you rarely have to think about throwing out old messages to keep your mailbox from bulging into overflow. On the other hand, letting all your mail hang around can clutter up your Inbox *fast*.

To help keep things under control, Gmail lets you *archive* older messages, which means that you can keep them around for historical reference, but you don't have to see them in your Inbox. If you archive a message or conversation, it moves from your Inbox to the mailbox called All Mail.

To archive a message, from your Inbox, turn on the checkbox next to the sender's name, and then, at the top of the column, click Archive. You can also archive an open message or an entire conversation, as shown in Figure 11-18. (When you archive a message that's part of a conversation, the whole conversation gets filed away in All Mail.)

Note: To archive more than one Inbox message at a time, simply turn on all the corresponding check-boxes before clicking Archive.

Figure 11-18:
*When you have an open
message or conversation,
clicking the Archive button
moves the selected
message—or the entire
conversation, if there is one—
out of your active Inbox and
into the All Mail area of your
Gmail account, where you
can find it if ever you need it
again.*

If you want to see the archived messages, click the All Mail link on the left side of the Gmail window. You can send a message back to your Inbox by selecting it in the All Mail list and then, at the top of the screen, clicking "Move to Inbox."

Note: If someone sends a reply to a message you've archived already, the *whole conversation* containing that message thread shows up in your Inbox again. This can be a good thing, as it shows you the whole exchange and saves you the trouble of remembering what you were writing about with this person in the first place. (If you don't like the behavior, however, you can't turn it off.)

Taking Actions with Messages

Clicking the box next to the sender's name in your Gmail Inbox selects that message for a specific action. For example, if you're in the middle of a hot email session with a friend and you get called away before you can reply to the last note, you can "star" the message by clicking the More Actions pop-up menu and then choosing Add Star. This action applies a little yellow five-point star to the message's entry in your Inbox (Figure 11-19), so you remember you have to go back and send a reply.

You can apply stars to a bunch of messages at once by turning on the checkbox next to each message and then choosing More Actions → Add Star from the menu at the top of the Inbox.

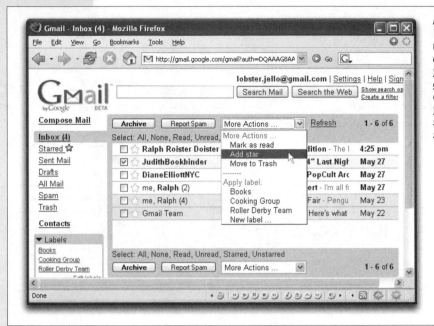

Figure 11-19:
The star can mean whatever you want—it doesn't have to remind you to reply. If you often get messages from celebrities, for example, you can use the star to signify who is, in fact, a star.

Tip: If you have a bunch of starred messages, you can separate them from the rest of the stuff in your Inbox by clicking the Starred link on the left side of the Gmail window.

In general, once you turn on the checkbox next to the sender's name in the Gmail Inbox, you've selected that message or messages for an action. You can archive all the selected messages, move them out of your life and into your Trash area, or even give them all the same *label,* a trick described in the next section.

If you want to get fancy with your selections, the Select line near the top and bottom of your Gmail Inbox gives you a lot of power. With just one click, you can select:

- **All.** This choice turns on the checkbox next to every message in the Gmail window.

- **None.** Here you can deselect any currently selected messages.

- **Read.** This command selects the messages you've already opened and read.

- **Unread.** Likewise, you can also select all the messages you haven't read yet.

- **Starred.** This command selects all the messages you've starred for future reference.

- **Unstarred.** You can also mass-select all your common, unstarred mail.

Creating and Applying Message Labels

Instead of folders for separating your mail into categories, Gmail gives you *labels*. You create a label and attach it to any relevant messages, and then Gmail lets you sift out all the messages with that label.

In your Inbox, the label shows up in small green type to the left of the messages' Subject line. But that's not the best way to find labeled messages. Instead, you can use Gmail's search (page 408), or you can use the label link. Here's how it works: Every time you create a new label, Gmail adds to the left side of the screen a link for that label. When you click the label link, Gmail automatically shows you all the messages with that label.

For example, if you want to keep all the messages from members of your book club separate from the messages from people in your duckpin bowling league, you can create a message label called Book Club to apply to all the messages from people in the group. Gmail then gives you a link for Book Club, and when you click it, you see a list of only those messages with the Book Club label. It's similar to having a folder for your Book Club messages, but more flexible because you can leave a message in your Inbox or All Mail box *and* label it Book Club at the same time *and* label it From Sister, too. That means you don't have to decide the best place for a message—you can tag it in all the ways that you deem relevant.

You can quickly create a label by heading to the left side of the Gmail window, and then clicking the green "Edit labels" link (if you have any existing labels, they're already listed here). That link takes you to the Labels screen, shown in Figure 11-20, where you can not only create a new label by typing it into the "Create a new label" box and then clicking the Create button, but you can also see any existing labels, plus how many mail conversations you've tagged with each label.

Tip: You can also create a new label from any mailbox by opening the More Actions pull-down menu at the top of screen and then choosing "New label…" to get a dialog box where you can type in your new label name.

Once you've created a label, Gmail adds it to the More Actions menu, which you can see back in Figure 11-19. To add the label to new messages, you have two choices:

- **From the Inbox (or any mailbox),** turn on the checkbox next to the message or conversation you want to label, open the More Actions pull-down menu at the top of the screen, and then choose the label you want.

- **When you're looking at an open message,** head directly to the More Actions menu and then apply the label you want.

Note: When you add a label to a message, Gmail automatically adds it to its whole conversation.

You can rename older labels if they've become outdated (if your book club morphs into a Harley club, this is the feature for you), or remove a label entirely (who needs that NCAA Final Four Pool label after the tournament's over, anyway?). On the Labels screen (Figure 11-20), just click the links on the right side of the screen to get a dialog box letting you type in a new name or confirm your deletion.

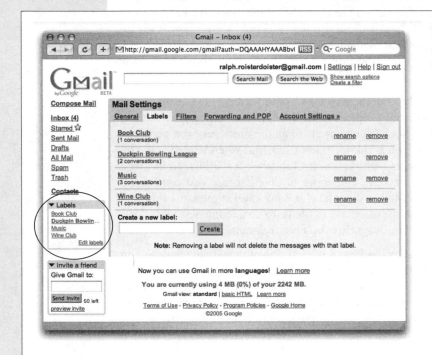

Figure 11-20:
On the left side of the window, clicking Edit Labels opens this screen.

Note: Luckily, removing or renaming a label doesn't delete or rename the messages themselves.

Want to see all the messages with a particular label? From the Labels screen or from the Labels list on the left side of the Gmail window, click the label name to get a list of all the messages with that tag. If you want to remove the label from a single message or from a few messages in the list, turn on the checkbox next to the ones you want to un-label, and then, at the top of window, click "Remove label *<label_name>*".

Tip: Page 411 tells you how to search for messages with a particular label or labels.

Mail Filters

Mail filters are like air-traffic control for your Gmail: They check and direct incoming messages and route them to the right place.

Say you subscribe to a mailing list of people all discussing a certain topic, like 19th century American literature or pet chinchillas, over email. Depending on how many people are on the mailing list and how chatty they are, you could be in for a lot of messages bombarding your mailbox along with all the mail from friends, family, your book club, and other correspondents.

With a mail filter, however, you can instruct Gmail to look out for all messages coming from the mailing list, and then have it automatically slap a label on them, add a star to them, or even forward a copy to another email address. They're a great way to help you maintain control of a busy Inbox.

Note: You can create up to 20 different message filters for your Gmail account.

To create a filter for incoming messages, click the Settings link at the top of the page, and then click Filters to get to the screen shown in Figure 11-21. You can also click the "Create a filter" link at the top of the Gmail window, right next to the "Search the Web" button.

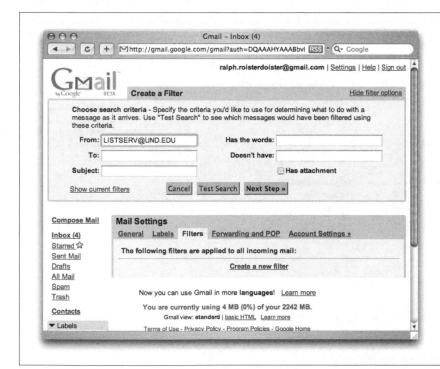

Figure 11-21:
The area labeled "Create a Filter" is the part you care about at this stage.

The first step in making a filter is telling Gmail what to watch out for in an incoming message. You can specify that it look for messages from a certain correspondent or email list, or that it look for messages to a particular group, with a specific subject line, or including certain body text. You can also turn on the checkbox that flags messages with attachments. Just type in the criteria you want, filling in one or more of the fields.

Tip: To test whether your filter is working, click Test Search to see which of your existing messages would have made the cut with the criteria you've set.

Once you've told Gmail how to recognize a certain type of message, you need to click the Next Step button and tell it what to *do* with the message.

As shown in Figure 11-22, you have several actions to choose from. You can have Gmail automatically star the message, archive it, label it, forward it to a different address, or dump it directly in the Trash (a popular option for the still-bitter and unexpectedly single). Once you've decided on all the actions you want to take with messages that match your criteria, click the Create Filter button to set the whole thing up. From here on out, Gmail performs these actions without any further work on your part.

Tip: If you want to change or remove a filter, in the upper-right corner of your Gmail window, choose Settings → Filters. That gives you a list of filters and what each of them does, along with links to edit or delete each one.

Figure 11-22:
If you click the "Show current filters" link, Gmail abandons the creation process and opens a list of existing filters.

Googling Your Gmail

If Google is known for anything, it's for being a top-notch search engine. And it can search your Gmail just as deftly and accurately as it can dig up results on the Web for *"cute pictures of baby ducks"*. You can use many of the same search techniques and operators (page 65) you use for regular Google Web searches on your own Gmail, too.

Gmail Address Plus One, Plus Two...

Lots of people keep multiple email addresses around: one for work, one for personal mail, one for a mailing list, one for online shopping, and so on. But it can be difficult to keep track of all those account names and passwords. Lucky for you, Gmail has the power to give you a whole bunch of different addresses to keep track of the various mail compartments of your life—all based on your one Gmail account.

Gmail does this through a neat trick called *plus-addressing*. With plus addressing, you can tag your own email address with significant keywords or phrases and tie them all together with a plus sign in front of the @ in the address.

For example, if your email address is *boo.radley@gmail.com* and you want to download a trial version of a program from a company that requires an email address to proceed, you can enter your address as *boo.radley+demoware@gmail.com*. When delivering messages to that address, Gmail conveniently ignores all those bits behind the plus signs, and then it deposits all the mail in your Inbox as if it were simply addressed to *boo.radley@gmail.com*.

The cool thing is that even though the plus-addressed mail arrives along with all your other messages, you can set up a filter to route and label any message with the plus address into the Trash, to All Mail, to Spam, or wherever. That way, if you find your plus address has been snagged by spammers, you can set up a filter to round-file the junk and then make up a new plus address to use for your next download adventure.

By adding a plus-address in the Cc field of a message to a bunch of friends planning a party or engaged in a seriously long email chat, you can filter all the responses by your plus-address (*boo.radley+BBQbash@gmail.com* or *boo.radley+batman+cooler+than+superman@gmail.com*) and organize the responses with labels, forwarding, or other special mail-handling instructions. With the power to create many addresses out of one, Gmail's plus-addressing feature is definitely a plus all on its own.

If you're just doing a quick search for words or phrases you know are in a message or subject line but can't remember anything else about it, just type the keywords into the blank box at the top of the Gmail window and then click the Search Mail button. Gmail will scour the contents of your mail account and give you a list of any messages containing those keywords. The list contains up to 20 messages per page, sorted by most recently received first; to see older messages, click the Older link in the upper- or lower-right corners of the window.

Note: The search function doesn't search text within file attachments—just the contents of the messages themselves.

Gmail won't automatically check your Spam and Trash bins for matching messages. If your results don't include the message you're looking for, click the "Show search options" link at the top of the Gmail page, and then on the next screen, choose Search → All & Spam & Trash, as illustrated in Figure 11-23, to search *all* your mailboxes.

Alternatively, if your list of results is too big to be useful, adding criteria is a good way to narrow it down. Click "Show search options" to get the screen in Figure 11-23, where you can home in on a message. In fact, you can use this form to *start* a search, a handy trick when you want guidance in defining a lot of criteria for your hunt. Just click "Show search options" from any screen.

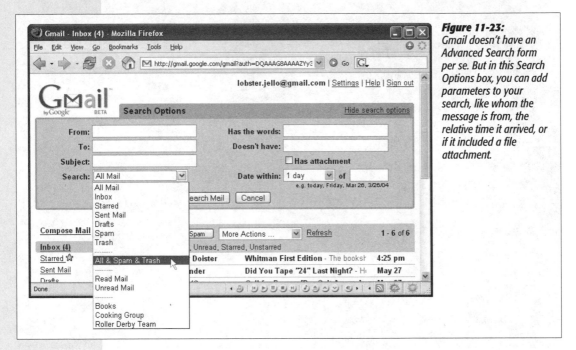

Figure 11-23:
Gmail doesn't have an Advanced Search form per se. But in this Search Options box, you can add parameters to your search, like whom the message is from, the relative time it arrived, or if it included a file attachment.

To close the Search Options box, in the upper-right corner of the box, click "Hide search options."

Note: If you type keywords into the search box at the top of the Gmail window and then click the "Search the Web" button instead of the Search Mail button, Gmail pops open a fresh Google window with the familiar Web search results.

Power searching

Just as you can get Google to rustle up definitions for you by typing *define:* before a word in the search box (page 38), Gmail can respond to a series of simple commands (called *operators* by database divas) designed for finding messages that contain certain elements, like a specific sender. For instance, if you want to find all the mail your pal Kermit has sent you, type *from:kermit* in the Search Mail box to have Gmail show you a list of messages just from him. Likewise, you can search for message you've sent to Kermit by typing *to:kermit* in the box. While you can similarly limit searches by using the Search Options box described previously, operators save you some clicking around and give you more choices. (Figure 11-24 shows you how it works.)

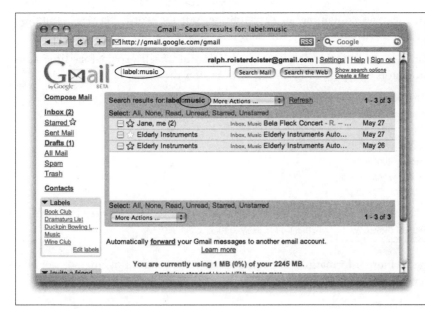

Figure 11-24:
Here, a search for label:music
*rounded up all the messages
labeled "music."*

Here are additional operators you can use with Gmail (in each case, you'd swap in your own keyword or phrase instead of the word "something"):

- *subject:something.* Searches for words in a message's Subject line. For example, if you search for *subject:online*, Gmail gives you any message that includes the word *online* in the subject—even if the subjects have other words, too.

- *label:something.* Searches for messages tagged with one of your custom labels.

- *has:attachment.* Searches for messages with attachments.

- *filename:something.* Searches for attachments by their file names.

- *cc:something.* Searches for messages by names in the Cc: field.

- *bcc:something.* Searches for messages by names in the Bcc: field.

For real power, you can combine operators. If you want to search for messages from either Kermit or Teddy, string it together as *from:kermit OR from:teddy*. If you have a ton of messages from Kermit but want to find the one where he sent you a photo of his pet chinchilla, type *from:kermit has:attachment* to narrow things down.

Punctuation marks can get pressed into duty as search operators as well. Think of the hyphen (-) as a minus sign and put it in front of any words you don't want to appear in your search results. For example, searching for *games -doom* looks for messages where you discussed games, but not Doom.

Typing words between parentheses lets you search for messages that contain all of those words. If you want to find all the messages where you discussed both baseball and football with Kermit, type *from:kermit (baseball football)* to dig up results.

To find messages containing an exact phrase, put the words between quotation marks in your Search box, as in *"live long and prosper"* or *subject:"Star Trek"*.

You can also track down messages with a handful of self-explanatory time-and-place operators by typing in a location or time after the colon:

```
in:inbox
in:spam
in:trash
in:anywhere
after:2005/05/17
before:2005/07/13
```

Note: The *before* and *after* keywords search for when a message was sent, not when it was received. Email is so fast these days, though, that it's not likely to make a difference.

Tacking in more information, like if the message was starred or unread, can help produce precise search results as well:

```
is:starred
is:unread
is:read
```

When you get a bunch of these operators working all at once, you have searches that look like your keyboard's colon key is out of control, like *from:kermit is:starred subject:(death OR taxes) before:2005/04/14*.

Deleting Messages Forever

When you're done with a message and never want to think about it again, you can dump it out of your Inbox in two ways:

- Move one or more messages from your Inbox to the digital dumpster by ticking the checkbox next to each message and then choosing Actions → Move to Trash.

Note: If the message you selected is part of a conversation, Gmal now trashes the *entire conversation*. If you want to delete only the message itself (and none of the others in the conversation), open the conversation, click the subject snippet you want to toss out, click the "More options" link next to the sender's name, and finally click "Trash this message."

- When a message is open, choose More Actions → Move to Trash.

Tip: Click the "More options" link at the top of an open message and then click "Trash this message" for more instant gratification.

While either of these actions moves the unwanted email into the Trash box, it doesn't permanently erase it immediately. Instead, Gmail waits for 30 days before automatically clearing out the Trash box. (Until then, you can still see the old messages by clicking the Trash link in the Gmail window.) To permanently dispose of all the old mail right away, click the Trash link and select all the messages by clicking the Select: All link at the top of the column. Click the Delete Forever button (Figure 11-25) to permanently zap the selected messages.

Figure 11-25:
If you've inadvertently trashed a message, you can use this screen to restore it to your Inbox; just click the "Move to Inbox" button. However, if you just can't wait to erase a message forever—like a particularly racy message from your extramarital lover—click the Delete Forever button so your spouse never stumbles upon it.

Printing Messages

When you want to convert a digital note into a paper copy, Gmail is on your side. This feature is useful when, say, you buy movie tickets online and want to print out your bar-coded proof of purchase so you can skip the line at the ticket printer in the theater's crowded lobby. To print a solo message, just open it and click the Print icon on the right side of the window.

Printing can get confusing, however, when you have a 20-message conversation onscreen but just want to print out the one message in the bunch. To print out a single message buried in a Gmail conversation, open the conversation, click the Expand All link on the right, and then find the message you want to print. Since each message in the conversation has its own "More options" link, click just the "More options" link in the *desired* message, and then, from the list of choices below the Subject line, click Print.

The Contacts List

Contacts are nothing more than a stored list of email addresses. The cool thing about them is that they let you fill in the To field of a message with just a click or two—and without having to remember whether your brother's e-address is *bro@workplace.com* or *bro@workplace.net*.

For example, instead of typing out *president@whitehouse.gov* every time you get the urge to tell the President how you feel, you can call up your Contacts list by heading to the left side of the Gmail window and then clicking the Contacts link. When you do so, Gmail presents a list of names and e-addresses of people you frequently send messages to (click All Contacts to see the entire list of people you've added to your email address book, as shown in Figure 11-26). Turn on the checkbox next to the entry for "President," and then click Compose to open a pre-addressed message form all ready for you to fill in with your latest thoughts.

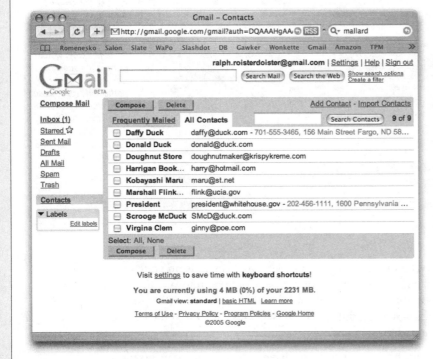

Figure 11-26:
Keeping your pals nicely filed away in your Gmail Contacts saves you a lot of message-addressing. You have the option of storing more info besides name and email address, too; within each contact file, you can add a snail-mail address, phone number, and other pertinent information. Page 415 tells you how.

Tip: You can send the same message to multiple Contacts all at once. Just turn on the checkbox next to each name on the list that you want to use (or, to include everyone, at the bottom of the Window, click Select: All) and then click the Compose button. It's a quick way to tell everybody about your new Gmail address, for example.

A great benefit of having addresses in your Gmail Contacts is that whenever you're working on a new message and you start typing a few letters of the recipient's address in the To field, Gmail's auto-complete function kicks in and shows you a list of contacts that match the letters you've already typed. So when you type *pre*, Gmail shows you *prefontaine@running.org, preppy_girl963@aol.com, president@whitehouse.gov,* and so on. Just select the one you want and then press Enter to have Gmail finish filling in the field for you.

There are three ways to add people to your Gmail Contacts. The first is to send a message to somebody; Gmail automatically stores the recipient's address in your Contacts. The other two ways—doing it manually and importing a batch from another program—are described next.

Tip: Want to import old mail as well as contacts into your Gmail account? Check out Mark Lyon's GMail Loader program at *www.marklyon.org/gmail/*, a free bit of software that harvests old messages from other accounts and plants them in your new Gmail Inbox.

Manually Adding Contacts to Gmail

You can add individual email addresses to Gmail when you're in the Contacts window (from the main window, just click the Contacts link). On the Contacts page, click the Add Contact link, and then fill in the form.

The basic screen allows for just a name, primary email address, and some random notes. If you're a completist and want detailed information on your pals, click the "add more contact info" link to add names, email addresses, mailing addresses, phone numbers, and more to the Contact file, as shown in Figure 11-27. When you're done, click Save to confirm and store all the new information you just added.

Figure 11-27:
When you opt to add more contact info, Gmail gives you some flexibility. For additional choices— like IM, Mobile, Fax, Company, and so forth— click the arrow next to Phone or Email to get a menu of choices. To add additional fields with this menu, click "add another field." If you want to nix a whole section, click "remove section"; to add a whole section (handy if you're storing work and home addresses, for instance), click "add section."

Tip: When reading a message from someone new, you can instantly add the person's email address to your Contacts list. With the message open, click the "More options" link next to the sender's name, and then, from the list of actions that appears, click "Add sender to Contacts list."

Addressing the Group Contacts Problem

At the time of this writing, Gmail does not support group or distribution lists. In other words, you can't have a contact name that contains multiple email addresses—like one contact name to address a message to all 23 people in your Oktoberfest beer-tasting club. As with many things in the software life, however, you can fake it 'til they make it.

The easiest method is to keep a text file around with all your group addresses typed in and separated by commas, as in the following: *tristram@shandy.com, barteleby@scrivener.com, betty@boop.biz, walt@leaves.net*, and so on.

When it comes time to mail the group, just open the text file so you can copy and paste the names into a new Gmail message header without having to type them all out or select them individually. To keep the list of contacts with you no matter what computer you use, you can also paste them into the Notes field of an *existing* contact to store them on the Gmail server. (If you have existing messages from the group in your Inbox you can copy and paste from there as well.)

Importing Contacts from Other Mail Programs

Manually adding address information into your Gmail Contacts is all well and good, but what if you have a nice full address book you've been working with for years—and it happens to be in another email program like Eudora or Outlook Express?

If your other mail program lets you export your address list to what's called a CSV file, you can import it right into your Gmail Contacts. (*CSV* is spreadsheet-nerd shorthand for Comma Separated Values, which means that each nugget of information is separated from every other info-nugget by a mighty comma.)

Converting contacts for use with Gmail varies depending on what email program you're using. With some, it's a simple export operation, while other mail programs make you jump through a few hoops. You may even have to muscle the file around in Microsoft Excel, Corel's Quattro Pro, or another spreadsheet program to get it to play nice with Gmail.

Keep in mind, however, that no matter what program you use, if you import a contact that has the same email address as an existing entry in your Gmail Contacts list, the newly imported contact will replace the older one.

Note: You can import up to 3,000 contacts at a time, but address-book entries formatted in mail-distribution lists or groups won't transfer. This means if you once made a Eudora nickname or Outlook group contact name to store the email addresses of all 67 members of the Film Society, Gmail won't accept it.

Some people get around this by manually adding each person's address to a message, sending the message, and then keeping that message around to cut and paste all the names into any future messages. It's a hassle, but it's the best you can do until Google adds group contacts.

Adding contacts from Eudora, Outlook, and Outlook Express

If you use a standalone email programs like Eudora, Outlook, or Outlook Express, you're in luck. They make it easier to wrestle out address-book information than do Web-based mail services like Hotmail.

To import contacts into Gmail, you must first export them as a CSV file from your existing mail program. Here's how to get started:

Note: These steps *should* work in older versions of each of these programs. If you're using a different version and you get hung up, however, search the program's help system for "Export" or "Exporting" to find the right steps.

- **Eudora 6.** With the address book open on screen, choose File → Export. In the dialog box, give the file a name, and then choose CSV format and export the file to your desktop or other easy-to-reach location on your computer.

- **Outlook 2003.** From the main menu bar, chose File → Import and Export to call up the Import/Export wizard. On the first screen, choose "Export a file," and on the next screen, select Comma Separated Values (Windows). From the list presented on the next screen, choose the Contacts file. Type in name to call the exported file, and then click Export. Finally, save the file to your desktop or other accessible hard disk location.

- **Outlook Express 6.** From the main menu bar, choose File → Export → Address Book. Select Text File (Comma Separated Values), and then click Export. Save the file to your desktop or some other place where you can easily find it.

Once you have your CSV file safely exported, you're ready to move the contacts to Gmail:

1. **Sign in to your Gmail account and then, on the left side of the window, click the Contacts link.**

   The Contacts page opens.

2. **Click "Import Contacts."**

   A dialog box like the one in Figure 11-28 pops up.

3. **Click the Browse button, mosey to the desktop or wherever you parked the CSV file, and then select it.**

   Click Open to return to the importing dialog box.

4. **In the importing dialog box, click Import Contacts.**

   Gmail imports your list and tells you how many contacts you've just added.

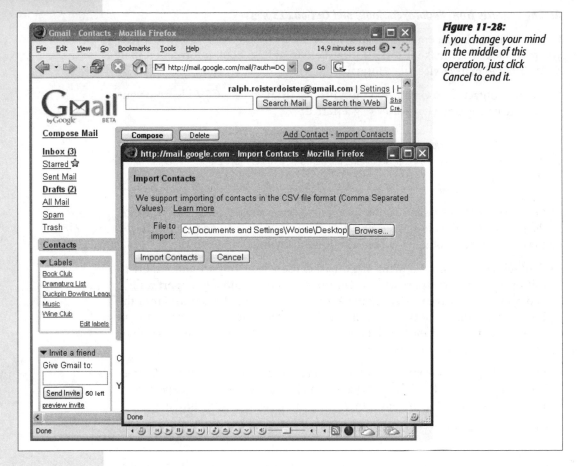

Figure 11-28:
If you change your mind in the middle of this operation, just click Cancel to end it.

Adding contacts from Yahoo Mail

Yanking a .CSV file out of Yahoo's address book is fairly straightforward:

1. **Sign in to your Yahoo Mail account, and then open your address book.**

   If you were sticking with Yahoo, this is where you'd add new contacts.

2. **On the right side of the Address Book page, click the Import/Export link.**

   If you ever decide to switch *back* to Yahoo, you can import any contacts you've accumulated in the meantime using the Import feature here.

3. **Go to the Export area, and then click the Export Now button next to "Microsoft Outlook."**

   Yahoo automatically creates a .CSV file called *Yahoo_ab.csv*, which you'll be able to then import into your Gmail address book.

4. **Save the CSV file to your desktop, or some other convenient location.**

5. **Follow the steps on page 417 for importing contacts into Gmail.**

GOOGLE: THE MISSING MANUAL

Adding contacts from Hotmail

Harvesting addresses out of Hotmail is possible, but it's a bit more complicated than in other programs. Here's one way to do it, but note that you'll need a spreadsheet program to crack open the exported file and fiddle with it:

1. **Sign in to your Hotmail account.**

   Click the Contacts tab.

2. **In the Contacts tab, click "Print view" and then select all of the contacts in the list.**

   You can select all the contacts by dragging the cursor over the list from the top of the Name column on down.

3. **Press Ctrl+C (⌘-C) to copy the selected text.**

4. **Open your spreadsheet program, and then click the top-left square.**

   In Excel, for example, this square would be cell A1.

5. **If you used Internet Explorer to log in to Hotmail, press Ctrl+V (⌘-V) to paste the text into the spreadsheet. If you used either the Mozilla or Firefox browsers, right-click the top-left cell, and from the menu that appears, choose Paste Special. A dialog box opens; choose Text (Figure 11-29) and then click OK.**

   Your contacts appear in the grid.

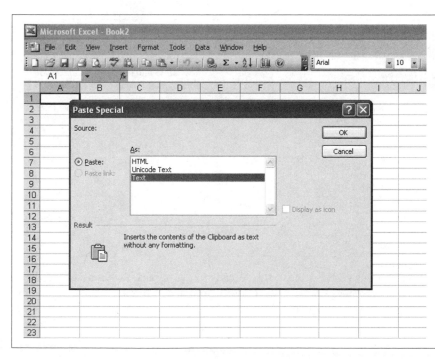

Figure 11-29:
The Paste Special command in Excel lets you choose the format to use for pasted text. If your browser was Firefox or Mozilla, when you copied your contacts, however, the browser added some gunk you don't want now. Choosing the Text option in this dialog box gets rid of the extra stuff.

6. **Save the spreadsheet as a .CSV file, and store it on your desktop or some other place you can easily find it.**

   In Excel, for example, choose File → Save As → CSV (Comma delimited).

7. **Follow the steps on page 417 for importing the contacts to Gmail.**

Adding contacts from AOL

Getting addresses, old mail, or anything else out of America Online's mail program can be tricky, and the variations are many. Luckily, there are links to plenty of address-extraction tools and other helpful programs on the eMailman site at *www.emailmain.com/aol/*.

Troubleshooting Importing Errors with Contacts

In most cases, Gmail will cheerfully import your addresses into its Contacts list without complaining. But certain things—like bad formatting in the CSV file—will trip it up, causing it to flash an error message at you.

In many cases, opening up the CSV file in a spreadsheet program and fussing with the formatting can take care of import problems. When you open the file in Excel or whatever spreadsheet program you use, make sure the file is formatted as a table. The table needs to include a header at the top of each column, describing what's in that column: name, email address, and so on (Figure 11-30). If the file doesn't have those headers, Gmail won't know what to do with the list.

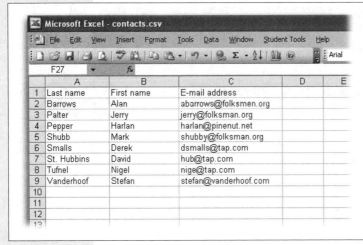

Figure 11-30:
Your spreadsheet can have names all in one column, or it can separate first and last names into their own columns—and it doesn't matter what order they're in.

Once you've adjusted the table in the spreadsheet program, save it as a CSV file—in Excel, choose File → Save As → CSV (Comma delimited)—and then try the Import Contacts process again.

Adding Contacts, the Hard Way

If Gmail, snorts, stamps its feet, and then hurls when you try to import your CSV file, there's still a way you can get those contacts imported—but it's not the most elegant thing in the world.

First, copy all your contacts in your old mail program to the Cc field of a message addressed to your Gmail account. Send a message off, and when you get it at your Gmail address, click the Reply All link and send everyone in your old address book a message telling them your new Gmail address.

Once you send off the message, everyone on the recipient list gets added to your Gmail contacts list. Since you're using the Cc field so you can see the addresses, though, remember that everyone *else* will be able to see who's getting the message as well. You may want to send multiple messages (friends, coworkers, fellow support-group members) to keep some degree of privacy.

Editing and Deleting Gmail Contacts

People are always on the move, and their email addresses may change in the process. If you need to edit somebody's address information, just open your Contacts page, click the name you want to work on to get a screen with just that person's name, and then click the "edit contact information" link to open an editable form for that contact. You can add data fields to include phone numbers, mailing addresses, pager numbers, instant-message screen names, and other useful coordinates as described on page 415—or you can just edit the information that's already there. When you're done, click Save.

Note: When you import information like birthdays or phone numbers into Gmail, they wind up in the Notes field of a contact. If you want to move the information out of the Notes field, just add an Other field and paste in the information. You may also find the Other field useful if you need room to store some serious intel on your pal, like dining preferences, parents' address, or whatever you want to remember.

If you decide to cross somebody off your list, you can delete the entire contact by clicking the checkbox next to her name and then clicking the Delete button at the top of the list.

Adjusting Your Account Settings

Gmail gives you the power to adjust many of the settings that affect how you see and get your mail. To get to these controls, click the Settings link at the top of the Gmail window, and you'll see a screen similar to the one shown in Figure 11-31.

There are five different Settings categories to fiddle with, as described next.

Figure 11-31:
*Whenever you tweak
something in the Settings
area, be sure to click the
Save Changes button at
the bottom of the
window to make it so.*

Mail Settings

The Mail Settings area holds many of the controls for what your messages look
like, including:

- **Name.** If you want to change the name on mail you send to people, adjust it
  here.

- **Reply-to Address.** Have your message replies come back to your Gmail account
  or choose another email address to collect the responses.

- **Language.** Select the language you want to use for the buttons, links, and other
  screen elements in your Gmail window. There are 13 of them to choose from.

- **Maximum page size.** You can opt to see a list of 25, 50, or 100 conversations at
  once on your screen.

- **Keyboard shortcuts.** Quick keystrokes can save time if you remember them (see
  page 424 for a list), but if they bother you, you can toggle the shortcut function
  on or off here.

- **Personal level indicators.** Gmail will automatically place single and double arrows next to messages in your Inbox, depending on whether they were sent to a group or just to you. You can turn on this feature here.

- **Snippets.** With Snippets activated, you have the option of seeing the first few words of a message in your Inbox alongside the Subject line. If you turn off Snippets, you just see the subject words alone.

- **Signature.** You can add or turn off a signature file (page 394) for all your outgoing messages here.

Labels

The Labels settings give you one place to create, rename, or remove the personalized tags that help you sort and organize your messages (page 405). Clicking a message name shows you all the conversations that Gmail has grouped under each label.

Filters

You can review all of your current mail filters (page 406) for rerouting or labeling incoming messages, and also create new ones within the Filters settings area. If you need to change a filter's action or delete one altogether, you can do so here as well.

Forwarding and POP

If you have multiple email accounts and want to automatically send incoming Gmail to another one of your accounts (page 429), turn on the forwarding option here and supply the email address you want to use to collect the rerouted Gmessages.

If you'd prefer to use a POP mail program like Outlook Express or Apple Mail to read your email messages, turn on the POP Download function. (You get to pick whether Gmail keeps copies of downloaded messages, archives them, or trashes them from your Gmail Web window.) Once you turn on POP downloads here, you'll need to open your POP mail program and add the Gmail account information, as described on page 427.

Account Settings

Gmail keeps all the settings concerning your account name, password, and security question here. Although you can't change your Gmail address after you set it up, you *can* change the password and the secret question that proves your identity if you forget your password.

You can delete your Gmail account here if you decide you don't want it after all, or add other Google gravy like having Froogle Shopping Lists (page 99) and Google Alerts (page 167) sent to your Gmail address.

Note: If you like Gmail but don't use it as your primary email address, be sure to sign in to it every few weeks to keep it active. If you don't use the account for an extended period of time, the folks at Gmail consider it dormant. After nine months of waiting around for you to come back, Gmail deletes all the messages in your account, closes it up, and tosses your address back into the pool of available names for somebody else to pick up and use.

Other Cool Gmail Tricks

As you get used to Gmail and want to earn your Power User merit badge, here are a couple of ways to make the service more fun and efficient.

Tip: Since Gmail launched, fans have complied Web sites full of tips, tricks, and tweaks. You can find a lot of information and discussion at sites like *www.gmailusers.com* and *www.gmailwiki.com*. Also worth a visit is Jim Barr's GmailTips site, *http://g04.com/misc/GmailTipsComplete.html*, and the GmailForums discussion board at *www.gmailforums.com*.

Gmail Keyboard Shortcuts

If you're tired of dragging your mouse around the Gmail window, try some of these keyboard shortcuts to perform many common commands with the tap of a button. The keyboard shortcuts are optional, though, and you have to tell Gmail that you want to use them in your Settings area. (To do so, click the Settings link at the top of the Inbox page, and then on the General tab, click the button next to "Keyboard shortcuts on.") Most shortcuts work for navigating around your Inbox window, unless otherwise noted, and all are lowercase letters. (If you don't have this book handy, you can also find the list of keyboard shortcuts in the Gmail Help area when you're logged in to your account.)

Shortcut Key	What It Means	What It Does
c	Compose.	Starts a new message for you to fill in. Pressing **Shift+c** starts the message in a new window.
/	Search.	Plants your mouse cursor in the search box.
k	Move to newer conversation.	Opens or moves the black cursor arrow to a more recent conversation in your Inbox list. Press **Enter** to expand a Gmail conversation.
j	Move to older conversation.	Opens or moves the black cursor arrow to the next oldest conversation in the Inbox's list. Hit **Enter** to expand a conversation.
n	Next message.	Moves your cursor to the next message. Press **Enter** to expand or collapse a message. (Works only in Conversation View.)
p	Previous message.	Moves the cursor to the previous message. Press **Enter** to expand or collapse a message. (Works only in Conversation View.)

Shortcut Key	What It Means	What It Does
o or **Enter**	Open.	Opens a mail conversation, and expands or collapses a message if you're already in Conversation View.
u	Return to conversation list.	Refreshes your current page and sends you back to the Inbox, or to a list of conversations.
y	Archive/Remove from current view.	Removes the message or conversation from your current view and sends the message elsewhere, depending where you're currently parked: • *Inbox*: **y** means Archive • *Starred*: **y** means Unstar • *Trash*: **y** means Move to Inbox • *In a label*: **y** means Remove the label If you're in Spam, Sent, or All Mail, pressing the **y** key does nothing.
x	Select conversation.	Automatically turns on a conversation's checkbox and selects a conversation so that you can archive it, label it, or choose an action from the menu for that conversation.
s	Star a message or conversation.	Adds or removes a star to a message or conversation.
!	Report spam.	Marks the message as vile spam and boots it out of your conversation list.
r	Reply.	Sets up a reply to the message sender. Pressing **Shift+r** opens the reply message in a new window (only in Conversation View.)
a	Reply all.	Sets up a reply to all message recipients. Pressing **Shift+a** opens the mass reply in a new window. (Works only in Conversation View.)
f	Forward.	Sets up the message to be forwarded to another person. Pressing **Shift+f** does the same thing in a new window. (Works only in Conversation View.)
Esc	Escape from input field.	Removes the cursor from your current field.

Once you've mastered the simple key shortcuts, you're ready for the one-two punch of combination keystrokes to jump around your messages and mailboxes:

Note: Press the first key, then the second key right after it.

Shortcut Keys	What They Mean	What They Do
Tab then **Enter**	Send message.	After writing your message, press this key combination to automatically send it. (Works only in Internet Explorer.)
y then **o**	Archive and next.	Archives the conversation and moves you to the next one.

Shortcut Keys	What They Mean	What They Do
g then **a**	Go to All Mail.	Takes you to the All Mail area, which is an online garage for all the mail you've ever sent or received (but haven't deleted).
g then **s**	Go to Starred.	Takes you to all the mail conversations you've marked with a star.
g then **c**	Go to Contacts.	Takes you to your Contacts list.
g then **d**	Go to Drafts.	Takes you to all drafts of messages-in-progress you've saved.
g then **i**	Go to Inbox.	Returns you back to your Gmail Inbox.

Turning Gmail into a Web-Based File Server

Considering all that space you get with your Gmail account, wouldn't it be great if you could use some of it for backing up big files that you could then snag from any Web browser? For example, if you had an 8-megabyte PowerPoint presentation you'd been working on at home and at the office all week, it would be cool to use Gmail as your Web-based file server, rather than toting the file back and forth on a CD?

Emailing yourself a copy of the file every time you make changes can get tedious, but a free little program for Windows machines running Internet Explorer 5 or later called GMail Drive (*www.viksoe.dk/code/gmail.htm*) turns some of that spare Gmail space into a virtual hard drive. The program adds Gmail to the list of drives that you can see in My Computer and lets you transfer files by dragging them onto it—just like any other hard drive or USB flash drive.

After you download and install the program, go to My Computer and then double-click the GMail Drive icon. In the dialog box that opens, type in your Gmail name and password (Figure 11-32). Now, when you drop files on your Gmail Drive icon, they copy over to your Gmail Inbox, just like you were dropping them on a file server or external hard drive.

When you want to grab a copy of a file you've backed up to Gmail, just log in to your Gmail account and you'll see the file in your Inbox with the prefix GMAILFS in the window. If you're running Windows XP on the retrieving computer, you can also install a copy of GMail Drive there to grab files using the GMail Drive icon in My Computer.

Three Other Ways of Reading Gmail

A lot of people love the storage space and freedom of Gmail but aren't fans of the interface. If you're part of that club, this section gives three ways to get your messages other than the standard Gmail window.

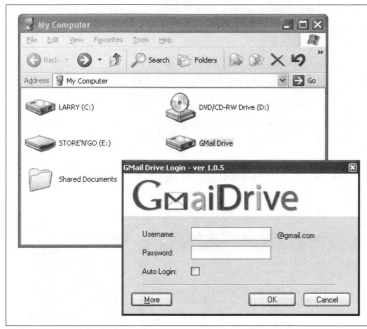

Figure 11-32:
You can drag files up to 10 megabytes in size into the GMail Drive to store them on the server and collect them later from any computer with a working Web browser.

Using Gmail with a Different Mail Program

Describing Gmail as "Web-based" email doesn't give the service full credit, because you can also send and receive your Gmail in a standalone mail program that handles POP mail. *POP* stands for Post Office Protocol, and it works with mail software like Outlook Express, Mozilla Thunderbird, Apple Mail, and Eudora.

Routing your Gmail through your existing mail program—especially if you have multiple mail accounts that you'd like to check all at once—saves you the trouble of remembering to fire up your Web browser to scope out your Inbox. It's also a good choice if you happen to prefer your email software to Gmail's Web interface.

Of course, if you ditch the Web browser window and download your Gmail with any ol' email program, you lose the neatly stacked Conversation view that's a big part of the Gmail experience. That's about the only big thing you lose, though; even if you're on the road and check your Gmail the old-fashioned browser way, all your messages will still download to your mail program (like Outlook Express) when you return home.

You need to do two basic things to run Gmail in the mail program of your choice:

- Adjust your Gmail account settings to allow POP downloading.

- Add the Gmail server information to your mail program's settings.

To adjust your Gmail so that it sends copies of your messages on to your POP mail program, sign in to your Gmail account from your Web browser, and then click the Settings link in the upper-right corner of the page. In the Settings area, click the tab for "Forwarding and POP" (shown in Figure 11-33), and in the POP Download section, set the following:

• Whether you want to download *all* your existing Gmail or just Gmail that arrives from now on. (Click the button next to the choice you want.)

• Whether to keep a copy of each message in your Web Inbox, archive them (page 402), or dump them in the trash (since you'll already have read the message in your mail program). Choose from the pull-down menu.

• The Gmail account settings for your e-mail software of choice. This step requires leaving the Gmail POP Download area and bopping over to your email program.

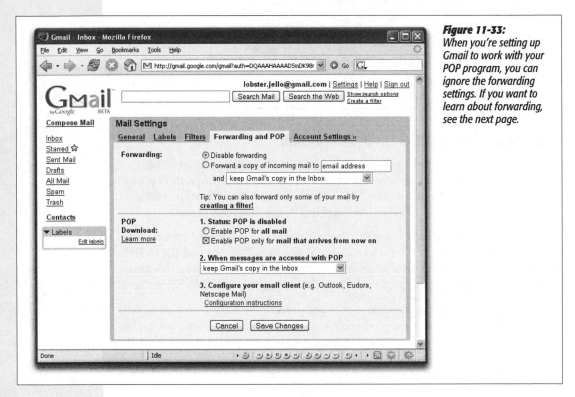

Figure 11-33:
When you're setting up Gmail to work with your POP program, you can ignore the forwarding settings. If you want to learn about forwarding, see the next page.

When you're done telling Gmail what you want, click Save Changes.

Next, you have to set up Gmail as an account in your other mail program. The exact configuration steps vary slightly depending on which program you use, but the basics are the same: you need to create a new account in your mail software's Preferences or Settings area, and then type in information to help the program find your Gmail.

The things you need to tell the mail program about your Gmail account include:

- **Your Gmail account name,** which is the same as your Gmail email address.
- **Your Gmail password,** which you should keep a secret everywhere but your POP program.
- **The name of the incoming mail server,** which is *pop.gmail.com.*
- **The name of the outgoing mail server,** which is *smtp.gmail.com.*

The Gmail *server* (the computer that's in charge of Gmail) uses a secure Internet connection and requires *authentication* to send messages, which means you need to tell it your user name and password every time you want to send a message. Web-based Gmail authenticates automatically. You can have your POP program authenticate automatically, too, by supplying the information in the Outgoing Mail server settings. Figure 11-34 shows some examples of account settings with a couple of different mail programs. You can find specific instructions for just about any current mail program—as well as BlackBerry wireless email devices—in the POP section at *http://gmail.google.com/support.*

Tip: Don't configure your mail software to hit up the Gmail server for new messages every few minutes. If you do, you may addle the server into locking you out of your own account. If find yourself locked out, wait an hour and then try using your Gmail account again.

Auto-Forwarding Gmail Messages

If you don't want to add your Gmail account to your existing POP mail program, but you *would* like see your incoming messages without having to log into Gmail, you can *auto-forward* your Gmessages. Auto-forwarding simply means that the Gmail server always forwards a copy of all your incoming messages to another email address. Auto-forwarding can be helpful if, say, you don't have access to a computer and are reading your mail on an Internet-enabled wireless phone for the day.

To turn on the auto-forwarding feature, sign in to your Gmail account, and then click the Settings link at the top of the screen. Click the "Forwarding and POP" tab. In the Forwarding section at the top of the screen, click the button next to "Forward a copy of incoming mail to," and then type in the email address you want to use for collecting your Gmail. Underneath that setting, use the pull-down menu to choose whether to save a copy of the original message, archive it (page 402), or trash it completely. Click the Save Changes button when you've adjusted the Forwarding settings to your liking.

Note: If you just want to forward incoming mail from a certain person, domain, or containing specific keywords, you can create a filter (page 406) to forward just those messages to your other account, and leave the rest waiting for you when you get back to your computer.

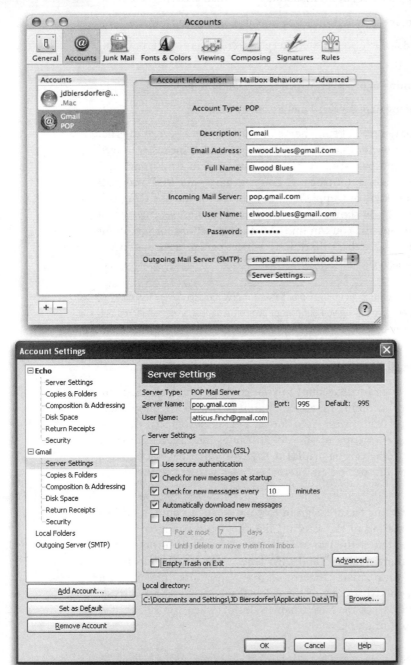

Figure 11-34:
After you turn on POP Download in your Gmail settings, you need to create another mail account within your standalone email program and give it the information it needs to find and download messages from your Gmail account. Adding accounts in Apple Mail (top) or Mozilla Thunderbird (bottom) requires that you type in your Gmail account name and password. You also need to supply addresses for your incoming and outgoing Gmail in the right fields. You'll need to turn on the checkbox for an SSL connection—and fill in your user name and password for the outgoing server—to let Gmail's servers know it's really you sending the message. Full instructions for most mail programs are at http://gmail.google. com/support.

Using Gmail with a News Reader

With people hoping to keep on top of all the 21st century information, it's no wonder programs known as *news readers* (or the more wonkish *news aggregators*) have caught on so quickly. With news-reader software, you can view freshly updated headlines and capsule summaries from hundreds of Web sites all in one window, without having to plod through site after site looking for new content.

These updates are called *feeds*. Many Web sites—from the *New York Times* to your favorite rant-a-day blog—have news feeds available to anybody who wants to sign up or *subscribe* to them. The summary text in the feed includes a link to the full version of the article or post in its original location, which makes it a breeze to scan the headlines and follow though to the full story of the articles that interest you.

There are two popular standards for serving up news feeds: Atom and RSS (which either stands for Rich Site Summary or Really Simple Syndication, depending on whom you ask). Some news-reader programs work with both systems. Moreover, some browsers, like Safari and Firefox, have Atom-ready newsreaders built right in.

You may think all of this news-reader stuff has nothing to do with Gmail, but in fact, you can browse summaries of your fresh, unread Gmail messages right alongside your news updates from the BBC and the *Washington Post*. Then, when you want to read a message, you can just click through to see the whole thing. All you need is a news reader that supports Atom feeds.

Note: Getting feeds of your Gmail doesn't alter the messages in your Inbox in any way. They're still there when you log into Gmail.

Modern Web browsers that work with Atom feeds, like Safari 2.0 and Firefox, can display your new Gmail messages in summary form (Figure 11-35). To find out if your browser can handle Atom feeds, check the Client Software list in the Atom Enabled directory at *www.atomenabled.org/everyone/atomenabled* to see if your program is on the list.

Adding a feed for your Gmail with Atom-ready browsers is simple. In Safari, log in to Gmail, look at the top of the page for the RSS button and then click it to open a dialog box like the one in Figure 11-36, where you provide your Gmail account name and password so the browser has permission to download and display summaries of your unread messages.

In the Firefox browser, you can see the subject lines of all your unread Gmail messages by making a Live Bookmark to round up the Atom feed. To do so, choose Bookmarks → Manage Bookmarks. In the Manage Bookmarks box, choose File → New Live Bookmark and get ready to do some typing in the URL box. When you've warmed up your hands, type in:

```
https://yourUserName:yourPassword@gmail.google.com/gmail/feed/atom
```

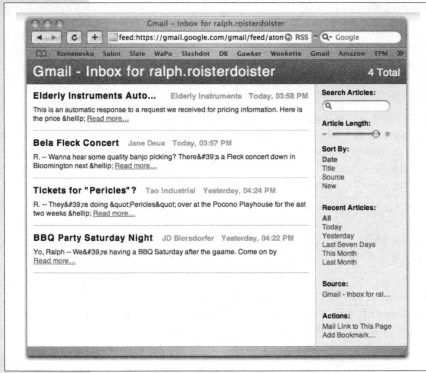

Figure 11-35:
You can have your Web browser give you brief summaries of your new messages without having to log all the way in to your Gmail account.

Figure 11-36:
When you set up an RSS feed in your browser, you're not giving your private info away; you're simply storing it in a place where your browser can find it, so it can pull down your Gmail messages.

The subject lines of any unread messages now show up in the submenu of Gmail Live Bookmark so you can keep an eye on your Inbox. If you don't have any new messages, the Live Bookmark fails to load—and sometimes even when you *do* have new mail, the Live Bookmark is a few messages behind. If you suspect that might be happening, right-click the Live Bookmark and choose Refresh Live Bookmark to update the list.

Note: The security-savvy will note that this URL puts your Gmail password in plain, unscrambled text. If that makes you nervous, perhaps it's best to stick to the Old Ways and the Web browser.

If your browser doesn't have an integrated newsreader, there are dozens of dedicated programs that can do the job. Newsreader programs that work with Gmail's Atom feed include the open source BottomFeeder program (*www.cincomsmalltalk.com/ BottomFeeder*), which works on most Windows, Macintosh, and Linux systems out there; FeedDemon (*www.feeddemon.com*) and NewsGator (*www.newsgator.com*) for Windows; and Shrook for Mac OS X (*www.fondantfancies.com/apps/shrook*).

Once you've decided which newsreader to use, you need to tell it where to look for your Gmail. While most reader programs come with a stock set of feeds, you can add new ones of your own (look for an "Add new feed" command or button within the program). When the software asks for a URL to use for the new feed, type in *https://gmail.google.com/gmail/feed/atom* to point it toward the Gmail server. (The program also asks for your Gmail account name and password in order to snag your new message summaries.) Figure 11-37 shows an example of a Gmail Atom feed displayed in the FeedDemon program for Windows.

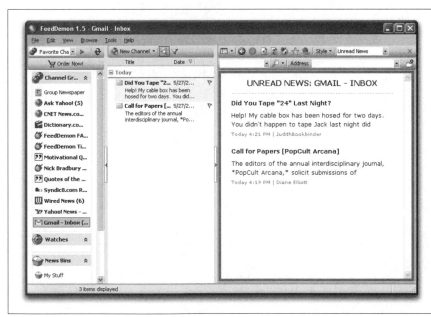

Figure 11-37:
Dedicated news reader programs like FeedDemon don't just give you a peek at your new Gmail messages; they also round up current headlines and news from Web sites around the world to keep you in the loop.

Tip: Google keeps an extensive, updated Gmail Help section online at *http://mail.google.com/support*. If you want an alternate route to Helpville, click the Help link at the top of the page when you're logged in to your Gmail account. In either case, the section covers pretty much anything you can do with Gmail, from configuring different email programs for downloading Gmail messages to creating filters to bounce bozos out of your Inbox and into the Trash.

Part Five:
Appendix

5

Appendix: The Google Wide Web

The Google Wide Web

Google is a phenomenon so huge, it's inspired a cottage industry of third-party sites either discussing it or using its index to do funky search tricks. Here are just some of the best and brightest.

Note: As of this writing, all of these Web addresses are working in the most recent versions of most modern browsers. If you have trouble using one of these services, upgrade your browser or try a different one. Should you find a URL that doesn't work (it happens), report it at *www.missingmanuals.com*.

Sites That Use Google

- *www.googlefight.com.* This site lets you type in two queries, and then it runs a search to see which is more popular. Find out who's mentioned more often on the Web, *cats* or *dogs*; *Janet Jackson* or *Justin Timberlake*; *George Bush* or *burning bush*. Don't miss the funny fights (found under the links on the left side of the page). Another site, *www.onfocus.com/googlesmack/down.asp* offers a similar service.

- *www.googlism.com.* Find out what the Web is saying about nearly anything. Type in a word, choose whether it's a Who, What, Where, or When, and then click the Googlism button to get a nifty list of comments from Google results that mention your term. For example, if you try *Tivo*, you learn that people have said: "Tivo is theft," "Tivo is god," "Tivo is exhausting."

- *www.googleblaster.com.* Here you can type in multiple queries at once, then click a single button to run the searches simultaneously. The results look like a regular Google page, but each of your searches has its own tab at the top. Handy when you want to compare a couple of searches to each other. The site also has a fun feature that automatically searches Google for every individual letter of the alphabet or the numerals (0–9) and then shows the results for each character on its own tab.

- *www.freshgoo.com*. Lets you limit search results to pages Google has added to its index within a certain time frame (the date pages were created is a different thing; see page 52 for an explanation). The next Web page on this list offers a similar feature, along with a nice, geeky explanation of how Google deals with dates.

- *http://www.researchbuzz.org/archives/cat_google_hacks.shtml*. The place to go to use Google to find recipes. Type in your ingredients, then choose a recipe genre, like vegetarian, Atkins, or seafood—and voilà! You get Google results with recipes. This site, by search guru and *Google Hacks* (O'Reilly) contributor Tara Calishain, hosts a bunch of fun Google tools, like the Search Sinker, which lets you emphasize the word in a Google query that is most important to you; Google Does Poetry (self-explanatory); and a nice collection of Google-specific bookmarklets (page 212).

- *www.googlerace.com*. Type in a word or phrase to find out which political candidates are most highly associated with your terms.

- *www.staggernation.com*. A bare-bones site with three interesting Google searches: GAPS (lets you enter two search terms and find out how closely they appear on Web sites that contain them both), GAWSH (lets you search for terms by domain—a useful way to find out which sites pay the most attention to your search terms), and GARBO (lets you search by URL to find a list of related pages or pages that link to the URL). The "Read Me" file on every page gives tips on using each search.

- *www.marumushi.com/apps/newsmap/*. An extremely cool visual representation of Google News headlines.

- *www.kryogenix.org/code/browser/aqgoogle/*. Technically, this site doesn't use Google; it lets you automatically post electronic artwork in Google Groups. The awesome part is that you create the art on this site by filling in a grid with blocks of color. Sounds dull, but it's actually a procrastination tool not to be mocked.

Note: This book contains discussions of a few other sites that use Google: FaganFinder.com (page 56) and Soople.com (page 59), for example.

Sites That Discuss Google

- *www.elgoog.nl/*. The mother of all Google-obsessed sites, this one has pages about every aspect of Google, including a very useful listing of Web forums and groups about Google. The Googlemania page lists more sites that use or discuss Google.

Google Bombing

Because Google uses a page's popularity to help determine its rank in search results (page 3), people constantly try to manipulate the Web in order to rise in the ranks. Most of the time, Google foils those attempts. But the company has ignored one kind of maneuver, known as *Google bombing*.

Despite its name, the effect of Google bombing is subtle: When you run a search for a word or phrase, an unexpected site or two may appear at the top of your results. For example, the query *"miserable failure"* brings up the official White House biography of George W. Bush, followed by Michael Moore's site, and later down the list, Hillary Rodham Clinton's official site. Yet the phrase "miserable failure" doesn't appear on any of those sites. What gives?

One of the ways Google associates a phrase with a page is by analyzing the text in the anchors linking to that page (anchors are words you click to jump to another page). If a lot of sites—particularly popular sites—link to a page using specific text, Google will show that page when somebody searches for the text—even if the words aren't anywhere in the destination page itself.

Google bombing requires a *group* of people to set the same anchors on their sites. And for those who can get enough people to join them, the coveted prize is forcing a page to the first position in a listing of Google results for a particular phrase. Political bloggers are among the most successful at marshalling a sufficient number of Web jockeys to influence search results.

Although targets of Google bombing sometimes ask Google to remove their pages from results for certain searches, the company has so far declined. It contends that its search results simply reflect what's on the Web and that Google bombing is limited enough that it doesn't pose a threat to the integrity of searches.

- *http://google.blogspace.com/.* This site keeps a tidy list of new features and subtle developments. The site gets tips from Googologists, so if you spend 25 hours a day checking your Google results for new font sizes, file your observations here. You can also sign up for email updates from the site, or for an RSS feed (a geek way of summarizing Web site text).

- *http://www.topix.net/com/google.* A collection of news stories on Google, updated constantly. Another site, *www.watchinggooglelikeahawk.com*, provides a similar service (despite its name, the site is not anti-Google).

- *www.squarefree.com/archives/cat_google.html.* This blog, by the guy who developed a few bookmarklets discussed in Chapter 7, makes occasional, quirky observations about Google. The site also includes a downloadable Google Relatedness tool, which you can use to measure how often two terms show up together in Google results. *Angelina* and *Brad*, anyone?

- *www.googleguide.com.* A site so comprehensive, you could use it as alternative to Google's online help.

- *www.googlewhack.com/.* Frivolous but fun: a site about Google queries that give you exactly one result.

- *www.google-watch.org/.* A site for those who believe, correctly or not, that Google is evil. Another site, *www.google-watch-watch.org*, comments on Google-watch.

Google on Google

Google has an email list for press announcements; anyone can sign up. It's not always the best way to learn about things Google, because Google watchers tend to figure out what's new and blitz the Web before Google gets around to making official announcements. But occasionally, Google slips something in that you wouldn't otherwise know about. And there's no need to worry about overloading your inbox: the announcements are so infrequent, you might wonder whether you've even made it onto the list. Sign up at *www.google.com/press/index.html*.

And don't overlook the Google Groups on Google. Like most Usenet groups (page 119), the Google discussions about Google can be wildly random, but they can also be a good place to ask questions or search for exchanges on a particular issue. To find the Usenet groups devoted to Google, head over to *http://groups.google.com/*, and search for *google.public* to get a list of groups covering Google.

Index

GOOGLE: THE MISSING MANUAL

Colophon

Sanders Kleinfeld was the production editor and proofreader for *Google: The Missing Manual*, Second Edition. Marlowe Shaeffer and Claire Cloutier provided quality control.

The cover of this book is based on a series design by David Freedman. Marcia Friedman produced the cover layout with Adobe InDesign CS using Adobe's Minion and Gill Sans fonts.

David Futato designed the interior layout, based on a series design by Phil Simpson. This book was converted by Keith Fahlgren to FrameMaker 5.5.6. The text font is Adobe Minion; the heading font is Adobe Formata Condensed; and the code font is LucasFont's TheSans Mono Condensed. The illustrations that appear in the book were produced by Robert Romano, Jessamyn Read, and Lesley Borash using Macromedia FreeHand MX and Adobe Photoshop CS.

Better than e-books

Buy *Google: The Missing Manual,* 2nd Edition and access the digital edition FREE on Safari for 45 days.

Go to www.oreilly.com/go/safarienabled
and type in coupon code G9F3-DEUG-TYQF-TQG1-HCL9

Search
thousands of
top tech books

Download
whole chapters

Cut and Paste
code examples

Find
answers fast

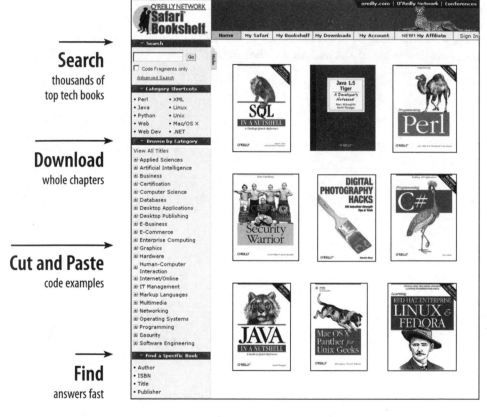

Search Safari! The premier electronic reference
library for programmers and IT professionals.